THE JUDGMENT OF PARIS

HUBERT DAMISCH

THE JUDGMENT OF PARIS

Translated by John Goodman

THE UNIVERSITY OF CHICAGO PRESS

CHICAGO AND LONDON

Hubert Damisch is director of studies at l'École des hautes études en sciences sociales in Paris. John Goodman is an independent art historian and translator.

Originally published under the title *Le Jugement de Pâris: Iconologie analytique 1*, ©Flammarion, Paris, 1992.

The University of Chicago Press, Chicago 60637
The University of Chicago Press, Ltd., London

Printed in the United States of America
05 04 03 02 01 00 99 98 97 96   1 2 3 4 5

ISBN 0-226-13510-1 (cloth)
0-226-13512-8 (paper)

Library of Congress Cataloging-in-Publication Data

Damisch, Hubert
[Jugement de Pâris. English]
The judgment of Paris/Hubert Damisch; translated by John Goodman.
p. cm.—(Analytic iconology; 1)
Includes bibliographical references and index.
1. Feminine beauty (Aesthetics) 2. Art—Psychology. I. Title
II. Sereis.
N7630.D3613 1996
701′.15—dc20   95-42081
CIP

∞ The paper used in this publication meets the minimum requirements of the American National Standard for Information Sciences—Permanence of Paper for Printed Library Materials, ANSI Z39.48-1984.

For Teri

Contents

Illustrations

. . . . .

Translator's Note

All English-language Freud citations are from the Standard Edition, but in accordance with current Lacanian usage *Trieb* has been translated as "drive" instead of "instinct" and placed within brackets. The German word *Reize,* which also figures prominently in this text, can mean both "charms" and "attractions." Strachey hedged over this term, sometimes opting for one rendering and sometimes for the other. For the sake of clarity, I have consistently translated it as "charms," even when the alternative rendering might seem more idiomatic; but note that on two occasions when passages from the Standard Edition are cited in which "attractions" was preferred by Strachey, I have changed this to "[charms]."

All citations from Kant's *Critique of Judgment* are from the recent edition by Werner Pluhar (Indianapolis: Hackett, 1987), but I have rejected his substitution of "powers" for the traditional rendering of *Vermögen* as "faculties," preferring to retain the latter term. Homer's *Iliad* is quoted in the Lattimore translation (Chicago: University of Chicago Press, 1951), but all other classical citations (except for a few from Plato) have been taken from the renderings in the Loeb Classical Library.

A few remarks about the author's literary style, and my approach to it here, are in order. Damisch's voice is highly self-conscious and rhetorical: his sentences tend to be long-breathed, with gerunds sustaining the momentum between their many successive clauses. He often deploys these long sequences—they sometimes jump over periods, forming series of grammatically "incorrect" constructions—to circle around the object of his scrutiny with a circumspection that can seem maddening ("When will he come to the point?" one occasionally finds oneself asking). Add to this a certain penchant for playfully cryptic formulations in the Lacanian mode, and it might seem that we have a recipe for preciosity. But not so: there is method, and a rare writerly intelligence, behind these choices. Damisch's idiom takes some getting used to, but then this could be said of many great stylists. The symphonic rhythms of his prose—alternately clipped and majestic—and its teasing, circumambulatory patterns are integral to the book's design: for his theme here is the relation between the sexual drive and aesthetic response (especially as triggered by sight), and, as he says in chapter 2, paraphrasing Lacan, "the drive can never find satisfaction, save by circling around a perpetually absent object."

In translating Damisch's French I have tried to retain its idiosyncratic flavor and organizational strategies, even at the risk of the occasional awkwardness. Traditional rules of punctuation have been handled rather freely. Although the result might seem off-putting and unfamiliar, I would argue that the prose of the original, too, produces something like the same effect at first encounter. It will be for others to judge of the degree of my success or failure in rendering *The Judgment of Paris* into English. But I encourage the reader to overcome any promptings toward resistance that he or she might initially feel, whatever their cause. The reward for such persistence will be considerable, for this book is as exhilarating as it is troubling.

J. G.

PART ONE

Beauté Mon Beau Souci

. . 1 . .

This Nothing That Psychoanalysis Has Had to Say about Beauty

"Nothing? Nothing."

Freud himself frankly avowed it: psychoanalysis has little or nothing to say about beauty—less, in any case, than about many other subjects.[1] And although he could take a certain satisfaction in having successfully used the analytic method to clarify a few problems relative to art and artists, very early on he found himself obliged to concede that in all important respects they slipped through his net: in 1913, assessing the contribution of psychoanalysis to related disciplines, he acknowledged that "most of the problems of artistic creation and appreciation await further study, which will throw the light of analytic knowledge on them and assign them their place in the complex structure presented by the compensation for human wishes."[2]

The statement that psychoanalysis has little or nothing to say about beauty can be understood in various ways. We can read it, against the grain of its inventor's own earlier boast that it would throw new light on the domains of art, literature, and mythology,[3] as an admission of failure or impotence—one over which many would rejoice. Or we might follow Lacan's lead and see it as an indication of exceptional caution on Freud's part ("On the nature of the creation that is manifested in the beautiful, the analyst has, by his own admission, nothing to say"[4]): as though it did not necessarily follow that the psychoanalyst had to be bound by the limits Freud set in denying him any capacity to judge the quality of works of art or of the formal elaboration of which they are the fruit. Finally, we might interpret it as a rhetorical ploy, or even the result of a compromise, in other words—to propose a subtler reading—as a kind of ruse, one intended to circumvent the expected resistance against the intrusion of psychoanalysis into such a highly sacralized field, a field that had not yet been exposed—at least where the "fine arts" were concerned—to such radical criticism.[5]

But the problem can be framed differently, in terms which place this profession of ignorance or of inarticulateness parallel to other formulations of the same type also found in Freud, for example concerning feminine sexuality. In this context, the establishment of a limit would take on the quality of a challenge, daring us to explore a bit further and to learn—and perhaps to speak—a bit more about it. Unless, that is, it is to be taken literally, in which case the question becomes one of what psychoanalysis has to say, or is capable of saying. About psychoanalysis itself, about its *not saying*—about its *saying nothing*, or its *saying less*. If the boundaries assigned to analytic discourse within the field of art and/or beauty can indicate a refusal of all "applied" psychoanalysis, then the choice of silence has the value of a sign or symptom: in his essay "The Theme of the Three Caskets," Freud reminds us that in dreams, as in analysis and already in *King Lear* in the person of Cordelia, muteness is a common representation of death.[6]

If we should opt for the hypothesis of a ruse on Freud's part—a ruse that would be not only rhetorical but structural, and connected, like a symptom, to the "speech" of psychoanalysis, not excluding its omissions, its continuities and points of suspension, its gaps—then we would have to concede, on listening to the clamor which I'm echoing here, that it has not had the intended effect: what is generally remembered of certain passages in his work—regularly cited out of context, or even through secondary sources—where beauty is discussed is that psychoanalysis has little to say about it—nothing, at least, that would merit special attention. But perhaps this ruse is too obvious—like the message it conveys surreptitiously, which can now be seen to function in the manner of a Freudian denial. If this hypothesis is to be accepted, it must be developed in the following way: without doubt psychoanalysis has little to say about beauty (and we can pretend along with Freud to deplore this); but what it does have to say can be expressed in very few words, words that, what's more, are hardly acceptable, words that lack the most elementary level of decency; words that cannot (in brief) be heard and that haven't been; words (to say all) it would have been better not to pronounce; words it would have been better not to write, the better part in this business being, it would seem, to let well-enough alone, and say "nothing."

There is at least one passage in Freud's work that seems to conform to this rhetorical or deceptive schema, one that presents to the reader's scrutiny, in quite explicit terms, this "nothing" which psychoanalysis would decidedly not have known how, or wanted, to silence. Curiously enough, the passage in question is from *Civilization and Its Discontents*, a work that at first glance seems to have little to do with aesthetic considerations. But an initial observation comes to mind, prior to any reflection on the relation that might obtain between the uneasiness certain to be inspired by the statement which psychoanalysis has to make about beauty (and which, I repeat, can be made in very few words) and Freud's much more general analytic project in this short text, which appeared in 1930 and which Lacan, and Marie Moscovici after him, recognized as a key work.[7] In the guise of a pamphlet, and in a theoretical landscape profoundly transformed by the introduction of the second topographic model and the notion of the death drive, *Civilization and Its Discontents* treats one of the most consistent themes of Freudian reflection, namely, the sacrifices necessarily made by man in exchange for the establishment and maintenance of something resembling "culture." What is generally regarded as Freud's avowal of impotence assumes a different meaning in this context, for here the beauty in question is not, or is not exclusively, or is not initially, the one whose name is usually associated with that of art, but rather a beauty conceived of in the vaguest, most general terms and which doesn't necessarily refer to the idea of *creation*, much less that of "art," its correlative. To couch this in the notably precise terms of Lacan, the analyst might well have nothing to say about "the nature of the creation that is manifested in the beautiful," in other words, about the work of artistic production. But then how are we to characterize what Freud could not prevent himself from saying, from the perspective of psychoanalysis, about beauty considered in itself and for itself, whatever its relations to art? Once again a "nothing," but one attaching itself (if this is possible) to the sign of "less": a "less than nothing" (in the sense in which we say this of an individual we hold in low esteem) which most definitely would not be worth dwelling on?

At the beginning of *Civilization and Its Discontents*, Freud set aside two separate places for art and beauty in his catalog of the methods and techniques used by man to attain happiness or, more modestly, to protect himself against suffering, in conformity with the program imposed by the pleasure principle. Methods and techniques in addition to what might be considered the "arts of living" in the most fully ethical sense of these two words, "art" and "living" encompassing everything from the use of drugs—given spectacular prominence here—to the flight into madness or collective delusion, notably religion. Which is to say in what terms the question of the goal (*die Frage nach dem Zweck*) toward which art and beauty could be posed, there where Freud pushed aside, not without contempt, the idea of assigning one to human life—a pretention in which he recognized one of many manifestations of human pride. As he drolly remarked, we never speak of the aim of animals' lives, unless specifying their destiny to serve man. "But this view is not tenable either, for there are many animals of which man can make nothing, except to describe, classify and study them; and innumerable species of animals have escaped even this use, since they existed and became extinct before man set eyes on them."[8] It is true that specialists in animal behavior scarcely concern themselves with the "aim" of animal lives; but they nonetheless feel justified in investigating, from a perspective that is not purely descriptive or taxonomic, the biological significance of the "beauty" they recognize in certain specimens, as evidenced by Konrad Lorenz's celebrated studies of the sexual display of birds or the notably aggressive behavior of certain varieties of brilliantly colored tropical fish.[9]

If religion alone is in a position to make pronouncements about the purpose of human life, this is because it originated the question, which is meaningful only on its own terms. But what of art? What of beauty? What is their relation to religion, which would have it that they contain a hidden meaning, a profound significance which it is our task to reveal? Or must we concede with Freud that art, like religion and perhaps even like science, has not only a vital but an economic function, in the libidinal sense of the word? Such is life's burden, replete as it is with suffering and deception, with insoluble problems and impossible tasks, that if man is to bear it he must have resort to sedatives (*Liderungsmittel*) and "succoring aids" (*Hilfkonstruktionen*), to use the words of Theodore Fontane cited by Freud. These sedatives can assume various forms: "powerful deflections, which cause us to make light of our misery; substitutive satisfactions, which diminish it; and intoxicating substances, which make us insensitive to it. Something of the kind is indispensable."[10]

In one way or another, art participates in all three of these categories. This makes it all the more significant that, in addition to the "substitutive satisfactions," the "ersatz" satiations (*die Ersatzbefriedigungen*) provided by it, Freud felt obliged to ascribe a distinct development to what he called "the interesting case in which happiness in life is predominantly sought in the enjoyment of beauty, wherever beauty presents itself to our senses and our judgement." Which implies a clear distinction between the slightly enervated feeling associated by him with purely aesthetic pleasure and the mild narcosis (*die milde Narkose*) into which art momentarily plunges its adepts—possibly at the risk, in both cases, of clouding the faculty of judgment. "The beauty of human forms and gestures, of natural objects and landscapes, and of artistic and even scientific creations":[11] if in the fields of art and science necessarily implies the idea of creation, it is not this which initially attracts the attention of the aesthete. The latter has chosen—this is his entire ethics, his "art of living"—to consider beings and things, including the works of man, solely under their aesthetic aspect, which is to say (as was already maintained by Kant in his *Critique of Judgment*, a work whose influence will be sensed beneath my reading of Freud even before it takes center stage) in strictly subjective terms. The aesthete's "thing" is beauty, just as for others it can be drugs, religion, love, or art itself.

* * *

The distinction Freud makes between the enjoyment (*der Genuss*) accorded by works of art, which doesn't necessarily entail beauty, and that inspired by beauty outside the field of art raises, however, more questions than it answers. If art is the domain of the most elevated "satisfactions through fantasy" (*die Phantasiebefriedigungen*), these latter derive first and foremost from creative activity and are only accessible to those other than the creator himself through the intermediary agency of the artist.[12] On the other hand, the pleasure that beauty grants its adepts implies no activity on their part other than a critical one (what Kant called the "judgment of taste"). Does this mean that beauty, including that resulting from art, should be conceptualized in terms of reception rather than production, even though the idea of it, in the case of natural beauty, resists dissociation from "Creation" or, at least, from a "plan," whether divine or other, in which man would have his assigned place?

This question—which evokes the central preoccupation of *Civilization and Its Discontents*, if it's true that Freud undertook to write this work in order to refute the idea, accepted since Aristotle, that there is a preexisting harmony between man and the world—prompts another, one that speaks to the relation between art and beauty on the one hand and reality on the other. If it's not only the products of human genius but also human forms and gestures, natural objects and landscapes that are capable of striking our senses and judgment as beautiful, should we conclude from this that "beauty" is situated in the exterior world and that specific instances of it in beings or objects of that world are irreducible to simple illusion but, rather, participate in one way or another in "reality," and not only on a formal plane, as is the case with scientific and artistic creations? Then again, aren't these last (that is, artistic creations) intended to procure for their authors—and through them, for ordinary mortals—substitutive satisfactions, "ersatz" pleasures (and an attempt will be made in the following pages to give the word *Ersatz* a special valence), which are nothing but illusions in relation to reality?[13]

The rather crude formulations concerning art in *Civilization and Its Discontents* find some rhetorical justification in the prominence—most unusual in Freud's work—accorded beauty, insofar as this text allows for its conceptualization apart from art, in isolation from the so-called artistic field. If art is reduced to a source of pleasure and consolation,[14] and if it aims only at satisfactions that are substitutive and as such illusory, but whose psychic effectiveness is proportionate to the size of the role played by fantasy in mental life,[15] then it becomes necessary to consider the recurrent aspiration to "realism" which figures so prominently in its history as a singularly twisted manifestation of fantasy and likewise the requirement of "truth" (whatever this might be taken to mean) prompting it either to put down roots (to use Alberti's metaphor) on the side of science or, alternatively, to attempt to uncover—this was Cézanne's project—those (the roots) of perception.[16] Even though the question does not allow of a single answer and must be formulated anew in each instance, it cannot easily be contained within programmatic boundaries dominated by pleasure. In fact, Freud himself was fully aware that art stubbornly works to reconcile the two principles of pleasure and reality. When the artist makes a work he is also attempting to return to the real, to give form to his fantasies, transforming them into objects that impress other human beings as "very precious images of reality" (in a letter to Freud, Lou Andreas Salomé evokes the "fantasy-laden realism" with which the artist commits himself to his work during the creative process[17]): which he succeeds in doing only because his fellow humans feel the same frustration as he does with the renunciation of primal satisfactions imposed on them, the consequences of which (this dissatisfaction, this frustration) are inseparable from what constitutes "reality" for us.[18]

Reality testing plays no role in unconscious processes, in which a mental reality functions as the equivalent of an exterior one, and a desire equals its satisfaction. But while art is of necessity linked to the unconscious, mining it for many of its effects and even, on occasion, imitating its specific operations, it does not reside in it. Resorting as it does to perception, it necessarily establishes ties to consciousness, from which perception is indistinguishable and which is not exclusively concerned with pleasure/unpleasure, devoting its attention primarily to sensory qualities; just as art is linked to the work of thought prompted by the activity of representation, which simultaneously implies and empowers a suspension of the motor discharge by means of which the psychic apparatus rids itself, under the reign of the pleasure principle, of excess excitation. Given the way art can work two systems at once—namely, memory and perception/consciousness—and its tendency to reverse their respective roles, one cannot and should not discuss art save in terms proper to it. As Freud stated, "One is bound to employ the currency that is in use in the country one is exploring"—the "neurotic currency"[19] in the case of analysis, and the "artistic currency" in that of the history and theory of art.

The essential point here is that in *Civilization and Its Discontents* Freud explicitly severed the question of art and art-derived pleasure from that of beauty considered as a possible source of happiness. Since Hegel, philosophy has tended to reduce aesthetics to what Alain called "the system of the fine arts," and the extent to which we remain in thrall to this tradition is indicated by our propensity, even today, to substitute "art" where the text—whether by Freud, Kant, or even Plato—says "beauty," and vice versa. And this in a time (our own) characterized by a tendency to forget what "art" means, and "beauty" as well, but one still haunted, secretly, by a nostalgia for their immemorial alliance. Isolated from beauty, is art anything other than a name? And beauty itself, what relation does it retain to the desire that confers the appearance of necessity upon it, one which is now denied to art? To put it another way: If desire there be, and ought to be—desire for art, desire for beauty—how can this be shored up by reality, when—to invoke Freud's metaphor once again—only the "aesthetic currency" is acceptable tender where it is concerned?

For, however distinct, the pleasure provided by works of art and that inspired by beauty have one thing in common: both of them act like a drug. But while intoxicants provide immediate pleasure as well as an unequalled sense of independence from the external world, two effects that are not only simultaneous but intimately bound up with one another,[20] the subtle narcosis into which art plunges its adepts is fugitive and never so intense as to make them forget their real misery,[21] whereas the slightly enervated feeling accompanying aesthetic pleasure (*der Genuss an der Schönheit*) is of little help against the misfortunes threatening man, even though it might well lighten his burden somewhat.[22] The parallel with what Freud termed the influence (*die Beeinflussung*) of drugs (the effects of which are sufficient to place it in the front rank of those "techniques for living" aiming at pleasure and the avoidance of suffering) is no less symptomatic. And this is all the more the case given that, according to Freud, no one completely understands the mechanism of chemical intoxication. Given that normal mental life features rapid, unpredictable oscillations between pleasure and unpleasure, Freud found it all the more regrettable that what he called the "toxic side" of mental processes had not yet been plumbed by scientific investigation.[23] Doubtless psychoanalysis has little—perhaps nothing—to say about the operations of art; but if art is capable of inducing in its adepts a certain intoxication, however slight, doesn't it follow that its "toxic side" has, or could have, a counterpart in the mental processes, just as intoxicants do? In other words, doesn't the "chemistry" of art function only to the extent it echoes the imagination?

The problem makes sense only if we are correct in drawing a distinction between the artistic and aesthetic registers, as we are encouraged to do by *Civilization and Its Discontents*, in whose problematic this distinction figures prominently. Freud insists that the slightly enervated feeling associated with aesthetic pleasure has a specific character (*ein besonderer Empfindungscharakter*): but how are we to understand this, if not within the framework and in accordance with the perspective of, precisely, civilization, *Kultur*? A kind of paradox follows from this, which Freud expresses concisely: "Beauty has no obvious use; nor is there any clear cultural necessity for it. Yet civilization could not do without it."[24]

The question of use value is, of course, not an innocent one in this context: if beauty must have a certain utility, this will tend precisely to situate the beautiful—in this instance, pleasure—on the side of reality. But how is this to be understood? And how are we to comprehend a statement that while beauty is apparently unnecessary to civilization or *Kultur*, the latter can't jettison it without unpleasant consequences? The divergence, the difference Freud throws into relief by stressing the specific character of aesthetic pleasure is inextricable from this paradox, which is that, precisely, of a utilitarian or use value that is inherently aesthetic. Culture certainly has no need of beauty to establish itself; but it remains to determine the role played by beauty in its development, and how it might prove indispensable in smoothing its operation.

But I am getting ahead of myself. On this point, Freud allows himself to observe only that "the science of aesthetics investigates the conditions under which things are felt as beautiful, but it has been unable to give any explanation of the nature and origin of beauty." And it is precisely in this context that we must read his assertion that it is about beauty (unfortunately) that psychoanalysis has the least to say. Less, at any rate, than about other subjects not so directly implicated in the discontent Freud has undertaken to analyze; but more, without doubt, than aesthetics, the "science of the beautiful," which in his view makes extravagant use of empty, sonorous phrases to mask its repeated failures. For this "less" is not (fortunately?) without a certain residue. One thing (at least) seems sure: "All that seems certain [about the aesthetic emotion] is its derivation from the field of sexual feeling. The love of beauty would seem to be [note the conditional tense here] a perfect example of an impulse inhibited in its aim."[25]

"Is that all?" we might be tempted to interject at this point, with an ironic flourish prompted by the apparent failure to come up with anything better to help us understand art and its works than this notion that echoes Kant's "purposiveness without purpose." But the irony proves misplaced when we pay close attention to Freud's text (as well as, when the time comes, to that of Kant). For what is in question, in this instance, is not art but beauty. And what psychanalysis has to say about it does not stop there. It also says this: "'Beauty' and ['charm'] are originally attributes of the sexual object. It is worth remarking that the genitals themselves, the sight of which is always exciting, are nevertheless hardly ever judged to be beautiful; the quality of beauty seems, instead, to attach to certain secondary sexual characters."[26]

Assuredly, these are unseemly terms (just as representations of the genitals in painting or sculpture always seem a bit indecorous): terms, in any case, that have provoked scandal when they have not been condescendingly dismissed. Is that really all that psychoanalysis has to tell us about beauty, such that analysts find themselves reduced to hunting down anything in works of art that might evoke, visually or symbolically, organs of the two sexes (a sport in which many have indulged freely, as we know all too well)? It goes without saying that beauty is somehow linked to sexuality; but surely it would have been preferable to remain mute on the subject rather than express it in such terms as these. Had Freud invoked a Platonic Eros, or referred to desire in a poetic mode, then he could have been accommodated: it is well known that humanist discourse has made a specialty of erotic rhetoric and dialogue between the various personifications of love—sacred and profane, carnal and spiritual—that often figure in art; and Freud himself observes that "anyone who looks down with contempt upon psychoanalysis from a superior vantage-point should remember how closely the enlarged sexuality of psychoanalysis coincides with the Eros of the divine Plato."[27] But was it necessary at this point in his argument to introduce the so-called sexual object, and in such crude, quasi-pornographic terms: as if it hadn't sufficed for him to observe that "beauty" and "charm" were originally (*ursprünglich*) attributes of the said object, as if it seemed important to him, in this context, to clearly indicate a difference between the excitement induced by looking at the genitals (which, I stress, are nonetheless rarely *judged* to be beautiful, *doch fast nie als schön beurteilt werden*) and the character of beauty seemingly attached to certain sexual traits described (without further specification) as "secondary"? And this from a perspective that ought to be that of an aesthetic—if, that is, the word and the project it designates still have any meaning?

. . 2 . .

The Future of Emotion

"It is not the eye that sees, it is the soul."

The remarks on beauty and the pleasures it can inspire, scattered throughout *Civilization and Its Discontents* without apparent order, are not unprecedented in Freud's work. The passage I have just cited is a repetition, somewhat developed and modified, of a note he added to the *Three Essays on Sexuality* in 1915: "There is to my mind no doubt that the concept of 'beautiful' has its roots in sexual excitation and that its original meaning was 'sexually stimulating.' This is related to the fact that we never regard the genitals themselves, which produce the strongest sexual excitation, as really 'beautiful.'"[1] Similar ideas are encountered here and there in very different contexts, though it was in these same *Three Essays* that Freud first introduced a theme he would take up again, fifteen years later, in *Civilization and Its Discontents:* namely that sexuality remains the weak point in the process of human cultural development.[2] And it is in connection with this theme that it will be appropriate to investigate the place finally accorded, in *Civilization and Its Discontents,* to Freud's question about beauty: If the aesthetic emotion derives from the sphere of sexual sensation, then what is the role—positive or negative—played in it by repression or denial, operations applied by *Kultur* to the sexual drive? And reciprocally: What has civilization to do with beauty, seeing that it (civilization, *Kultur*) exacts so many sacrifices of man, notably in the realm of sexuality?

The question is posed in completely different terms in the first of the *Three Essays* and, in particular, in the passage glossed by the note quoted above. This text examines a problem which had long interested Freud: that of "sexual aberrations" and the many deviations which could manifest themselves in what he then termed the sexual drive (*Sexualtrieb*), with regard to both its object (the person toward whom the drive was directed) and its aim (the desired act). Along the path leading to the act considered to be "normal" (heterosexual intercourse), certain relations, qualified by Freud as "intermediary," assume the character of "preliminary sexual aims": touching the object, for instance, or looking at it—activities themselves accompanied by pleasure at the same time that they help sustain and intensify excitement, which should be maintained until the achievement of the so-called normal act. To this end, a certain amount of touching (kissing, skin contact, etc.) seems indispensable, at least (as Freud himself specifies) between human beings. The same holds for sight, which in the last analysis is subsidiary to touch: "Visual impressions remain the most frequent pathway along which libidinal excitation is aroused; indeed, natural selection counts upon the accessibility of this pathway . . . when it encourages the development of beauty in the sexual object." With the following qualification, inserted in the text at about the same time as the note on the sexual roots of "beauty": "if, that is, such a teleological form of statement is permissible."[3]

The note to the *Three Essays* seems to contain a contradiction: If we admit that, originally (*ursprünglich*), the concept of "beauty" designated that which is sexually stimulating, how are we to understand that the genitals can never be found "beautiful," despite the fact that the sight of them provokes the most intense sexual excitement? And further: What could be the link between these two seemingly antithetical statements? In *Civilization and Its Discontents*, this problematic is given a still more subtle twist: while "beauty" and "charm" were, originally, attributes of the sexual object, the attribution of beauty depends less upon the genital organs considered in themselves than upon sexual characteristics designated as secondary. But the contradiction, quite pronounced from the start, is not absolute, as is evidenced by the assertion that the genitals, the sight of which always spurs excitement, are nonetheless almost never considered "beautiful" (it being implied that, under certain conditions and in certain contexts, they can be). We should not conceive the divergence or hiatus that can exist between sexual excitement and aesthetic emotion only in topographical or economic terms, but equally and perhaps primarily from a dynamic perspective, given that beauty is discerned in consequence of—or more accurately, in correlation with—a displacement, or even a repression. But does it follow from the fact that the genital organs, the sight of which is supposed to provoke the most intense sexual excitement, are rarely, if ever, considered beautiful—does it follow from this that the attribution of beauty to secondary sexual characteristics can (or should) be dismissed as "deviant" or "perverse" from the moment its principal effect becomes that of diverting the sexual drive from the aim which society has assigned and which psychoanalysis has embraced and defined as the genitalization of desire? If the drive's exclusive aim is to bring the two sexes together, why then wouldn't the excitement that results from viewing the genitals be sufficient? To maintain that "no healthy person, it appears, can fail to make some addition (*Zusatz*) that might be called perverse to the normal sexual aim"[4]—this experiential datum has no direct bearing on the question at hand, which comes up repeatedly in the Freudian text, notably in *Civilization and Its Discontents.* But Freud says something quite different in the *Three Essays:* there, his primary concern is to demonstrate that perversion can only be declared pathological from the moment such an addition comes to occupy the foreground, takes on the exclusivity and permanence of a "fixation" (*Fixierung*), and supplants what it is supposed to augment.

Just as—the parallel seems unavoidable—sadism would correspond to a hypertrophy and autonomization of the supplement or admixture (*Beimengung*) of aggression figuring in normal sexuality and to its displacement into a central position.[5]

Beauty as an admixture or supplement, including the pathways, sometimes perverse, that it opens up for the sexual drive? The paradox confronting us here is that in artistic matters beauty is regularly ("normally"?) associated with characteristics or traits designated as secondary, while excessive attention to the genitals raises the issue of pornography: as in the case of Courbet's now-famous painting *L'Origine du monde* (a foreshortened female torso, its vagina—with carefully articulated cleft—given foreground prominence by the chosen vantage point), executed for Khalil Bey, the former Ambassador of Constantinople to Saint Petersburg, who had it installed in his dressing room, and which came into the possession—by route unknown—of Jacques Lacan (Figure 1).[6] To say nothing of the last assemblage conceived by Marcel Duchamp, the *Étant donnés* in the Philadelphia Museum, in which the effect created by the framing of a simple mannequin—headless but with legs spread—is intensified by the position of voyeur to which the beholder finds himself relegated. Quite different is *L'Évidence éternelle* by René Magritte (Figure 2), in which the painter has cut the image of a nude woman into a vertical sequence of small paintings, each of which—including one picturing her groin—bears a manifest relation, thanks to the mischief worked by their simultaneous presentation, to visibility of a kind that's deemed perfectly acceptable, whereas Courbet's small canvas, by contrast, had to be exhibited beneath a veil, a nicety observed even by Lacan. As Freud noted at an early date, in the *Three Essays*, after the remarks already cited about the role of "visual impressions" in the evolution of the sexual object toward beauty: "the progressive concealment of the body which goes along with civilization keeps sexual curiosity awake. This curiosity seeks to complete the sexual object by revealing its hidden parts. It can, however, be diverted ('subli-

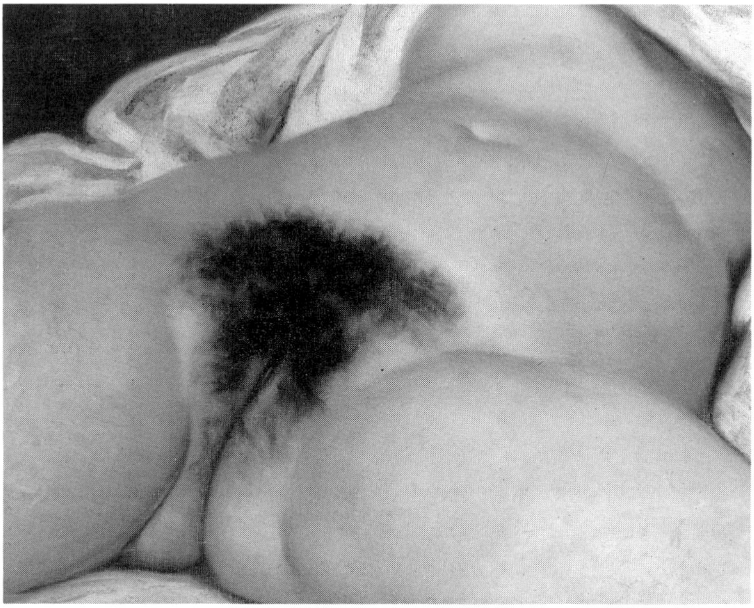

Figure 1 Gustave Courbet, *The Origin of the World*, 1866 (private collection).

mated') in the direction of art, if its interest can be shifted away from the genitals on to the shape of the body as a whole."[7]

This passage merits close scrutiny on several counts. First, because it was at this point in the *Three Essays* that Freud inserted, in 1915, his note on the sexual derivation of beauty. Second, because the notion of sublimation makes its first, rather furtive appearance here. And, finally, because of the opposition Freud felt obliged to note at this juncture between a posited regime of sexual curiosity, determined to seek out the missing parts of the object, and a more diversified, polymorphous regime centering on art: insofar as it is more "elevated," the aesthetic emotion paralleling the "overvaluation" of the sexual object as a *Wunschziel* or aim of desire, which is rarely limited to the genitals alone, tending rather to play over the entire body and involve every sensation derived from it.[8]

However, the aesthetic emotion plays only an indirect role

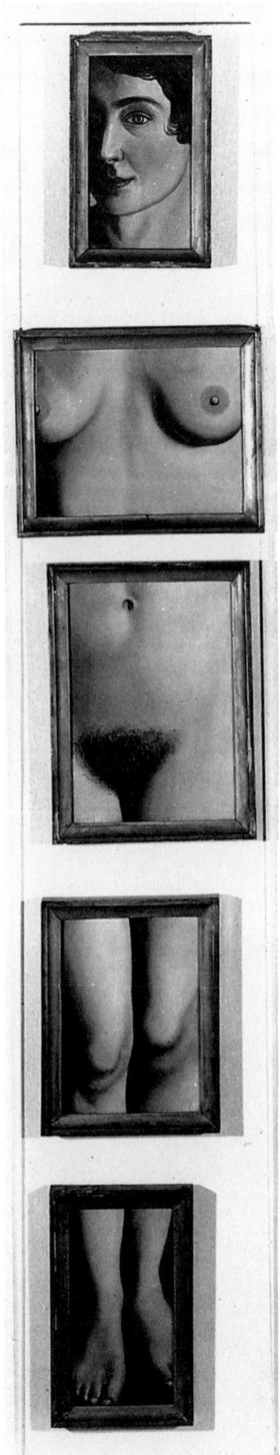

Figure 2. René Magritte, *L'Évidence éternelle*, 1930 (Collection William N. Copley, New York).

in the elevation of non-genitally-centered activities to the level of a sexual aim. It does nothing more than divert the sexual drive: it inhibits it from reaching its aim by, eventually, diverting it in the direction of art (in which case we should speak of "sublimation"), but does not necessarily have any effect on its object. And it was primarily to this object that Freud was referring, in *Civilization and Its Discontents*, when he asserted that "beauty" and "charm" were originally its attributes. "Originally" (*ursprünglich*): the fact that evolution of the sexual object toward beauty could result from natural selection is consistent, in the phylogenetic order, with inhibition of the aim (though not of the object?) which is its final intent, without there being any need for art to intervene.

A reading of the first of the *Three Essays* should lead us to modulate somewhat the emphasis seemingly given, in *Civilization and Its Discontents*, to the object of which beauty is an attribute. In a discussion of sexual inversion (what we now call homosexuality), Freud affirmed that there was as yet no satisfactory explanation (*keine volle Aufklärung*) of its genesis. Another added note, this one dating from 1910, indicates that psychoanalysis nonetheless has significant things to say about this subject. If Freud saw no need to resolve this apparent contradiction—to be more precise: if he chose to be a bit coy about it (as he would later be with regard to beauty and what psychoanalysis might or might not have to say about *it*)—one reason for this might be found later in the text, where he states that analysis encourages a way of seeing things that could, ultimately, be more important than a resolution of the problem (this observation, too, relegated to a note). The clinical study of cases considered abnormal reveals, indeed, that a solderlike relation obtains between sexual drive and sexual object (*eine Verlötung zwischen Sexualtrieb und Sexualobjekt*) which is not present in normal formations, where the object appears to be part and parcel with the drive (*wo der Trieb das Objekt mitzubringen scheint*). Contrary to the popular prejudice holding that the sexual drive, absent in childhood, comes to maturity during puberty as a result of the attraction exercised by one sex over the other, "we are thus warned to loosen the bond that exists in our thoughts between [drive] and object. It seems probable that the sexual [drive] is in the first instance independent of its object; nor is its origin likely to be due to its object's [*charms*] [my emphasis]."[9] The same goes for the "perversion" associated, at its entry into Freud's text, with the enigma of beauty: it is less important to explain its genesis (about which psychoanalysis nonetheless has something to say) than to liberate this question from that of its object and the "charms" it might have in order to attach it once more to the realm of the drives.

A bit of history (or perhaps archeology) should help us conceptualize the drive apart from the object—beauty itself in this instance—if it is true, as Freud thought, that the most important difference between our approach to sexual life and that of the ancient world (which, as is well known, was greatly preoccupied with the search for beauty) was precisely that, whereas we lay stress on the object, the ancients emphasized the drive itself.[10] Such an assertion only has meaning, of course, in a Platonic context: doesn't the text that has exercised the greatest influence on humanist reflection concerning the relations between beauty and love, Plato's *Symposium*, indicate that aesthetic education is the first step in an initiatory process leading to the revelation of love's final mystery, the older man being charged with overseeing his disciple's passage from the love of the beautiful body to that of the body in general, and then with helping him understand that beauty of soul is superior to physical beauty, encouraging him "to contemplate the beauty of laws and institutions," such that he finally comes to realize that "nearly every kind of beauty is akin to every other" and that "the beauty of the body is not, after all, of such great moment"?[11] If Socrates maintained that we ought to honor love above all things, this was precisely because he had managed to detach himself progressively from simulacra in order to arrive at contemplating beauty in itself, "through the organ that makes it visible" (*orōnti ō oraton to kalon*).[12] From which follows Freud's statement, according full acknowledgment to what psychoanalysis has to say about beauty, even if the latter—or at least our own relationship to it—is considered *historically:* "The ancients glorified the [drive] and were prepared on its account to honor even an inferior object; while we despise the activity of the drive in itself, and find excuses for it only in the merits of the object."[13] With the caveat that art, especially contemporary art, has taught us that this object (but are we still discussing the same one?) lends itself to all sorts of variations, even aberrations, some of them singularly perverse, and others so crude that we would prefer to know nothing about them—as Freud wrote concerning the choice of particularly repulsive objects—*aus ästhetischen Gründen*, "on aesthetic grounds."[14]

Freud never wavered on this point: the object of the drive is eminently variable; it "is not originally connected with it but becomes assigned to it only in consequence of being peculiarly fitted to make satisfaction possible," its position in the circuitry of the drive being determined by the fact that it is through it, or rather thanks to it, or yet again—as Lacan put it—*en en faisant le tour*, that the drive can attain its aim: so true is it that this object is but the presence of a void, a lack, and that the drive can never find satisfaction save by circling around a perpetually absent object.[15] That the object has no importance within the drive, at least in the beginning, that it is, to use Lacan's language again, a matter of total indifference there, such an assertion should prompt one "to prick up one's ears."[16] Doubly so for us, if it's true, as is maintained in *Civilization and Its Discontents*, that the aesthetic emotion offers a typical example of a drive "inhibited in its aim," which is to say—returning to Freud's definition—of a process that, having first evolved in the direction of satisfaction, is subsequently thwarted or detoured. To view the aesthetic emotion in terms of the drive is to deny that it has its cause in the object. Then how are we to accept, how grasp, that the concept of the "beautiful" could have its roots in the domain of sexual excitement, as indicated in the *Three Essays*, and that originally it designates what is sexually stimulating? Doesn't this stimulation proceed from the object, and initially from the sexual organs, the sight of which is supposed to provoke the most intense sexual excitement, even though we can never find them beautiful, properly speaking? Isn't the eye, the erotogenic zone "perhaps the most remote from the sexual object"—to use Freud's language in the *Three Essays*—also the one that, "in the situation of wooing an object, is liable to be the most frequently stimulated by the particular quality of excitation whose cause, when it occurs in a sexual object, we describe as beauty"? And don't we, "for the same reason," describe "the merits of a sexual object as 'charms' (*Reize*)"?[17]

It must be admitted that the question is poorly formulated and biased—perhaps doubly so, due, on the one hand, to the status assigned the excitation of the drive, which Freud believed emanated not from the exterior world but from inside the organism, its satisfaction being obtainable only through appropriate modification of its internal source; and, on the other, to the paradoxical role explicitly vested in sight, according to the speculative hypothesis that Freud was to propose in a long note to *Civilization and Its Discontents:* while the erotogenic zone corresponding to the eye can be stimulated only from a certain distance, the resulting excitation is among the most vivid, even when the sexual object attracts attention precisely by thwarting it, as is most often the case. And yet, however stimulating the view of the sexual object might be, especially of its sexual organs, the intensity of visual excitation is not, in human beings, a primary given: phylogenetically speaking, it is a consequence of the "organic repression" (*organische Verdrängung*) leading to the permanent substitution of visual excitation for olfactory sensations initially linked to a specific physiological function, namely the periodic production of menses: as evidenced by the menstrual taboo, which Freud thought was intended to preclude reversion to an earlier phase of human development.[18] This note was appended to a discussion of the institution of the family, which should not surprise us: it might indeed be supposed that the establishment of the latter coincided with an evolution of the need for genital satisfaction, which "no longer made its appearance like a guest who drops in suddenly, and, after his departure, is heard of no more for a long time, but instead took up its quarters as a permanent lodger."[19] Once intermittent, the excitation, and with it the need for sexual satisfaction, became continuous, at least theoretically, regardless of the effects entailed by becoming accustomed to the pleasure deriving from the act itself. But this organic repression would follow, according to Freud's hypothetical scenario, upon man's adoption of an upright posture, which, by giving prominence to the previously obscured genitals, prompted feelings of shame and an impulse to cover them. Such that the straightening or "verticalization" of humankind initiated an irreversible process: "From that point the chain of events would have proceeded through the devaluation of olfactory stimuli and the isolation of the menstrual period to the time when visual stimuli were paramount and the genitals became visible, and thence to the continuity of sexual excitation, the founding of the family and so to the threshold of human civilization."

Freud found this hypothesis so important that he expected the study of animals whose living conditions were closest to man's would verify it, and this only throws into greater relief the bias of which I spoke above. A bias one can only regard as having been carefully calculated, as it very effectively precludes the operation of any strict apportionment between nature and culture, as well as between animality and humanity, obfuscating this question entirely. In this respect, *Civilization and Its Discontents* fits quite comfortably into a line of speculation initiated by Freud in *The Future of an Illusion.* The focus of this investigative project is the future of man and civilization, even though it must proceed by returning to the remote past. Despite appearances (the comparison with other forms of animal life suggested by the hypothesized link between man's "verticalization," "organic repression," and the institution of the family), the problem, for Freud, was not one of situating man in a zoological series. In the matter of developmental sequences, the one that retained his attention was not consistent with—nor did it preclude—the received evolutionary idea holding that *Homo sapiens* is the last link in the chain climaxed by the primates. The importance Freud ascribes to the upright posture by no means implies his rejection of the traditional image of the man-ape, or his embrace of the idea, which first attracted attention after the discovery of Sinanthropicus and Australopithecus at about the time *Civilization and Its Discontents* appeared, that the human line might be radically distinct from that of the anthropoids, as the prehominids had previously adopted an upright posture, which was a necessary condition for human status.[20] Nonetheless, the essential point here is that the chain of events he describes, which is supposed to have led ineluctably to the institution of what he calls *Kultur*, unfolds entirely within the hominid line, and that, as a result, any comparison with other animal species should be couched not in terms of anatomy but rather in those of behavior.

The role devolving upon visual excitation in the reproductive cycle is not in itself an exclusively human trait, nor even one of human evolution. The sexual display characteristic of numerous animal species, like the vivid colors of the genitals in some apes, can function only as a signal or a lure: here engagement of the imaginary is secured through visual means, without any kind of "organic repression" being implied. On the other hand, the olfactory relation as understood by Freud does not seem to be limited to a strictly reflexive conditioning, for he implies that the corresponding sexual excitation effects the psychic economy, stating that the sense of smell performs an intermediary function enabling menstruation to act on the "male psyche" (*auf die männliche Psyche*). A being that rises above the ground and resolves to walk upright is thus already a man, and not a "super-anthropoid," even though the criteria used by Freud are quite distinct from those of comparative anatomy. The plaster figure of Anthropopithicus, the intermediary stage between ape and man, presented at the International Exposition of 1900 boasted at least one indubitably human trait according to Freud's criteria: the fig leaf obscuring his genitals—perhaps solely intended to honor the scruples of visitors, but which nonetheless appears retrospectively as a corollary of the happy inspiration prompting those responsible for the reconstruction to confer upon this purported human ancestor a quasi-vertical posture: an idea that, despite its being prominently displayed at the exposition, met with considerable resistance before being accepted in paleontology (see Figure 3).

If according to Freud's hypothesis we must take "verticalization" as the point of departure not of man but of the process leading to the advent of *Kultur*, this is because—a point well worth repeating—an erect posture, by making visible the genital organs that had previously been hidden, necessitated their being protected while at the same time initiating shame, entailing the depreciation of olfactory stimuli and the increased importance of visual ones. The emergence of civilization is thus inextricably linked (though not in a cause-effect relationship) to an affirmation not only of the sexual drive per se but also of the scopic drive (*Schautrieb*)—originally focused on the genitals—discussed in the *Three Essays:* the ambivalence of the two terms combined in *Schau-Lust*, the German neologism designating scopic pleasure, pointing up the decided ambiguity of every drive and every pleasure deriving from the sphere—as we're discussing man—identifiable with looking, whether in a passive or an active mode. The pleasure experienced in looking and exhibiting oneself (*Schau- und Exhibitionlust*) indicates that the eye corresponds to an erotogenic zone of the sexual drive emanating from it, like the skin, which in certain parts of the body "has become differentiated into sense organs or modified into mucous membrane, and is thus the erotogenic zone *par excellence.*[21]

As applied to man, the hypothesis of an "organic repression" following upon the acquisition of an upright posture also raises

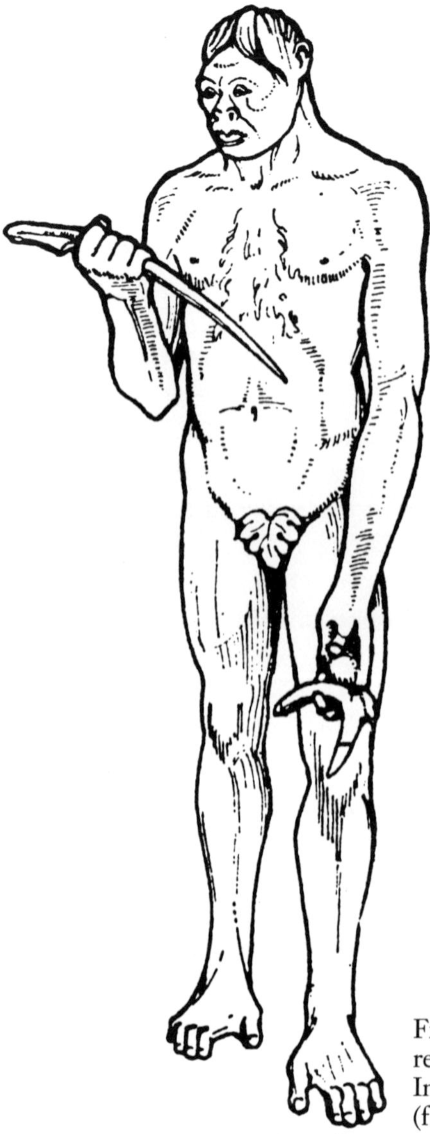

Figure 3. *Pithecanthropus*, as reconstructed by Dubois for the International Exposition of 1900 (from Leroi-Gourhan).

problems with regard to a repressive factor that must be designated as "psychic." The displacement of one sensory organ in the process of sexual excitation by another does not guarantee that the sensations formerly assuming the primary role will be diverted into the register of the unconscious: at most, it is justifiable to maintain that visual perception implies a zone of consciousness distinct and more extensive than that tied to olfactory sensations. If Freud used the term "repression" here, this is because he understood the process to entail not only the substitution of visual excitation for olfactory sensation but also a depreciation of the latter, thereby clearing the way for that repression (also qualified by Freud as organic, and for the same reasons) to which infantile anal eroticism is condemned—and "condemned" is indeed the appropriate word here, if this repression is what Freud says it is: something analogous to a "condemnatory judgment" (*Urteilsverwerfung*) in the field of logic.[22] Freud further notes that education, which sets out with particular determination to instill a sense that excrement is disgusting, succeeds in doing so only because its strong odor makes it susceptible to the fate reserved for all olfactory impressions in the wake of man's becoming erect[23]: the designation "man" being truly merited only by those who, having opted for an upright posture, agree to pay the price of an initial renunciation and accept the transformation of a source of pleasure into a source of unpleasure.

It is at this point that the repression begins. A repression that is literally paleontological, to the extent that it puts in place a structure constitutive of the human being, its ontogenesis being reduced to a strict repetition of its phylogenesis, the former's development being a close imitation of the latter's, even where the "prehistory" wiped out by infantile amnesia is in question.[24] But the substitution of visual for olfactory excitation produces additional effects that are in complete rupture with the organic register. Not only is the eye, as was already maintained by Aristotle, the most "theoretical" of all the sense organs, but visual perception prevails over every other in the construction of man's image of the world (to such an extent that consideration of how a blind person might gain access to it makes us uneasy: see Diderot's *Letter on the Blind*). Its aesthetic dimension (even in the transcendental sense of this term), accentuated by its serving as one of the subject's primary means of getting its bearings, justifies the role assigned to it in the

Platonic tradition: a path leads from the sensible world to the ideal world, corresponding to the successive degrees of initiation into the secrets of Beauty. The metaphor of vision and visibility was prevalent in Plato, and to an even greater extent in the Neoplatonists, as a means of qualifying how thought contemplates the Idea, as well as the relation that can obtain between Beauty, on the one hand, and Truth and sovereign Goodness on the other, as is signified unequivocally in the Greek *idein*, "to see."

This path is not exclusively that of perception, and still less that of optics, geometry, or physiology, but that of love, and initially that of desire. How is the latter introduced into the picture, and what is its claim to relevance here? As Lacan never tired of repeating, the drive manifests itself at the level of the scopic field by means of the split between the eye and the gaze. Man doesn't just look, he gazes, and it is this gaze that justifies adding the scopic to the catalog of other drives.[25] Its *addition:* as though both beauty and the scopic drive in which it finds its primary anchor participated, to some extent, in the register of the supplement. A man looks; in looking, what does he see? That what he sees gazes back at him. According to a teaching of Merleau-Ponty that was embraced by Lacan: I see from one point only, but in my own existence I'm gazed at from everywhere. The gaze of the other, however, though it disorganizes the field of perception, is not, any more than is my own, that of a purely reflexive subject. If there is a reciprocity or dialectic of the gaze, it is not solely an affair of points of view, of perspectives, nor is it one of shame, but rather one of desire. As was also emphasized by Lacan, the presence of the other in the scopic field concerns not the organ of vision but rather the subject's sustaining itself in a relation of desire.

In order to arrive at this integration of vision within the privileged field of desire that is the gaze—the gaze assuring passage from excitation to desire as a properly human structure, to the point that another *Letter on the Blind* becomes necessary in relation to the question of desire—an "organic repression" must lead to the prevalence of visual excitation over olfactory sensations, such that the scopic drive becomes all the more important because, to cite from the *Three Essays*, "the optical impression remains the means by which libidinal excitation is most frequently stimulated," with the acknowledged beauty of the sexual object playing a determinant role in this process. Does the explicitly teleological[26] relation described by Freud in the *Three Essays* between natural selection and the evolution of the sexual object toward beauty have a "biological significance"—one that follows from Freud's hypothesis, with regard to sadism and masochism, that the biological meaning of aggression, of the tendency to "force things" in the sexual relation, could derive from a necessity to overcome resistance to the sexual object in some way other than wooing?[27] If there is necessarily a component of violence in sexuality, this is because the means at the disposal of the sexual drive to impose its will are limited. In other words, this impurity, this admixture (*Beimengung*) of aggression bears witness to the boundaries of seduction, "whether this consists of a show of things or of words." Does it follow from Freud's "biological" necessity that natural selection favors the evolution of the sexual object toward beauty in order to increase its capacity for exerting attraction and, simultaneously, to increase libidinal excitation by opening the way to seduction—the very notion of "natural selection" (*Zuchtwahl*) being understood as implying the possibility of a development, if not an advance, that would nonetheless implant the properly aesthetic destiny of the scopic drive in the biological?

* * *

The Freud of *Civilization and Its Discontents* unambiguously rejects biologism and even naturalism, according the breadth and weight of reality to the "sexual theory" developed in the *Three Essays*. Nonetheless, the later text stresses a "reality" of another kind, one in which the culturally imposed renunciation of drive-linked satisfactions plays an integral role. Which entails certain paradoxical consequences with regard to "beauty," as long as one remains committed to a clear division between nature and culture—the question then becoming one of determining what role civilization, in implementing its project to reduce human pretensions to happiness, can assign to beauty, and whether it merely tolerates it or knows how to manipulate it to achieve its ends.

But what meaning can the word "beauty" have in the order or register of "nature," insofar as it remains distinct from that of art? If "natural objects" or landscapes have their own beauty, like the human body, does it follow that this particular kind of beauty—one making a show of things only, words being left to the eventual devices of art?—is subject to strictly natural determinants which civilization must preserve within itself as it cultivates and develops them? "We require civilized man to reverence beauty wherever he sees it in nature and to create it in the objects of his handiwork so far as he is able."[28] But how are we to justify this requirement, which we readily acknowledge to be a signal indicator of evolved civilization, if not in terms, once more, of pleasure? And how are we to understand the passage from a beauty necessarily characterized as "natural" to one that is the product of artifice, in all senses of the word? Does nature deceive us, as art does, when it offers us substitute satisfactions? And how is the part played by delusion to be apportioned between the natural and the artificial, given that, if delusion there is and ought to be, there would be no way to exclude it *a priori* from the field of "culture"?

Freud's way of broaching the question in *Civilization and Its Discontents* undermines the prevalent tendency to see in the beauty of nature a confirmation of the generous intent of Providence, as well as the notion of a preexisting harmony between man and the universe. If it's true that the supposedly prior and immediate feeling of unity with the world, the so-called oceanic feeling susceptible to consideration as the source of all religious feeling, calls for a psychoanalytic explanation (which is to say a genetic one, as Freud notes[29]), and if it's true that it is the expression of a need for protection linked to the infantile state of total dependence and a longing for the father, then the attraction of so-called natural beauty could be the result of an analogous defense mechanism. The cult of beauty would then be but one among several means used by man to exorcise the power of a nature decidedly hostile to him: an affair, as Freud implies, not only of sensibility but also of judgment (*Urteil*), as is also true of the beauty inhering in perishable bodies and thus vulnerable to decay and death. In both cases, the attribution of beauty would serve to reassure us.

But beauty does more than compensate us for the sacrifices imposed by social life. It also satisfies a requirement of civilization that Freud associates with its characteristic penchant for order and cleanliness. While the utility of both of these criteria seems obvious, neither is absolutely vital to survival, and it is difficult to see how they could function as sources of pleasure. On the other hand, "That civilization is not exclusively taken up with what is useful is already shown by the example of beauty, which we decline to exclude from the interests of civilization . . . ; something else must be at work as well."[30] As is proven by our regarding the care lavished by human beings on "things" whose vital necessity is far from apparent as a reliable index of culture. Freud cites the example of green spaces, which are certainly necessary in towns as playgrounds and reservoirs of fresh air, but which we also (*auch*, to indicate a supplementary status?) take pleasure in adorning with flowers, just as we do balconies and windowsills.[31]

Beauty settles in where it can, and one might be tempted to object that, insofar as "things" are concerned, civilization gets its money's worth in this case, as flowerpots on balconies might well have aggressive connotations, corresponding to territorial markers. But the example of urban green spaces brings to mind another, that of the preserves established by more advanced societies to husband their natural resources, a phenomenon invoked by Freud in his discussion of the question of art and its function in the human psychic economy. The case of the American National Parks, where man's intervention is kept to a minimum and nature is effectively left to its own devices, held particular interest for him: here there are no ornaments or addenda, no supplements or pretensions to "embellishment" (cities apparently offering, at least in the United States, a sufficiently large field for the work of "beautification"), though these areas provide superb "natural" decors that Hollywood was quick to exploit. Likewise for art: however "cultivated" it might be, it nonetheless remains, in some sense, a repository of what Jean Dubuffet called "savage values," the contradiction in question encompassing all that relates to beauty. Art, insofar as it is governed by the pleasure principle, can indeed function as a kind of preserve (which doesn't necessarily imply restricted access) in which man is allowed to give his fantasies free reign; nonetheless, in the passage to implementation, which is to say to reality, it plays (however reluctantly) a definite civilizing role; thus positions advertising themselves as "anticultural"—in the case of *art brut*, for example—can be perfectly consistent with and even owe their very existence to a culture of great sophistication, as is observable precisely in the case of Dubuffet. And, likewise, civilization can develop and extend itself at the expense of nature as well as of beauty's part in it: if beauty there is and ought to be, its idea is imposed by culture, which also formulates the demand for it, even as it furnishes man, through education, with the means to make judgments about it.

The connection, apparently crucial to civilization, between the beauty imperative and the requirement for order and cleanliness is not, however, as innocent as it seems. The considerable emphasis placed by Freud on the relation between anal eroticism and the compulsion for order and cleanliness might well prompt us, here again, to prick up our ears. Did not the aesthetic emotion itself proceed from an "organic" repression that supposedly entailed a depreciation of olfactory sensation and paved the way not only to civilization but also to the repression of anal eroticism, the drive toward cleanliness proceeding from an imperious need to make excrement, now an object of repugnance, disappear?[32] This repugnance, which itself serves to thwart the sexual drive, can—there is nothing paradoxical in this—extend its reach to the genitals, beginning with those of the opposite sex; if the sexual drive "in its strength enjoys overriding this disgust,"[33] that is because what's in question is not merely a hysterical response but one of more general import, as is confirmed by our never finding the sexual organs in themselves "beautiful," even though the sight of them can provoke the most intense sexual excitement.

Freud says, also in *Civilization and Its Discontents*, that beauty and charm are originally attributes of the sexual object. But if it seems incontrovertible that the concept of beauty has its roots in sexual excitement, how are we to comprehend that this category does not and cannot apply, as a general rule, to the genital organs in and of themselves (*die Genitalien selbst*)? The distance Freud implicitly marked out between seeing them, which is always exciting, and that element precluding our finding them "beautiful," far from resolving the apparent paradox, only further intensifies it: as is the case with the connection posited—explicitly—in the *Three Essays* between the assertion that "beauty" originally designated that which is sexually stimulating and that one *cannot* find the genitals beautiful. At the very moment in which a veritable craze for "applied psychoanalysis" was developing, Freud studiously maintained that psychoanalysis had nothing to say about beauty. But if he felt compelled to write in *Civilization and Its Discontents* that psychoanalysis had less to say about beauty than about other subjects, this was because he sensed something in play that, far from operating on the level of taste and judgment, was linked rather to resistance and repression: something—a "less than nothing"—affiliated with the lack (or as Lacan preferred to designate it, the *minus-phi*) of castration, as symbolized by the gaze.

As Freud stressed, the importance accorded by female hysterics to the sexual organ's role in urination is not sufficient to justify an attitude of repugnance toward it; but the fact that this is at least as true, if not more so, of the female as of the male sexual organ (due to oscillation between the cult of the phallus and castration anxiety) does not preclude, far from it, our suspecting that what psychoanalysis might have had to say about beauty, at least in the writings of its founding father, conformed to an essentially male point of view. The same could be said regarding the irresistible attraction exerted over Freud by certain of his hysterical patients (which would lead him to the discovery of the "transference"): an attraction comparable to that of the most exquisite flowers, but also the most sterile, precisely because of their disgust with sex. In the years following the second edition of the *Three Essays* (1910), we are far removed from the problematic of hysteria. At this time, Freud was interested in very different things: fantasy, literary creation, and narcissism. But his handling of the question of beauty nonetheless bears witness, in its discrete formulations, to a kind of secret insistence, to an obstinate determination to return to that which occasioned the beginnings of psychoanalysis: as though for Freud beauty was necessarily linked, not only with perversion, but with hysteria.

The possibility that disgust might play a role in the genesis of the aesthetic emotion would seem to necessitate a reconsideration of the question of the *beau idéal* and its civilizing function—of its very status as a question, or as an enterprise, which is not explicable in terms of reason alone. But one point is clear: the divine Plato was not mistaken in maintaining that beauty is linked with desire, although the statement does not necessarily hold up if the terms are reversed. Even so, psychoanalysis has nothing to do with a renewal of Neoplatonism, and if some think they can look down on it from a superior vantage, they have good reason. Certainly the notion of "sublimation" implies no idea of ascension, elevation, or even advance, but rather that of an uncoupling, a slippage, or a displacement originating in the substitution of secondary sexual traits for the genitals as a source of excitation, as well as that of a fixation or blockage of scopic pleasure. Freud states this plainly, although it might appear that in doing so he is once again deferring to a sacralized image of art: "It is usual for most normal people to linger to some extent over the intermediate sexual aim of looking that has a sexual tinge to it; indeed, this offers them a possibility of directing some proportion of their libido on to higher artistic aims."[34]

The aesthetic emotion as typical example of a drive inhibited in its aim? That depends completely on the aim assigned to the scopic drive. If the latter inclines only toward release through the "normal" sexual act of heterosexual coupling, then any deviation from, and to an even greater extent any blockage of, this path will run the risk of appearing deviant or aberrational. On the other hand, if the drive finds insufficient satisfaction in the preliminary pleasure born of excitation of the erotogenic zone, then the need for the greater pleasure corresponding to the "normal" pathway can cede its place to pleasure of a different kind, but one whose sexual derivation will be no less marked. Careful readers of the *Three Essays* will hesitate before declaring the aim linked to this pleasure "more elevated." As is well known, the scopic drive can fix upon aims so far removed from sanctioned aesthetic norms that one is tempted to declare them pathological; and it can also overcome the shame, disgust, horror, and even pain opposed to the achievement of scopic pleasure in order to play itself out in "performances" as "astonishing" as those inventoried by Freud as "perversions." In either case, the same observation holds: Freud writes that it is in the most abominable perversions that psychic participation in the transformation of the sexual drive is most fully evident, and whatever the eventual results, it seems clear that Freud is here engaged in idealizing the drive. "The omnipotence of love [like that of art, its derivative?] is perhaps never more strongly proved than in such of its aberrations as these"; and Freud then cites a passage by Goethe (*Vom Himmel durch die Welt zur Hölle*), which he paraphrases and elaborates as follows: "The highest and the lowest are always closest to each other in the sphere of sexuality."[35]

It might seem a contradiction in terms to speak of "idealization" in connection with the scopic drive's most disgusting aims. But the contradiction is only apparent and ultimately derives, like that between art's anticultural component and its civilizing role, or between the biological meaning of beauty and the economic requirement behind it, from a much deeper conflict: the one that follows, for the eye, as for every other organ or system of organs, from having to serve two masters at once, namely the ego-drives and the sexual drives: "The mouth serves for kissing as well as for eating and communication by speech; the eyes perceive not only alternations in the external world which are important for the preservation of life, but also characteristics of objects which lead to their being chosen as objects of love—their 'charms' (*Reize*) . . . The closer the relation into which an organ with a dual function of this kind enters with one of the major [drives], the more it withholds itself from the other."[36]

The view of the aesthetic emotion as "a typical example of a drive inhibited in its aim" raises certain difficulties. For what drive is in question here: the so-called sexual drive (*Sexualtrieb*) as a whole or that component of it dubbed "scopic" by Lacan? This partial drive would indeed be inhibited from attaining its aim, if its normal destiny were that of opening a pathway to the sexual act. But why, then, should the exclusive focus of scopic pleasure on the genitals be considered perverse, as Freud maintains in the passage of the *Three Essays* to which he appended his note on the sexual derivation of the concept of "beauty"? Why couldn't the pleasure obtained by viewing the sexual organs be counted among the so-called preliminary pleasures that prepare the way toward one that's greater and more intense, a "terminal" pleasure assessable in terms of satisfaction as opposed to excitation? Why should there be a displacement of the drive such that its object becomes not the organ itself but the sexual characteristics or signs, the traits (*Merkmalen*) classified as secondary—those "beguilements" or "charms" into whose catalog the genitals could not be admitted without qualifying as perverse, or even pornographic? And how are we to account for the fact that in the first rank of these "beguilements" are maternal traits, the breast above all, which here occupies a paradoxical place because its acknowledged status as the first sexual object would seem inconsistent with that to which it is reduced when it is pronounced a "secondary" trait to which beauty can attach itself? Clearly, beauty has a certain relationship to lack, to loss. The nursing infant is certainly incapable of appreciating the beauty of the breast. In order for an object, even a phallicly determined one, to be judged beautiful, it must first have been posited as lost, if only on an unconscious level. But the spectacle of this loss, of its figuration in genital terms, can under no circumstances occasion aesthetic pleasure—or so some would have us believe.

All of these questions tend, we might say, toward the same aim: beauty, insofar as it derives from the sexual sphere and is preeminently linked to the scopic drive, should lend itself to a dismantling analogous to that operated by Freud on the drive, distinguishing the latter's object or aim, as well as the pressure or *Drang* animating it (whose constancy utterly precludes assimilation of the drive to some biological force), from satisfaction, which can borrow the pathways of sublimation: however inhibited the drive might be from reaching its aim, it nonetheless tends toward and obtains satisfaction, and it does this without repression. As Lacan insists, this state of affairs can only lead us to question what, exactly, is meant by satisfaction.[37]

The attribution of beauty, then, is not solely a function of relationships (as Diderot would have it), given the paradoxical resemblance of the drive, in Lacan's view, to a montage or surrealist collage that seems, at first glance, to have neither head nor tail.[38] That vision is called upon to serve not one but two masters simultaneously—the ego-drives and the sexual drives—only further confirms this. But the essential thing, with regard to what is known as "art history," remains the following: What psychoanalysis might have had to say about beauty, through Freud, which assuredly is not something simple and straightforward, is linked to the scopic drive, seeing as beauty is a derivative of the sexual drive pressed into the service of civilization, just as the ego-drives subject vision to their aims. Freud's according sight such a privileged status in the genealogy not only of the idea of the "beautiful" but of beauty itself (if we accept his naturalist hypothesis), as it is tied to the emergence of desire, is rather astonishing, given that he never stopped insisting, perhaps with a complacency that's somewhat suspect, on his not being a visual creature and having only a limited interest in music, on his preference for literature as opposed to the plastic arts. It is well known that Freud's artistic tastes ran to the classics, and anyone hoping to find in the pages of *Civilization and Its Discontents* a justification of the modernist critical stance as this relates to the visual arts will be disappointed. Beauty, even insofar as it is visible, is not exclusively optical or retinal (a term used by Duchamp to dismiss a certain kind of painting he found as disagreeable as "the smell of turpentine"). To be sure, words are not its initial means of transmission (though there's no denying that language has an effect on the scopic field and that passage from the imaginary to the symbolic is possible). But its being drive-linked, whether in its essential nature or by derivation (as André Breton wrote in these same years, "Beauty is convulsive or it is nothing"), is consistent with Descartes' view that it's not the eye that sees, but the soul. And it is with the soul—*die Seele* recurs constantly in Freud's original German—that we must come to terms. For the question around which we've never stopped circling, like the drive around its object, is this: What exactly is satisfaction, if the soul has any purchase on it? And what is the soul itself—the seeing soul—if it has any purchase on satisfaction, deviant or otherwise?

3

Freud with Kant? The Enigma of Pleasure

I have already stated that this reading of Freud, and of what he could have had to say about beauty, will be oriented and framed by his implicit reference to Kant's third *Critique*, more specifically to the analytic of the beautiful which opens its "Critique of Aesthetic Judgment." There is nothing in Freud's text that calls for this reference or explicitly justifies it.[1] In an attempt like this one to assess historically the passages in which Freud evokes the problem of beauty, other names also have some claim to consideration, beginning with that of the "divine Plato." Kant was certainly not the first to bring what Lacan called the "pleasure index" to bear on aesthetic matters, but his formulation of the question of the judgment of taste is echoed in Freud's text; these echoes are decidedly problematic, but I will undertake to amplify them, to set them reverberating, in hopes of revealing something that otherwise would have remained obscure.

First, the thesis consistently advanced by Freud that the object of the drive is, at least initially, of no importance, its only point of interest being its capacity to provide satisfaction (at least initially: the problem consisting in part of determining at what moment, under what conditions, in what context, as a result of what evolution, and in virtue of what displacement the object ceases being, as Lacan would have it, a matter of total indifference). Would we be justified in comparing Freud's uncoupling of the question of beauty, insofar as it is derivative of the drive, from its object with the "Copernican revolution" operated by Kant with regard to the faculty of judging "beauty"? The analytic of the beautiful posits that the judgment of taste is not logical but aesthetic, with the latter term designating "that of which the determining principle can only be subjective": to decide whether something is beautiful or not, we do not relate the representation to the object by means of the understanding; rather, we relate it by means of the imagination to the subject and its feeling (*Gefühl*) of pleasure (*Lust*) or unpleasure (*Unlust*). It is a question of *affect:* while Diderot already maintained that beauty is relational, what counts for Kant is no longer the objective relation of representations among themselves but the subjective relation of representations to the feelings of pleasure or unpleasure accompanying them, feelings that designate nothing in the object itself but rather the positive or negative affect produced by its representation within the subject.

The parallel would make sense if the analytic of the beautiful did not explicitly exclude from satisfaction, from that *Wohlgefallen* crucial to the judgment of taste, all connotations of drive or libido as well as all links with the realm of desire. The paradox and enigma of what Kant terms "pure" pleasure begins here. Speaking of feelings of pleasure and unpleasure might be another way for Freud to designate the subject's "feeling of life," the *Lebensgefühl* that grounds the faculties of discrimination (*Unterscheidungsvermögen*) and judgment (*Beurteilungs vermögen*): if there is any such thing as this life feeling, it is and must be—insofar as it has anything to do with taste—independent of the faculty of desire (*Begehrungs vermögen*). In determining whether or not something is beautiful, the judging individual asks himself whether its representation gives him satisfaction, his "indifference" (*die Gleichgültigkeit*) being determined less by the object than by the subject itself, for whom it is not so much the object (or rather the latter's representation within him) that is a matter of indifference but its reality, the fact of its existing or not existing. As Kant himself said, in terms we would do well to remember, a judgment concerning beauty in which the slightest bias or interest (*das mindeste Interesse*) plays a role is decidedly partial (*sehr parteilich*) and cannot be considered a judgment of pure taste; to play the role of judge in matters of taste, one must first silence within oneself all desire, and be not the least bit (*im mindesten*) interested with regard to the object's existence but rather totally indifferent to it.[2]

So it is difficult to see, at first glance, what might be the meaning within a Freudian context of a "satisfaction" such as that posited by Kant as the basis of the judgment of taste: one that is "pure and disinterested"—disinterested to an extent inconsistent with the nature of the drive. For there to be a judgment of "pure" taste, the subject must pay no attention to the object and what he might think of it, heeding only the feeling of pleasure or unpleasure awakened in him by its inner representation. A work of art might well be, as Walter Benjamin maintained, a document of barbarism as much as of culture, and, to use Kant's example, a palace might bear simultaneous witness to the vanity of the great and to the exploitation of the working class; but Kant maintains that *such is not the subject at hand* (*nur davon ist jetzt nicht die Rede*): "The important thing in declaring an object beautiful and demonstrating that I have taste is not my relation to the existence of the object, but what I do with this representation within myself (*was ich aus dieser Vorstellung in mir selbst mache*)." The representation is related not to the object but to the subject. But what the latter "does" with it does not adhere to the register of knowledge, not even that through which the subject knows himself (*auch nicht zu demjenigen, wodurch sich das Subjekt selbst erkennt*): judgments of taste convey nothing about the object in question, and they likewise tell us nothing about the pronouncing subject, except that the latter has—or does not have—taste, which is to say that he is capable of declaring an object "beautiful" on the sole basis of affect, of the satisfaction he derives from it.[3]

In Kant's view, where there is *Interesse*, whether positive or negative, there can be no "pure" judgments of taste. Any more than there can be *free* judgments of taste, freedom being paired here with purity and vice versa. Interest of any kind either presupposes or produces a need (*ein Bedurfnis*), and this precludes the pronouncement of judgments that are truly "free." The same holds for satisfaction deriving from the "graceful, lovely, delightful, enjoyable" etc., and generally for "everything pleasing to the senses in sensation." Whereas feeling (*das Gefühl*) must remain subjective and manifest itself in simple approval, in pure assent (*Beifall*), sensation, by contrast, corresponds to an objective representation that determines an inclination, a penchant (*eine Neigung*)—the sole criterion of the value of things being pleasure, in the sense of the enjoyment (*das Vergnügen*) they procure, or that they promise (*welches sie versprechen*). "Of that which is agreeable, we don't say 'I like it' (*es gefällt*) but 'it gratifies me' (*es vergnügt*)." *Annehmlichkeit ist Genuss:* "The agreeable is pleasure"; and pleasure (*jouissance*) goes beyond assent, implying use or consumption. Gratification of this kind is so impure, so interested, that it will always induce a desire (*eine Begierde*) for objects of the same kind that are capable of providing analogous gratification. Beyond a certain point, when the enjoyment becomes most intimate, when it attains a certain level of creaturely pleasure (*das Geniessen . . . das ist das Wort, womit man das Innige des Vergnügens bezeichnet*), judgment of taste is no longer in question: those in search of such gratification willingly dispense with judgment.[4]

Roland Barthes has demonstrated that psychoanalysis provides us with a criterion for distinguishing pleasure from *jouissance*. Pleasure is verbally communicable while *jouissance* is not (Barthes cites Lacan on this point: "What one must bear in mind is that *jouissance* is forbidden to the speaker, or cannot be spoken except between the lines").[5] But we must go farther, at least as regards pleasure—above all that pure pleasure free of any taint of gratification, the one supposedly at the root of the judgment of taste. Jacques Derrida has grasped that the enigma posed by this pleasure must be assessed in light of what's in question, namely, the *discourse on the beautiful*—not only a discourse about the beautiful, but the discursivity inherent in the very structure of the beautiful.[6] Properly speaking, there is no "beauty" that isn't spoken, declared to be such in and by means of a discursive act, a judgment. I can have no pure pleasure insofar as I exist, only insofar as I can speak. Pure pleasure is inseparable from utterance: it is what makes me speak (judge), because the first condition (the *a priori* principle) of the judgment of taste stipulates that in this discursive act the pleasure must be posited as pure, *which is to say* (a phrase to be understood literally in this case, as the index of an enunciatory task) as a pleasure that's not a function of experience, but rather of pure affect—so pure that it can only be measured by its discursive effects (the affect is "to be spoken," and spoken in its function as a feeling of pleasure—"pure" pleasure).

The paradox here is that the affect seems to bracket the subject as much as the object—both the subject as empirical being and as desiring subject, man in both his reasoning and animal aspects. The enigma doesn't lie so much in its being a "pure" pleasure as in its link to feeling, to affect. How can we have a "feeling of life" so utterly unconnected to desire that the subject can properly pay no attention to the existence of an object whose representation is a source of pleasure for it? How can we have a pleasure in which gratification plays no part, when gratification designates pleasure's most intimate component? How can we have a satisfaction in which—to use Kant's term—there is nothing "pathological," which is to say, nothing passive, a satisfaction that's not induced by a stimulus? How can we have an affect stripped of all accompanying emotion which, while pure, belongs to the register of activity (the free play of the faculties)? A pleasure, a satisfaction, an affect whose "purity" is commensurate with that of the judgment of taste, in discursive terms? If these questions have a bearing on the discursive element in the structure of the beautiful, they also concern the relation of pleasure, satisfaction, and affect to the very discursivity that produces them in all of their "purity," insofar as this latter is a condition of the judgment of taste.

Formulated in this way, these questions prompt a reconsideration of one of the most difficult passages in the analytic of the beautiful, section nine, where Kant investigates whether the feeling of pleasure precedes judgment (*die Beurteilung*) of the object or derives from it, the solution to this problem constituting for him the key to the critique of taste (*der Schlüssel zur Kritik des Geschmacks*). If pleasure comes first, it is reduced to a simple sensory gratification and is immediately dependent on the representation in which the object is *given*. To sensory taste (*Sinnesgeschmack*), which has a purely individual value, is opposed considered taste (*Reflexionsgeschmack*), which issues judgments with pretensions to universality: the very foundation of the judgment of taste, the condition of its subjective condition, is unanimity with regard to satisfaction (*die allgemeine Stimme, in Ansehung des Wohlfallens*), the universal communicability of this "mental state" (*die allgemeine Mitteilungsfähigkeit des Gemütszustandes*), each individual considering that the satisfaction he experiences is rooted in something he can take for granted as being shared by everyone, and so can speak of beauty as if it were a property (*Eigenschaft*) or a structure (*Beschaffenheit*) of the object, something determined by a concept. Insofar as it is universally communicable, the "mental state" or *Gemütszustand* is a thing of words. So a purely subjective (aesthetic) act of judgment logically precedes the pleasure induced by the object and provides the basis for the pleasure proceeding from the harmony of the powers or faculties of knowledge and their free play (free because not limited by a concept) in a representation. But the pleasure experienced in communicating, the interest (*Interesse*) inherent in sharing the state of mind that is its point of departure, is not sufficient to account for the judgment of taste in its most intimate manifestation, which is not intersubjective. However dependent on verbal expression it is and must be, beauty, like pleasure, even when shared, is not a matter of consensus: in itself, independent of its relation to the feelings of the subject, it is nothing.[7]

It is principally in this respect that the analytic of the beautiful might seem to overlap with Freudian analysis, which tends to depict the subject as split, divided, separated from itself. What relation can possibly obtain between the attribution of beauty to the unconscious and the repression thanks to which the conscious subject is separated from a portion of its representations? The essential thing here is that, for Freud as for Kant, beauty is a matter of judgment, and "the beautiful" essentially has the value of a predicate. Kant does not investigate beauty in and for itself, but rather taste, defined as the power or faculty of discerning (*unterscheiden*) whether something is beautiful or not: the analytic of the judgment of taste should establish what is necessary to declare an object "beautiful" and clarify its source, its root, in the speaking subject. Likewise with Freud: psychoanalysis, he feigns to avow, does not have much to say about beauty. But this is immediately to displace the question toward that of the attribution of beauty: the concept of "the beautiful" originally designated what was sexually stimulating, even though the genitals, however exciting to the eye, are rarely judged (*beurteilt*) to be beautiful. This prompts a question that might be formulated as follows: Is it "taste" that prohibits us from judging them to be "beautiful" and discourages their representation, which is declared to be "pornographic"? To reframe the question in Freudian terms: What is the relation between "taste" and repression—and between "the beautiful" and the repressed?

The displacement preliminary to the attribution of beauty is inextricable from the function here performed by negation (the genitals are not judged to be *beautiful*). This might well make us prick up our ears once we know that, for Freud, the capacity to make an impartial judgment (*die unparteilische Urteilsfällung*) as to whether a property does or doesn't belong to a thing depends on the creation of the symbol of negation, under whose cover thought acquires a semblance of independence with regard to the repression and achieves a kind of intellectual acceptance of the repressed.[8] Judgment goes in tandem with the repression for which it is a substitute: for judgments of taste to be possible, first of all the "organic repression" bearing on the genitals must be replaced by a judgment of denial or condemnation thanks to which a representation of the excitation they stimulate nonetheless rises to consciousness. Positive, approving judgments are predicated upon a double displacement, that of the genital organs onto so-called secondary sexual characteristics, and that of the stimulus (*Reiz*) prompted by seeing them onto the "interest" awakened by these "charms" (*Reize*), which—it is worth repeating—are so-called because of "the particular quality of excitation whose cause, when it occurs in a sexual object, we designate as 'beauty'"—the discrepancy between the two meanings of the word *Reiz* being indicative of an evolution, perhaps even a history, belonging not only to the sexual object but also to the subject here constituting itself, discursively, by uttering an aesthetic judgment.

Thus Freud's text renews, within a perspective that is not critical but rather genetic, the question of the role of "discursivity" in the structure of the "beautiful." Judgment as such is a matter of the "ego"—which, under the cover of negation, sets itself apart from the unconscious even as it frees itself from the constraints of the pleasure principle. The judgment of taste in the Freudian sense is so paradoxical as to presuppose, in its capacity as *judgment*, the passage, by the ways and means of discourse, from a strictly subjective position in which the subject adheres to its internal representations—that of the pleasure-ego, the *Lust-Ich*—to an objective position—that of the *Real-Ich*, the reality-ego—from which a question arises as to the reality of these representations, of their correspondence to the external world. The paradox, which we have seen also finds its echo in visual art, resides in the fact that judgment of taste cannot be perfectly disinterested, even though it corresponds to a sublimation of the drive through withdrawal of its libidinal components. The very act of judging implies the reality principle's dominance over the pleasure principle, if only, as Freud says, as a way of serving it, of assuring its continued supremacy over the long term.[9]

* * *

It would be absurd to maintain that the solution to the enigma of the judgment of taste is to be found in psychoanalysis. And yet this enigma is present and operating whenever the question of beauty arises in Freud's work—an enigma that, once again, must be understood in discursive terms. Kant's project was not genealogical but critical: he set out to build a bridge between understanding and reason by introducing judgment as a third term, a *Mittelglied.* Freud's project, by contrast, was psychoanalytic, and thus genetic. He set out to determine whence the very concept of "beauty" proceeded, or from what it derived. The paradox consists in the fact that this process or derivation is at the origin of, or at any rate contemporary with, the passage from nature to culture inherent in the acquisition of an erect posture: the judgment of taste is predicated upon an initial displacement, a transfer of "interest" from sexual excitation to the realm of desire. And the origin of desire and emotion, and perhaps even of aesthetic judgment, is to be sought in the schism between the eye and the gaze. There can be no aesthetic emotion unless it declares itself as such in the form of a judgment; but this judgment, in turn, presupposes that, through the operations of desire, the "charms" of the object of amorous interest have overwhelmed or obscured the primary source of excitation, the possibility now presenting itself of a fixation on strictly scopic pleasure and, through this same means, of a diversion of the libido toward goals declared to be—as soon as they're designated "artistic"?—"more elevated."

Though the moment of passage from the one to the other is clearly marked in Freud's text, the opposition between nature and culture has no operative value: if we think, as psychoanalysis would have us do, in terms of derivation, or better yet of *sublation* (to use a Hegelian one), we soon realize the impossibility of precisely situating, if not the point of departure of the evolution in question, at least the threshold beyond which the passage from sexual excitation to judgment of taste becomes thinkable, as soon as it's allowed that something of the initial state must survive in even the most elaborately "sublimated" structures. Freud insists on this point from the very beginning of *Civilization and Its Discontents:* in the realm of psychology, primitive elements frequently survive alongside more advanced ones deriving from them, just as in animal evolution primitive characteristics tend to persist in subsequent stages of development.

The problem here doesn't concern the potential pathways to sublimation, to "idealization" of the drive, though it is perhaps worth stressing once more the necessarily discursive character of the process. The important question is the following: Can sublimation or "idealization," however diverted, lead to an aesthetic emotion of sufficient purity to satisfy Kant's criteria for the judgment of taste? Doubts begin to arise when we observe how fearlessly Freud associates in a single derivation the two terms Kant took such care to distinguish from one another: "beauty" and "charm." Kant writes: "Taste needing a mixture of charms (*Reize*) and emotions to attain satisfaction will always be barbaric, all the more so if it makes these the standard of its approval."[10] If, as the third *Critique* would have it, beauty concerns form exclusively, then it would be a misunderstanding (*ein Missverstand*) to value over beauty a charm or attraction that enlivens a representation and makes it more vivid (color, for instance), in other words to make it pass as itself beauty, when it is not integral to the representation but rather a mere addition, ornament, external trapping—or, to employ a Greek term used by Kant and recently given renewed currency by Derrida, a *parergon*.

It remains that, as Kant himself admitted, such misunderstandings often have "some basis in truth" (*etwas Wahres zum Grund*). Here again we must operate on the level of discourse: if indeed there is a misunderstanding, the only way to avoid it would be through rigorous conceptual definition. In which case the only judgments to qualify as pure judgments of taste would be those in which charm and emotion play no part and whose sole determining principle is form.[11] But Freud's thesis is, precisely, that it is impossible to anticipate the derivation of concepts. And isn't the "basis in truth" of which Kant speaks linked to the fact that if the beautiful, if "that which pleases," is meaningful only for man because he is endowed with reason, this same man is also an animal being and thus just as subject to the pull toward "gratification" as animals not endowed with reason? In Freud, it is beauty itself that is presented, at least initially, as a *supplement* ultimately intended to reinforce sexual excitation, to support and reinvigorate it despite the ever-present risk of deviation. The problem, again, is to discern whether sublimation can have as its aim beauty in itself, abstracted from any possible link with the sexual realm—a matter, as Kant would have said, of "conceptual rigor." For if, in the wake of the transition to an erect posture, the coprophilic component of the sexual drive is revealed to be incompatible with what we might call the "aesthetic exigencies" of our civilization, these developments concern only the superior forms of beauty, while the basic processes leading to amorous excitation remain essentially unchanged. "The excremental is all too intimately and inseparably bound up with the sexual; the position of the genitals—*inter urinas et faeces*—remains the decisive and unchangeable factor. One might say here, modifying a well-known saying of the great Napoleon, 'Anatomy is destiny' (*Die Anatomie ist das Schicksal*). The genitals themselves have not taken part in the development of the human body in the direction of beauty: they have remained animal, and thus love, too, has remained in essence (*im Grunde*) just as animal as it ever was."[12]

It was Kant's explicit intention to isolate the question of pleasure from that of desire. By contrast, Freud set out systematically to constitute desire as an autonomous energy by freeing it of any immediate dependence on gratification: according to his schema, desire is educable but the sexual drive is not. Excitation finding release in discharge does not always go hand-in-hand with desire, and vice versa. We have seen how, for Freud, the institution of the family facilitates a transition from sexual behavior that is reflexive, and thus intermittent, to a desire capable of sustaining itself continuously to the extent that it manages to remain independent of the pleasure principle—at least partially, as in the case of the drive. This question encompasses the aesthetic realm: art's participation in a psychic economy that is ultimately subject to the pleasure principle does not preclude the possibility of change in the regimes of pleasure, or in those of beauty.

What holds in the aesthetic realm also holds in that of ethics. In Freud's theoretical construct, the genesis of the ethical dimension is rooted precisely in desire itself, a thing's value being commensurate with its desirability.[13] The same could be said of the aesthetic dimension, with the following caveat: here something analogous to a censor detaches itself from the energy of desire, such that the beautiful presents itself as an "ideal" opposed to the obscure root of beauty. This transformation of the energy of desire makes possible a conceptualization of the genesis of its repression: the ideal of beauty maintains a relation with that of human love that might seem paradoxical to the extent that the genitalization of desire stands in opposition to attraction to the secondary sexual characteristics, which are declared to be "beautiful." But the paradox is only apparent: beauty can sustain a relation with that which gives "body" to sexual desire only on condition of the partial drive's first being detoured away from the sexual "parts"—just as, it's tempting to add, "taste" itself detaches from its gustatory component to assume another, strictly discursive form of orality. Such are the detours of metonymy echoed by beauty even in the more perverse guises of the genitalization of desire, detours which, without the relationship necessarily being one of cause and effect, tend to discourage *judgments* that the genital organs are beautiful, however exciting the sight of them, and furthermore (as if the relation obtaining here between subjective and objective were identical to that between cause and effect) haven't *become* beautiful: if beauty is a matter of form, the *genitalia* belong—by a kind of necessity in which anatomy, figuring as destiny, also has a part to play, if not its word to say—to the realm of the unformed, *l'informe.* But the relation of the unformed to the formed is not one of simple substitution, nor is it one of unambiguous advance: the very mechanism of "sublimation" presupposes that the reign of the unformed will persist, as an undercurrent, *im Grunde*, throughout that of form.

. . 4 . .

Cherchez la femme: Beauty in Relations between the Sexes

If love remains, essentially (*im Grunde*), animal can the same be said of beauty? Even when an attempt is made to establish order through rigorous conceptual definition, the misunderstanding addressed by Kant, which consists of attributing beauty to mere "charms," has some basis in truth (*etwas Wahres zum Grund*). But what is the precise nature of this fundamental relationship, given that the analytic of the beautiful sets out to establish that satisfactions deriving from judgments of taste are pure and disinterested? This operation corresponds to a displacement that should be deemed basic (*gründlich*), in the most literal sense, because it implies passage from something linked to the faculty of desire at the level of its determining ground or *Bestimmungsgrund*[1] to another kind of foundation or principle that the third *Critique* sets out to establish: one that is transcendental, proceeding exclusively from the authority of the faculty of judgment itself. In the matter of judgment there is no place for the "misunderstanding" denounced by Kant: "The faculty that exercises it is the same one that invented it."[2] Such is the curious nature of the "subjectivity" laid down by the faculty of judgment as its own governing principle.

Beauty is a predicate, and as such it is a matter of judgment;

further, the judgment ascribing it is the same one that posits it, that declares it to be such. But as Freud was to say, aesthetic judgment presupposes the mark of negation as its condition. Didn't Nietzsche see in Schopenhauer's philosophy a "brilliantly perverse" attempt to subject life's most exuberant forms to a radical, nihilistic denigration—beginning with beauty, which in his view corresponded to a negation of the reproductive drive and a liberation of the will, which is centered in sexuality? Fortunately, as Nietzsche hastened to add, the "divine" Plato (and Plato was "divine" for Schopenhauer himself, as he was also to be, with a dash of irony, for Freud) maintained the exact opposite. But then philosophy was practiced *otherwise* in Athens, in the company of beautiful adolescent boys, just as it was practiced *otherwise* in Paris, in the presence of women.[3]

Cherchez la femme, seek out the woman: clearly this injunction cannot mean the same thing in the vastly different contexts of seventeenth-century France and ancient Greece, of *l'amour galant* and so-called Greek love. But the *difference* between them only assumes that much greater relief in light of the question of beauty, as the latter is linked fundamentally, *im Grunde*, to the difference between the sexes. Does Nietzsche's conception of a beauty that was *relative* because inseparable from "the pleasure that man takes in man," and of a judgment of taste expressing the "vanity of the species" taking itself to be the measure and criterion of perfection—a conception that goes so far as to see in the sublime an effulgence of the most primary instinct of all, namely, that for preservation of the species and of the self—have a specifically gendered connotation? Doubtless beauty is "human, all too human," being linked to the "subjectivity" of the species and thus so circumscribed that we must ask ourselves whether the pleasure man derives from looking at certain animals doesn't depend on his seeing in them a beauty that is *other*, an animal beauty expressive of the no less narcissistic "vanity" of other species (as Freud suggested was the case with cats). But it cannot be maintained with regard to either Nietzsche or Freud—or the "divine" Plato himself—that what they said (or could have had to say) about beauty and its ties to the realm of desire, whether direct or indirect, was (or could have been) clearly stamped from the beginning with the imprint of sexual difference.

Things are very different in the case of Kant: twenty-six years before the *Critique of Judgment*, he devoted an entire section of his *Observations on the Feeling of the Beautiful and Sublime* to a discussion "Of the Distinction of the Beautiful and the Sublime in the Interrelations of the Two Sexes," beginning with the observation that women, like men, are human beings, *but not of the same gender.*[4] Since their philosophy is supposedly more a matter of feeling than of reasoning, even in the intellectual arena they have their own *specialty*, which is concerned precisely with the difference between the sexes and is described by Kant in terms not so unlike what we would today call "gender studies": he suggests it is woman's lot to examine the influence of the female sex in culture and to study the conditions stipulated to her by men in other periods and lands—including what Kant calls "the changing taste in amusements," which for him encompasses gallantry, a new kind of "beauty in customs and manners." "These comprise [woman's] whole history and geography."[5] But it is in relation to aesthetics that sexual difference is most marked: all qualities that set the "fair sex" apart from our own "noble sex"—I am still paraphrasing Kant—tend to exalt the character of the beautiful, while the sublime is more properly associated with men.

Women have a natural sense of beauty, insofar as this is consistent with the art of *appearances* or even *maquillage* and cannot be separated from elegance, ornament, and finery.[6] But what kind of beauty is meant here? Beauty as opposed to utility, which is more consistent with "nobility" or the sublime? Beauty as inconsistent with *disgust*, since cleanliness, modesty, and shame are among the preeminent virtues of the fair sex? These oppositions are not as simple and straightforward as they might seem. Shame itself begins by throwing a "curtain of mystery" over nature's purposes (and associated refinements are here understood to derive all their allure from that very source) "so that a too familiar acquaintance with them might not occasion *disgust* [my emphasis], or indifference at least, in respect to the final purpose of a [drive] onto which the finest and liveliest inclinations of human nature are grafted."[7] Disgust is the reverse of taste, which is ultimately rooted in sexual appetite. Even if we make a leisurely circuit, as we might paraphrase Kant, around nature's great purpose, the outcome of judgments of taste retain their subjective character: our inclination for the opposite sex is fundamentally (*im Grund*) the motor of the charms we find in it—with the caveat that while the natural appetite directs itself indiscriminately toward any individual of the opposite sex, taste, being more fully regulated, is directed precisely toward none, being "occupied only with an object that the enamored inclination creates in thought."[8]

Is the judgment of a woman's beauty a matter of taste, of aesthetic judgment? For the Kant of the *Critique of Judgment* the matter admits of no doubt, even though in this instance aesthetic judgment lacks that "purity" to which it should by rights aspire. In judging natural beauty, there is no need to refer to a concept of what the thing ought to be (*was das Ding sein soll*) or, more precisely, of what the object ought to be as a thing (*was der Gegenstand für ein Ding sein soll*): the form is pleasing in itself, whatever its ultimate destination or utility. Matters are very different when the object presents itself as the product of art, which on principle presupposes an aim that is its reason for being and its cause (*in der Ursache und deren Kausalität*). Judgments of artistic beauty cannot be based solely on the object itself; in addition to form, they must take into account that which makes for the perfection of the "thing" (*die Vollkommenheit des Dinges*), that which constitutes it as a thing, *für ein Ding:* namely, the harmony of the whole, the submission of its parts to an internal determination posited as its aim. Considered aesthetically, a mountain is an object without apparent purpose; by contrast, a work of art is an object in which its nature as a thing is in question, an object that imparts an idea of *what sort of thing it ought to be* (or to put it another way, parodying a celebrated dictum of Freud's, where formerly there was an object, there is now a thing, *wo ein Gegenstand war, soll das Ding werden*). But what about a woman? What do we think—it is Kant himself who poses the question, in section 48 of the *Critique of Judgment*—when one says "That is a beautiful woman," *Das ist ein schönes Weib*? Nothing other than the following, according to Kant: in her form (*in ihrer Gestalt*)—and I would add, in anticipation of my argument: in what the Greeks called her beauty, her *eumorphia*—nature handsomely represents the purposes inherent in the female build (*die Natur stellt . . . die Zwecke im weiblichen Baue schön vor*). In this instance, judgment is not exclusively a matter of taste but also doubles as a teleological judgment concerning her nature as a *thing* and not a simple object. "We then judge nature no longer as it appears as art, but insofar as it actually *is* art (though superhuman art)."[9]

The position could hardly be stated more clearly. And the fact that, from the start, the *Critique of Judgment* appeals to the feeling of life (*das Lebensgefühl*) under the aegis of the pleasure principle proves, at least where aesthetic questions are concerned, that Kant, like the Greeks (if we are to believe Nicole Loraux), "*ne pensait qu'à ça*"*—despite all of the effort, all of the work of the third *Critique* in view of *displacing* the question of beauty, of uncoupling it from that of the "charms" and substituting pure and disinterested pleasure for more transient ones, to the point of replacing the euphemistic *ça*, "that" (that is, sex, the sexual drive) with the would-be speaking and judging subject. That he, and they, thought only about the thing that's in question in beauty, if not in art, as it is in woman. Only about the thing to which the question of beauty, if not of art, returns us, as does the question of woman. For the thing that psychoanalysis could have had to say, by way of Freud, about beauty amounts to Nietzsche's injunction *cherchez la femme*. An injunction already implied in Balzac's *Chef d'oeuvre inconnu*. In other words, there's a woman behind it somehow.

* Note that *ça* does double service here, for it is the standard French translation of "id."—TRANS.

. . PART TWO . .

The Judgment of Paris

In the end it's always the woman who judges. (The legend of Paris obscures this a little, but even Paris is only judging which goddess has the strongest final judgement.) . . . Who can claim to know the judge's secret thoughts?

Franz Kafka, *Letters to Milena*

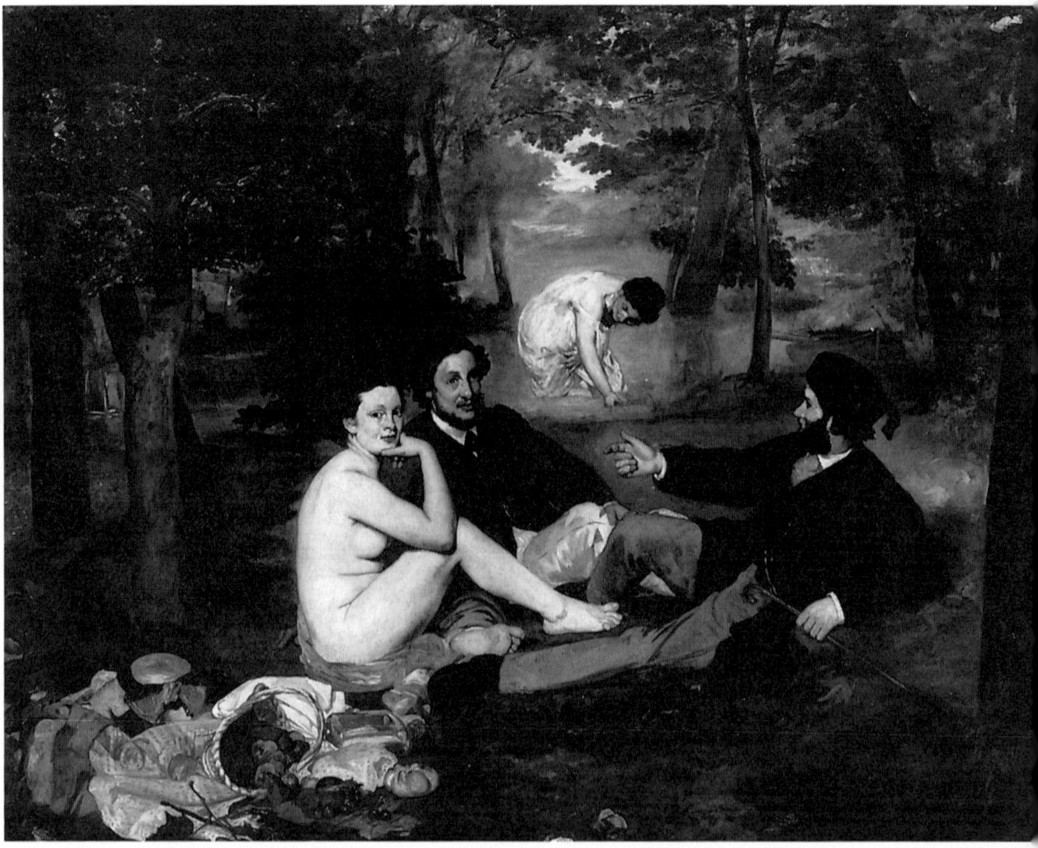

Figure 4. Édouard Manet, *Le Déjeuner sur l'herbe*, 1863 (Paris, Musée d'Orsay).

. . 5 . .

A Woman, Then: *Le Déjenner sur l'herbe*

A woman, then, who is unclothed and seated in a clearing with two elegantly dressed men, looking at us (the woman) with an incipient smile apparently so natural and familiar that in context it assumes something of the quality of a challenge, while in the background another woman still wearing her chemise takes a dip in some shallow water (Figure 4). Whether historians or critics, those professionally licensed to speak about painting have not managed to conceal the embarrassment, uneasiness, and discomfort this canvas still inspires in them, as it does in everyone—"like listening to a joke that goes on too long," to cite the catalog of the centenary exhibition.[1] And it is only too true that this particular joke has had an exceedingly long life. Just as it is only too true that, if joke there be, it has to do above all with the difference between the sexes—a difference with which Manet's masterpiece continues to play with an insolence that neither time nor evolving morals have managed to blunt. And this despite the fact that the abovementioned embarrassment, uneasiness, and discomfort are prompted in part by other considerations which we might provisionally describe as pictorial, if only to avoid making precipitous judgments about art's relation to difference in general, and to sexual difference in particular.

Manet was not the first to depict clothed and unclothed figures in the same picture, of course. His most visible stroke of audacity, even insolence, is the air of contemporaneity with which he imbues the scene, an effect similar to that produced in the theater when we see characters in works by Sophocles or Wagner dressed in raincoats and blue jeans. While this parallel might also be drawn with *Le Concert champêtre* in the Louvre (Figure 5), then attributed to Giorgione, a fine copy of which (by Fantin-Latour) was kept by the artist in his studio, this comparison worked to Manet's detriment, because the *Déjeuner sur l'herbe* could lay so little claim to the historical distance associated with masterpieces that it seemed to make a mockery of the very notion of the masterpiece. As a London critic wrote at the time,

> I ought not to omit a remarkable picture of the realist school, a translation of a thought of Giorgione into modern French. Giorgione had conceived the happy idea of a *fête champêtre* in which, although the gentlemen were dressed, the ladies were not, but the doubtful morality of the picture is pardoned for the sake of its fine color . . . Now some wretched Frenchman has translated this into modern French realism, on a much larger scale, and with the horrible modern French costume instead of the graceful Venetian one. Yes, there they are, under the trees, the principal lady, entirely undressed, . . . another female in a chemise coming out of a little stream that runs hard by, and two Frenchmen in wide-awakes sitting on the very green grass with a stupid look of bliss. There are other pictures of the same class, which lead to the inference that the nude, when painted by vulgar men, is inevitably indecent.[2]

One did not have to be English to deliver similar judgments. By affixing the same descriptive term "indecent" to the picture

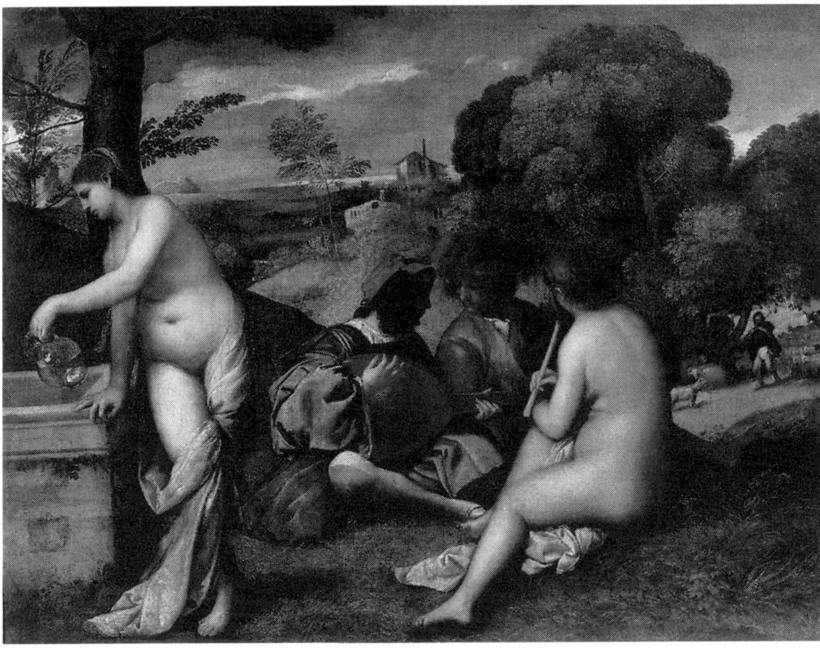

Figure 5. Titian, *Le Concert champêtre*, 1511 (Paris, Louvre).

at the start, the French Emperor launched the *succès de scandale* provoked by the *Déjeuner sur l'herbe* at the Salon des Refusés. The dodges of repression: the ruler's reaction was to be echoed all the more strongly because it was he himself who ordered Count Nieuwerkerke (the Director of Museums responsible for the Salon) to organize an official Salon of works refused by the jury, such that—as he himself said—the public might be free to judge for itself. As though the Emperor had understood that censorship, in order to be truly effective, should not remain the exclusive province of state-controlled institutions but should seek reinforcement in public opinion: the so-called cultural administration reserved the right, given that it could not strictly control the production of works of art, to intervene at the level of their reception by delivering them up to public scrutiny under conditions guaranteed to provoke scandal, the repression in question being all the more effective because it concerned material already *refused* by the same administration, and expressly exhibited as such. But isn't "the rubbish-heap of our observations," to use Freud's own phrase, the preferred raw material of psychoanalysis, to say nothing of modern art?[3]

* * *

What was it, then, about the *Déjeuner sur l'herbe* that should not have been presented to view—that perhaps couldn't have been without the model's smile inducing in the beholder, paradoxically, the same feeling of strange uneasiness that's born, according to Freud, of a familiarity sensed to be false or equivocal, something that, to cite Friedrich Schelling (as does Freud in this context), would have been better left in the shadows[4]—the public's embarrassment betraying itself in its initial inclination to laughter?[5] And why the scandal, when female nudes of another cast—and exhibitionistic in another way—met with triumph in the official Salon in the form of Cabanel's *Birth of Venus* and Baudry's *The Pearl and the Wave* (Figures 6 and 7), praised by the critics for their technique and "exquisite" taste? To a certain extent, this was a matter of "distinction" or "distancing," as Manet's painting refuses all poetic or mythological alibis. But note—and we will be returning to this point—that mythology itself was at this time no longer safe from attack, having suddenly been accused by science, which had taken it as an object, of the same *indecency* that outraged the critics and the public in Manet's painting. For a science was then taking shape that considered the store of fable that had long nourished European culture as an object of scandal and demanded that it be regarded as such. As though an ancient spell previously safeguarding its authority had been broken; as though there had been a sudden realization that ancient mythology, like the art soon to be christened "modern," was full of obscene stories and spoke an absurd language touched by madness. With the result that the classical heritage central to academicism was subjected to converging assaults that, while differ-

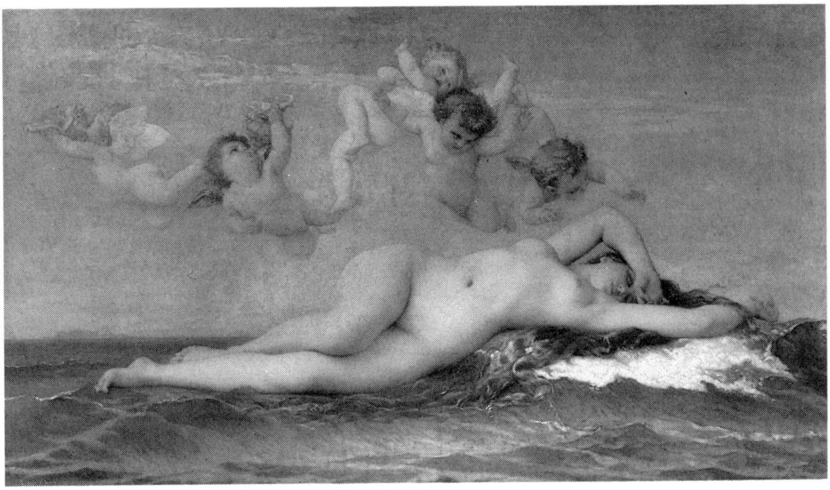

Figure 6. Auguste Cabanel, *The Birth of Venus*, 1863 Salon (Paris, Musée d'Orsay).

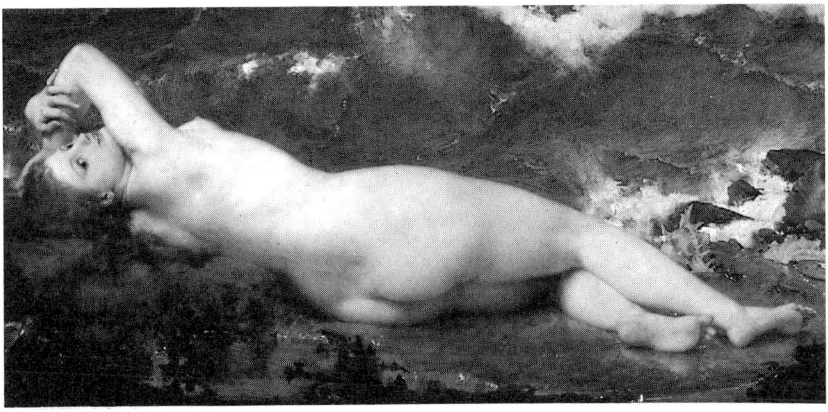

Figure 7. Paul Baudry, *The Pearl and the Wave*, 1863 Salon (Madrid, Prado Museum).

ently motivated, contributed to a single undermining process, as the critique of mythology proceeded from the same distaste and resistance brought into play in the responses to the *Déjeuner sur l'herbe*.[6]

We are fairly well informed about what constituted—after an initial moment of hilarity, itself something relatively new in the history of "reception"—the critical reaction to what was regarded by many at the time as a deliberate provocation, or, even worse, as evidence of the painter's lack of taste and even technical skill. But it is far from clear that the reconstitution of this critical response in all of its nuances and occasional contradictions, a project embraced by art historians, will help us to see Manet's painting any better; nor is it clear that it will enable us to view the work through contemporary eyes, especially as we have access only to written testimony. The fact that the British critic already quoted mistakenly describes the two male figures in the *Déjeuner* as wearing "wide-awakes"—soft felt hats with broad brims and low crowns—raises certain suspicions about his objectivity in examining the painting. To such a point, in fact, that we might be tempted to see in this slip the effect of a kind of blindness endemic in critical writing and that should be carefully investigated as such: perhaps what people mistakenly thought they saw in Manet's painting served to screen out what was there and remains there, doing its work despite the refusal to see it.

However "indecent" the (feminine) nude "when painted by vulgar men," it would seem—judging from the remarks of this same London critic—that the violation of decorum had less to do with the treatment of the female figures (undressed in the Manet as in the "Giorgione," though without the attenuating circumstance of its "fine color") than with the "horrible costume" imposed on the two men, which being "modern"—and French?—could only appear at the time as an insult to beauty (just as their black jackets might be construed as an affront to color). And it mattered little that only one of them was equipped with head-gear—not a hat or "sombrero" (as was claimed by another critic, probably as a result of the proximity in the Salon des Refusés of two other paintings by Manet in a "Spanish" mode: the *Young Man as a Majo* and *Mademoiselle V. as an Espada*), but a student *faluche* or tasseled cap, the presence of which can't be justified by this figure's being a student—he is too old—or *un homme coiffé* (an expression with phallic connotations).* Once this "thought" had been translated into modern language, it would seem that beauty (like color) could only depart the painting, an event encompassing the bodies of the two women, who seem to absent themselves from it, one by means of the look she directs at the beholder—which effectively makes her the focus of attention—and the other through total absorption in her toilette, an effect intensified by the marked inattention to them on the part of the men.

Thus the nude is declared "indecent" on the basis of contrast or antithesis. Which is a matter of context, not only internal (it's not so much the nude in itself that is indecent as its presence in such a painting, and perhaps the character of this presence) but external as well: for the painting is also, and perhaps above all, indecent by comparison with other works, whether the—perfectly chaste—images of picnics that proliferated in late nineteenth-century painting (see Figure 8) or classic works whose age and renown effectively inoculated them against such charges, to which they would otherwise have been vulnerable. Meyer Schapiro has clarified how, in the Louvre *Concert champêtre*, the difference between the sexes is blurred by class distinctions, the shepherd being opposed to the young courtier just as the rustic beauty is contrasted with a more refined one and the simple flute with the poet's lute, while the painting as a whole "intimates a comparison of nature and artifice in love" as in music, though not without "a deep unity of forms" that links the contrasting figures to one another and to the paradisal landscape. But things are very different in the *Déjeuner sur l'herbe:*

> With Manet the contrast of the sexes becomes obtrusive through the detachment of the figures; it is an abrupt opposition in mode of being, social as well as biological, and is reinforced for the eye by the setting in the cavernous green landscape. Woman here is an impersonal sexual ob-

* This French phrase would normally mean "a behatted man" or "a smitten man," but its implicit reference to a man's "head" gives it indecorous overtones.—Trans.

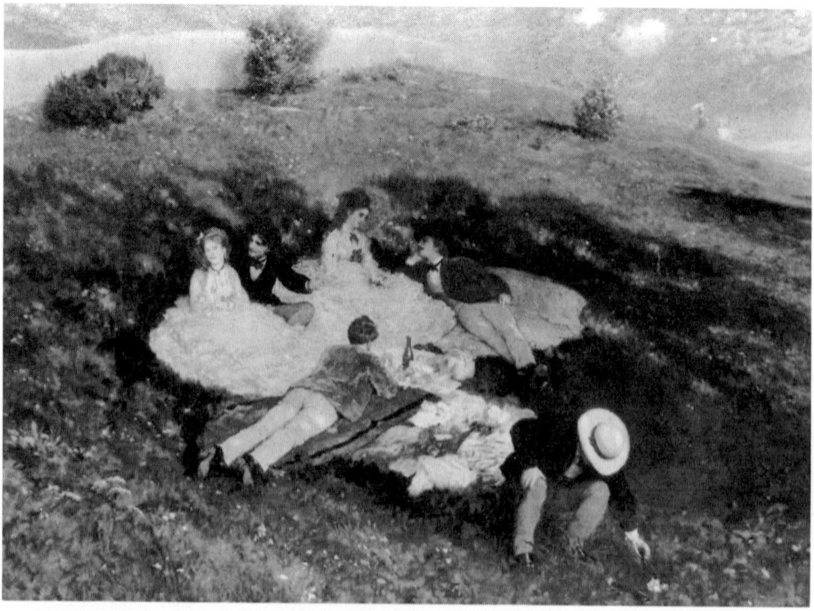

Figure 8. Pal Szinyei-Merse, *Picnic*, 1873 (Budapest, Museum of Fine Arts).

> ject, with a wonderfully painted still-life of pears, apples, cherries and a brioche beside her . . . Manet's painting does not simply translate Giorgione's . . . imagery into modern clothes; the meaning of clothes and of nakedness as signs has changed. No current of feeling unites the sexes and nothing of the model's myth and music remains. The starkness of naked white flesh is allied to the equal starkness of the men's black clothes. The woman's glance is addressed to the spectator and calls for his own glance, as if her nakedness in this context of conversing Parisian men represented her normal social self.[7]

Schapiro strongly suggests that the social self in question is that of a prostitute—he sees in the *Déjeuner sur l'herbe* an ironic reminiscence of *The Romans of the Decadence* (see Figure 9), the "masterpiece" by Manet's former teacher Thomas Couture

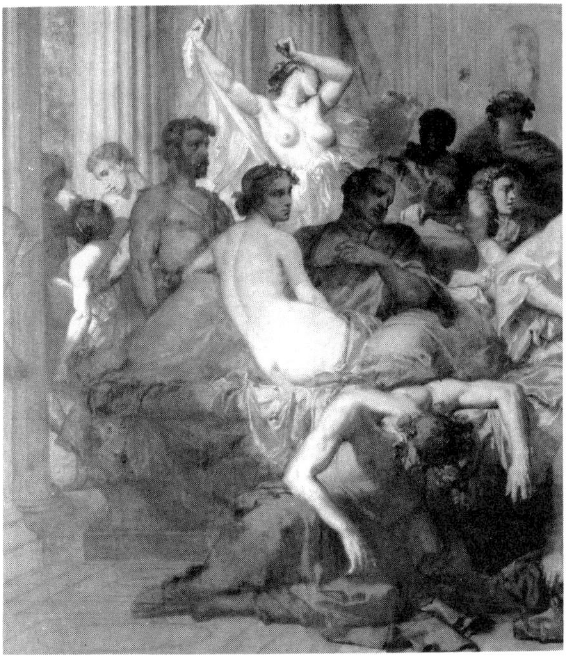

Figure 9. Thomas Couture, *The Romans of the Decadence*, 1847, detail (Paris, Musée d'Orsay).

now enthroned at the center of the Musée d'Orsay where Courbet's *Studio* should be—or a professional model (a very different matter), one whose name is known to us: she is Victorine Meurent, the painter's favorite subject.

The resistance (in the psychoanalytic sense, for that is what is in question) that even today is brought into play by looking at Manet's painting is, of course, a reaction to the woman's nudity—a nudity so incongruous and seemingly aggressive that at least one viewer felt obliged to imagine that the men were *coiffés* in order to block out or compensate for this insolent display of femininity by exacerbating the fact of difference. But we must also take into account the pictorial context of this nude, beginning with the way the figural group stands out against the background of greenery, whose artificial, even theatrical appearance makes it difficult to decide whether the bathing woman is within the "backdrop" or a figure in front of it. This same sharp contrast between figure and ground discussed by Schapiro is undermined at yet another point, in another area of the canvas and through strictly pictorial means: the clearly articulated edge between the black clothing and the green grass becomes indecisive along the curve of the model's back, which when examined closely seems to have an odd, totally incongruous crest or dorsal fin running down it, one that is admittedly evanescent because it fuses with the background—an echo, perhaps, of the elusive line of the back of the seated woman on the right in the *Concert champêtre*, which is blurred by the same reddish shadow that falls over the meadow. "Is this drawing? Is this painting?" Castagnary was to ask.[8] For amateurs accustomed to a technique without imprecision, to the "finish" of academic nudes, there was something here, something about what this critic called a "fine sketch" (though one that, as such, had no place in the Salon, not even the Salon des Refusés, at least not the one befitting a "masterpiece" that it seemed to claim for itself) that provoked astonishment and even indignation.

A watercolor from Manet's hand, doubtless based on a tracing taken from a photograph of the painting, retroactively clarifies not only the outlines of the figures but also, more generally, the "montage" or "collage" technique—what we might refer to as the "cut and paste" approach—employed here. The *Déjeuner* has a hodgepodge quality insofar as it has a *plein air* feeling but was in fact executed in the studio; interior becomes confused with exterior, and vice versa; the figure group seems pasted onto the wooded background; within this group, the figure of the woman—who, as we shall see, has just finished doing something very different from bathing (the work was exhibited at the Salon des Refusés with the title *Le Bain*)—seems blatantly superimposed on those of the men; the unclothed "model" is juxtaposed with other models who are clothed. And then, to go right to the heart of the matter, something like a cut-and-paste, hodgepodge quality is inherent in the *nude* as such: the nude—which was primarily female, though the rules of studio practice long dictated the use of male models, and this despite the attendant risk of producing female figures with overly muscular anatomies—the nude, then, regularly associated in the classical tradition with the idea of beauty, without this association's necessarily entailing any lessening of the desire potentially induced in the spectator looking at it. But what does it mean to desire a body in painted form? What does it mean to desire a woman *in painting*—in the sense that we say of someone that we can't see their likeness in a portrait, which brings us back to painting and through it to the effigy, to the portrait as a kind of trial, as the touchstone of vision as well as of desire?

This particular nude—the remark also applies to the *Olympia*—certainly wasn't beautiful or desirable, at least not in the same way as Cabanel's *Venus*, which was immediately purchased by the Emperor, who seized the occasion to award its artist the Legion of Honor. But the *Déjeuner sur l'herbe* contains an intimation, not without a certain polemical edge, of what Wayne Andersen has called—playing on the homonymy of the two names: that of the shepherd, the son of Priam; and that of the city in which the Salon was held—the "Judgment of Paris"; more specifically, of the judgment of the Parisian public, seeing as here (as he would do again two years later, still more discretely, in the *Olympia*) Manet was challenging the image of beauty shamelessly exploited in official art. The image (the beauty?) of a morality at least as dubious as that opposed to it by Manet: in comparison with the equivocal, confectionary eroticism suffusing Cabanel's *Venus* (to say nothing of Baudry's *Pearl*), Manet's *Bain* and its "bather" must have struck the public eye, in its crudity and even irreverence, as something close to pornography; for such are the ironies of history—or perhaps the realities of power—that, considered in light of the soliciting, swooning nudity proffered by Cabanel and Baudry, Manet's nude was immediately identified as a prostitute from the rue Bréda.[9]

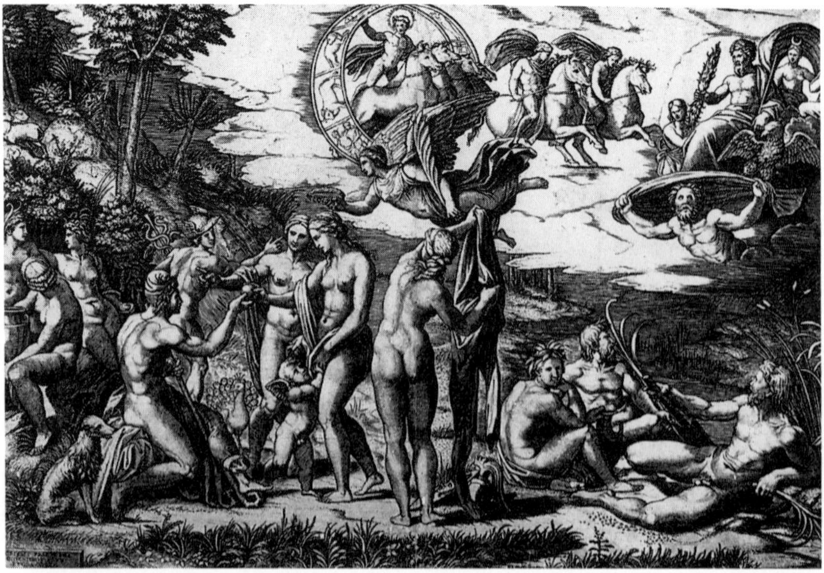

Figure 10. Marcantonio Raimondi, *The Judgment of Paris*, engraving after Raphael.

The wordplay on the name of the city of Paris—as well as the attempt to suggest parallels between what Manet himself called his *partie carrée** or (sexual) foursome and the story of the shepherd Paris—can easily be accommodated within traditional art-historical discourse and method. The critic Ernest Chesneau was the first to point out to his readers, in a note subsequently added to his review of the Salon des Refusés, that the focal group of three figures in Manet's composition was a direct quote from a print that was well known in artists' studios at the time.[10] And, in fact, in an engraving by Marcantonio Raimondi, traditionally held to be after a lost work by Raphael (Figures 10 and 11), we see on the right the group that served as Manet's model—or rather, after which Manet had his mod-

* The phrase *partie carrée* does not necessarily carry sexual overtones in French.—Trans.

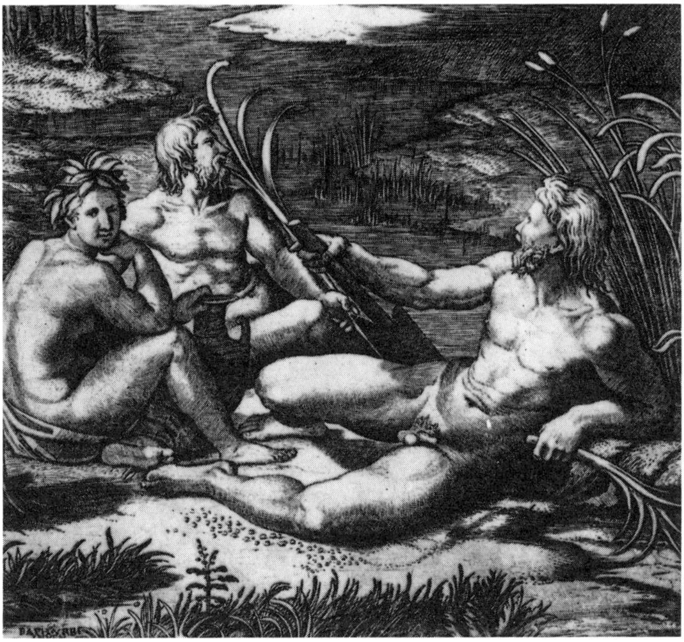

Figure 11. Marcantonio Raimondi, *The Judgment of Paris*, engraving after Raphael, detail.

els pose, a different, more subtle way of attaining a collage effect, in imitation of the postures of the nymph (if she is indeed a nymph, she is an oddly muscular, androgynous one) and two river gods, all sitting on the sidelines as though marginal to the story or fable, on which the first goes so far as to turn his back; while one has only to remove the oar held by the other river god to confer upon his uplifted arm the eloquence of a gesture accompanying speech.[11] Curiously, this "discovery," which is today generally accepted, had no impact at the time; it was not until 1908 that Gustav Pauli, curator at the Hamburg Museum, took it up again, in a form more likely to attract the attention of art historians—beginning with his friend Aby Warburg, who unhesitatingly saw the *Déjeuner sur l'herbe* as the last link in a long chain extending back through the Renaissance to the

Hellenistic period, while Manet, that pioneer of modernity, impressed him as a capable guide to what he termed the life and history of symbols.[12]

There is nothing surprising about this delay: Chesneau himself only noticed the citation after the Salon had closed and his review had already been published. If he chose to point out the connection, it wasn't to display his erudition but rather to exploit this new element in view of strengthening his earlier criticisms of Manet, those uttered before he'd discovered what could only appear, in the eyes of amateurs less perspicacious than Aby Warburg, to be a joke in the worst possible taste: according to Chesneau, not only did Manet lack basic skill in drawing and perspective and deliberately choose scandalous subject matter; he increased the provocation by tracing his composition after a model consecrated by tradition, a print to which a special prestige accrued because of its association with Raphael. All of which underlined just how important it was to *vendre la mèche*—to discover, by counterplot if necessary, the secret of this conspiracy directed against the *beau idéal* in view of rendering it harmless.[13]

If we except Warburg's commentary, which is essentially iconographic and to which we will return later, criticism has tended to minimize the importance of Manet's borrowings from masterpieces of the past. Far from viewing them as more or less cryptic citations that demand interpretation, there has been a tendency to see them as proof of a marked poverty of imagination on the part of the painter, who, it is maintained, was less interested in subject matter than in the way it was treated[14]; or they are cited as evidence of his "compositional difficulties."[15] Those who stress the parodic or farcical element in the painting, its status as a kind of "studio joke," come much closer to the true nature of the work, even if one is dealing exclusively with its reception: the same taste for parody, as well as an interest in the shepherd Paris himself, is to be found in Offenbach's *La Belle Hélène*, which was given its first performance a few months after the Salon of 1863, when the Goncourt brothers spoke of "corrupting jokes," "the assassin of respect," and "the *vis comica* of our decadence," evidently feeling that no words could be too harsh to denounce this new manifestation of the French spirit.[16] The continuing relevance of such responses is evidenced by the discomfort and embarrassment still inspired, in the words of Françoise Cachin, by this "live enactment" of a "classic," of a "museum piece," and the slight uneasiness we still feel in front of the *Déjeuner sur l'herbe* today, when we are supposedly no longer scandalized by it and when parodic allusions to past masterpieces have become so commonplace that they've lost all of their provocative implications.

But now we must direct our attention, by way of Raimondi's engraving from which Manet excerpted the main group of his *Déjeuner*, to the story or fable it illustrates. A story or fable with a certain pertinence, even with regard to the question of reception: once having passed through the turnstile separating the official Salon from the Salon des Refusés, the public felt licensed to choose between two forms of art or two forms of beauty (and perhaps three, if we take into account the works from the past providing an inescapable context). The conflict between a painting already declaring itself "official" and the one later designated "avant-garde" first became manifest in 1863; and the stakes of this conflict, of this attack against "good taste," were made clear by the contrast between Cabanel's Venus Anadyomedes and another image of female nudity—this one, too, of classical derivation, but stripped of all poetic and mythological connotations as well as of all erotic affectation. If the *Déjeuner sur l'herbe* caused such a scandal, this was above all because of the lack of decency it displayed in so blatantly posing questions about what beauty was, or could be, in art, by so openly considering the possibility that pornography might not be foreign to it, and this at a time when the notion of "ideal" beauty had been reduced to serving as a pretext for images that could hardly be more suggestive. What was not to be said, much less shown, even under cover of a disguised citation—one that connected this work and these queries, at least indirectly, to the judgment of the shepherd Paris—was that beauty, insofar as it is linked to the body and to sexual difference, is always to some extent indecent, and this of necessity.

. . 6 . .

RAPHAEL INVENIT: The Masterpiece of Interlude

According to art history, the Salon des Refusés of 1863 was simultaneously an effect and a symptom of repression, and it has become a critical commonplace that Manet's *Déjeuner sur l'herbe* marked the birth of modern painting—a distinction it is held to share with the artist's *Olympia,* which was exhibited at the 1865 Salon and provoked a comparable scandal, though this time within an "official" context. It's as though these works were twins, despite their having seen light of day two years apart: for both of them featured female nudes that constituted assaults against the singularly lubricious ideal of beauty embraced by the middle class under the Second Empire, an ideal typified by the swooning nudes of Bouguereau and Baudry. Within its own order, that of the history of modern art, a significance accrues to this event comparable to that assigned by the epic tradition to the mythological episode illustrated by the engraving used by Manet in what remains, in the words of Michael Fried, "perhaps his sheerest, most intractable masterpiece"[1]—a phrase underscoring not only its resistance to analysis conceived of along conventional art-historical lines, but also its irreducibility to the normative status of just another link in the continuous chain of works presented in museums.

From a historical perspective, what is the nature of the spell this "masterpiece" continues to cast over us? What is the nature of the ascendancy that this masterpiece has appropriated from another serving as its model, and what sort of prestige can this citation bestow retroactively on the earlier work? In order for the authority of the masterpiece to manifest itself fully in such an instance, must there be repetition or encoded reiteration that eventually affects our reading in both directions, in both cases? This question applies every bit as much to twentieth-century works variously based on the *Déjeuner sur l'herbe* (beginning with the series of some two hundred paintings and drawings by Picasso) as to the relation obtaining between this essentially "modern" masterpiece and those of the past. But the problem is complicated by the following considerations: the work serving as Manet's "model" was, by its very nature, itself caught up in the cycle of repetition, in the circuit of reiteration; and if there ever was a "masterpiece by Raphael," our only access to it has been through an engraving that occupies a singular position in the history of European painting.

The role in this story of *The Judgment of Paris* print engraved by Marcantonio Raimondi after Raphael is not merely anecdotal, nor can it be reduced to a mere studio joke. The longstanding popularity of this image among painters, who saw it not only as a pictorial resource but also as a kind of challenge, seems perfectly consistent with what we know about its original function. For according to tradition, it was—to adhere to current usage, at least provisionally—the first reproductive engraving and was executed, with the intent of its being widely circulated, not after a painting but after a lost drawing by Raphael. Fréart de Chambray, in his *Idée de la perfection de la peinture* of 1662, describes it as follows:

> The first sheet to carry the name of Raphael outside of Italy, making known to all the painters of his century that he was their Coriphée, was the noble and celebrated print of the *Judgment of Paris*, which proved such a fortunate

> enterprise for Raphael, as for his student Marcantonio, that he subsequently continued to employ the latter in this same capacity; toward which end he made several other beautiful drawings especially, ones we might well never have seen but for these circumstances, since he never painted them.[2]

A reproduction, then, and the first of its kind (or very nearly so[3]), but one whose original, since lost, was not a painting but a drawing, though in this particular case not one made "especially" in view of its being reproduced. Such a characterization sufficed to earn Marcantonio's engraving unique status in a history of art attentive to modes of dissemination and reception. But is "reproduction" the appropriate term here, given that we are dealing with productions that might never have been seen "but for these circumstances," since they never assumed the form, or the strength, of *paintings*? Might not this word, and the problematic associated with it since the publication of Walter Benjamin's now classic essay "The Work of Art in the Age of Mechanical Reproduction," put us on the wrong track? Although so-called reproductive engravings were to make Raphael's masterpieces well known in the seventeenth and eighteenth centuries, the many prints produced during the painter's lifetime by the studio that grew up around Marcantonio Raimondi would seem to have been ruled by logic of another sort, by ends that were not strictly reproductive, even though these works bore witness to—and were the instruments of—a production process of considerable complexity and sophistication, one based on a highly developed system of the division of labor.

In *The German Ideology*, Marx astutely seized upon the fact that Raphael did not himself execute most of the frescoes attributed to him, using it to denounce the error into which Max Stirner, author of *Uniqueness and Its Properties*, had fallen in proclaiming the solitary nature of both scientific and artistic work, and stressing the irreplaceability of one name for another in the matter of artistic authorship. For according to Marx, even though none of his colleagues could have taken his place,

> Raphael as much as any other artist was determined by the technical advances in art made before him, by the organisation of society and the division of labor in his locality, and, finally, by the division of labor in all the countries with which his locality had intercourse. Whether an individual like Raphael succeeds in developing his talent depends wholly on demand, which in turn depends on the division of labor and the conditions of human culture resulting from it.[4]

One recognizes here the program and the ideology embraced, under the aegis of "scientific rigor," by current practitioners of the "social" history of art, which, however, only rarely achieves penetrating analytical insight into the material conditions shaping artistic production. But when formulated in these terms, the argument hits a snag very early on; for the problem lies not in recognizing that Raphael's works were "conditioned" by the splendor of the Rome of his time, as Leonardo's were shaped by circumstances pertaining in Florence and Titian's by those in Venice, any more than it lies in demonstrating the degree to which the supposedly "unique" activity of artistic work is dependent on commissions and must come to terms with distinct forms of organization; it is rather a matter of determining the precise role and function of the individual (whether replaceable or not) behind the signature "Raphael" in an original studio configuration involving students and collaborators and the ways in which such a configuration made it easier for this small community to satisfy the specific, and formidable, demands made upon it. Thus a fuller understanding of the way engraving functioned within the framework of the studio will prove extremely instructive; for if, contrary to Marx's repeated assertions,[5] the word "history" can properly be applied to art, the process of production and reflection so designated should find in it one of its main points of anchorage; which brings us back, as we shall see, to the work for which art can provide a privileged site in the order of representability (to use Freud's term), as in that—the two orders are not unrelated—of reproduceability (in Benjamin's sense).

* * *

The principal source of information about the relations between Raphael and Marcantonio Raimondi remains Vasari's *Lives*, and it was on the canvas provided by the latter text that Fréart de Chambray embroidered his own account of the *Judgment of Paris.* What, then, do we learn from Vasari's "Life of Marcantonio of Bologna and Other Engravers of Prints"? That shortly after arriving in Rome, the latter

> made a magnificent copper engraving after a cartoon by Raphael, representing Lucretia killing herself, that was so accurate and beautiful of manner that, some of his friends having immediately brought it to Raphael, the latter determined to publish in the form of engravings some of his own drawings; and among these, a drawing he had previously made of the judgment of Paris, in which, by caprice (*per capricio*), he had represented the chariot of the sun, nymphs of the woods, those of springs, and those of rivers, with vases, oars, and other fine fantasies around them; and this having been resolved (*e cosi risoluto*), Marcantonio engraved the whole in such a way that all Rome was astonished.[6]

According to Vasari's "Life of Raphael," it was at the instigation of the master himself, who was so full of admiration for Dürer's engravings that he wanted to emulate them, that Marcantonio undertook to master this skill, with splendid success.[7] We must of necessity rely upon Vasari's account, which bears all the marks of a typical narrative of origin. Even so, the notion that a painter might have envisioned demonstrating his capacities in the art of engraving through an intermediary, without himself wielding the burin, is an indication of a conception of artistic work that, while current by the time Vasari was writing, Raphael had been the first to implement on a large scale; and what's more, he had pushed it to an extreme. This observation takes on added meaning in the context of Vasari's account of Marcantonio's years of apprenticeship. Having purchased a group of engravings by Dürer in Venice, the young Raimondi started out by counterfeiting them (*E cosi comincio a contraffare di quegli intagli d'Alberto*) as a method of studying them, going so far as to reproduce the initials AD that served as the artist's identifying mark; and his efforts in this line were so successful, according to Vasari, that amateurs were fooled and purchased these engravings as being from Dürer's own hand. On getting wind of this, the latter became very angry and went to Venice to plead his case before the Signoria; but all he could obtain from the authorities was a prohibition against Marcantonio's using Dürer's initials on his own plates, even when these were obviously copies.[8]

In the end, this dispute over what today would be called "authors' rights" came down to a question of *copyright*, and in a quite literal sense. Marcantonio was given free license to copy Dürer's engravings, print them, and sell the resulting copies—or should we say the resulting "reproductions"?—on the sole condition that he not use Dürer's name or initials. Knowing as we do that engravings by Dürer (originals or counterfeits by Raimondi?) were on the walls of Raphael's studio, and that in 1515 the two artists exchanged works with one another, the questions of "copy" and "copyright" (not to mention that of royalties) take on higher relief. All the more so, as the name of Raphael was not to appear on Marcantonio's plates until their second state, and the formula /RAPHAEL INVENIT/, followed by the initials /MAF/ (for *Marcantonio fecit*) began to appear only in 1515.[9] But the fact that Marcantonio contented himself with *executing* something whose "invention" was explicitly attributed to Raphael demonstrates that, in this instance, the question of attribution—like that of "hands," and like that of the distinction, or even opposition, between the functions of conception and execution—was vexed from the start.

Marcantonio didn't "reproduce" engravings by Dürer, he *copied* them. But can it be said that he copied the drawings provided him by Raphael, or that he contented himself with reproducing them with their dissemination in view? Whether we speak of "copies" or "reproductions," a way of organizing artistic work is at issue that seems inconsistent with the very notion of the "artist" as defined, precisely, during the Renaissance, and with that of the "genius," essentially "unique," around which the romantic century would rally at the very moment of the birth of the discipline known as "art history." Somewhat uneasy about certain nudes in the *Fire in the Borgo* and the Loggia that seemed to lack the grace and suavity proper to Raphael, Vasari was the first to propose that differences in the quality of certain figures resulted from the master's having allowed others to execute them after his own drawings. This same concern over distinguishing, within the body of work bearing Raphael's name, between its autograph portion and that executed by assistants would lead connoisseurs—beginning with the most prominent among them, the celebrated Morelli, whose work and methods were of interest to Freud[10]—to considerably reduce the number of works distilling, in its pure state, the essence of his art, a matter that would largely reduce itself to a question of "hands."

* * *

Henri Zerner has astutely observed that the distribution of work within Raphael's studio imposed constraints upon execution so rigorous as to make distinguishing among various "hands" especially difficult, perhaps rendering the very notion meaningless. For the constraints in question were binding on the master himself, and the authority he exercised over his students and collaborators implied his own submission to the rules he laid down for everyone else; to such an extent that not only the notion of "hand" but that of "personality" itself becomes blurred, and we are forced to admit that "the triumph of art over personality [allowed] the painter of the Stanze a kind of artistic imperialism, a veritable colonization of others' talent, such that even when examination permits us to ascribe not only specific passages but even certain tendencies or stylistic traits to one or another of his assistants, the work as a whole . . . remains that of Raphael . . . In the history of art, his name is not that of an individual but rather of an artistic enterprise."[11]

But we must go farther and ask ourselves whether those works regarded by us today as the most precious components of Raphael's oeuvre, namely his preparatory drawings (subject to the increasingly rigorous analysis of connoisseurs), themselves obey, in principle as well as in their very form, the rules we've just posited as indispensable to the proper functioning of the studio. In order for "colonization of others' work" to exist or even be possible, the "imperialism" imputed to Raphael would have to have certain means at its disposal: the faculty of adaptation, the power of assimilation already attributed to him by Vasari, the capacity for systematic exploration of the possibilities—not only the formal ones but the symbolic and expressive ones as well—of classicism, in a word everything favorably regarded by Vasari under the rubric of that "universality" inherent in any imperialism worthy of the name tends in this direction, even as they explain and justify, as Zerner correctly observes, the immense effort exerted by the academies (the first of which appeared shortly after his death) to extract from the work of Raphael something like a code or a system of rules. Such being the case, it was inevitable that these imperatives should find an echo in studio practice, beginning with the very first stage of the production process, with the first ideas or "thoughts" (*i primi pensieri*) reflected in the preparatory drawings.

What was the role played by engraving in this process? Specialists have not yet managed to clarify the precise nature of the collaboration between the master and his assistants, including the engravers of Marcantonio's circle. While there is no consensus about the degree of finish of the preparatory drawings provided them, one thing is clear: the establishment of an engraving workshop within this painting studio was a circumstance we are justified in describing as "unique"—especially as it was linked to the name of Raphael, if not to his initials—and in part experimental, given the novelty of a practice whose difficulties with regard to painting Raphael seems to have been the first to grasp. As is indicated by the fact that in the century's first decades only preparatory drawings for frescoes or paintings were engraved in the studio, to the exclusion of finished works, which would first appear in print form only in the 1550s. All of Marcantonio's engravings, with the probable exception of the *Galatea*, were executed after drawings, and Vasari's suggestion that Raphael made drawings expressly to be engraved is generally accepted by scholars, some of them even including the *Judgment of Paris* among those works realized after drawings executed with this end in view, though they assign it a date (c. 1515–16), notably later than that implied by Vasari's account, in which it is said to be among the first engravings completed by Marcantonio after his arrival in Rome.[12]

Thus we should not speak in this instance of a "reproduction," but rather, following the usage of the specialists, of a "translation,"[13] in the sense of the transferral of a figural statement from one idiom into another—in the way that Manet, in his *Déjeuner sur l'herbe*, was said to have "translated" a "thought" of Giorgione into modern French: such a transferral necessarily entailing labor and specific effects to the extent it implies passage from one medium or mode of expression to another.[14] But things become more complicated as soon as we concede that the material or graphic documents corresponding to the first stage of the production process might have been informed or programmed, reciprocally, by the very end for which they were devised: the function the work was intended to serve must have crucially influenced the way in which it was initially conceived, as can be discerned from the engravings as well as from the cartoons developed in the studio for execution on wall or canvas (and I point out in this connection that, according to Vasari, Marcantonio began by engraving a cartoon by Raphael before the latter decided to provide him with drawings from his own hand). What makes for the originality of the kind of drawing associated with Raphael's name is that these drawings were designed to serve a project of reading and interpretation necessarily involving the intervention of other "hands," with all of the effects and constraints that this entailed.

The initial goal of reproduction was not the dissemination of masterpieces; it was, rather, the furthering of their production in a form proper to itself. In the process leading from "first thoughts" to the finished engraving and/or cartoon by way of so-called preparatory drawings, the actual moment of *invention*—defined by Vasari as the combination of a variable number of figures into an *istoria*, such that each of the said figures has the posture, gestures, and action appropriate to it[15]—is not easy to pin down. If the precise origin of these productions eludes us, this is because any effort to comprehend them in their initial moment confronts an operation bearing the stamp, from the very beginning, of "reproduceability" or "translatability," for these works must be informed from the start by considerations bearing on their ultimate "reproduction" or "translation." With the caveat that the latter must be conceived of in terms other than mechanical or biological ones—rather as an "identical" reproduction, or as like reproducing like, with the print playing a decisive role in the process: that of an indicator under whose influence the "idea" given form in the initial drawing should find itself verified even as it is fixed. Which is sufficient to render irrelevant, in this instance, any idea of a primordial "sketch" in an umbilical relation to the painting, there being no masterpiece (according to Delacroix) save where a completed work renews, in its very execution, with the ardor and liberty of the rough approximation from which it was born, a conception of the masterpiece, and of the latter's relation to its "creator," totally foreign to the one current in Raphael's time.

* * *

Whether from the hand of Raphael himself or "mere" copies, a few drawings are known that can be linked with engravings by Marcantonio.[16] To say nothing of two Roman sarcophagi that supposedly inspired Raphael—a point to which I will return—and that served as the point of departure for Aby Warburg's study of the *Déjeuner sur l'herbe.* But while the process of invention can, to a certain extent, be reconstructed upstream, such is not the case closer to its final issue: unlike other pieces engraved by Marcantonio, *The Judgment of Paris* left no trace in the painted work of Raphael.[17] This fact merits our attention, given that the comparison of engravings and finished works can often be quite instructive. A telling example is provided by the *Saint Cecilia* in Bologna (Figure 12): whether Marcantonio's engraving of this composition (Figure 13) was made after a lost sketch by Raphael or after a drawing by Gian-Francesco Penni sometimes attributed to Raphael (Paris, Petit Palais), the remarkable fact remains that the holy Magdalene—who, on the right in the painting, seems to absent herself from it to look at the spectator with a gaze as fixed and indiscreet as that of the woman in the foreground of the *Déjeuner sur l'herbe* (to say nothing of the nymph serving as the latter's model)—in the engraving lifts her eyes toward heaven and its concert of angels, invention having finally rectified an apparent absurdity: for this is the representation of a "vision" of Saint Cecilia, and she is so positioned that she can't see the angel-musicians appearing behind her but can only *hear* them.[18] Unless, by contrast, the engraver merely altered a trait suitable for an altar-

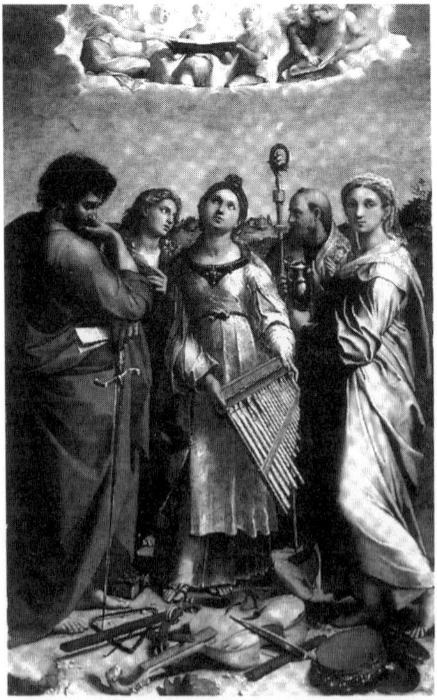

Figure 12. Raphael, *The Ecstasy of Saint Cecilia*, ca. 1515–16 (Bologna, Pinacoteca).

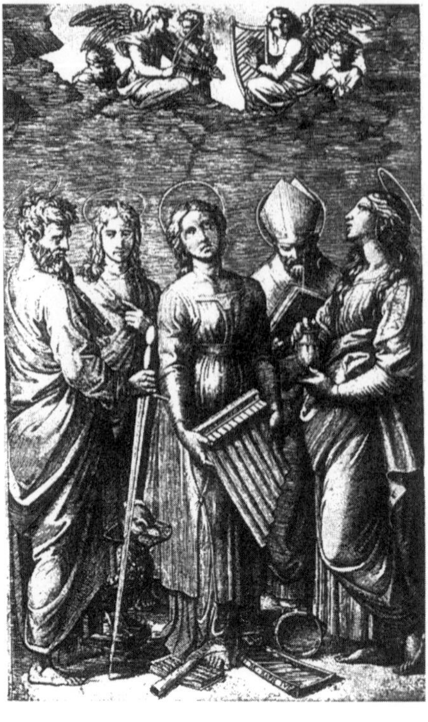

Figure 13. Marcantonio Raimondi, engraving after Raphael's *Saint Cecilia*, first state (?) before insertion of the cartouche.

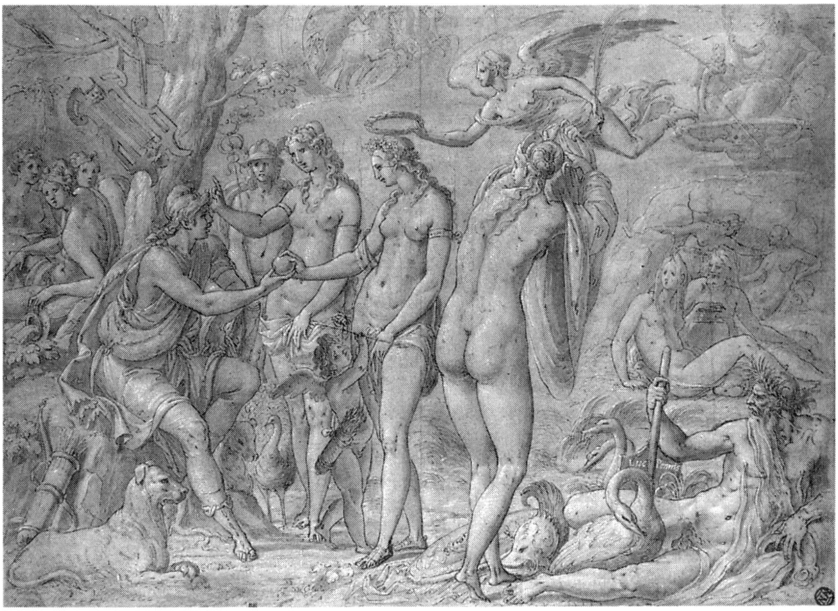

Figure 14. Luca Penni, *The Judgment of Paris*, after Raphael, pen and wash (Paris, Louvre, Graphic Arts Department, Inv. 1395).

piece but not for a print: there is a drawing by Luca Penni that paraphrases Marcantonio's *Judgment of Paris*, but relegates the nymphs and river gods to the background, showing them—as by rights it should—looking directly toward the scene unfolding in the foreground, in the center of the composition (Figure 14).

Marcantonio's *Judgment of Paris* engraving contains two figures that would subsequently attract the attention of artists: that of the nymph to serve as Manet's model, directing her gaze toward the spectator; and that positioned as the latter's pendant on the other side of the principal scene, turning her back to us. Is their presence here an index of the high finish that would earn this plate a special status in the Raphaelesque corpus, justifying at the same time (at least in part) its critical renown? There is no simple answer to this question, but it prompts another that brings the desired answer within our reach: Doesn't the division of labor in Raphael's studio interest us here precisely because it bears upon the legitimacy of our speaking of the "work" carried out by art, by the image, in the sense Freud spoke of the "dream-work"? The process of production perfected by Raphael opened up the possibility of such "work" from the moment that something—easily encompassing the term "invention"—was operating in the interval—or joint—between drawing and painting, something related to what Freud called "representability" (*Darstellbarkeit*) in his writings on dreams: in other words, to that aspect or portion of a story or fable lending itself to visual representation through an ordered set of "ideas" and "thoughts," with the engraving simultaneously bearing witness to it and crystallizing a key point in its evolution. In this process, the subject "Raphael" (assuming that this tag has not been reduced to functioning as a kind of brand name) has no readily discernable place. As a unique entity, it can get its bearings only in the context of an activity whose sole sphere of operations is situated in the interval between the successive stages of the production process and the various practices mobilized by it, with the engraving operating, in this field of *interplay* or *Zwischenspiel,* as an *interlude* or *intermediary* in which invention manages to fix itself and assume a properly communicable form.

For this is indeed the paradox associated with Marcantonio's engraving—a paradox we should keep in mind during our investigation into the reasons behind artists' persistent interest in this print, and into its singular role in the history of European painting. As understood and practiced by Marcantonio after Dürer's example, engraving did not lend itself to the sketchy, nor to the expression of "first thoughts." On the contrary, it corresponded to a later stage in the process, that of "invention," if it hadn't already, of necessity, matured and taken on the trappings of something relatively stable and explicit (RAPHAEL INVENIT). In this sense, the print amounts to an instance of determination, of verification—or, as we might say today, of an "exposure" in invention's developmental process. But the engraving did more than reveal, fix, or verify the initial "idea" by means of translation and interpretation: as a means of multiplying the image, it performed a function of communication and dissemination totally alien to drawings—its being understood that the two terms "fixation" and "communication" constitute, as in writing generally and (as already noted by Husserl) in mathematical writing in particular, two mutually inextricable aspects of a single process of inscription. In the context of the Raphael studio, this trait takes on even greater relief, because the practice of engraving was then something new and original. Raphael does indeed have a legitimate claim to being Dürer's rival in this medium: from the first, he inflected it so that it might better serve a carefully designed production process in which reproduction played a key role.

However diversified the regimes of production, in their means as well as their ends, there's no denying that engraving has served a crucial function in the history of post-Renaissance Western art, as both a means of dissemination and as an instrument furthering the sedimentation of works and models. And this development encountered resistance. In a letter written late in life and addressed to his faithful friend Chantelou (the brother of Fréart de Chambray), Poussin bemoaned the reduction of "poor painting . . . to prints, or I might better say to its grave (if anyone other than Greeks has ever seen it alive)."[19] He was alluding to painting as becoming, in the hands of "the more commonplace painters" (*le vulgaire des peintres*), a matter of repetition and proliferation somewhat analogous to the model of engraving, which allowed for multiple proofs. But there is more: he was also pointing out that in this stage or moment execution was strictly programmed. Raphael's placement of Baviera in charge of the commercial operations of the engraving studio—even stipulating in his will that its profits were to revert to La Fornarina[20]—assumes particular importance in this context: its production and dissemination campaigns were to focus not on completed works but on "invention" itself, seized in the moment of its fixation, even if this were only transitory. As if the only meaning ascribable to the idea of the "model" were inseparable from its functioning as an intermediary within a system of production in which conception and execution were understood to be mutually complementary. Or better still: as if it were necessary, as in Delacroix's conception of the "masterpiece," for the model to retain something of the movement attendant upon the moment of invention and—despite its manifest air of finality—a portion of its virulence, power of suggestion, and fecundity.

If the engraving of the *Judgment of Paris* has repeatedly attracted the attention of artists over a period of several centuries, there can be absolutely no doubt but that this has been due—in addition to the intrinsic interest of the motif, with its choice between three women incarnating as many types of beauty—to its marked quality of *invention:* beginning (a point stressed by Vasari) with its element of "caprice," for this was the term used by Vasari to describe the group used by Manet in developing his *Déjeuner sur l'herbe*. And this quality would seem to be all the more present, all the more active, because the engraving did not issue in a finished painting in the "Raphael" corpus: the power of attraction exercised by this image was only increased by inventions here having been discernably left in suspension, as it were, there being no subsequent masterpiece to supersede it, such that the print tends to function like an open proposition or a question put to painting, perhaps even to art itself and the thought animating it. The exchange or interplay between drawing and painting, between line and color, as well as between myth and fable, image and allegory animating—over a period of several centuries—the history whose scene I am here trying to set, was possible only because it had been programmed into the engraving from the beginning, the latter image providing a pretext for work that would have been impossible without its intercession, without the kinds of interaction necessary for its production. In short, the model's authority was all the more secure precisely because of its being devoid of anything authoritarian, because of its explicitly allowing for the play of fantasy in the operations of reproduction, repetition, translation, multiplication, and even—to use a Hegelian term—sublation, to which the *Judgment of Paris* was subjected in the *Déjeuner sur l'herbe*, constituting an absent but conjectured masterpiece as the ultimate authority.

7

The Story without the Picture: The Myth-Work

If such is the role allotted engraving in what we conventionally refer to as the art of Raphael, it is easy to see how Fréart de Chambray, in his *Idée de la perfection de la peinture*, could bestow so choice a position—the first, in fact—to the *Judgment of Paris* as engraved by Marcantonio Raimondi without worrying about the fact that it was only a print—and, at that, one not even from the hand of the studio's master and proprietor. Fréart begins this short work by listing the principles fundamental to the art of painting and goes on to illustrate them with examples from antiquity, proposing that these latter are paralleled by certain works by the most renowned of modern painters, beginning with Raphael himself and "his celebrated print of *The Judgment of Paris*." But before examining this image to determine "whether the painter has adequately satisfied the five fundamental considerations" of his art—namely, invention, proportion, color, expression, and figure placement (which Fréart elsewhere calls perspective)—beginning with the first of them (invention), the author judges it "absolutely necessary, if our discussion is to be reasonable, for us to know the circumstances of this poetic story."[1] Taking as his model Poussin, who upon delivering his *Manna* had advised the other

Fréart, known as Chantelou, to "read the story and the picture (*tableau*), so as to know whether each thing [was] appropriate to the subject,"[2] Fréart de Chambray provides, "in a few words," the following version of the story of Paris:

> Paris, the son of King Priam, having been exposed on Mount Ida immediately after his birth and abandoned to the wild beasts (because of a sinister dream, one fatal to his country, experienced by his mother Hecuba during her pregnancy), was taken in by one of the local shepherds and raised by him as his son. Though neither his foster father nor he himself was aware of his princely birth, by some secret virtue of his royal blood his development proceeded so perfectly that he soon surpassed all others of his age in strength, beauty, intelligence, and all else considered important among those people. Everything thus far has some resemblance to a true story: but poets, who are in a sense the comrades of painters, proceeded to introduce several capricious fantasies into it; saying that all the gods had been convened at that time for the wedding of Peleus and Thetis, with the sole exception of the goddess Discord; and that this malicious being, to gain revenge for the contempt so shown for her, secretly threw into the assembled crowd a golden apple on which were written the words *To be given to the most beautiful woman.* Mercury, the greatest schemer of all the gods, having perceived it and picked it up, read aloud the message borne by the pernicious gift, thereby inciting such jealousy among the goddesses, all of whom prided themselves on their beauty, that Jupiter himself refused to be the judge, for fear of offending his wife Juno if he should pronounce in favor of another, or of raising suspicions of bias should he choose her. Juno's only rivals were proud Minerva and pleasing Venus. Once the question had been referred, by common consent of the three contenders, to the judgment of the royal shepherd Paris (who was him-

self a perfect model of beauty), Mercury immediately rushed to him in Jupiter's name with the apple, which he was to give to the one among the three judged by him to be the most beautiful.

This is what Raphael set out to depict in his drawing, where in accordance with a general usage that is almost always necessary he placed the subject's principal figures in the center of his design, giving them a great variety of aspects and expressions. Minerva, filled with disdain because she had not won the coveted prize, turns her back on the judge, her face indicating extreme contempt. Venus, in whose favor the judgment was pronounced, is between her two rivals, receiving the token of her victory with a modesty as graceful as can be imagined. The painter wanted us to see her in profile, which is the most flattering view, in order to show the form and regularity of the parts of a beautiful face. Juno, the proudest of the competitors, extremely vexed at not having won, seems about to inveigh against Paris, who nonetheless doesn't seem worried and remains where he is, seated, as befits his quality as judge here, and delivers his decision by awarding the fatal apple that subsequently caused such disorder in Greece, and finally the complete ruin of the wretched city of Troy, the birthplace of Paris. This last goddess is depicted from the front, being more audacious than the other two: and Raphael deliberately drew all three of them from different points of view [*aspects différents*], to create as much contrast as possible between his figures. I point out that even the profile of the shepherd Paris differs somewhat from that of Venus: while this beauty exposes the profile of one of her breasts to us, by contrast we see both of Paris' shoulders [from the back]. So careful has our painter been to instill diversity in his painting.

In addition to these four figures, which suffice to recount the entire story, he also introduced Mercury in a

> posture making it clear that, having executed his commission, he is ready to return to Jupiter with news of the event, and of who had been crowned the happy victor.[3]

I interrupt this long citation here, at the moment Fréart is about to turn his attention—as we shall soon do ourselves—to the other elements of the composition, to the many figures and accessories surrounding the group recounting the story's essentials (which is not, strictly speaking, at the center but is, rather, shifted slightly to the left): those same portions—the chariot of the sun, the wood and water nymphs, the river gods etc.—which are, I repeat, the only ones Vasari saw fit to mention, under the rubric of "caprice" (*per capriccio*), in the passage of his "Life of Marcantonio" devoted to the *Judgment of Paris*. But let it be noted immediately that whereas Chantelou's brother sees fit to devote an unusual amount of attention to the events leading up to the fable (events which, at least as regards Hecuba's dream and the exposure of the child, had "some resemblance to a true story"), and then to recount what poets added to the narrative, he limits himself, with regard to the episode of the judgment itself, to describing the "story" as Marcantonio had represented it, only appending a summary evocation of the disastrous consequences of the choice imposed upon Paris: which means that he passes over in silence elements—namely, the rewards or "gifts" promised by each of the goddesses in hopes of thereby obtaining the prize—that might seem irrelevant to the Raphaelesque "invention," but that are nonetheless an integral part of the fable itself, which we will now consider independently, apart from all visual representations of it. It might seem only logical to read the story before "reading" the painting, or rather the engraving (though in this instance we in fact began with the image), but, all the same, we must not forget that the account of the shepherd Paris related by Fréart is but one singularly late and long-winded version among many of a narrative whose origins date back to the pre-Homeric era, and which is now accessible to us—supposing things had ever been otherwise—only in derivative form, one that's more or less faithful, in the same way the supposed lost drawing by Raphael is known to us only through the intermediary of Marcantonio's engraving purporting to reproduce it, and—perhaps—through another drawing from a copyist's hand retaining only the idea of the principal group.[4]

* * *

The story, then, without the picture (*tableau*), but all the same not the story without that painting whose *storia* is supposed to represent, according to Alberti's well-known formulation, the goal, the ultimate form, the greatest work[5]—what we might have to say about the first (the "story"), and even the questions we might be prompted to ask about it, being meaningful only with regard to the second (the painting), while the reverse is not necessarily the case. The same goes for the difference we might be tempted to posit, as I myself have just done, between myth and fable. A difference that becomes problematic as soon as the frontier between a properly mythic activity and a more strictly fabulist one becomes blurred, myth being summoned sooner or later—and sometimes very soon, as was the case in Greece—to follow what Georges Dumézil has called "a proper literary career," and to such an extent that it can become all but "unfindable," to use Marcel Detienne's term.[6] Which might well give pause to the reader of Greek "myths," prompting him or her to "rethink mythology rather than continuing to recount it while revelling in the complicity, ancient and continually recycled, between the Greeks and us"[7]—or, to put it another way, rather than pretending that the stories of the Olympian gods mean essentially the same thing to us as they did to the ancients. But what additional significance does this question assume when myth and fable embark on another career, which we might dub representational or pictorial, and which depends on a memory that's neither oral nor written, a "visual" or imaged memory? What interest does this question hold for painters and art-lovers and for those specialists in images called iconologists? Can't they make do with the story or *storia* that's the subject of the painting without worrying about its status or about a possible distinction between myth and fable, or between myth and legend?[8]

This distinction will only hold up in a field we might call "analytic" iconology (see below) if distinguishing traits can be discerned in the paintings themselves, with the differences between these two modalities of the *storia* becoming evident on the register of "representable" effects. Are we justified in drawing a distinction in the work performed by painting as well as that performed by the "story"—the *storia*, in which this art supposedly attains its highest point—between a fable- or legend-producing activity conforming to narrative constraints like those found by Vladimir Propp in popular tales and an activity we might call myth-producing that's shaped by determinations of an entirely different order, an order we might designate as "deeper," or even—following Lévi-Strauss—as "unconscious," if such a posited depth or unconsciousness didn't in turn become problematic, entailing that these determinations be situated, localized, acknowledged, defined, and characterized as such? Does the story of the shepherd Paris, and to an even greater extent that of the judgment associated with his name, have another dimension, is it more than a straightforward narrative? If so, how are we to understand it, and on what basis can we advance such a hypothesis? How does it signify, this story; what sensitive spots in our culture does it touch, what depths does it plumb, such that even today it holds a particular resonance for us? Questions all the more difficult to ignore given that this story or legend is situated, according to literary criteria, at a key turning point if not of myth then at least of mythology and the epic. And given that it corresponds to a relatively autonomous episode in Greek mythology, a fable complete unto itself, the dispute between three Olympian deities and the judgment intended to end it having been inscribed in human memory at the beginning of an event—the Trojan War—of considerable interest to European humanity, as it marks the latter's entry into history*: a history which, though it was to continue—as far as Greek tragedy—to borrow from fable and even legend, seems to no longer owe anything to myth.

* * *

The oldest reference to the judgment of Paris in Greek literature seems to be the brief allusion made to the event at the beginning of the last book of the *Iliad.* When the Olympian gods see how disrespectfully Achilles has treated the body of Hector, dragging it in the dust around the tomb of Patroclus and then leaving it there, face down, they take pity on the dead hero and propose that Apollo withdraw the body from Achilles' wrath:

> There this was pleasing to all the others, but never to
>   Hera
> nor Poseidon, nor the girl of the grey eyes [Athena],
>   who kept still
> their hatred for sacred Ilion as in the beginning,
> and for Priam and his people, because of the delusion of
>   Paris
> who insulted the goddesses when they came to him in
>   his courtyard
> and favored her who supplied the lust that led to
>   disaster.[9]

Modern philologists were not the first to doubt the authenticity of this passage. As early as the third century, the critic Aristarchus proclaimed it to be an interpolation, "for a thousand good reasons," if we are to believe Albert Severyns:[10] be-

* *L'histoire:* The reader should bear in mind that this French noun can mean either "history" or "story," or both at once. Damisch exploits this ambiguity throughout the chapter, beginning with its title.—TRANS.

ginning with the term rather freely translated by Lattimore as "lust" and less freely in other translation as "luxury," *machlosunē*, which seemed suspect to Severyns because it normally applied only to women (which could well have implications other than strictly philological ones, a point to which we shall return). Severyns goes so far as to see in this allusion at the poem's end to a mythological episode "originally" without any relation to the Trojan War as evidencing the dubious taste of an epigone; but then it was that scholar's intention to stress the merit of Homer, who, while deforming the Trojan legends according Paris the leading role in the *Iliad* by making Hector the leading character, still would not have stripped Priam's son of his legendary inheritance and reduced him to those utterly human proportions allotted to Hector, Paris being less the effeminate coxcomb the latter proclaimed him to be, in deliberately provocative terms, than a warrior prepared to fight courageously to retain control over the erotic object bestowed upon him by Aphrodite. But isn't the fact that Paris was a man—complex and with a pronounced "feminine" aspect, perhaps, but still a man—precisely what confers significance and resonance on the judgment associated with his name? To the point, perhaps, of giving it the strength of myth, if not of an enigma?

* * *

In fact, it makes very little sense to suggest that the story of the judgment of Paris was originally unconnected to the Trojan War. For one thing, the idea of a primitive version of the fable is inapplicable to myths and legends first transmitted orally, even when what's in question is not an account of an epic's underlying causes.[11] More important, the dispute between the three goddesses is a recurrent theme of the Homeric poem in its written form: not satisfied with fighting each other through human proxies, Hera, Athena, and Aphrodite descend into the arena themselves, at the risk of personal injury, to lend assistance to "their" forces, the Greeks in the case of the first two, the Trojans in that of Aphrodite—their intervention culminating in book XXI when they engage in hand-to-hand combat with a violence (as has been emphasized by George Dumézil) that has every appearance of being a settling of personal accounts.[12] Even Zeus himself could not remain indifferent to this dispute; in the end he had to become involved. His opting to take no part in the war between the Greeks and the Trojans would only be consistent with his position at the beginning of the affair, when he delegated the responsibility of choosing between the three rival deities to Paris. But in the first book of the *Iliad*, Thetis implores him to grant victory to the Trojans for as long as the Greeks continued to insult her son Achilles, and the placement of such a scene at the poem's beginning gives it unusual force. For wasn't it at the marriage of Peleus and Thetis that the quarrel was initiated, a quarrel in which human beings were to find themselves implicated despite themselves, over an extended period and with the most tragic consequences?

That the judgment of Paris has a certain autonomy as a "story" is evidenced by the many depictions of it on Greek vases. But here the autonomy—a notable characteristic of fables—is only relative, if we assess it in accordance with criteria appropriate for legend or epic; and the very brief allusion at the end of the *Iliad* to a choice made by a single mortal unleashing a long sequence of events only a few of which are in fact recounted by the poem, this allusion, however suspect on textual grounds, nonetheless participates—whoever its author may have been—in the poem's overall functional economy. For readers of Homer, it appeals even today to a memory that is not exclusively, nor even initially, rooted in books: aside from a handful of specialists, how many of us have read the versions of the judgment of Paris story in Euripides or Lucian, much less those in Ovid or Fréart de Chambray? And Raphael himself may well have known this "fable" only by hearsay, having encountered it in spoken form, which was the way the Homeric poem was transmitted over a period of centuries—

the epic poet's recitation appealing to the oral memory characteristic of cultures "without writing," which a simple allusion sufficed to mobilize, because all of the story's episodes, and all of those potentially associated with it, had become familiar to his audience through prior recitations. Which made for an economy of the signifier analogous in more ways than one with that operating through the visual arts in our own culture, with its constant interplay, exchange, and dialogue between the spoken and the written, as well as between text and image, or even between drawing and painting, through the possible intermediary, the *Zwischenspiel*, of engraving.

For the dispute between the goddesses, and the ensuing choice made by a mortal, must have belonged to the corpus of ancient legend in the repertory of the epic poets contemporary with Homer, and it was taken up again, in the eighth or seventh century B.C., in a poem called the *Cyprian Lays*, now lost but known to us secondhand by fragments published by the grammarian Proclos in his *Chrestomathy*.[13] Even if Albert Severyns is correct in his supposition that it was the author of this poem who definitively integrated the episode into the complex epic of the Trojan War, still we cannot ignore the fact that the material of the epic invited this integration and justified it, facilitating it and perhaps even rendering it necessary: by making a mortal responsible for settling a disagreement between three Olympian deities, the legend simultaneously accounts for the involvement of human beings in divine business (and vice versa) and states its cause. And it does these things all the more effectively because the judge does not shrink before the task assigned him. There might well be justification for dismissing the allusion to Paris in book XXIV of the *Iliad* as an interpolation, but it is not at that moment that the reader discovers "the lust that led to disaster" through Aphrodite's decisive offer to sate it. This scene would have been added as a kind of reprise, without veils or paraphrase, of another passage in the *Iliad*, one that is not controversial on textual grounds, in which the goddess, after having interrupted the combat between Menelaus

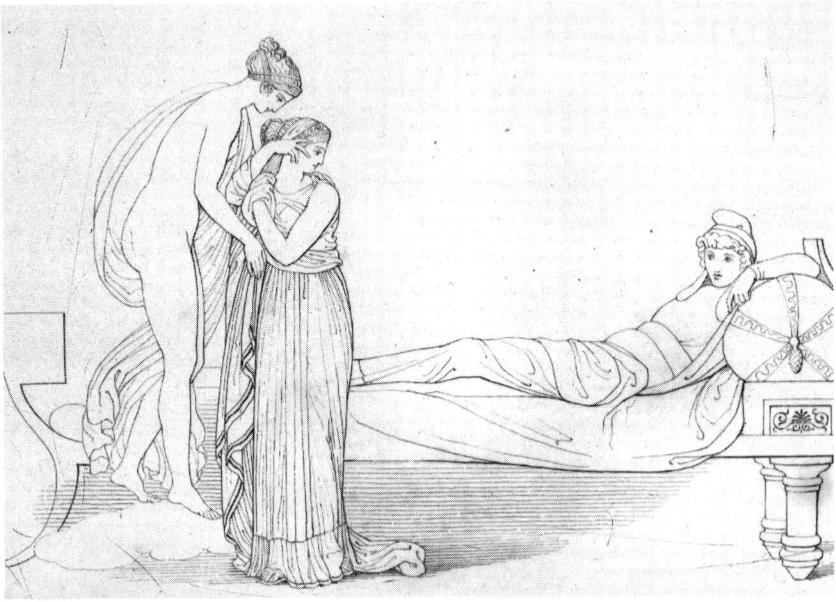

Figure 15. *Aphrodite Bringing Helen before Paris*, from *The Iliad of Homer*, engraved by Thomas Piroli after a composition by John Flaxman (Rome, 1793).

and Paris that by common agreement was to have settled the war, transports the hero into his bedroom (see Figure 15) and brings Helen to his bedside (Paris is speaking):

> Never before as now has passion enmeshed my senses,
> not when I took you the first time from Lakedaimon the
> lovely
> and caught you up and carried you away in seafaring
> vessels,
> and lay with you in the bed of love on the island Kranae,
> not even then, as now, did I love you and sweet desire
> seize me.

Thus in the *Iliad* the intrigue is already knotted, and intricately knotted (in a way consistent with what Aristotle called *mūthos* in the *Poetics*[14]), however obliquely, into the framework and the fixed form of a poem intended to be read (and not just heard) in its entirety. Helen is clearly the name of that bitter, painful (*algeinē*) lust or luxury given Paris by Aphrodite. Its name, and not its object, which justifies the use of the word *machlosunē*, though this need cast no doubt on the effeminate character of the hero: it is woman's own desire, as much as that inspired by her, that's in question here, as Helen fearlessly makes clear to the goddess toying with her:

> Strange divinity! Why are you still so stubborn to
> beguile me? . . .
> Go yourself and sit beside [Paris], abandon the gods'
> way,
> turn your feet back never again to the path of Olympos
> but stay with him forever, and suffer for him, and look
> after him
> until he makes you his wedded wife, or makes you his
> slave girl.

Woman's desire, or, to put it more accurately, a desire or pleasure—despite the repeated assertions in official discourse that sexual pleasure was an exclusively male province—that must be discussed (as indicated by Nicole Loraux) *in the feminine*,[15] and as a gift bestowed on man by Aphrodite. And the latter did not shrink from making it clear to Helen that she was merely her instrument in this affair:

> Wretched girl, do not tease me lest in anger I forsake
> you,
> and grow to hate you as much as now I terribly love
> you . . .[16]

So the gift bestowed on Paris by Aphrodite indeed has its place in the *Iliad*, where it constitutes, through its very repetition, one of the essential reference points of the plot: the goddess only supports the hero in the face of Menelaus's anger in order to reawaken in him a desire that would be stilled only by his death, which would be followed by the ruin of his country. But while there are no references in the Homeric poem to the gifts offered Paris by Aphrodite's rivals, this should not lead us to conclude that the theme of the three promises was unknown in Homer's time. That the theme was used, without notable inconsistencies, by a number of authors of the pre-Christian era might suggest that the episode took on its definitive form in the *Cyprian Lays*,[17] and this is confirmed by the summary account appearing in the *Epitome* of Apollodorus's *The Library* ("And they promised gifts to Alexander. Hera said that if he preferred her to all women, he would reign over all men; Athena promised him victory in war, and Aphrodite the hand of Helen"[18]). Even though lost, this poem does not have an originary value and status; while it perhaps served as the version of reference over an extended period, it nonetheless corresponds to only one state of the myth (or the legend).

Rather than surrender to fascination with an original that—as Marcel Mauss never tired of telling his students[19]—*does not exist*, surely it is better to squarely accept that our only access to myths (like dreams) is through texts contrived after the fact, texts that in Greece assumed literary form very early on. In this connection, it is remarkable that, aside from Homer and the *Cyprian Lays* fragments, the oldest surviving references to the judgment of Paris are to be found in relatively late works written for theatrical performance and thus also intended to be heard: this hiatus of several centuries in the poetic tradition offers a striking contrast to the seamless continuity of the visual tradition, beginning with vase painting. But this temporal gap makes all the more noticeable the remarkably altered character of this episode linked to the Trojan War as evoked by the Greek tragedians. And their evocations are numerous: the ancients called Sophocles "the tragic Homer," and Aeschylus himself described his dramas as "crumbs from Homer's banquet," while "Trojan" works make up almost half of Euripides' surviving production, with the judgment of Paris itself being the object, in no less than five plays, of references that seem to become ever more numerous, to such an extent that the story seems to be constantly on the characters' minds (how could it have been otherwise, given that this fable seems inscribed at the very dawn of history and of tragedy?).[20]

Sophocles wrote two plays (both lost) dealing with the story of Paris, *The Quarrel* (*Eris*) and *The Judgment* (*Krisis*), in which it would seem that a marked tendency toward allegory and moralizing first entered the ancient poetic tradition: "Once preference had been given to Aphrodite, in other words to pleasure, everything was overthrown." (It is Athena who speaks, as the embodiment not only of military strength but also of thought, reflection, and virtue.)[21] But in Euripides, the legend of Paris assumes an entirely different character, one bearing witness to the considerable distance between tragic poetry and the myth, which was henceforth regarded as belonging to the remote past, but as nonetheless present in people's minds, its being tragedy's responsibility to assess its dubious heritage, the better to control it.[22] The moment had long since passed in which Zeus could be said to have contrived everything, as was maintained in the *Cyprian Lays:* if tragedy still springs from the will of the gods, the very incommensurability of the quarrel among goddesses and the long-term consequences of a decision rendered by a man called upon to deliver it, the disproportion between a choice made by one and the ruin of all, furnished Euripides and his characters with a pretext for reflection on the question of the extent of man's mastery of his own affairs, of the degree of his responsibility for his own misfortunes. In the opening scene of *Iphigenia in Aulis,* Agamemnon himself evokes the visit to Sparta of this man "with his garments flowered in gold and his dress blazoned with barbaric gems," who pretended to be the arbiter of goddesses, or "so the Argives have the story."[23] The king himself making an initial distinction between what might be categorized as fable and what as historical event, as was, for him—and for Herodotus—the rape of Helen: but, here again, there is a marked disproportion between the fury of a deceived husband, the disarray of a sovereign ruler, and Iphigenia's choice in favor of a glorious death enabling the fleet to depart the ruins of Troy, on the one hand, and, on the other, the stakes, both real and symbolic, of the expedition and war to come:

> A right thing that Greeks rule barbarians,
> Not barbarians Greeks.
> It is right,
> And why? They are bondsmen and slaves, and we,
> Mother, are Greeks and are free.[24]

(It is the human race that speaks here through Iphigenia: man as the generic being, and not woman or the sexed being—to use the distinction for which Nicole Loraux has argued so persuasively.)

That said, the judgment of Paris appears in Euripides' text in two instances that might seem equivalent from a structural point of view, as suggested by Georges Dumézil, but that are quite different from one another if assessed in iconographic terms:

a) The first version, the one followed by Euripides in his *Iphigenia in Aulis*, makes no reference to the three promises but has the goddesses appear before their judge with identifying paraphernalia reminiscent of their depictions in vase paintings: the cunning Cypris (Aphrodite) being as proud of the power of desire (*a men epi pothō truphōra Kupris*) as are Pallas (Athena) of her spear (*a de douri Pallas*) and Hera of sharing the royal bed with her divine husband (*Hera te Dios enaktos eunaisi basilin*). This is the way the vase painters were to represent the judgment of Paris, depicting desire in the guise of one or two cupids flying around Aphrodite, giving Athena a spear, a helmet, and, more rarely, a shield bearing the Gorgon's head, and having Hera carry a scepter;

b) the second version, in which the theme of the three promises does appear, is that recounted in *The Trojan Women* (v. 925 ff.). I cite it first in a translation after the version that Jean-Paul Sartre penned for performance—once more, a matter of *history*—during the Algerian war, when this Greek tragedy seemed to speak to current events, once again through the mouth of women.

(It is Helen who speaks:)

> "So Paris, aged twenty, climbed Mount Ida;
> He met three goddesses who accepted him as judge.
> 'Who among us three is the most beautiful?'
> Do you know what Pallas offered him to sway his
> judgment?
> All Greece, nothing less. With Athena's aid
> he would have conquered it in a flash.
> And Hera: 'If I win you shall have Asia entire
> and everything within Europe's borders.'
> Cypris, should she win, promised only myself.
> She described me, and she won!"[25]

Or, in Lattimore's more faithful rendering:

> First then!
> *She* mothered the beginning of all this wickedness,
> For Paris was her child. And next to her the old king,
> who would not destroy the infant Alexander, that dream
> of the firebrand's agony, has ruined Troy, and me.
> This is not all; listen to the rest I have to say.
> Alexander was the judge of the goddess trinity.
> [*Ekrine trisson zeugos ode trissōn theōn*].
> Pallas Athene would have given him power, to lead
> the Phrygian arms on Hellas and make it desolate.
> All Asia was Hera's promise, and the uttermost zones
> of Europe for his lordship, if her way prevailed.
> [*ei sphe krineien Paris*]
> But Aphrodite, picturing my loveliness,
> [*Kupris de toumon eidos ekpagloumenē*]
> promised it to him, if he would say her beauty
> surpassed
> all others. [*ei theas hyperdramoi kallei*].[26]

* * *

If the summary evocation of the judgment of Paris in the *Iliad* has been suspect since antiquity, this is because it seems somehow out of kilter with the epic tone of the poem. Homer is indeed prone to multiply the signs of divine intervention in human affairs, but it is the anger of Achilles that is the central theme of the *Iliad*, not that of Hera or Athena (an anger, as noted by Ernst Robert Curtius, paralleling that of the Greeks in its having been provoked by the abduction of a woman, the captive Briseis, which the hero had been constrained to cede to none other than Agamemnon[27]). And while the poet stresses the divine ancestry of Achilles, he pointedly ignores that of Helen, as well as that of her two twin brothers Castor and Pollux, all three born, according to legend, from the loves of Zeus and Leda. With regard to the gods themselves, in the sixth century B.C., Xenophanes was already indignant about Homer's having conceived of them in the image of humans, going so far as to attribute to them "everything about them that is dishonorable and blameworthy: theft, adultery, deceit." But, like Plato, he would never have dreamed of casting doubt on the historical truth contained in the epic, visible beneath what he already regarded as its mythological trappings.

Outdoing Xenophanes, certain moderns, dubbed "the vivisectors of Homer" by Dumézil,[28] supporters of the "historicist" approach that has long held sway in Hellenic studies, maintain that the divine interventions scattered throughout the Homeric narrative and, *a fortiori*, in the contested passage of book XXIV of the *Iliad*, are but secondary, superfluous ornaments, that they resemble a *supplement* that can be eliminated to recover the historical matter, the real events that were Homer's raw material, beginning with the Greek siege of Troy. Everything else, all of the interpolated mythological elements whose proliferation supposedly obscures this datum, being considered by them, as it had been by Fréart de Chambray, as the effect or product of poetic license, or even of pagan superstition, as redolent of a taste for allegory consistently denounced as having no bearing on the question,[29] and as being all the more incongruous for seeming to contradict one of the most characteristic features of the Homeric poems. For as Eric Auerbach has demonstrated, Homeric narrative not only doesn't invite interpretation, it positively resists and even opposes it, as is demonstrated by the fact that all attempts made by nineteenth-century mythologists to read the epics in allegorical or symbolic terms proved as futile as those proliferating in the Hellenistic era. "Homer can be analyzed . . . , but he cannot be interpreted . . . [proposed] interpretations are forced and foreign, they do not crystallize into a unified doctrine. The general considerations which occasionally occur . . . reveal a calm acceptance of the basic facts of human existence, but with no compulsion to brood over them, still less any passionate impulse either to rebel against them or to embrace them in an ecstasy of submission."[30] This trait, which is characteristic of epic, assumes even greater relief if we compare the "style" of the Homeric poems to that of the Old Testament. The world described by Homer is entirely self-sufficient: even if pure fiction, the narrative produces its effect without there being any need to search for hidden meaning, for any final cause. By contrast, the religious intent behind the biblical text manifests itself through a pretention to absolute authority justifiable only in terms of a teleological reading of each episode of the Old Testament as well as of sacred history in its entirety.[31]

To those maintaining that Homer was the educator of Hellas, Plato retorted that he was most assuredly the first and the greatest of tragic poets, but that all poetry should be banished from a well-made society. It is not that he rejected Homer's notions of justice and the gods, of good and evil, as Moses Finley claimed a bit hastily.[32] For Auerbach was correct: it is not possible to extract a philosophy or an ethics from the Homeric texts. What's more, as Finley himself notes, the speeches the poet has given his heroes contain no trace of anything resembling a social conscience, not a hint of the Decalogue; they evince no sense of responsibility other than familial, no obligation to anyone or anything but one's own prowess and one's own drive to victory and power.[33] The actions recounted by the poem have meaning and validity only insofar as they are "heroic." If it's true that the Homeric poems correspond to a decisive moment in what Dumézil called the "literary career" of myth, nothing in the *Iliad* contradicts the first principle of mythic narrative: namely, that the objects of myth are not so much ideas, creeds, or symbolic representations as happenings, events, occurrences.[34]

And occurrences, as has already been established, which are anything but historical. As Finley astutely observes, "the Trojan War is lost to us," and there is little chance now that it will ever be recovered: the Homeric poems are inconsistent with almost everything we know about the actual functioning of Mycenean society; and what's more, their Troy, while in the right location, precisely where Schliemann later sought it out, has only the barest resemblance to the one excavated by archeologists.[35] Which is not to say that the society described by Homer did not exist in a moment Finley situates, "allowing for anachronisms and fictions," in the centuries following the end of the Mycenean age but before the rise of the Greek city-state civilization, a period at the beginning of which the *Iliad* and the *Odyssey* assumed what was by and large the form familiar to us, because they were first written down at that time[36]: its being maintained by historians that an attentive reading of the poems allows us to extract from them a picture of social institutions and values that have every appearance of being historically reliable.

However, what concerns us here is not the historians' real world made by real men—"a world of history and not of fiction"[37]—but rather what Finley thinks he should call the "fiction" (even though it was accepted by Herodotus, "the father of history") holding that "the wrong done Menelaus was at the origin of the Trojan War, even though the priests, indignant at Paris's behavior, kept Helen in Egypt."[38] As well as that other "fiction" whose evocation toward the end of the *Iliad* has every appearance—and it is only an appearance—of being a decorative addition, a mere ornamental flourish, the one holding that the gods themselves were the cause of the entire episode. In other words, a "history" or "story"—or, if one prefers, a fable, a *muthos*—that, whatever the nature of its relation to the Trojan War, was only too well suited to provide material for recitation and memorization, whether in poetic or visual form.

There are many surviving Greek vase paintings that represent either the judgment itself or subject matter closely related to it.[39] Some of these depict events immediately preceding the actual competition (such as Hermes leading Hera and Athena forward while Aphrodite lingers in front of her mirror,[40] or the messenger of Zeus leading the three goddesses in procession (Figures 16 and 17)[41]); while in others Paris contemplates the three beauties among whom he must choose, sometimes deliberating in a seated position, with the rivals in front of him (Figure 18),[42] and sometimes seated among them,[43] as was common in the Archaic era—when, that is, he didn't flee in great haste, apparently frightened by the apparition, as was frequently the case toward the end of the sixth century.[44] On other, later vases, the scene is given a more picturesque inflection: Paris is seated on a rock near a tree, while the goddesses are preoccupied with their toilettes. A remarkable Archaic tripod pyxis now in the

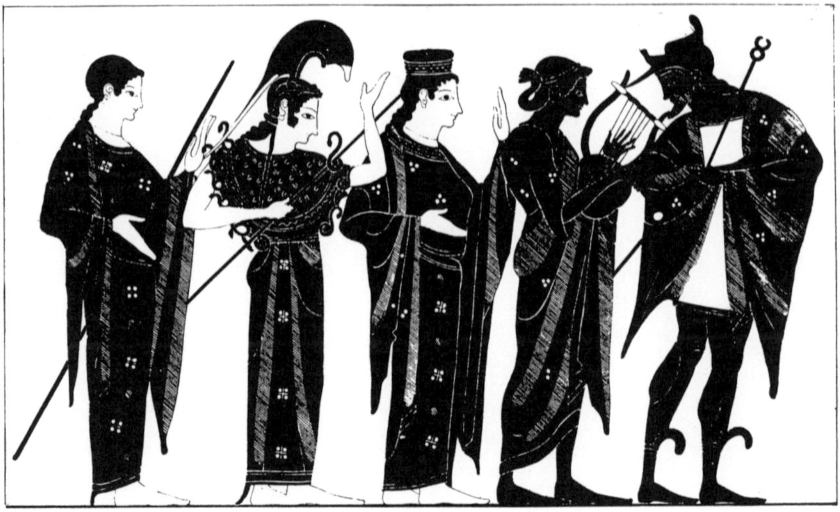

Figure 16. *Aphrodite, Athena, Hera, Paris, and Hermes*, black-figure amphora (Auckland, New Zealand; as drawn by Gerhard).

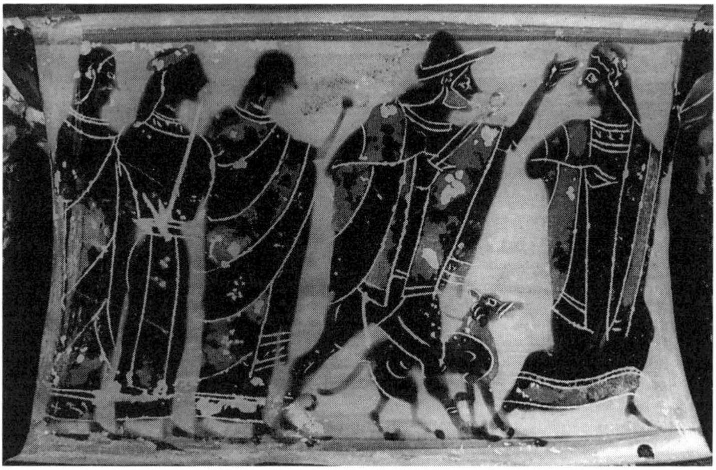

Figure 17. *Hermes, Followed by the Three Rival Goddesses, Hailing Paris,* black-figure pyxis (Paris, Louvre [MNB 508]).

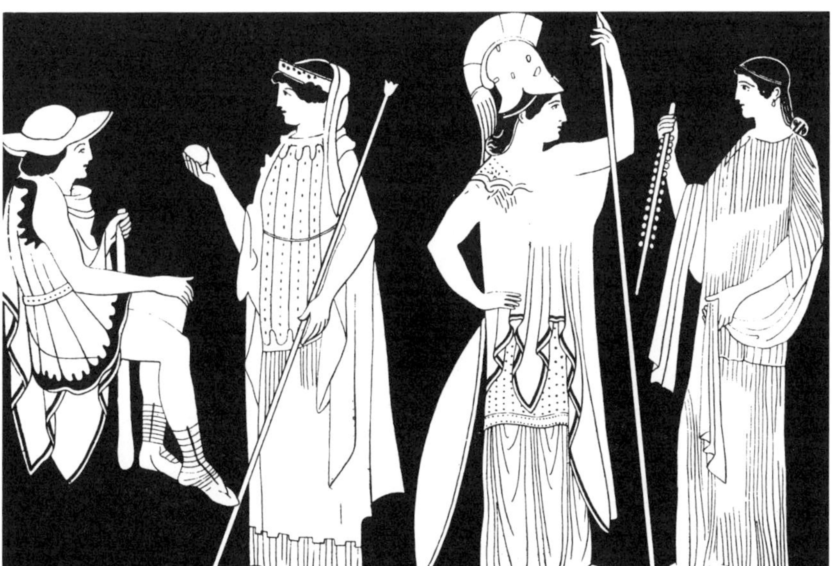

Figure 18. *The Judgment of Paris,* red-figure amphora attributed to the Niobid Painter (London, British Museum [E 257]; as drawn by Gerhard). On the back, *A Warrior Mounting His Quadriga.*

Louvre, attributed to Beazley's "painter C" (it is patently influenced by the Corinthian style), proposes a variation on the theme that's as precocious as it is enigmatic: Hermes leads the three goddesses forth, turning back toward them, while a fourth female figure stands directly in front of and facing Paris (Figures 19–21). She is perhaps Iris, the other messenger of the gods, the female double of Hermes, unless she is Eris, or Discord.[45]

But the image of the judgment was not always presented in isolation. It was frequently associated, on the same object, the same cup, the same receptacle, the same amphora, with other scenes and other figures, represented on what is designated, somewhat arbitrarily, as the back of the vase, or, as with the pyxis in the Louvre, on its cover, around whose periphery is a series of notable combats, while on the other feet of the tripod are represented the birth of Athena, emerging fully armed from Jupiter's head (the oldest known depiction of this subject; Figure 20), and a couple in a wedding chariot pulled by two horses toward which three women advance, holding out crowns (Figure 21). Archeologists have paid very little attention to these juxtapositions and combinations, considering them *a priori* to be meaningless, but this makes Christoph Clairmont's survey of them all the more interesting, even though he only notes the associated images for a few of the vases he considers.[46] While it is difficult to discern a connection between the judgment of Paris and the retinue of Dionysus, quite a few vases associate the image with an evocation of the wedding of Thetis[47] or of episodes from the Trojan War. Several Attic black-figure vases juxtapose the episodes corresponding to the beginning of the story of Paris (the judgment) and its conclusion (the restoration of Helen to Menelaus), while the sequence of events is summarized on certain red-figure vases on the back of which are represented either the abduction of Helen or her arrival in Troy (the only implicit allusion to be found in vase painting to the gifts with which the three rivals attempted to influence the judge's decision, or

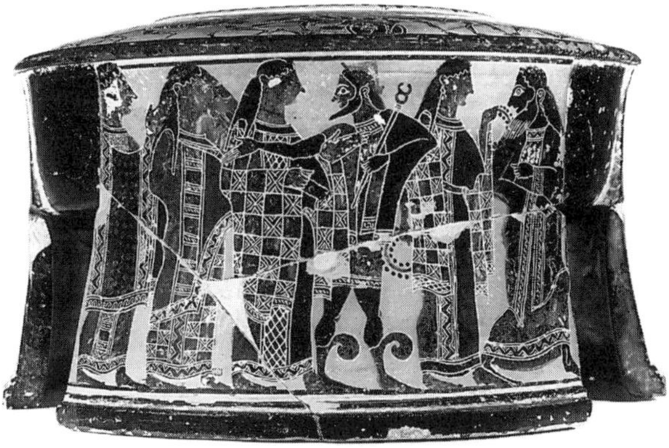

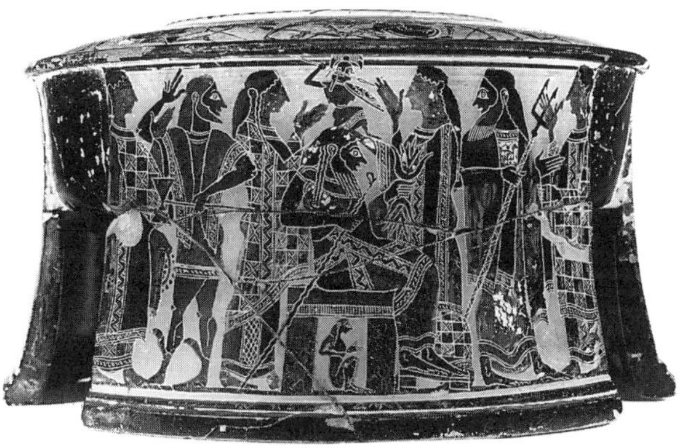

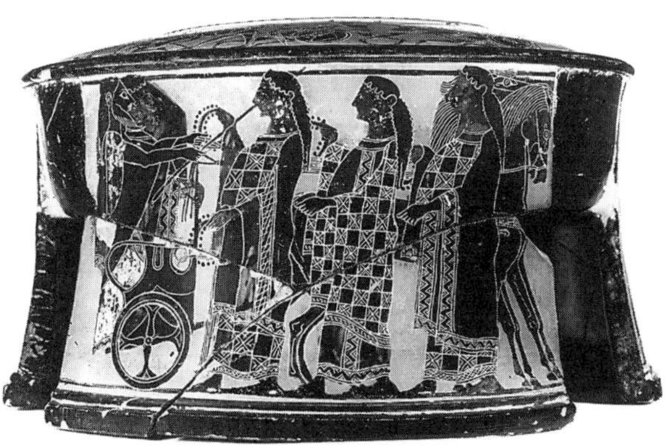

Figures 19–21. Black-figure cothon: (Paris, Louvre [Ca 616]). [19]. Support B, *The Judgement of Paris*; [20]. Support A, *The Birth of Athena*; [21]. Support C, *Wedding Chariot*.

at least to that of Homer's "lust that led to disaster"). In other cases, the judgment of Paris is paired with images of the body of Hector being dragged through the dust (which in book XXI of the *Iliad* corresponds to the moment of the evocation of the dispute between the three goddesses), of the death of Troilos (which Homer mentions only in passing, three books later[48]), or of that of Anchises and his son Aeneas. To say nothing of more generic subjects, such as a hero departing for combat, war scenes, or chariots presented in frontal or side views, often bearing Athena, helmeted and carrying the aegis, her shield outfitted with an image of the Gorgon's head.[49]

Thus the myth, the legend, or, as we might be tempted to say, the "history" or "story," has a certain autonomy, at least a relative one, within the representational order and lends itself to various associations and combinations: on some Attic vases, among them another tripod in the Louvre, the judgment appears along with a wedding procession. Could it be that Paris is here depicted as an allegorical suitor?[50] It is difficult to say, and the question of his status in the Homeric poem remains just as open. That the myth as presented there has all of the outward appearances of being an adventitious element could be a consequence of the very form of the epic, which may have dictated the maintenance of a certain distance from the myth even as it periodically resorted to it as a kind of extratextual commentary: as though it should continue to play its role surreptitiously, with the dispute among the goddesses—and before it the anger of Thetis, which is explicitly introduced at the beginning of the narrative, and Zeus's promise to her that the Trojans would remain victorious as long as the son of Peleus should hold himself aloof from battle[51]—running through the *Iliad* like a thread of its backing that regularly surfaces in the text, a thread giving it much of its strength, even if in a kind of delayed-action effect: as though the reminder of an always possible, though long-deferred, intervention of the gods (beginning with the first among them[52]) had been devised to make all the more affecting the eventual leveling of something that initially presents itself to the reader's eye as a distinctly human story; with the result that the apparent relation between figure and ground comes to be reversed, with the mythological element constituting the mainspring of the plot presenting itself as a purely ornamental trait, a kind of *supplement*.

By the same token, the "myth-work" here reclaims its rights, and those of interpretation as well, on condition that this is understood in a completely nonallegorical way. Georges Dumézil has shown how the legend of the judgment of Paris lends itself, in the mythological order, to structural interpretation. Indeed, it constitutes—this is perhaps one reason for its longevity—a rare Greek example of a manifest application of that trifunctional schema to be regarded as characteristic of Indo-European ideology, which has left very few traces in Hellenic institutional structure, theology, and even mythology. "Ransom to the Greek miracle . . . , in this corner of the world the critical and creative spirit set to work quite early, transforming even as it preserved. None of the characters acting around Achilles, from the king who offended him to the object of his affections . . . , imitates the gods."[53] As Dumézil emphasizes, the Homeric poems, unlike India's *Mahabharata*, did not result from a projection of mythology onto epic: and this makes it all the more remarkable that the long war between the Greeks and the Trojans seems to have been the result of a strict application of the tripartite structural model.

Grounded in an ancient tradition, the legend clearly articulates the three canonical functions: Hera, representing sovereignty, and Athena, representing military strength, join forces to combat the rich and voluptuous Troy, which they accuse of having preferred, through the person of Paris, the third function or party, that of riches and fecundity, represented by Aphrodite (see Figure 22). With the fundamental difference, in contrast to the ordinary modalities of the interaction of the three functions in the mythologies of peoples more conservative than the Greeks, that free will had its own role to play in the affair, if not by right, then at least in principle (and without

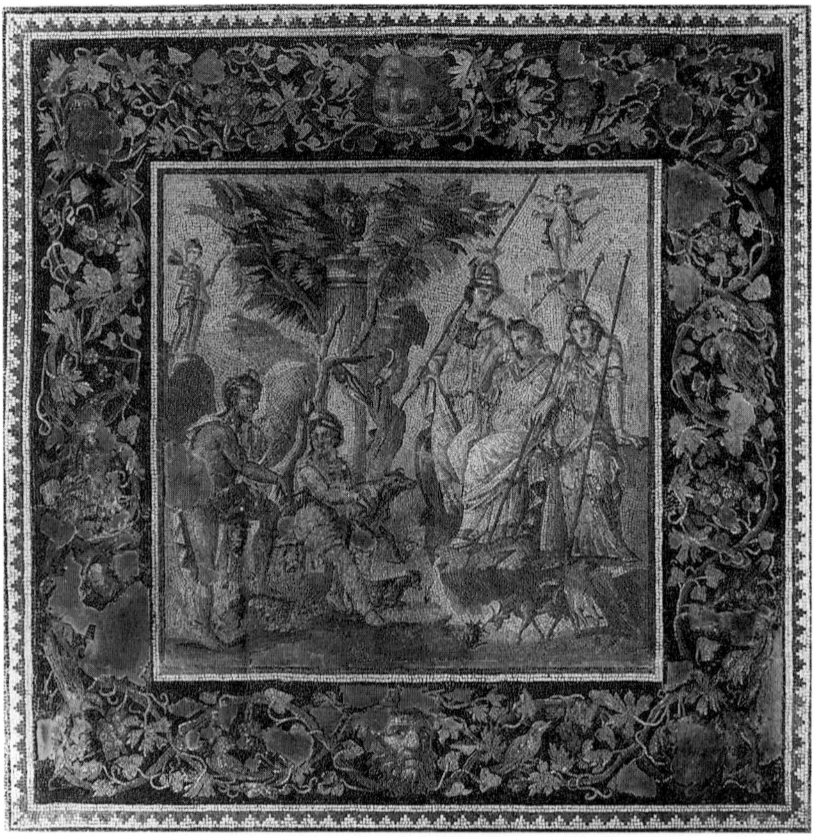

Figure 22. *The Judgment of Paris,* floor mosaic from Antioch, c. 115–150 (?) (Paris, Louvre [MA 3443]).

there being any juridical considerations in play): while the shepherd prince paid no heed to the possible consequences of his choice, according to Dumézil, it is nonetheless true that mankind, through him, disposed of "a short but decisive moment in which he could *orient history,*" whereas in the Roman world he would be reduced to reading his destiny in divine signs.[54]

The motif of the promises made to their judge by the three rival goddesses corresponds in every respect to the interpretation of the legend in terms of the trifunctional ideology. Unless we choose to view it as an instance of the typically Archaic ritual of the mutual exchange of gifts (the suitors' promises being premised on a like gesture being made by their judge), certainly the idea of the possible corruption of the judge raises questions about the nature and character of the decision expected of him. Was it indeed a judgment, in the juridical sense of the term, that Paris was expected to deliver? Was the decision of the judge—if judge he was—really free? We shall see that the ancients posed this question themselves, though in somewhat different terms. If we continue to adhere to Dumézil's point of view, maintaining that the judge deliberated in complete independence, then we appeal, in advance, to the perspective of the history that begins from this point, and we also privilege fable as opposed to myth. Being a shepherd, wasn't it preordained from the moment Zeus charged Paris with this perilous task that he would pronounce in favor of the goddess of the third function? Such a view cannot be sustained in the face of the fact that this shepherd was also the son of a king,[55] and that in the *Iliad* he is presented not only as a pleasure-seeker but also as a warrior who, in the end, is courageous: which means that the judge called upon to settle the differences among the three rivals combined in his person all three functions. To such an extent that it's tempting to see him as the reversal of an Indo-European theological construct associating with the gods of the three functions, rather like their spouse, a single but trivalent goddess operating in some sense as their synthesis[56]—a connection all the more justifiable in that the forced alliance (though one that constitutes, I repeat, one of the mainsprings of the *Iliad*) between Hera and Athena in opposition to Aphrodite echoes an important structural feature of the *varna*, the three social classes in which India, from very early on, is held to have incarnated the three functions in atrophied form: it is, in effect, a commonplace of the *Brahmana* that the first two *varna*, the priests (*brahman*) and the warriors (*ksatriya*), closed ranks in opposition to the third, the cultivator-farmers (*vaisya*).[57] And the choice attributed to Paris is consistent with a pervasive inflection of the tripartite ideology, one holding that the third functional category is always defined by a single one of its aspects, namely its beauty.[58]

Does this amount to saying that Paris had to choose not so much between three kinds of beauty as between three functions, and that it was only natural for his choice to have fallen on the one of these most regularly associated with beauty?[59] In Homer, Aphrodite's function is stated quite clearly—proof that the myth is very much at work there, and with it the ideological construct shaping it: when the goddess complains to her mother Dione about having been wounded in combat by Diomedes, the Father of the Gods smilingly reminds her that her lot was not the "works of warfare" but rather the "lovely secrets of marriage"[60]; secrets to which he himself was to succumb happily after Aphrodite, more or less willingly, entrusted to Hera the girdle embroidered with all of the beguilements allowing the latter to trick her royal spouse through deception, love, and sleep.[61] That three goddesses associated with three quite distinct functions were able to compete in the same beauty competition attests to the distance between the myth and Dumézil's "ideology": one based on "three functions," to be sure, but one that's nonetheless irreducible to a simple reflection of a real tripartite social division.[62] As though work performed by the myth on itself had determined that the choice expected of Paris would take on a dimension that was not exclusively "ideological," and that the question of "beauty" would exceed the boundaries of ideology, accruing a significance other than the strictly functional one. But not such that the equilibrium upset by the disputing goddesses could not be reestablished on another level: the apportionment of functions is even more explicitly affirmed by the nature of the gifts offered their judge by the three rivals, in the hope of carrying off the prize, than by their respective appearance and attributes.

It was not only the choice made by the judge that established a link with the fundamental determinant of the system: if we can believe, following Dumézil, that beauty was accorded a privileged status in the third category, this is a sure indicator of Archaism. "This notion is completely at home on a level whose conceptual peopling results from fecundity and multiplication, which is to say in the final analysis from the sexual act as performed by human beings as well as animals, and consequently from sexual attraction. As Indian reflection and institutions evolved, this root was forgotten; the most powerful expression of the tripartite structure, the hierarchy of the three *varna*, effectively excluded it: for how could beauty be one of the attributes and means of action of the cultivator-farmer, of the *vaisya*?" Which brings us back to Freud, as well as to the proposition figuring in our inquiry from the beginning, which we might now reformulate in terms consistent with those which Dumézil made his own: In Vedic India, as elsewhere, civilization or *Kultur* performed the important office of liberating beauty from its primordial tie to the reproductive function, resituating it on a more elevated level and eventually associating it with other, more cultivated functions—"sublimated" ones—in which the social dimension seems to have prevailed over the "sexual root."[63]

. . 8 . .

The Theme of Choosing

"I will willingly love her,
goddess and immortal."

Our comparative analysis has clarified the value of *signs* conferred on the story's protagonists through the myth's operations beneath the surface of the narrative: beginning with the three goddesses, whose attributes and functions, as well as the promises made to their judge, enable us to recognize them as champions of the three levels of the tripartite structure inherited from the Indo-European conquerors. This insight already identifies an important interpretive reference point within the Homeric poems, though one strictly governed by the ideological context in which the fable came into being. As regards the judge himself, the question must be formulated rather differently: within the context of the tripartite functional division perhaps constituting the primary substratum of what Dumézil presents as a "legend," the figure of the "shepherd-prince," as we've seen, is replete with ambiguity. But conceptualizing Paris and the role assigned to him in terms of the period is no easy matter: within the perspective of Greek myth, what could have been Zeus's rationale for designating a simple mortal, and a male at that, to settle a dispute involving three of the most important goddesses in the Hellenic pantheon? On this point, should we credit Fréart de Chambray, who merely repeats Lucian's remarks in a short comic vignette about the judgment of Paris, to the effect that Zeus (here called Jupiter) had refused to intervene personally for fear of being accused of bias in favor of one of the disputants, and of the two losers subsequently turning against him?[1] But if such were the case, why would he designate a man as arbiter, thereby making him responsible for a choice which the master of Olympus knew only too well would have repercussions among the gods and, consequently, among humans?

In what respect would a man have been a better judge of feminine beauty than a god[2]—not to mention a goddess, or a woman? To reframe the question: If the Greeks held that a mortal's view of the matter was decisive, doesn't this mean that for them beauty had something to do with death? And that it also had something to do with sexual difference, given that a man (and not a woman) was called upon to deliver the judgment, *de visu*? It was another mortal, once again a man, though one who according to Ovid knew the pleasures of both sexes,[3] upon whom Zeus and Hera called to settle the debate—which arose between them in the course of playful banter—over whether man or woman experienced the greater pleasure in lovemaking. Tiresias reputedly lost his sight because his answer ("Woman!") provoked the anger of the stern Juno, guardian of the marriage bed. As for Paris, he could not have foreseen the devastating consequences of his choice in favor of Venus, namely the ruin of his country and his own death in battle before the walls of Troy. Nonetheless, these tragic overtones impart to the choices imposed on man by the gods their true dimension, a mortal one, in every sense of the word: the gods do not have to pay for their mistakes and errors of judgment, at least not with their lives or with the loss of a sense as precious as sight. But how are we to understand that this concern, if not with *beauty* per se then with their *own* beauty, came to preoccupy the goddesses to such an extent that they agreed to take part in a competition to be judged by a man? Or are we to believe that in their natures *woman*—or more precisely, given that these are divine and therefore immortal beings: *sex* (as opposed to *gender*)—so prevailed over the *theos*, the divine element, that they found themselves reduced to deferring to a man's verdict, though retaining the right to seek vengeance should he rule against them?

It is perhaps tempting to respond to these questions along lines established by Xenophanes when, six centuries before the beginning of the Christian era, he saw fit to denounce the idiocy of human beings who attributed their own desires and feelings to the gods. That a man, whether Paris or Tiresias, was selected to arbitrate a disagreement among the gods, and one fundamentally linked to sexual difference, would seem to manifest that same "projective" fallacy denounced by Xenophanes: doubtless men do have something to say to this question, because it is they who willed that the gods have, like themselves, "clothing, speech, and a body"[4]—and consequently a sex. From the very start, the argument was destined to take a critical turn, one avowedly preordained to change its meaning quite radically, with irony giving way to indignation, and even denunciation, in the context of the Christian polemic against "false gods": its being understood that monotheism simply reversed the terms of the problem, organizing itself around the mystery of the "Christian body" and the incarnation of a God "made man," but one believed to have started by creating man in his own image, an essentially masculine one. Hence the necessity of removing ourselves from the optic of "truth" put in place by Christianity in order to consider the possibility of an Archaic Greek notion of a "divine body" constituted within the framework and consistent with the perspective of ancient polytheism, a project undertaken by Jean-Pierre Vernant in a text that concludes, quite strikingly, with an explicit reference to the story of Paris.[5]

It was all very well for Xenophanes to make fun of or to deplore the practice, but if the Archaic Greeks wanted to conceptualize or represent a being, of whatever kind, they could only do so in terms of what Vernant calls the "code of corporeality."[6] For them, individual existence entailed having a name and a body. And this was the case for gods as well as human beings, for ancient polytheism held that the divine world was organized like a society of the beyond, one constituted by a multiplicity of singular characters such that the gods, like human beings, represented "a set of recognizable features facilitating their identification and differentiation."[7] In this divine world, divided as it was by the plurality of the beings composing it, each divinity was allotted a limited, specific existence, the division—as well as the individuation, and so the finitude entailed by this—being at the origin of the many conflicts between them, that arbitrated by Paris being only one among many.

The gods, like human beings, have bodies. But how are we to conceive of these bodies in all of their difference and divergence from those of human beings? How are we to comprehend a body that can bleed, but only with blood that isn't blood, that is immortal, as was the case with Aphrodite when she was wounded beneath the walls of Troy while aiding her son Aeneas against the Greeks (in the Lattimore translation, "and blood immortal flowed from the goddess, ichor, that which runs in the veins of the blessed divinities; since these eat no food, nor do they drink of the shining wine, and therefore they have no blood and are called immortal")?[8] And what sort of body is it that remains invulnerable to hunger and fatigue, that has no need of either nourishment or sleep, unless *purely for pleasure*,[9] or in direct relation to it? One can only regret, in this connection, that Vernant did not see fit to discuss another question bearing on the "divine body," namely: To what extent was this body capable of experiencing not only pleasure, but desire as well? Admittedly, there are few texts that would allow us, if not to answer the question, at least to frame it in appropriate terms. A celebrated passage in the *Iliad* describes Zeus sleeping tranquilly, his wife between his arms, subdued by both sleep and desire (XIV, 346–51)—this as a result of Hera's having convinced Aphrodite to empower her erotically under false pretenses ("And when he saw her, desire was a mist about his close heart as much as on that time they first went to bed together and lay in love, and their dear parents knew nothing of it"; XIV, 294–96). Nicole Loraux correctly pointed out to me that Zeus here describes his desire in the same words as those used by Paris in his seduction of Helen, which provides explicit confirmation that the same desire (*eros*) is in question for both mortals and immortals: "But come, let us take our joy, couched together in love" (*en philotēti trapeiomen eunēthēnte*). And if he dares go on in the same passage to enumerate his conquests for the jealous Hera (his list is in fact quite selective), this is in order to persuade her, once again appropriating words previously uttered by Paris, that "never before has love for any goddess or woman so melted about the heart inside me, broken it to submission, as now."[10] *For any goddess or woman:* the fact that the gods, in their amorous affairs, so long ignored the distinction between the divine body and the human body (before limits were placed on those couplings entailing too many difficulties, even if these were only logical or taxonomic), and that the metamorphoses occasioned by these encounters sometimes resulted in violations of the boundaries between the divine and the human, as well as between the divine and the animal, constitutes compelling evidence of a complicity between the divine and the human bodies insofar as they were both *sexed.*

The gods, like human beings, as well as animals in general, have a sex, which is sufficient to qualify them as beings of desire (and of pleasure) and introduces into the Greek pantheon an organizational principle that must be considered constitutive: the difference between the sexes is fundamental to the society of the Immortals to the extent that this society, like that of mortals, relies upon the function of reproduction. Doubtless this function played only a marginal role, one bordering on the anecdotal, in the context of the pantheon as definitively codified in Hesiod's *Theogony*—a "third generation" pantheon, according to Vernant's definition, and one corresponding to that of Homer. Nonetheless, the fact remains that it is in the domain of sexuality that the limits set to the gods' existence and activity are most apparent: the gods, including their master, Zeus himself, were not free to dispose of their sexual objects however they pleased: they were obliged to honor certain forms and bow to certain constraints, not the least of which was the necessity for them to metamorphose or disguise themselves so that their human partners might enjoy sexual intimacy with the divine refulgence, the divine splendor, without being immediately stupefied, or even reduced to ashes.

While the role of difference—beginning with sexual difference—in the world of the gods has its importance with regard to the problem that concerns us here, and while it was not without consequences for humans themselves, it is nonetheless true that the choice of a mortal to arbitrate a dispute opposing three female deities finds its ultimate justification in the dissimilarity, the distinction marked by the Greeks—whatever Xenophanes may have said—between the body of the gods and that of human beings. The splendor attributed to the divine body manifested itself in various guises, including linguistic ones, such as the use of the superlative and, conversely, of negative formulations leading symptomatically to the definition of beings whose lives and bodies are characterized by utter positivity in terms of absence and privation: the gods are nonmortal (*athanatoi*), just as they are nonperishable (*ambrotoi*). But they are also much larger and "a hundred times stronger" than men.[11] The "super-body" attributed by the Greeks to their gods was conceived of after the model of their own body. But while they had to base their representations of the divine life and body on conditions familiar to them, this was, as Vernant stresses, in order to separate themselves from their mortal envelope and, setting themselves apart from it through a series of dodges and denials, constitute a kind of purified body, a "sublime" body, an ideality of the body which might appear to be "the source, the foundation, the model of that which, on this earth, we have but a poor reflection, an attenuated, deformed, derisory image."[12] In fact, a good deal more was at stake than merely decking out the gods in human corporal costume: the Greeks had to posit a divine "super-body" to facilitate their conceptualization—in all its limitation, deficiency, and incompleteness—of the mortal, perishable body that was their own.

"The divine being is one that, while endowed with a specific existence like that of men, knows neither death nor anything associated with it, because in its very specificity it has the value of an atemporal essence, of an inexhaustible and universal power."[13] And that applies to beauty as much as to any other attribute that might be ascribed to the gods. "Beauty?—I will willingly love her, goddess and immortal": the response Baudelaire placed in the mouth of "the stranger" (at the beginning of *Le Spleen de Paris*) is perfectly consistent with the views of the Greeks. If a man was retained as judge in this matter, this was first of all because the idea of a beauty impervious to decay and destruction of any kind, including old age and death, was very much the product of a specifically human anxiety, and of an intellectual operation, a work of idealization and passage to the *Idea*, that was rooted in the human condition. As Vernant emphasizes, Calypso was quite right to maintain that, in the matter of corporal beauty and appearance, she need cede nothing to the human wife for whom Ulysses longed so ardently, as was acknowledged by the hero himself in his response, to the effect that however perfect Penelope might be, she "would seem a shade before your majesty, death and old age being unknown to you, while she must die."[14]

From the perspective which is our own, the manifest Platonic connotation of this analysis poses no difficulties: the idea of beauty that Vernant thus traces back to its anthropological premises is the same one that would consolidate its position in Western culture through Neoplatonism and humanist culture and was to shape all readings and interpretations of the legend of Paris proposed within this framework. Certainly the competition to be judged by the shepherd-king did not pit mortal against immortal women. But Zeus's resolution to have a man settle the debate among Hera, Athena, and Aphrodite was consistent with yet another motivation, one that doesn't take us very far from Plato and that might seem to contradict a specifically human concern about escaping the cycle of generation and corruption. In the matter of beauty, the work of idealization neither can nor should go so far as to liberate the Idea (in this case, that of Beauty) from its intimacy with the reign of desire. If the judge awarded the prize to Aphrodite, in the end it was because he recognized that this goddess was not only *one* beauty among others, and thus one with whom they might be compared, but rather incarnated *Beauty par excellence* and thus had a privileged relation to what was beautiful and desirable in anyone else.[15] For however beautiful they might be in their different ways, neither Hera nor Athena could pretend to incarnate an ideal of beauty so closely associated, as was already the case not only with the Greeks but also with the Indo-Europeans before them, with what Freud called "the sphere of sexual sensations."

"In its magnificence, the body of the goddess is the very power of Eros as a universal force."[16] But a difficulty remains, one not without its importance with respect to the representational order: If he was in fact confronted by this same "splendor," how was Paris able to look upon it if its blinding intensity was such that no human eye could withstand the experience, and "its radiance escaped vision through an excess of clarity, just as darkness makes light invisible"?[17] Without doubt, the ancient law of Kronos that had been the undoing of so many humans, stipulating that no one can contemplate the gods against their will, was not applicable to Paris, given that the three goddesses had agreed, more or less willingly, to arbitration of their dispute by the shepherd-prince. Sight of the gods at close range and in all their refulgence was always perilous—to such an extent that, as already noted, divinities were obliged to assume another form when manifesting their presence to simple mortals. But in this instance the circumstances differed considerably from those generally prompting the gods to metamorphose or disguise themselves: for Paris to assess the respective charms of Hera, Athena, and Aphrodite accurately, they would have to present themselves to him in person, for what was in question was precisely the divine body. Lucian gives us a Paris who is pale and trembling, and who, being a mortal and a creature not of the city but of the country, is amazed to be permitted to contemplate so astonishing a spectacle, but one who nonetheless is bold enough to ask that Hermes request the goddesses to disrobe so that he might better judge of their beauty.[18] In the short tragedies in epistolary form that make up Ovid's *Heroides*, and which constitute the classic Latin version of the legend, Paris, addressing Helen, is more discreet: when the three goddesses first place their delicate feet on the grass, he is so frightened that his hair stands on end, and it is only after Mercury commands him to be the arbiter of beauty (or literally: the arbiter, not of *forms* but of *the form*, *Arbiter formae*) that he recovers his composure and his eyes their audacity[19]; it falls to his abandoned lover, the nymph Oenone, to let the cat out of the bag: Venus, Juno, and even Minerva herself do indeed present themselves to his judgment unclothed, though the latter would have been more comely in armor.[20] Which, to return to the Greek version of the legend, may have posed no insurmountable problem for Aphrodite or Hera, both of whom were preeminently carnal goddesses—even though Anchises, after having spent a night with Aphrodite, found it difficult to look at her on awakening[21]—but which was far from a self-evident matter in the case of Athena, the divine virgin. Was Paris, by warrant of an unexampled privilege, permitted to contemplate the three divine bodies in all of their splendor without being blinded or punished for his audacity, as was the case for so many heroes of fable: beginning with Tiresias, who, according to the late version of the story recounted by the Hellenistic poet Callimachus, lost his sight for having seen Athena, and having seen her nude—that same Athena of whom Callimachus asserts that her virginity was so fiercely cherished that she did not deign to look at herself in a mirror to assess her chances against her rivals in the distant time of the judgment of Paris?[22]

The fact that in the ancient tradition, literary as well as visual, the three goddesses never present themselves to their judge without covering of some sort (this happens only in Ovid and Lucian) does not constitute a decisive argument in the matter of visibility: as Vernant observes, for the Greeks, dress was completely integral to the body, including its attraction and allure. On an Etruscan silver plate Athena does indeed appear with her rivals in the nude, in a representation of the scene, invented by Euripides, of the goddesses bathing prior to the judgment; but Nicole Loraux has shown that the real problem posed by this image (to say nothing of subsequent depictions of an undraped Athena) arises not in connection with Paris, nor with Athena's rivals, but with the divine virgin herself, goddess of the gray eyes and the unseizable body, prohibited because impossible, and perhaps invisible *as a body*, being as inseparable from her *peplos* as from the cuirass and shield protecting her.[23] But sexed nonetheless, this body, and sufficiently female, this goddess, however eminently virile her "function," to compete for a beauty prize.

* * *

A mortal, then. And a man. But why this particular man, in his corporeal, desiring being? Why Paris? The question concerns not only his competence but the equity, and perhaps the ethics, of this choice. Smitten as they were with allegorical interpretations and even interpolations allowing them to infiltrate their doctrine into texts whose wide dissemination would thus serve to propagate their cause,[24] the Pythagoreans were not the only ones, nor even the first, to maintain that Helen's abductor could not be considered an unbiased, impartial judge: Hector himself finds that there are no words too harsh for admonishing this "beautiful boy, chaser and seducer of girls."[25] As for

Priam, he has good reason to hold the gods entirely responsible for the war with the Greeks: for then Helen would have had no part in its outbreak, having been but their instrument in this affair.[26] But Paris? Paris the barbarian, and as such a slave (as Iphigenia would have it), above all else a slave to his own senses? If we are to credit the allegorical reading of the myth advanced by Sallustius (or Sallust the Platonist) in the Hellenistic era, the choice made by the judge was not a free one: "The soul that lives in accordance with sense perception (for that is Paris) seeing beauty alone and not the other powers in the universe, says that the apple is Aphrodite's."[27] But perhaps Zeus revealed himself to be even more cunning than was supposed by Fréart de Chambray. Perhaps he was secretly aware that the pleasure-loving character of Paris would compel him to make a choice that would lead to a vicious war, one in which the gods themselves would be implicated, in order, if not to wipe out an overpopulous humanity, as was maintained by the *Cyprian Lays*,[28] to bring definitively to an end the age of heroes and of direct personal communication between humans and the gods. Being more cunning, or perhaps a subtler mythologist, did the master of Olympus understand that the shepherd Paris, linked as he was, precisely in his capacity as shepherd, to the third function (agriculture, fertility, reproduction), and despite his being the son of a king (which only augmented his authority and increased his similarity to Anchises, that other Trojan beloved of Aphrodite), would necessarily pronounce in favor of the goddess of love, thereby acting in accordance with the secret logic of the system?

According to Dumézil, man, "as is only natural in the land of the philosophers," on this occasion disposed of a brief but decisive moment in which to exercise his free will and influence the course of history. Whether "interested" or not, the fact remains that rarely has a judgment of taste entailed such serious consequences: namely, if we consider exclusively human beings, a ten-year war, the associated calamities for the Greeks, the destruction of Troy, and the death of the very prince who had delivered the judgment in question. The same holds for the selection of Paris as for Cleopatra's nose: if the judge had preferred Hera or Athena, would the world have been different? Euripides himself asks the question through the mouth of Helen when she confronts the anger of her first husband (a scene sometimes depicted, as we have seen, on the back of vases decorated with the judgment of Paris). All things considered, things would have gone even worse for the Greeks if Paris had chosen Hera or Athena and thereby acquired the political or military means to obtain victory:

> Think what this means, and all the consequence.
> Cypris prevailed, and I was won in marriage: all
> for Greek advantage. Asia is not your lord; you serve
> no tyrant now, nor take the spear in his defence.
> Yet Hellas' fortune was my own misfortune. I,
> sold once for my body's beauty stand accused, who
> should
> for what has been done wear garlands on my head.[29]

* * *

Seeing as what we are dealing with at present is not the arbiter, the judge himself, but something long designated by tradition as "the judgment of Paris," it might seem that a problem of anachronism comes into play here, at least if we focus on the history of language and of institutions. The very term *krisis*, which Sophocles used as the title of his (lost) play on this theme and which Lucian took up again for his short play *The Judgment of the Goddesses* (*Theōn krisis*), appears at a relatively late date, the verb *krinein* progressively displacing the older *dikazein*, though without eliminating it altogether. But the notion of *dikē*, which designated the code of law governing the relations between families of a tribe, was opposed to that of the *themis* or "established rule," of divine origin, which regulated conduct within the family group and prescribed the action to be taken when the order of the *genos* was in jeopardy. In the Homeric era, both of these concepts were dominated by the empire of custom: if the life of the *genos* allowed for a certain judicial apparatus, and if the root *deik* implies, as Benveniste has demonstrated, the idea of showing what one ought to do, of prescribing the norm, then the *dikē*, and *a fortiori* the *themis*—literally, the established rule—allowed no place for deliberation in the mind of the judge: "Rendering justice is not an intellectual operation requiring meditation or discussion. Formulas have been transmitted which are appropriate to given cases, and the role of the judge is to possess and apply them."[30] The idea of judgment, in its strictly judicial sense, was introduced only when the order of the *genē*, based on tradition, was replaced by that of the city-state.

As has been pointed out by Louis Gernet, in Greek, as in French and English, the word "judgment" is equivocal: it can designate either the intellectual operation *par excellence* (and the deliberation presupposed by this) or the weighing of an offence, including the sentence and the choice implied by it.[31] This second meaning became current in Greece rather late, with the development of legal institutions and a judicial apparatus. Whereas *dikazein* referred to a mode of judgment that was essentially predetermined, whether by precedent or by objective considerations such as the presence and number of witnesses, *krinein* implied an element of appreciation as well as of personal responsibility on the judge's part. Disintegration of the *genos* led to group intervention in family matters: finding himself obliged to judge cases in which there were no witnesses, the judge imposed the idea of a kind of justice that was specifically human and social, one that was impersonal but that ought to have a certain resonance in the individual conscience, beginning with that of the judge himself.

While the etymology of the verb *krinein* predisposed it to express the idea of "discernment" or "discrimination," and perhaps even of personal "choice," the word, as Gernet also notes, may not have originally corresponded to a new notion: there are known instances of its use from a very ancient period in religious language, where it designated the interpretation of dreams or the flight of birds, or even—its first judicial usage carried decidedly unfavorable connotations—the selection of victims. Which fact is altogether consistent with what has been said of the "judgment" of Paris. While the story includes several features suggestive of a trial, beginning with its agonistic aspect,[32] the "sentence" handed down was aberrant in every respect, in both its underlying justification and its long-term effects. Far from furthering the reestablishment of an equilibrium or *eunomia* that had been disturbed, the choice made by the shepherd-prince might seem, at least retrospectively, when it came time to assess it in ethical terms, closely related to that form of *hubris*, of an attack against the established order, automatically forfeiting that authority of a king-judge from which the *themis* followed. While the judge violated no family rules and his choice followed quasi-automatically from his position in the trifunctional hierarchy, the sentence pronounced by him (better described in terms of *dikē* than of *krisis*) nonetheless lent itself to contradictory interpretations. But we have seen that the system itself did not prohibit equivocations of this kind, far from it: it actually encouraged them, insofar as on principle every judgment in the strict sense of the word implied a kind of leap or rupture, as well as an oath that, while ultimately referring to a body of rules or laws, was not bound by any constraining premise.

> Why then do you marvel, if the lowest of the people, the lawyers, beasts of the courts, and advocates that are but vultures in gowns, nay if all our judges nowadays sell their judgements for money, when as in the beginning of the world [from the exordium, the beginning of things: *cum rerum exordio*] one only bribe and favor corrupted the sentence between gods and men, and that one rustical judge and shepherd, appointed by the counsel of the great Jupiter, sold his first judgement [*et originalem sententiam:* the

> originary or primordial sentence] for a little pleasure, which was the cause afterward of the ruin of all his kin?[33]

There is nothing surprising about this sally by Apuleius when considered in context, for it appears in *The Golden Ass* shortly before a bestial coupling reserved for the hero in the same theater where a curious pantomime on the theme of the judgment of Paris has just been presented. It would have been meaningless in an age in which epic poets tried to persuade their listeners that everything in this story was determined solely by the will of Zeus, despite the fact that those who eventually paid for Paris's choice with their lives made a point of verifying for themselves, *de visu*, as had previously been done by the judge himself, whether Helen's beauty was such as to justify so much effort and misfortune: according to the summary of the *Cyprian Lays* provided by the grammarian Proclos in his *Chrestomathy*, Achilles, having asked to contemplate Helen, was permitted to do so in a rendezvous arranged by Aphrodite and Thetis before the Greeks laid siege to Troy.[34] In Troy itself, the Council of the Ancients (*demogerontes*) proceeded in precisely the same way when Helen approached the door close to where the old men were seated.[35] As recounted by Homer, the scene lacks that special quality characteristic of Gérôme's *Phryne before the Areopagus:* in both cases, the question of beauty, being posed publicly, and even to the point of nudity, was nonetheless intended to disturb institutions (but the image by Gérôme reproduced in the *Grand Larousse illustré* was too carefully constructed to move me as a child).

To speak, as I did just now, of the "judgment of taste" in connection with the story of Paris is doubly anachronistic. For it is not enough merely to assert that a semantic slippage is attributable to the story—even though (to cite Gernet again) objective explanations are based on necessary relations and not solely temporal ones[36]—and then, without further ado, to invoke this fact as a justification for using a language that would, after two millennia, be that of Kant. And yet, if we adhere to the terms of the story as recounted in the fable in its "classic" form, what Ovid was to call the *arbiter formae* (beauty being explicitly confounded in this instance with form, as was already implied in the Greek), Paris was indeed instructed to award the apple to that goddess among the three judged by him to be the most beautiful: which supposed that he had the requisite competence, taste (*Geschmack*) being nothing other, in Kantian terms, than the ability to judge of the beautiful.[37] Does the fact that the judge himself is attractive, even passing for a "model of beauty," amount to a sufficient qualification for his deciding the question, as Fréart de Chambray seems to suggest, and as is affirmed by Zeus himself, at the beginning of Lucian's playlet, though not without his uttering a qualifying remark concerning Paris's libidinous tendencies, implying the likelihood of their influencing the outcome?[38] Is it sufficient to be beautiful oneself to be in a position to judge the beauty of others, even if they are of the other sex? Does beauty (*la beauté*) know itself, in its principle as well as in its various manifestations (*le beau* being masculine, like the genus "man," *la beauté* being gendered as feminine)?

But what exactly do we mean—to repeat Kant's question—when we say that a woman is beautiful? If we are to believe Fréart de Chambray, Paris was not called upon to pronounce with regard to ideas or principles, but to designate which, among the three goddesses agreeing to submit to his arbitration, he found to be the most beautiful. Although we know from other sources that his choice was anything but "disinterested," and that therefore he could not pretend, in Kantian terms, to "universality" of any sort (it will be recalled that according to Fréart, who here conforms to tradition, Jupiter had renounced settling the debate himself, out of fear, precisely, of appearing "biased" or "interested"): the barbarian, the man of pleasure[39] who was Paris could not but decide in favor of Aphrodite. And all the more so as the goddess had not hesitated to sway her judge by promising him, should he decide in her favor, the most beautiful of women: which implied, on her part, another judgment of taste, one setting Helen apart from other mortals, which means that the feeling of pleasure on which Paris based his judgment was not determined solely by the representation of the object presented to his view. The existence (the presence) of Aphrodite had a special interest for him: in her very appearance the goddess constituted proof of the pleasure attending contemplation of beauty at its apogee, as well as the promise of a recompense—again in terms of pleasure, but of a very different order, the announcement of a surplus pleasure (*plus-de-jouir*) that would be not only a function of the scopic drive but would also imply possession of the object of desire. The myth thus posits that Aphrodite made her appeal to Paris's desire even as she channeled it toward another goal: doubtless she did not herself want the object, except insofar as it could influence the choice in her favor; but the pleasure experienced by the arbiter or judge in looking at it still implied an indirect or deviated reference to the faculty of desire under auspices that were not exclusively scopic. To cite Kant once again: "That a judgment by which I declare an object to be agreeable expresses an interest in that object is already obvious from the fact that, by means of sensation, the judgment arouses a desire for objects of that kind."[40]

It should be noted that in the ancient versions of the legend, Aphrodite does not see fit to offer herself to her judge: this gesture figures only in smutty versions of the modern era, as well as in the libretto of Offenbach's *La Belle Hélène* by Meillac and Halévy. The essential point remains that neither the goddess of Love nor her rivals were content to rely exclusively on their own beauty to carry the day: Hera appealed to Paris's desire for power, Athena to his desire for victory, and Aphrodite to his desire for woman—a desire that it was within her power to satisfy insofar as she oversaw matters of love. Apparently respectful, in this case, of the difference between mortals and immortals, she promises her judge to deliver to him, in return for the golden apple, the most beautiful of women, though leaving him to make sense of a pure concept ("the most beautiful of women"), which was certainly not the case when he contemplated her herself, even if only to recognize her as Beauty personified. But there is nonetheless a certain parallelism between Paris's having to choose the most beautiful of the goddesses and Aphrodite's promise to select the most beautiful of women for him. As the goddess of love, Aphrodite had her own ideas about feminine beauty, just as Paris, the shepherd-prince, was inclined to consider the goddesses with the same eye he would use for simple mortals. If Hera, rather than Aphrodite, had promised him the most beautiful of women, Paris might well have been able to resist the temptation: what made an irresistible appeal to his "interest" was the most beautiful of women *in Aphrodite's terms*, and not in those of Hera or Athena. Paris could not but desire the most beautiful of women as chosen for him by the goddess he was to prefer to her rivals. If he awarded the prize to Aphrodite, it was because the latter had promised him, as recompense, the woman she judged to be the most beautiful in conformity with the same standard of beauty personified by her herself in his eyes, one that in this capacity excited his desire, that *interested* him (the problem being, in terms of painting, that of determining by what means or through what forms, as opposed to attributes alone, painters have set about differentiating the three rivals).

Thus the paradox of Paris consists in his having been reduced to imagining the object of his desire in terms of what was present to his vision. "I see her," Lucian's Paris says of Helen ("Not so fast!" Aphrodite then cautions him, wanting to retain his complete attention). And Ovid's: "It was you that filled my vision as I waked, and you my soul saw in the night, when eyes lie overcome by peaceful slumber. What will you be face to face, you who won me yet unseen? I was fired with love though here, far away, was the flame."[41] In itself, the prize offered the judge was only a simple promise of pleasure (how would it have been possible for Paris to desire, even in a dream or in a hallucination, what remained for him nothing but a concept, unless he did so through the model presented to him by the goddess of Love?). A promise of pleasure, and as such agreeable, though it was not then reinforced by an objective sensual representation. To put it another way: in this instance, it was not so much beauty that swayed Paris as it was the premium of pleasure accompanying it, the promise of a surplus pleasure. The very notion of the promise (as well as a correlative one, that of expectation) implying a delay, a *différance* with an *a*, as written by Derrida, and with it the possibility of a diversion, even a deception—something like a trap.

* * *

But, once again, what does it mean to invoke Kant or Freud in connection with the judgment of Paris? How can we justify reading the fable in our own terms, in the light of our own time? What authorizes us, from a historical or a critical point of view, to manipulate and even alter the very substance of the ancient legend by recasting it in a mold foreign to it, in the same way that Chrysippus and his successors deformed and denatured the Homeric narrative by imposing an allegorical form on it?

If we were proposing to interpret this Greek legend in terms of the *Critique of Judgment* or of *Civilization and Its Discontents*, there would be good reason for historians to criticize us for anachronism, even though in matters of art anachronism seems to be the rule. But it is quite another matter, and in no way contradicts either the accepted norms of historical writing or the way history is made, to use Kant as well as Freud (just as others have used Plato) to reflect on the myth's fortune in European culture: insofar as, even though it commences with Homer, this fortune cannot be confined within the boundaries of literature. If we are examining the work of the myth over a (very) extended period or *longue durée*, this is because we have chosen not to focus exclusively on its literary career and because, beginning, like Aby Warburg, with its incongruous echo in the work of Manet, with a mode of citation that is singularly cunning and cryptic, we have rebounded, via Marcantonio's engraving, back to the legend itself and to the roots—specifically mythic ones?—firmly securing it within Indo-European ideology. Further, we have resolved not to exclude *a priori* any of the echoes stirred up by this same legend, or any developments to which it might lend itself in other areas of thought and knowledge, beginning with philosophy and psychoanalysis. The idea that the myth-work is readily containable within a given temporal framework, however extended this might be, one that in some sense is logically antecedent to it, is difficult to reconcile with what we have begun to glimpse about the conditions shaping such an activity: specifically, with any marked distinction between expressive content and form and with a preliminary division between the fields or periods in which it unfolds. In the end, it is the very object of our investigation that necessitates the extended chronological parameters of the interrogation. If in this context something presents itself to our minds in the guise of a "framework" (temporal, substantive, formal, practical, ideological, regional, etc.), it cannot be conceptualized in the accepted terms of opposition between form and content: insofar as *work* is in question here, that of the myth (like that performed by art, or by the unconscious) must be conceived of as producing its own framework and even, something much more difficult to grasp, as implying or containing it, for the framework operates within the myth, just as it can operate—Marcantonio's engraving offers a fine example of this, as we shall soon see—within a painting, and not exclusively at its margins.

So described, the task we have set ourselves is quite consistent with Warburg's project and inevitably runs counter to historicist and positivist agendas. What, for instance, do we mean by "context"? What do we mean by "framework"? What do we mean by "*durée*"? What do we mean by "history"? And—to pose a question that sums up all of the others—what do we mean by "anachronism"? The very word, however obvious its conceptual incoherence, still carries a certain negative inflection, a decidedly pejorative connotation: anachronism is held to proceed from an inadmissable confusion of periods or eras. Which presupposes that the individual (generally a historian) making the accusation himself knows whereof he speaks with regard to time as well as history: the time of history (and of the story) as well as history's (and the story's) relation to time. A relation conceived of as being quite simple, rather like that of a container and what it contains: history and the story unfolding in time, inscribing itself and developing within it. And as for the *longue durée*, here again, Bergson to the contrary, we are dealing with the historian's time: a time as measurable as space, and which thus lends itself to all manner of reduction and manipulation, with all the attendant risks of confusion, against which we outfit ourselves with all sorts of instruments intended to strengthen our control over them. Whereas it is, quite obviously, the object under study (and for example the way in which an entire history can be woven, by means of a network of texts and works of art, around the theme of the myth) that produces the time, the very duration within which it is inscribed, and within which it must of necessity be known and studied. Which suffices to justify our undertaking, in a displaced, radical form, a project first articulated by a physicist: that of a *history of time*.[42] The *big bang* being inscribed, we might say, at the beginning of time, which is its product, or its effect, or its consequence, just as the judgment of Paris might be inscribed at the beginning of a history proceeding, in its very movement, from this false step.

* * *

Is the *Déjeuner sur l'herbe* a joke, then, and one that has *gone on for too long*? If joke there be, it has gone on even longer than might have been imagined. For as we began to glimpse with Manet, if not with Raphael and Fréart de Chambray, and as will soon be confirmed by additional further examples: art (to say nothing of the unconscious, which Freud maintained has no "history") seems to go about its business quite heedless of such questions, as well as of comparable scruples; it takes its materials wherever it finds them (which is not the same as saying haphazardly) and uses them in accordance with its own ends, diverting them, often quite deliberately, from their original contexts. This applies, notably, to fable and its imagery, from which it draws freely to satisfy its whims as well as its momentary needs, without manifesting the slightest concern about possible anachronism or arbitrariness, any more than about offhandedness or absurdity or irrelevance. What's in question here is a false debate: historicism and positivism cannot long hold out against the singular trajectory of the judgment of Paris in Western culture, a fact of which it cannot be said *a priori* that its key will be found in history.

Between history and myth, which one "traverses" the other? Seeing how it cuts such a wide swathe "through history"—and given that it has been recounted in many different ways that are not always mutually compatible—can this fable possibly have any meaning separate and distinct from that imprinted upon it by specific contexts of reception (if not, we would be obliged to deal case by case, in reference to the specific circumstances holding in each instance)? Or, by contrast, is the history of reception traversed by a portable meaning, such that the fable is not present and active in history save in a transitory or even a *transitive* state, with neither its final destination nor the effects it is capable of producing in a wide variety of fields ever being verifiable; such that its fortune would only be comprehensible by passing through—among others—Kant and Freud? What are we to make, what could we make, of a fable or story that has traversed time in this way without having lost its allure, a fable that has retained its enigmatic quality, a story that continues, even today, to prompt reflection? How can we not recognize in such an anecdote, in such a legendary motif, a problem, or at least a theme of more general and perhaps even universal interest, to which the myth directs our attention? In this connection we might cite the way Freud invokes, precisely, the story of Paris, or those of Psyche and Cinderella, both in the end selected over their two elder sisters, linking all of them to the motif of the choice imposed on the suitors in *The Merchant of Venice* among three caskets: of gold, silver, and lead; as well as to the old king's decision to divide his realm among his three daughters in *King Lear:* all of these tales, legends, or stories being, according to Freud, once stripped of their symbolic trappings, treatments of the same "human content" (*menschliches Motiv*)—the choice a man is called upon to make among three women, the outcome being, with a regularity so consistent as to suggest its predetermination by some internal necessity, that he settles on the third and last of them, who is acknowledged to be the most beautiful, the best, the most obliging, but also the least talkative, the most silent.[43]

Georges Dumézil has recognized in what he calls "dramas of choice" a theme that is quite persistent, one that recurs in the epics of many traditions and is widespread in folklore, although the specific circumstances of the choice vary considerably—as do the actors in the story and the objects in question. The Iranian epic, for example, tells of the three sons of Feridun, to each of whom their father-king consigns a region of the world, having resolved that the one favoring law and religion over riches and military might would win his crown, while in an *exemplum* of the fourteenth century, William the Conqueror selects as his successor the one of his sons, the last, who had preferred Prudence to Valor and Beauty. Sons or daughters, attributes, qualities, or functions, in every case these are variants of a single type, the essential point being that while the protagonists of the drama and the objects among which they choose may change, the basic structure remains the one familiar to us from the best known "epic" example in the West, namely the judgment of Paris.[44]

Does this mean that, comparative analysis aside, history should have the last word here, as the recurrence of the theme bears witness to the permanence of a system of thought which continued to prevail even though the medieval three-estate structure no longer corresponded to that of Indo-European society?[45] In this context, the judgment of Paris would occupy a singular position, less because of the place set aside in the narrative for feminine divinities, beings who do not readily accede to being reduced to the status of simple objects, or of the aberrant character of the choice made by the shepherd-prince, than because of the fate reserved for the fable in European culture, beginning in the Middle Ages and the Renaissance. In Dumézil's view, the tripartite ideology's having left so few traces in Hellenic institutional organization and mythology was a price paid for what is sometimes called the "Greek miracle" (a tag suggesting greater coherence than many historians feel is justified), the critical, creative spirit in Greece having very early on set about transforming the very thing it was preserving. But while it may be true that the choice confronting Paris, in the version of the story dating no later than the sixth century B.C., is independent of those speculations which, from the Pythagoreans to Plato, restored to the ideology of the three functions, which was forgotten in practice, a philosophical existence,[46] it is impossible to be satisfied with such a declaration, which reduces philosophical speculation to a kind of reversion to sources or a return of the repressed. The rule of structural thought (which is consistent with the project of Aby Warburg[47]) applies here as it does elsewhere: what counts is less what a work—whether of art or philosophy—represents or manifests as what it *transforms*, even if this entails altering or perverting its meaning, and if not its meaning then its form.

In the matter of transformations, if we are to judge the import of the work accomplished by European thought under the title of the "triad" considered in all of its manifestations, logical and dialectical, theological and mystical, literary and, above all, pictorial, then we must look beyond ancient literature. The judgment of Paris, as well as the theme of choosing among three women (or their symbolic substitutes, whether caskets or something else), offers a fine illustration, for, as has already been pointed out, it was to have a singular fortune in the culture of the Renaissance, a development that is not necessarily inconsistent with Dumézil's hypotheses. As Edgar Wind has shown, Renaissance Neoplatonists concurred with "antiquarians," who were responsible for the renewal of study into the ancient "mysteries," in recognizing that ancient myths and legends were the receptacle, under the veil of "mystery" and an imagery declared to be "hieroglyphic," of a wisdom and perhaps even a religion older than Homer and Hesiod (it will be recalled in this connection that the fable of the judgment of Paris seems to have originated in a period earlier than that in which the Homeric poems assumed written form, and that its linkage with the Trojan War in the *Iliad* was doubtless a more recent development). A wisdom, a secret religion that the humanists dubbed "Orphic," and manifested a hidden concordance with the Mosaic and even the Christian tradition.[48]

As a good Neoplatonist, Saint Augustine would have been the first to agree: the ancients, whether Jewish or pagan, knew the *res ipsa*, the "thing itself," which was called the Christian faith after the coming of Christ.[49] As formulated by him, the doctrine of the "vestiges of the Trinity" maintained that the Holy Trinity had left its traces everywhere and thus was one of those mysterious revelations supposedly shared by pagans and Christians,[50] the idea that the Trinity was the measure of all things echoing the theological axiom of Platonic derivation to the effect that everything divine exercises its power in a triadic rhythm.[51] Beginning with Venus, whose unity manifests itself in the three Graces (in Greek, the *Charites*), united by the knot of universal charity, whose attributes they are, like the unity of Necessity manifested in the Fates: in a pantheon such as that proposed by Neoplatonic doctrine, whose central focus is a Love mediating between Man and God, the group of the three Graces can be interpreted—following a lesson proposed by Marsilio Ficino, of which the Villa di Careggi, seat of the Academy of the same name, seemed to him predestined, by its very name, to become the *charitum ager*, the soil of the Graces, and which is illustrated on the medal by Pico della Mirandola serving as Wind's point of departure—as a tripartite though unsymmetrical configuration in which Love, while embracing Beauty, turns toward Voluptuousness in conformity with a procedure which, between procession (*emanatio*) and return (*remeatio*), is that of conversion or rapture (*raptio*).[52]

In his list of sisterly trios associated with the theme of choosing, Freud, while according ample space to the goddesses of destiny, curiously fails to include the three Graces. The reason for this omission is, of course, that the choice among the latter did not seem relevant before Neoplatonic exegesis had established order, determining that, within what was originally presented as an undifferentiated trio, pleasure (*voluptas*) should prevail, in the eyes of love, over beauty. But, by contrast, the most remarkable thing about humanist reference to the judgment of Paris is its elimination or, more accurately, its refusal of the theme of choosing, although the tripartite schema persisted. Marsilio Ficino himself used the fable as an *exemplum* lending support to his theory of a *triplex vita*, endorsing the argument of Fulgentius, the Latin grammarian whose *Mythologiae* (concerned with the pagan gods) constitutes, along with Gregory the Great's *Moralia* (whose focus is the Bible), one of the two great monuments of the allegorical literature of the early sixth century: this text includes, among its many edifying interpretations of antique fables, the first suggestion that the three goddesses among whom Paris must choose are symbols of the contemplative life, the active life, and the life of love or pleasure (*voluptaria*).[53] In the dedicatory epistle of his commentary on Plato's *Philebus*, which was addressed to Lorenzo de' Medici, Ficino insisted on the danger of favoring one of these three routes over the two others: Paris, like Hercules, like Socrates, was punished by the two goddesses he had offended; and Ficino flattered his prince by stating that, having been instructed by the oracle of Apollo, Lorenzo had been wise enough to acknowledge and adore all three goddesses in accordance with their respective merits, with the happy result that he had been accorded wisdom by Pallas, power by Juno, and grace, poetry, and music by Venus.[54]

Several fifteenth- and sixteenth-century morality plays involving the three goddesses pick up threads woven into those of the twelfth and even the ninth centuries, and in some cases as far back as the sixth century and beyond. In the words of Jean Seznec, "the scholar who believed that he had recovered the secret of the lost wisdom of antiquity was in reality merely returning to the hybrid doctrine that the Fathers had inherited from the last defenders of paganism." Among these was the Sallustius of the *De diis et mundo*, already cited, a kind of pagan catechism written at the instigation of the emperor Julian to serve as a tool in the battle against the Christians, and which was predicated on the belief that myth and fable contained, in disguised form, hidden truths which were translatable not only into moral doctrine but metaphysical doctrine as well.[55] Thus it is all the more remarkable that the judgment of Paris, presented as exemplifying a myth combining theological, physical, psychic, and naturalist features, figures so prominently in this little book, which was described by Father Athanasius Kircher, a great connoisseur of allegories in cryptic or "hieroglyphic" form, as "pure gold"[56]:

> The blended kind of myths can be seen in numerous examples; one is the tale they tell that at the banquet of the gods [Discord] threw a golden apple and the goddesses, vying with one another for its possession, were sent by Zeus to Paris to be judged; Paris thought Aphrodite beautiful, and gave her the apple. Here the banquet signifies the supramundane powers of the gods, and that is why they are together, the golden apple signifies the universe, which, as it is made of opposites, is rightly said to be thrown by [Discord], and as the various gods give various gifts to the universe they are thought to vie with one another for the possession of the apple; further [here we

> come to a portion of the text that has already been cited], the soul that lives in accordance with sense-perception (for that is Paris), seeing beauty alone and not the other powers in the universe, says that the apple is Aphrodite's.[57]

(Sallustius is here articulating as clearly as possible the allegorical interpretation of the myth and the dichotomy introduced by it: "So the myths represent the gods in respect of that which is speakable and that which is unspeakable, of that which is obscure and that which is manifest, of that which is clear and that which is hidden." They imitate the beauty of the gods, who willed that all of the good accessible through the senses be available to all mankind but reserved the good known through the spirit exclusively for the wise ("The myths proclaim to all that the gods exist, telling who they are and of what sort to those able to know it"). And they imitate their activities: on which basis Sallustius feels he can assert that "the universe itself can be called a myth, since bodies and material objects are apparent in it, while souls and intellects are concealed."[58])

Ten centuries later, *Les Échecs amoureux*, an allegorical poem written between 1370 and 1380 in which the game of chess serves as the controlling metaphor of a moral description of the world, also allots a prominent role to the judgment of Paris. But here the choice theme is viewed from another perspective entirely. In an illuminated manuscript painted around 1500 for Louise of Savoy containing a prose version of the poem, several of the images treat the theme or motif which concerns us (Figures 23–26): on folio 14 verso, the three Fates are depicted; farther on, Mercury introduces the author to Pallas, Juno, and Venus (folio 26 verso), while the two last illustrations in the volume represent Venus thanking Paris for having chosen her (folio 165) and the author being introduced by Deduit to the desired orchard to which Nature holds the key and in which are offered to him, in the persons of Venus, Juno, and Pallas, three ways of living which, being confined within the same walled enclosure, are not so much three different options as they are an indissoluble trio (though Venus, here again, is standing in the foreground, while her rivals are placed some distance behind her).[59]

But it was Giordano Bruno who, in his *Eroici furori*, went the farthest in this direction. Assembling a list of the suffering and difficulties encountered by the soul while returning to the One, the supreme Good, Bruno employs the rhetorical device of multivoiced commentary on a poem said to be by a mysterious poet referred to as *il furioso*, as he is possessed of the *furor divinis*. The moment arrives in which this poet perceives a golden apple bearing the device *pulchriori detur* ("for the most beautiful one"), said to be a transparent (*molto volgare*) allusion to the fable of Paris and the three goddesses submitting to his judgment: Venus, goddess of the Third Sky and mother of the blind archer who subjugates all beings, Pallas, born from the head of Jupiter, and Juno, the haughty wife of the master of the gods. Which provides the poet with an occasion to affirm that if his divinity had agreed to take part in such a competition (*Se la mia diva al paragone s'appone*), neither Pallas, nor Juno, nor Venus herself would have won the prize, for she alone possessed the measure of all beauty, wisdom, and majesty, uniting in a single subject (*come in un suggetto*) the different kinds of beauty, whereas each of the three goddesses could claim only one as her own, in whose terms she surpassed her competitors, who only possessed these alternate forms of beauty accidentally, as it were. If beauty, wisdom, and knowledge exist in things only to a greater or lesser degree, in the divine essence all perfections are as equal as they are infinite. In the face of an object prevailing over all others in terms of, simultaneously, beauty, wisdom, and power, the debate is rendered moot; and, in principle, *il furioso* himself can make but one choice: even if he has eyes only for beauty, he must concede that the latter is at its height when augmented by wisdom and power which equal it in stature, and which are likewise infinite. And if it is true that the dimensions of a sphere are not only equal but

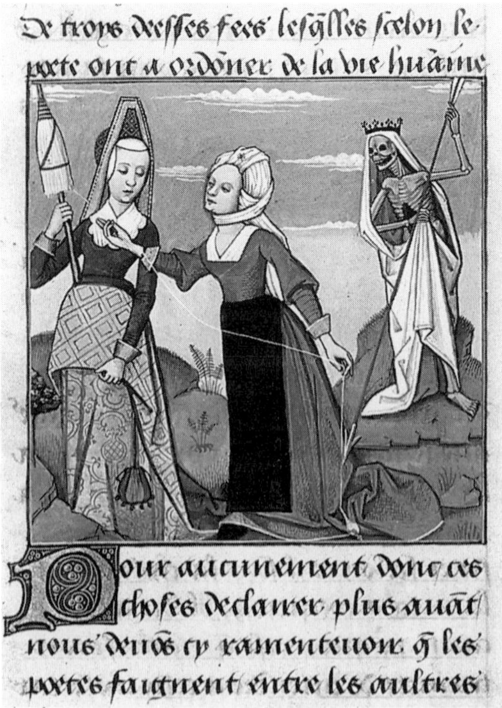

Figure 23. "The Three Fates," miniature from *Les Échecs amoureux*, c. 1500 (Paris, Bibliotheque nationale, ms. fr. 143, fol. 14 v.).

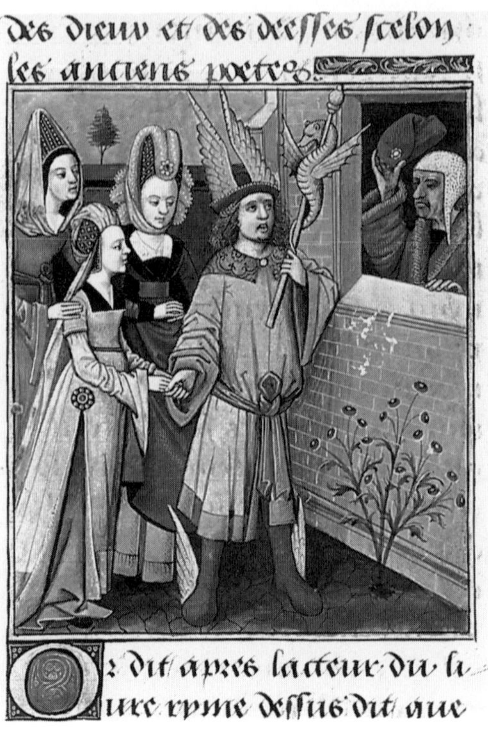

Figure 24. "Mercury presenting Pallas, Juno, and Venus to the author," *Les Échecs amoureux*, fol. 26 v.

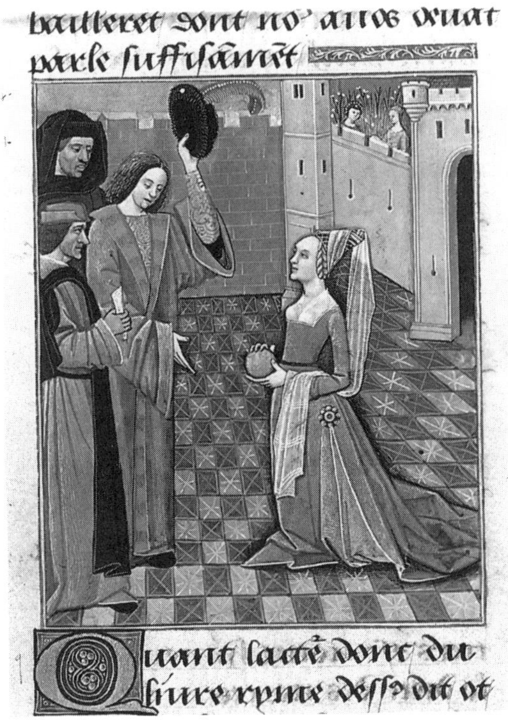

Figure 25. "Venus thanks Paris for his choice," *Les Échecs amoureux*, fol. 165.

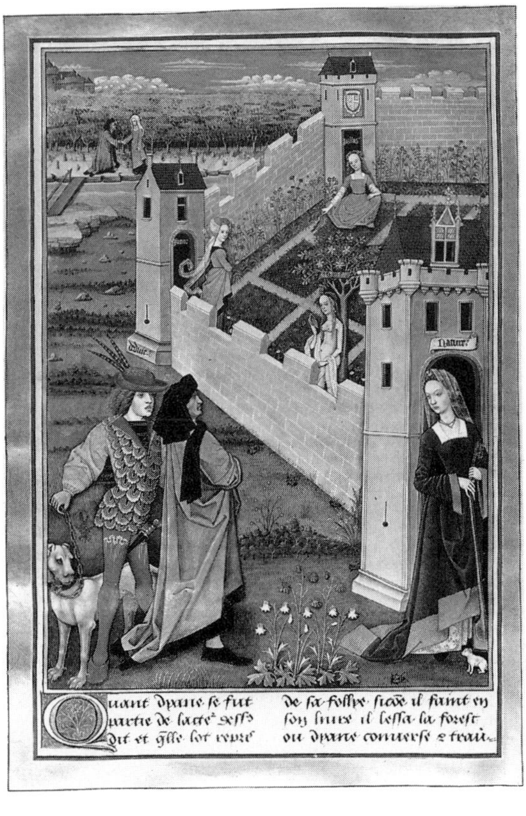

Figure 26. "The author introduced by Deduit to the desired orchard," *Les Échecs amoureux*, fol. 198 v.

identical, its length being indistinguishable from its width and its width from its depth, then the apple, itself spherical, must of necessity be awarded not to Venus, who is certainly beautiful but who in wisdom is surpassed by Minerva and in majesty by Juno, nor to Pallas, who lacks Venus's beauty and the majesty of her other rival, nor to Juno, who is the goddess of neither intelligence nor love, but rather to *she who is all in all.*[60]

. . 9 . .

"Remember Paris": The Genealogy of Europe

At the center of the *Dream of Poliphilus* is an allegory—which is also an image—corresponding to a key moment in the narrative, one sufficient to inscribe this rather aberrant Renaissance production, a novel of initiation in the form of a labyrinth in which (as André Chastel put it) every step counts within the ideological context I have just evoked: Poliphilus, led by the Queen of Free Will to a rocky outcropping pierced by three openings closed by bronze double-doors and surmounted by inscriptions in Arabic, Hebrew, Greek, and Latin—provided in full in the image but not in the text, which specifies only that the right door was inscribed *Theodoxia* and the left *Cosmodoxia*, while the third one bore the indication (*havea notato cusi*) *Erotrophos*.[1] Three doors, corresponding to the three routes among which the hero, having reached this point in his itinerary, was asked to choose, of his own free will and in full awareness of the stakes (Figure 27).

The fact that Poliphilus opted not for the doors under the signs *Gloria Dei* and *Gloria Mundi* but rather for the one marked *Mater Amoris* indicates his preference among three forms of life—the contemplative, the active, and the voluptuous—that had, by contrast, been synthesized in the *triplex*

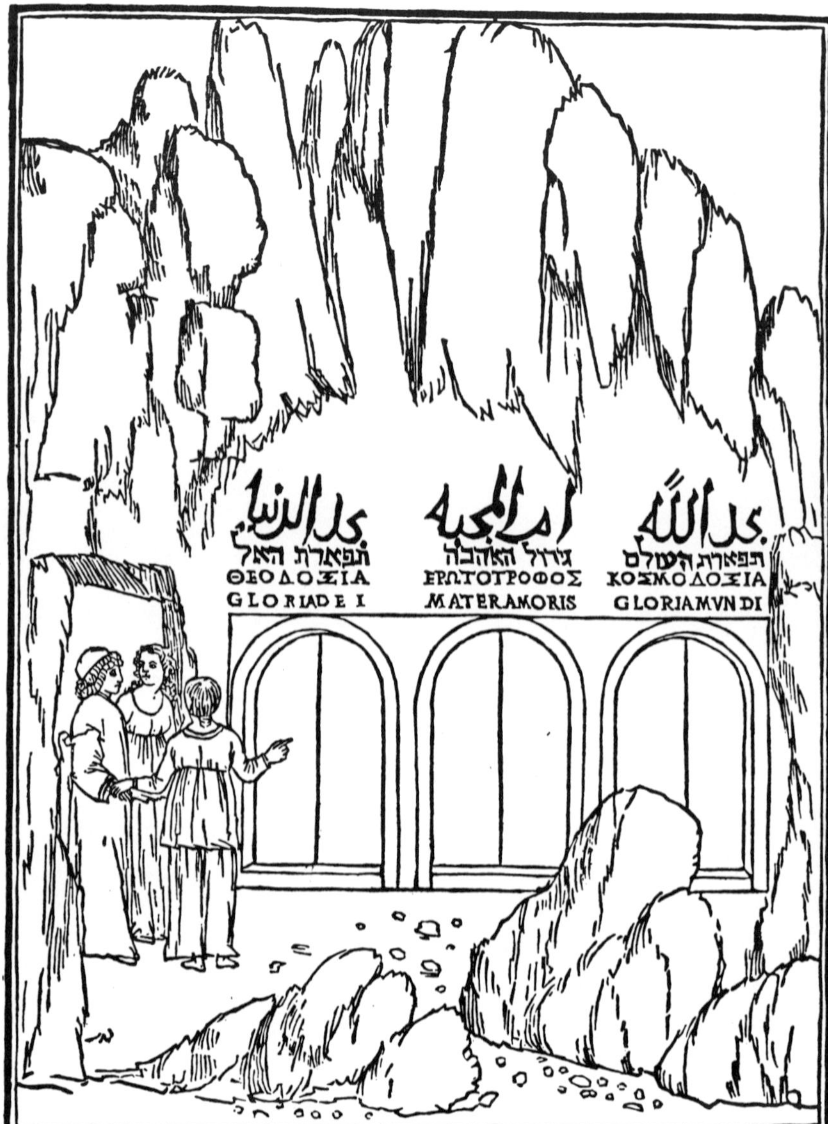

Figure 27. *Poliphilus Led by Logistics and Queen Eleuterilyda before the Three Doors*, woodcut illustration for the Aldus Manutius edition of the *Hypnerotomachia Poliphili* (Venice 1499), fol. h 8r.

vita extolled by Ficino. In this respect, the three doors in the *Hypnerotomachia* are substitutes for the three goddesses among whom the fable would have us believe the shepherd-prince was obliged to choose, though decidedly Pallas's function here has become more spiritual than martial. But the preference for the way of love (along which Poliphilus soon encounters the beloved object that is the goal of his quest), while implying a rejection of both austerity and power, was not in fundamental contradiction with Neoplatonic doctrine. In the Neoplatonic pantheon, two figures were given pride of place: Cupid, who assured communication between gods and mortals, and Venus, who personified the system of exchange by gift and answering gift that was held to regulate the circulation of divine gifts, in conformity with a tripartite rhythm (giving, receiving, bestowing in turn) allegorized by the three Graces. Ficino was fully aware of this image, which originated in the Epicurean tradition and was handed down by Seneca, and which Alberti, in his *Della pittura*, was to recommend to painters before any ancient depictions of this charming trio, either painted or sculpted, had been discovered:[2] borrowed from his commentary on Plato's *Symposium*, the trio of inscriptions—*Pulchritudo/Amor/Voluptas*—accompanying the three graces on Pico della Mirandola's medal corresponds to the circle of divine love aroused by beauty and traversing the world, eventually returning to its point of departure and attaining ecstasy.[3] As for Poliphilus himself, the route he chose to follow was not as exclusive as it might seem; Jean Martin's French translation conveys this with considerable subtlety: "Le desir et le desire, le savoir et l'avoir, le vouloir et le pouvoir s'estoyent accordes ensemble, si perfectement qu'il n'y avoit rien à redire" ("Desire and the desired, knowledge and possession, wishing and achieving were in such perfect accord the one with the other that nothing remained to be said").

The image of the three-door motif in this famous book—published by Aldus Manutius in Venice in 1499, to an ambiguous but ultimately favorable response attributable not so much

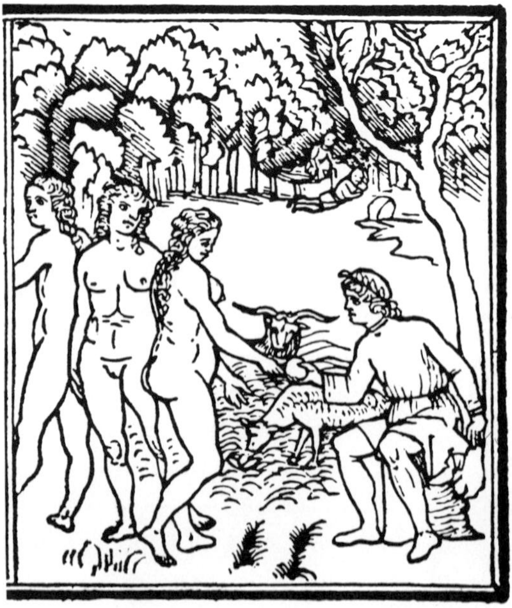

Figure 28. *The Judgment of Paris*, woodcut illustration from *Hypnerotomachia Poliphili*, fol. k 7r.

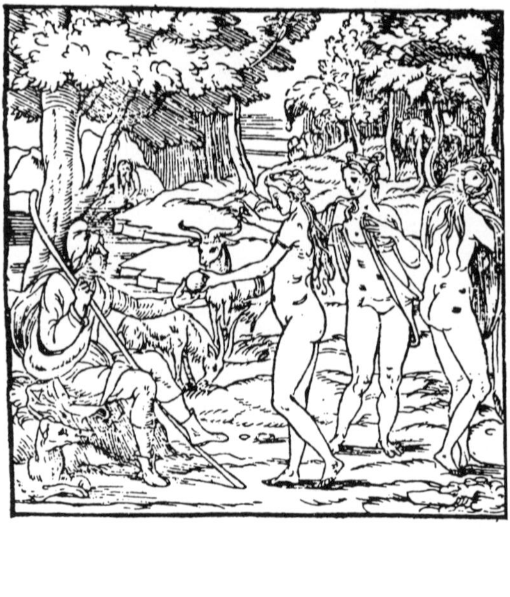

Figure 29. *The Judgment of Paris*, woodcut executed by the Jean Goujon studio for the French edition of the *Hypnerotomachia* entitled *Le Songe du Polyphile* (Paris, 1546), fol. K iij.

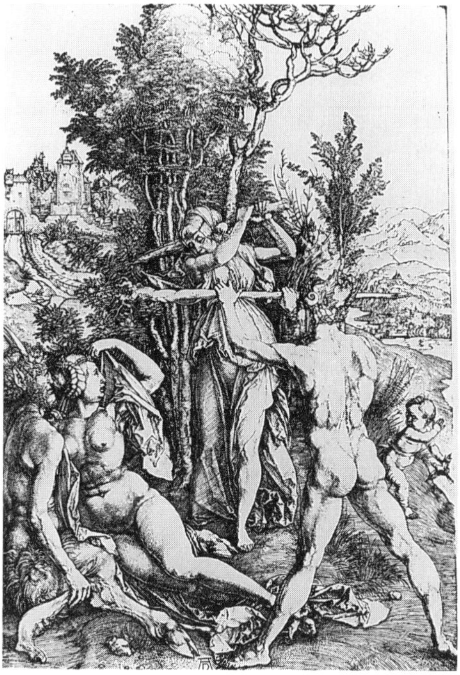

Figure 30.
Albrecht Dürer,
Hercules at the Crossroads,
engraving.

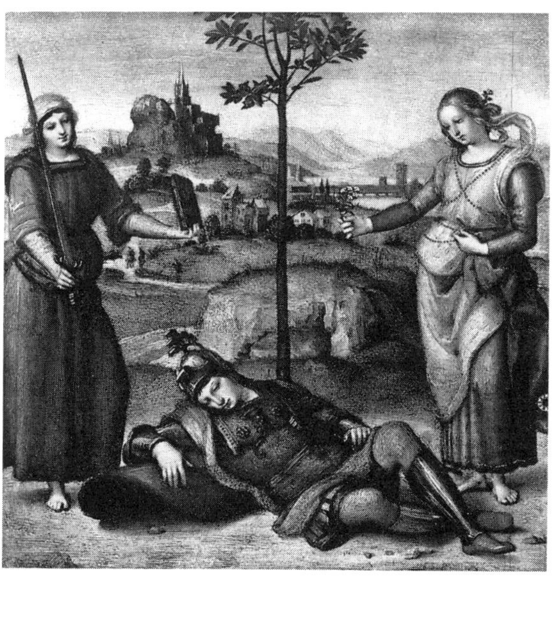

Figure 31.
Raphael, *The Dream of Scipio*,
1504–5 (London, National Gallery).

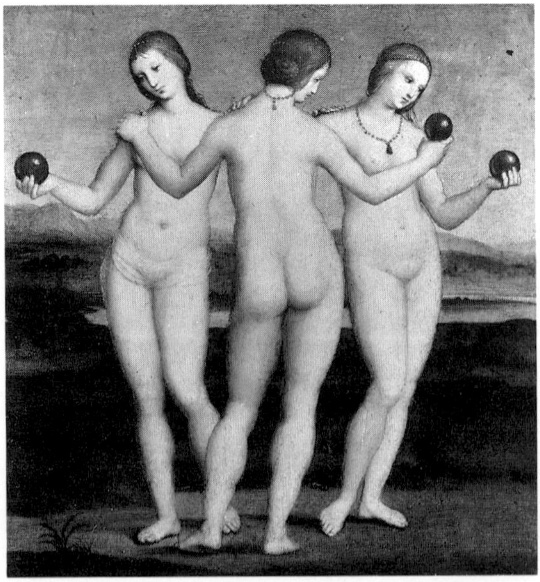

Figure 32. Raphael, *The Three Graces*, 1504–5 (Chantilly, Musée Conde).

to its text, which is mannered and rhetorical, as to the quality of its typography and its woodcut illustrations (recut by Jean Goujon or one of his followers for the French edition: compare Figures 28 and 29)—echoes not only the judgment of Paris, which is invoked a few pages farther on in association with the chariot of Leda,[4] but also, as Panofsky suggested in a famous essay, one of the favorite themes of the Renaissance, represented not only in depictions of Hercules at the crossroads (the same Hercules whose labors were sometimes associated with the story of Paris in Attic vase painting; see Figure 30)[5] but also in *The Dream of Scipio* painted by the young Raphael, a pendant to the so-called *Three Graces* now in Chantilly[6]: it represents two women approaching a young man asleep, the first offering him a sword and a book, the second a flower—three attributes which, according to Edgar Wind, refer to man's three routes to happiness: strength, mind, and pleasure (Figures 31 and 32).[7] As Ficino wrote to Lorenzo de' Medici, Paris chose pleasure, Hercules strength, Socrates mind—and all three were punished. But while Raphael's little panel echoes Macrobius's commentary on Scipio's dream, which culminates in an encomium of *tripartita philosophia* and a recommendation that the hero choose the active or contemplative life over a life of sensual indulgence, the gracious trio in the pendant, associated with it (to use Edgar Wind's formulation) like one side of a medal to its obverse, nonetheless makes an eloquent case against the overly intellectual and martial character of the *perfectio gemina* (*Sapientia-Fortitudo*).[8] And the chivalric code would do likewise.

* * *

Shortly after leaving his house astride Rossinante, Don Quixote found himself confronted with a parting of the ways that reminded him of "the crossroads where knights errant set about determining which course they would follow."[9] If, as again suggested by Wind, there is a secret relation between Raphael's *Dream of Scipio* and *Three Graces* and that other "mystery" constituted by the apparently paradoxical—and scandalous—loves of Mars and Venus,[10] it should first be considered in tandem with contemporary German images of the judgment of Paris, which undeniably have a Quixotic character *avant la lettre:* beginning with a large woodcut by Lucas Cranach dated 1508 that depicts Paris, like Scipio, dressed as a knight in armor who, having dismounted from his horse, sits at the foot of a tree not far from a waterfall, his extravagantly plumed helmet on the ground, an enormous apple at his feet, surrounded by a Mercury in theatrical costume and three graces who are completely nude (Figure 33).[11] The gesture of Mercury, who strikes Paris's chest with his baton as though trying to awaken him, is meant to signal that the hero is asleep (even though his eyes are open) and that the messenger of the gods and the three rival goddesses are appearing to him in a dream, in accordance with a device frequently used in Medieval illumination.[12]

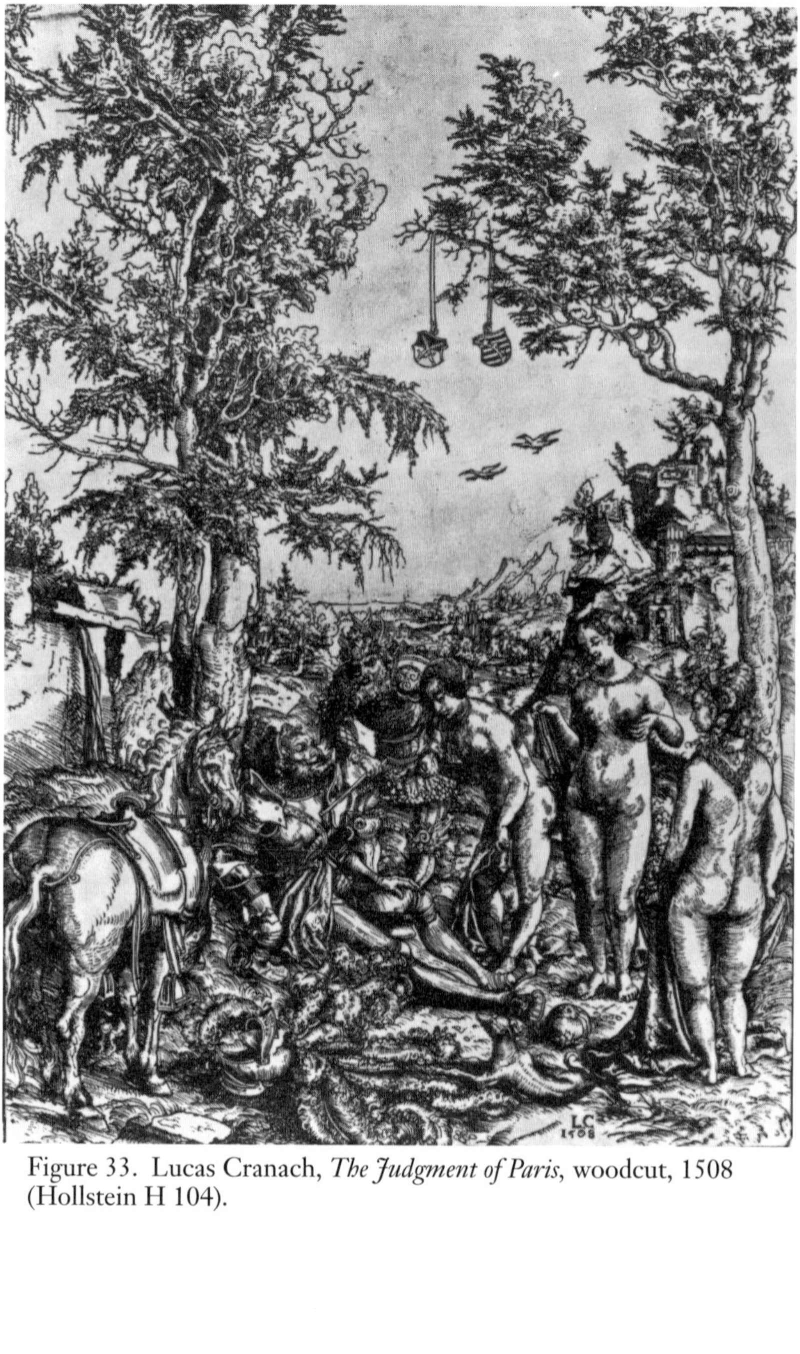

Figure 33. Lucas Cranach, *The Judgment of Paris*, woodcut, 1508 (Hollstein H 104).

A woodcut dated a few years earlier than the Cranach (it is an illustration for a translation of a poem by the Neapolitan humanist Giovanni Battista Cantalicio, the *Iudicium Paradis Troiani*, published in Wittenberg in 1504, and subsequently reprinted in the 1512 and 1513 editions of *De excidio Troiae historia* by Dares Phrygius, also published in Wittenberg, which will be discussed below; Figure 34) takes up this "dream" composition but treats it in a much cruder idiom: at the bottom of the image is the armored Paris, deep in slumber close to a fountain beside which stand the three goddesses, here nobly dressed, and Mercury, who wears a crown and carries a caduceus but makes no attempt to awaken the dreamer—who has already made his choice, for Venus holds the apple in her hand. Such is not the case in an image of Hercules choosing between Virtue and Pleasure from the *Concertatio Virtutis cum Voluptate*, another woodcut, this one by an artist from Basel, from the second edition, in Latin, of the famous *Stultifera Navis* or *Ship of Fools* by Sebastian Brant, published in Basel in 1497 (Figure 35): here again the hero lies asleep on the ground, his plumed helmet at his side, while in a dream there appear to him, at left, Voluptas, nude but wearing slippers (as in the 1936 *Nude beside a Fireplace* by Matisse, the model for which, it is said, had complained of cold feet),[13] behind whom lurks the figure of Death, and, at right, Virtus, wearing a long robe and holding a distaff (an attribute which recurs in Cranach's *Hercules and Omphale*, where it carries an almost precisely opposite meaning), a split in the road according separate access to either of them. This last image confirms the link between the two episodes in the stories, respectively, of Paris and Hercules representing moments of choice: Jakob Locher "Philomusus," the humanist who translated Sebastian Brant's book into Latin, added a preface emphasizing the combat between Vice and Virtue, and in 1502 he proposed to his students in Wittenberg a didactic playlet on the theme of the judgment of Paris, the idea for which came from Fulgentius, as he himself admitted.[14]

The theme was thus familiar to Cranach's contemporaries,

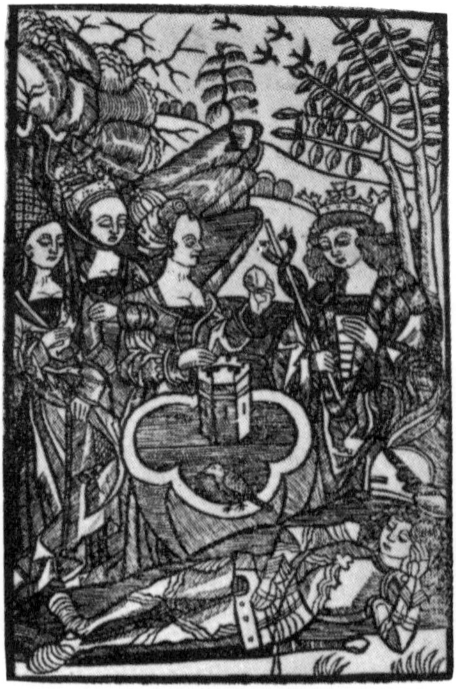

Figure 34. *Paris's Dream*, woodcut illustration from G.-B. Cantalycium, *Iudicum Paradis Troiani* (Wittenberg, 1504).

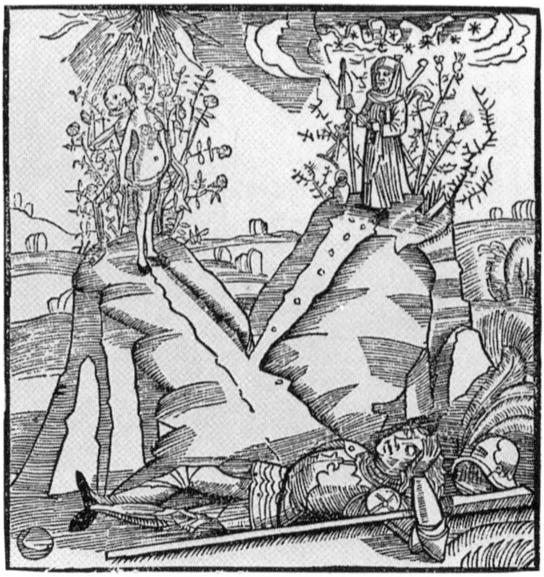

Figure 35. *Hercules at the Crossroads*, woodcut illustration from Sebastian Brant, *Stultifera navis* (Basel, 1497).

as it might well have been to those of Raphael. But in some instances different and even diametrically opposed meanings accrued to it. Often represented in the "minor" arts—pottery, tapestry, *cassone* panels, and book illustrations—the story of Paris was also dramatized in public Shrove Tuesday festivals of the late medieval period, and it was mounted as a *tableau vivant* on the occasion of the entry of Philippe le Beau into Antwerp in 1494, in the presence of Frederick the Wise of Saxony.[15] But it must also have provided raw material for contemporary exercises in edifying rhetoric, a corpus (exemplified by Jakob Locher's playlet) that often borrowed—to the point of placing Greek and Latin words in the goddesses' mouths—from Lucian's playlet on the same theme, despite the latter's complete lack of moralizing content.

The motif of the dream of Paris was to have a long life in German-speaking lands: Hans Sachs used it as late as 1561 in a *Beschluss*, or short moralizing poem, entitled "Der Traum Paridis."[16] Although this motif corresponded to a pervasive medieval *topos*, namely the dream vision, it was also consistent with the idea of an inner choice, as well as with the fundamental premise of medieval "moralizations," namely that ancient fables have an exemplary meaning for Christians when properly interpreted, something that was also believed to be true of dreams.[17] And there was at least one source to justify such an iconography: the *Historia destructionis Troiae* by the thirteenth-century Italian jurist Guido delle Colonne, published in 1287 (a German translation of which appeared in Augsburg in 1477), in which we read that Paris, having lost his way while hunting, fell into a deep sleep after tying his horse to a tree and that Mercury and the three goddesses appeared to him in his sleep.[18] This work is part of a long series also including the previously cited text ostensibly by Dares Phrygius, *De excidio Troiae historia*, an apocryphal work purporting to be a first-person account of the siege of Troy by a member of the expedition which enjoyed great success in the Middle Ages and in the German courts during the Reformation period, largely as

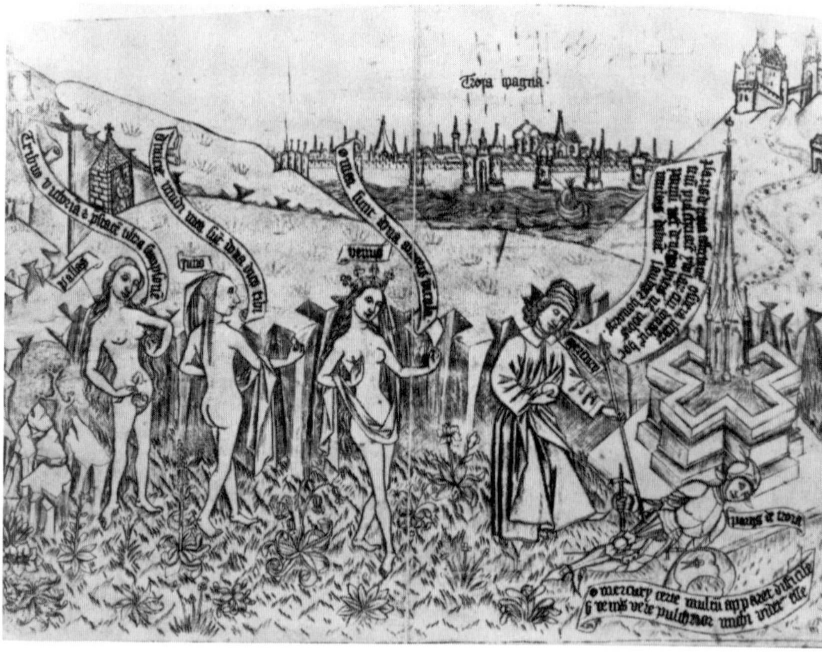

Figure 36. Master of the Banderolles, *Paris's Dream*, woodcut, c. 1470 (Munich, Bayerische Staatsbibliothek).

a result of its maintaining that the Franks and the Emperor Maximilian himself were the direct descendants of Francus, the son of Hector, just as the Romans were descended from Aeneas, the son of Venus and Anchises. Paradoxically, Paris was thus situated at the beginning of a long history that, while issuing in tragedy at Troy, was to provide a framework for the more or less phantasmatic exercises of an entire "Trojan" literature which, from the *Roman de Troie* by Benoît de Sainte-Maure, a French troubadour of the twelfth century, and the *Historia destructionis Troiae* by Guido delle Colonne, an adaptation of the previous work, to the *Illustrations des Gaules et singularitez de Troie* by Jean Lemaire de Belges, historiographer to the Burgundian court, nourished the medieval Western imaginary in much the same way as that of ancient Greece was nourished by tragedy.[19] (See Figure 36.)

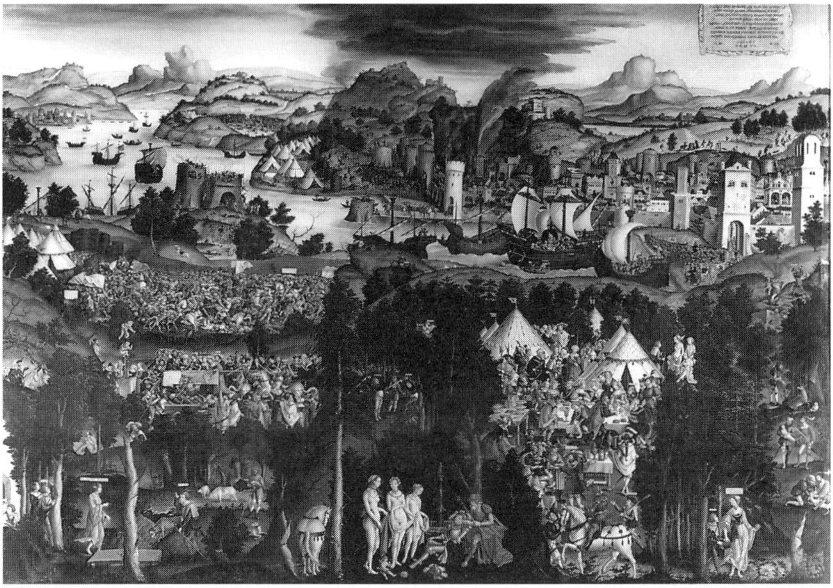

Figure 37. Mattias Gerung, *The Destruction of Troy and the Judgment of Paris*, 1540 (Paris, Louvre).

In this context, Paris could not long retain his identity as a simple shepherd, even one of royal descent: he was destined to take his place among the gallant knights-errant pressed into service as "ancestors" in genealogies—both legendary and moral—devised to legitimize princes, pagan epics cast as novels of chivalry that were understood to have a privileged relationship of some kind with the early history of the Christian West. Such is the intent behind the large, episodic painting by Mattias Gerung, *The Destruction of Troy and the Judgment of Paris* (1540, Louvre; Figure 37), in which the story of Paris is represented as a kind of rite of initiation, though one brought to an end by a false step whose disastrous consequences are detailed by the painter.[20] (See Figure 38.)

This widely disseminated theme was subjected to any number of operations and transformations by Cranach, in ways entirely consistent with his artistic enterprise. We might begin by discussing the previously mentioned print of 1508 (the year

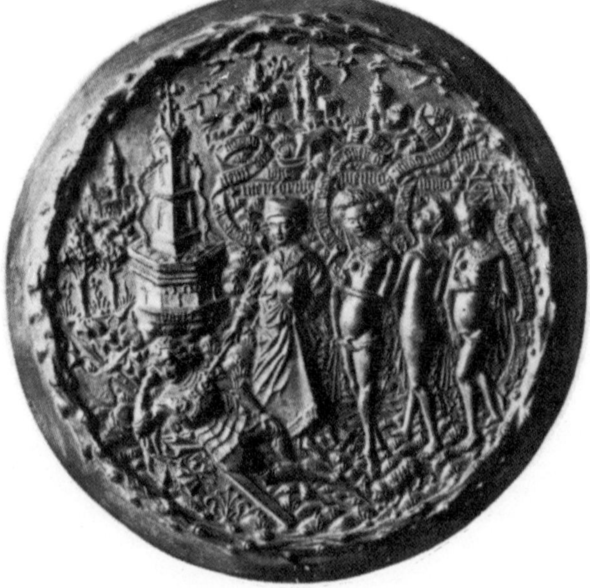

Figure 38. *The Judgment of Paris,* terra-cotta, Rhine valley, c. 1450–70.

of his trip to the Low Countries in the entourage of the Emperor Maximilian, at the moment in which Jean Lemaire was working on his *Singularitez de Troie*), which depicts the "dream of Paris" motif, but in a large format (36.3 × 25.2 cm) that sets it apart from the small images in illustrated publications issuing from Wittenberg humanist circles in the years preceding the painter's 1505 arrival at the Saxon court—not to mention its astonishing richness of detail, given that this is a woodcut, featuring precisely articulated figures, both nude and armored, complexly branching trees, and a landscape view dominated by a towering fortress. Some years before Marcantonio Raimondi engraved *The Judgment of Paris* for Raphael, also in a large format, Cranach paradoxically set out to ennoble the theme by means of a medium—the print—whose very essence was reproducibility, and then—another paradox, and one that again raises the issue of just what is meant by "repetition," "copy," and "reproduction"—turned out multiple painted images of the theme in the form of small works (usually studio productions bearing his trademark, like the engravings produced in Raphael's studio) included in series depicting Venus with mythological or biblical heroes who, from Hercules to Samson, from Paris to King David, had bones to pick with her and with the so-called weaker sex in general (see Figures 40–53).

One of the most remarkable aspects of the production associated with Cranach's name and trademark (a small dragon with extended wings) is the picture it presents, in the aggregate, of relations between the sexes and the role of women in contemporary society, to say nothing of that allotted them in the Lutheran Reformation, which was actively supported by the Cranach studio. The sex that Kant was to qualify as "noble" does not necessarily assume a positive character in this imagery rich in proto-feminist messages, and in which humor, if not derision, often prevails over all moralizing intent. Allegories of *The Age of Silver* in which men kill one another while women and children watch (Figure 39); hunting and tournament scenes in which violence and/or confusion carry the day, again as women look on; "heroes" who play the coxcomb by making vulgar displays of strength, such as Hercules suffocating Antaeus or Samson mastering a lion; sublime heroines like *Lucretia* with her dagger or the *Saint Catherine* in Budapest, beheaded by a male executioner with bulging genitals; and multiple seduction scenes which, from Adam and Eve to the dream of Paris by way of Hercules and Omphale, Lot and his daughters, David and Bathsheba, and Samson and Delilah, convey a great deal about the weakness and stupidity of the "stronger" sex as well as about the wiles of which women are capable in turning their condition to advantage: Cranach's brush can be positively ferocious when he sets out to depict ill-matched couples or the truth test to which women freely submit.[21] And when he joins forces with humanists and reformers to preach morality and issue warnings about the dangers of passion, priests are not the only ones to be heckled: the

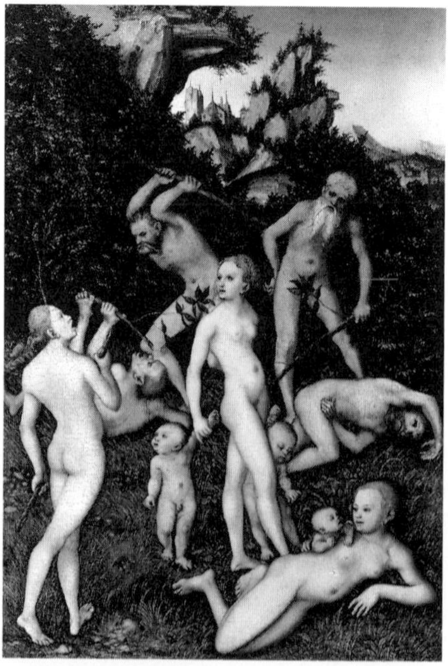

Figure 39. Lucas Cranach, *The Age of Silver*, c. 1530, Fr. 263 (London, National Gallery).

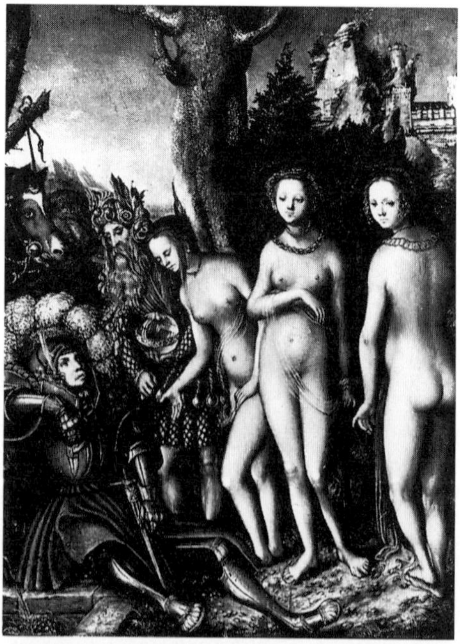

Figure 40. Lucas Cranach, *The Judgment of Paris*, c. 1512–14, Fr. 41 (Cologne, Wallraf-Richartz Museum).

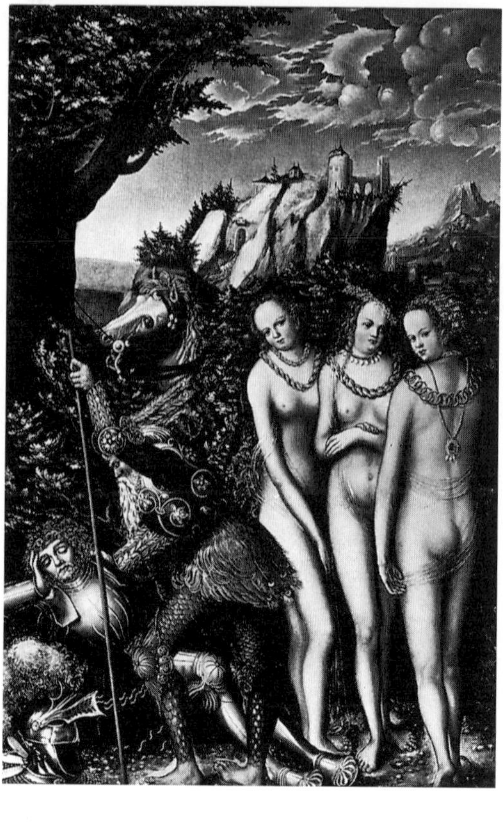

Figure 41. Lucas Cranach, *The Judgment of Paris*, c. 1516–18, Fr. 118 (Seattle Art Museum).

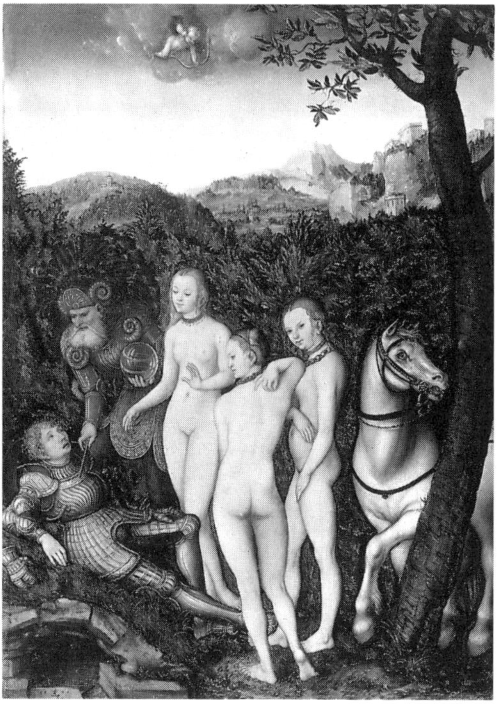

Figure 42. Lucas Cranach, *The Judgment of Paris*, 1527, Fr. 252 (Copenhagen, Statens Museum for Kunst).

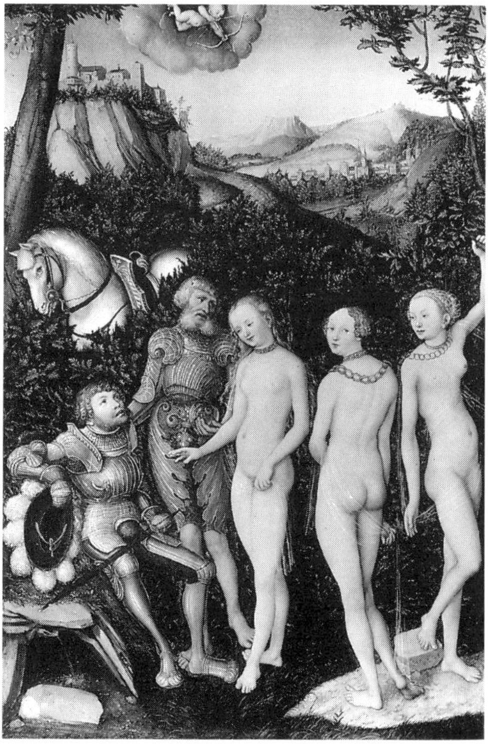

Figure 43. Lucas Cranach, *The Judgment of Paris*, 1538, Fr. 253 (Basel, Öffentliche Kunstsammlung).

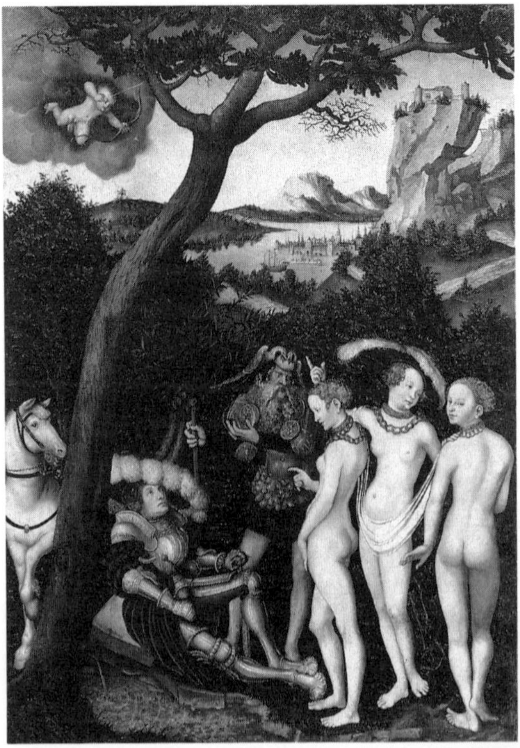

Figure 44. Lucas Cranach, *The Judgment of Paris* Fr. 254 (New York, Metropolitan Museum).

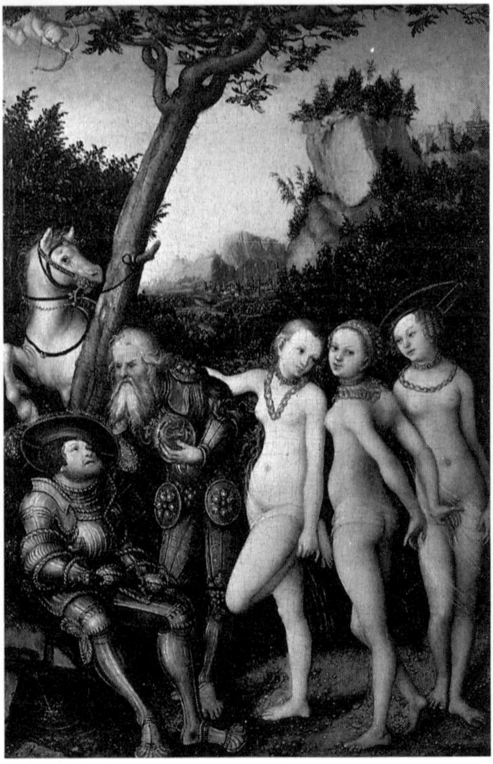

Figure 45. Lucas Cranach, *The Judgment of Paris*, 1530, Fr. 255 (Karlsruhe, Staatliche Kunsthalle).

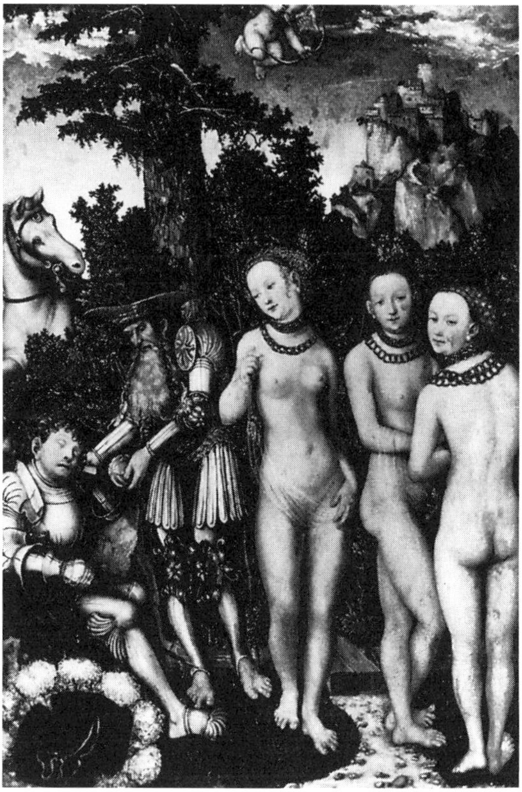

Figure 46. Lucas Cranach, *The Judgment of Paris*, c. 1530–35, Fr. 257 (Graz, Steiermarkirsches Landesmuseum).

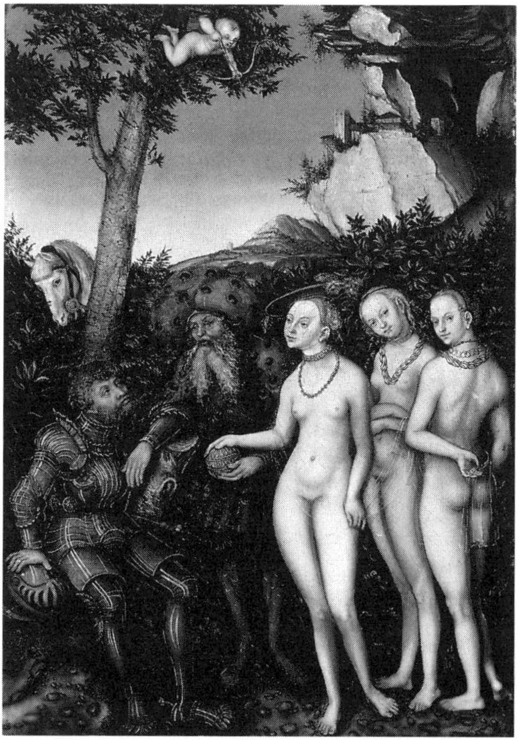

Figure 47. Lucas Cranach, *The Judgment of Paris*, 1537, Fr. 258 (Saint Louis Art Muuseum).

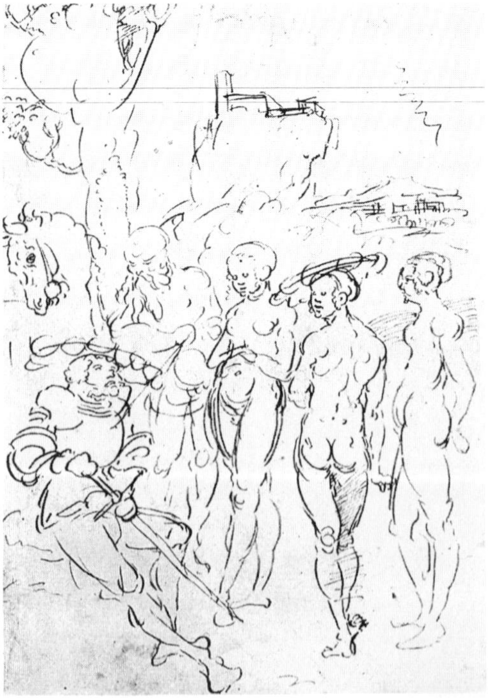

Figure 48. Lucas Cranach, *The Judgment of Paris,* drawing, c. 1530 (Braunschweig, Herzog Anton Ulrich-Museum).

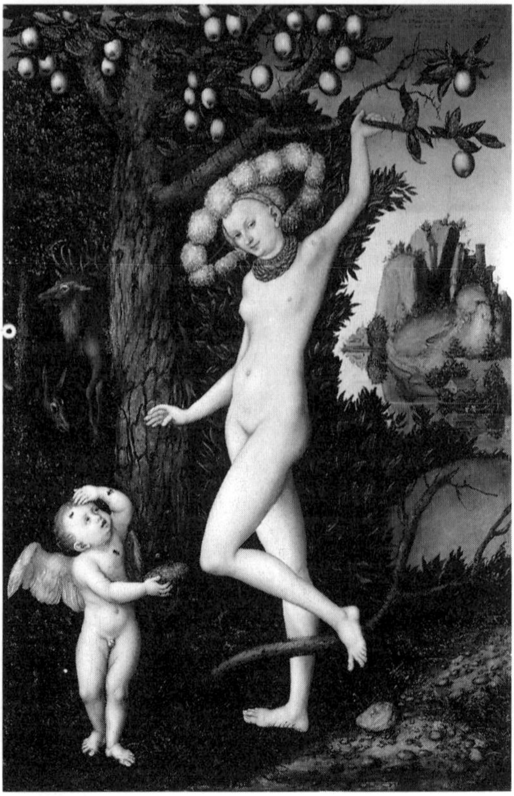

Figure 49. Lucas Cranach, *Venus with Cupid Stealing Honey*, 1531, not in Fr. (London, National Gallery).

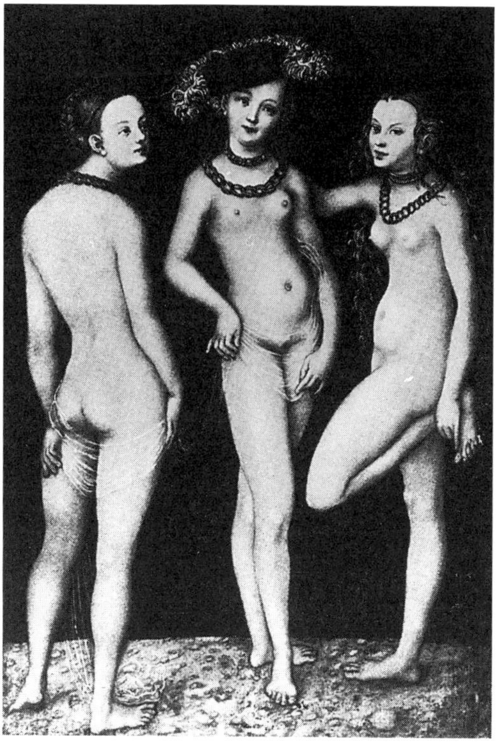

Figure 50. Lucas Cranach, *The Three Graces*, 1531, Fr. 250 (Paris, J. Seligman collection).

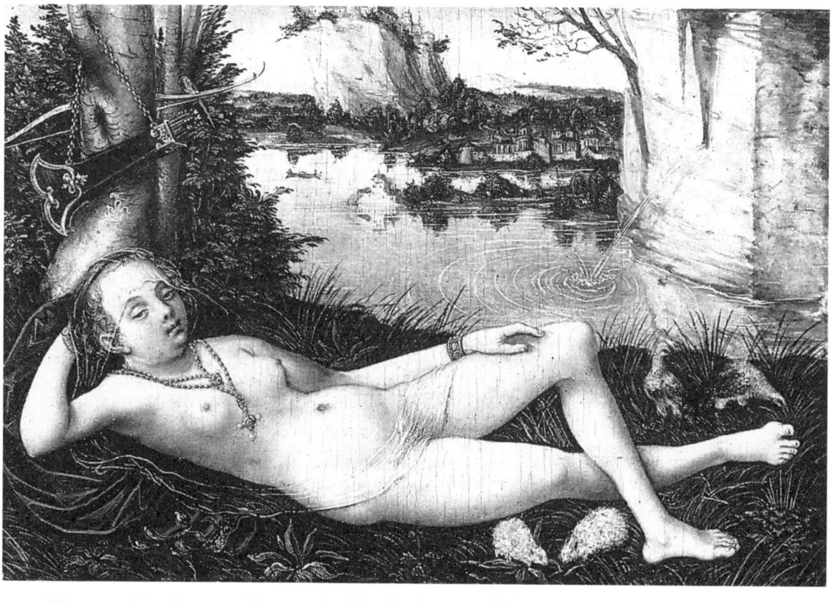

Figure 51. Lucas Cranach (?), *Reclining Water Nymph*, 1518, not in Fr. (New York, Metropolitan Museum, Lehman collection).

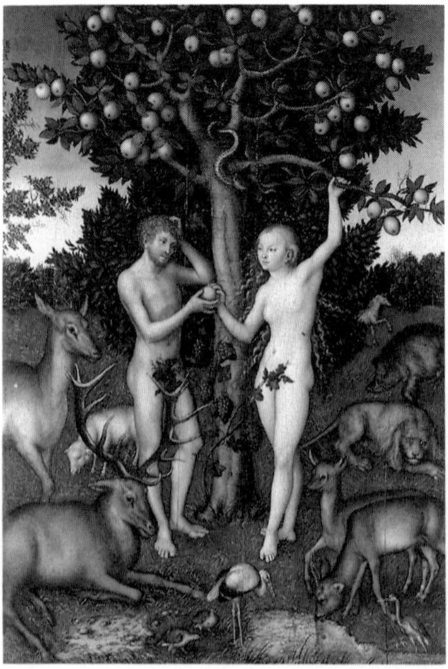

Figure 52. Lucas Cranach, *Adam and Eve*, 1526, Fr. 191 (London, Collection of the Courtauld Institute).

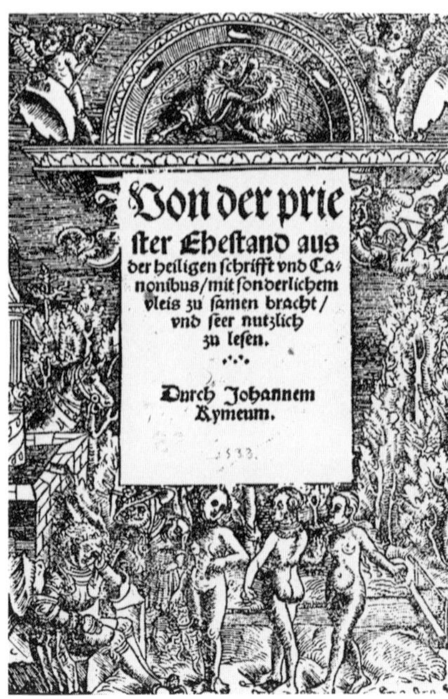

Figure 53. Cranach studio, title page, Johannes Kymaens, *Von der Priester Ehestand* (Wittenberg, 1533).

same princes who were his patrons are prominent targets in his art, in which women are regularly depicted as either virtuous or victorious and men succumbing to their charms are made the object of ridicule. One of the most interesting images produced by his studio is the frontispiece of a book about the marriage of priests, published in Wittenberg in 1533, in which the dream of Paris is given prominence (Figure 53);[22] but as early as 1513 Cranach had painted the same motif on the nuptial bed of Duke John of Saxony along with images of Hercules and Omphale, Lucretia, and Venus. The duchess, by contrast, had no need of such lessons: her apartments were decorated with scenes celebrating conjugal love, chastity, and fidelity.[23] For these images enjoined men to realize that they had less to fear from women and the *Weibermacht* or strength traditionally attributed to them than from their own fantasies: the "dream of Paris" (like that of Hercules) effectively signifying that, far from being victims of the other sex, in the end the responsibility for their choices and errors rested squarely on their own shoulders.

* * *

In the series of paintings associated with Cranach's name treating—as we might say of a poem or an essay—*The Judgment of Paris*, it would seem that in the matter of "routes" or "paths," if not of "doors," the painter set out systematically to cover his tracks. While the three women appearing to the hero in a dream are always distinguishable from one another in terms of posture, placement, and relations with their judge, they are denied any attributes that might make it possible to differentiate between them not only on moral or symbolic grounds but also on aesthetic ones, for they are all equally seductive. In the oldest version[24] it looks as though Venus has her hair untied while her companions wear hairnets. The three rivals (which in fact nothing designates as such) wear chokers and chains around their necks; and if one of them sports a hat, this is an accessory used by Cranach in several of his Venuses[25] as well as in depictions of the three graces.[26] As a general rule, Venus seems to be the nude closest to Paris, and she sometimes places her hand on the apple held by Mercury (in which cases it is she who wears a hat);[27] but in other instances the woman standing beside Mercury pays no attention to her judge and turns toward her companions, graciously clasping her upraised ankle, as she also does in one painting of *The Three Graces.* The woman who is shown from the back, sometimes wearing a hat,[28] twists to look at the viewer as though more interested in attracting his attention than in seducing her judge. As for the third figure, generally shown from the front, she sometimes places a hand on one of her companion's shoulders (a gesture unmistakably suggestive of the three Graces), or herself looks at the viewer, or lifts her hand toward the heavens, pointing out to her neighbor (again, as in depictions of the three Graces) Cupid, who seems to be pointing his arrow not at Paris but at one of the three women (indicating that she is Venus?).

That the three female figures are perfectly interchangeable, like their postures and accessories (when Venus is depicted holding the apple, she wears her hair in a net); that the trio of goddesses misleadingly evokes that of the three Graces, whose image excludes by definition any idea of rivalry or choice; that Paris himself, shown sleeping next to a spring, is likened to a reclining nymph who summons, in his turn, the inhabitants of the wood to his side[29]: all of these substitutions and exchanges indicate that what's in question here is not, or is no longer, a choice between three forms of life but rather one concerning, as much as beauty, the relations between the sexes insofar as both are implicated in the give and take of desire. In this context, which is constructed by Cranach's entire oeuvre, *The Judgment of Paris* should be linked not so much with images of the Golden Age (the same one that Don Quixote set out to revive) as with those of the original sin: with the signal *difference* that in this latter case it is Eve who gives the apple to

Adam, an action that—at least in the version in the Courtauld collection—seems to leave him a bit perplexed.[30]

If Cranach's art is less than ideally suited to hermeneutic games, that is because in his work allegory cedes pride of place to satire, or better yet to critique. Doubtless this shows him to have been a faithful student of his master Luther. But humor already occupies an important place in late examples of the "Trojan" literature, beginning with the *Illustrations des Gaules et singularitez de Troye* by Jean Lemaire de Belges, where we can already see early evidence of what was to become a pivotal moment in the history of the West, with the chivalric ideal retaining something of its prestige—even as late as *Don Quixote* this would remain the case—while new forms of social organization and economic activity were bringing about its final destruction. This same moment saw the development of the nation-state: the legend claiming to establish a common genealogy for Western princes began to accrue "European" connotations and was also in harmony with the revived project of a crusade, intended to return the descendants of the Trojan heroes to the lands of their origin (What better way to calm disagreements amongst themselves than to unite in a common cause against the Other, the "Turk"?[31]). But this was also a moment in which new interests came into being, ones with only the most distant relation to the chivalric ideal and to Neoplatonic culture, even though princes and merchants still professed allegiance to the latter: in matters of wisdom, the Minerva of Jean Lemaire de Belges, "goddess of Prudence and Fortitude," straightforwardly offers her judge knowledge of the "artifices of nature" and an understanding of "all divine and human sciences by which human life shines unimpeded."[32]

* * *

A century earlier, the *Epître d'Othéa* by Christine de Pisan had proposed a moralizing reading of the story of Paris entirely consistent with chivalric ideology (a point worth noting, given that Christine de Pisan was one of the most ardent "feminists" of her day[33]). Othéa, goddess of Prudence (perhaps I should mention here an exemplum, also dating from the fourteenth century, cited by Dumézil, in which William the Conqueror chooses as his heir the son who prefers Prudence to Valor and Beauty[34]), whose German cousin is none other than Temperance, addresses the young Hector of Troy, son of Mars, the "god of battle," and Minerva, "the powerful goddess who of arms is the mistress," and through him (the genealogical theme here coming into play once more) the successors of the noble Trojans, to teach him, and them, "those things necessary to high chivalric valor that can be acquired through proper education": all of which are virtues that Othéa says are known to her, given that she is a goddess, "through science and not through experience."[35] In the *Cent Histoires de Troye*, so named in reference to their fictional auditor (the prince of Troy), though not without an intentional invocation of the judgment of Paris, a hundred fables taken from ancient mythology and literature are recounted, each of them meant to convey a moral lesson and each lending support to the central precept that "strength derives from great virtue." The chivalric character of this educational program is consistent with the messages conveyed by the novels of knighthood that so delighted Don Quixote: while it is incumbent upon knights to emulate Hercules and his valor ("tirer vers Hercule" and "ses vaillances remirer"), they must also imitate Perseus, who, mounted on Pegasus, had delivered Andromeda and, "being a good knight-errant," had returned her to her parents. But while those aspiring to power ought to be capable of playing the executioner ("Autrement de porter heaulme / n'est digne de tenir royaume"), they must also possess good judgment and comport themselves differently from Paris, who passed over both Pallas, "goddess of chivalry and knowledge" ("The arms of knights and the science of scholars are owed to me. I can make you the most chivalrous and give you knowledge surpassing that of all others"), and Juno, "goddess of possessions and lordly status" ("All the world's treasures belong to me. If you give me the apple, you will be rich and powerful"), opting instead for her who "by soft amorous words . . . offers instruction in love and feminine attractions and who makes madmen wise and wise men rave, who reduces the rich to beggary and enriches the most base," namely Venus, who had promised him only Helen. But then he was neither chivalrous nor wise: "En amour furent toutes ses pensées" ("All his thoughts dwelt on love").

Such is the central argument of the *Epître d'Othéa* and the moral of the story of Paris, that "histoire de Troye" *par excellence*, which can be broken out into five points:

1. The good knight should remember Paris ("De Paris ayes record") and not follow his example:

> De Vénus ne fays ta déese
> Ne te chaille pas de sa promesse
> La poursuivit en est travailleux
> Non honorable et pouilleux.
> [. . .]
> Comme Paris ne juge pas
> car on reçoit maint dur repas
> Par male sentence octryer
> Maintz en ont eu mauvais loyer.
>
> [Do not make Venus your goddess
> Succumb not to her promise
> Pursuing her is hard work
> Dishonorable and mean.
> [. . .]
> Do not judge as Paris did
> For handing down a bad decision
> Can lead to much hardship
> Many are those who have reaped its sorry reward.]

2. He must beware of Cupid, the "grand enragé," as well as of women:

S'il advient que d'amours affolles
Gardes au moins a qui tu parolles
Que ton fait ne soit emmesles
Souveigne toy de femelle.

[If cupids should bewitch you
At least take care with whom you speak
So that your deeds do not become entangled
Remember the ways of women.]

3. Though his noble status entails his following in the footsteps of his father as in the poem, he must make every effort to avoid the trap into which Mars fell:

Se amour raccourcist la nuyt
Gardé que Phebus ne te nuyt
Pourquoi tu puisses estre prins
Es liens vulcan et surprins.

[If love should shorten the night
Take care that Phoebus is not your undoing
You might be a prince
But you can still be surprised like Vulcan.]

4. Thus it is not Venus whom the knight will choose as his goddess, but Minerva: she whom the poem says is his mother, without any mischievous intent (Had Paris followed the advice of Prudence, Troy would not have fallen and Hector would not have perished in combat):

Adjouste Pallas la deese
Et met avec ta prouesse
Tout bien te viendra se tulas
Bien siet o minerve Pallas.

[Make Pallas your goddess
And prowess will be yours
All that is good will come to you
If you opt for Pallas Minerva.]

5. But he must also beware of Discord, who is at the origin of the entire episode. And Othéa here cites Pythagoras: "Avoid the route crossed by hatred." Which brings us back to the more specifically political agenda of Lemaire de Belges.

* * *

The Trojan legends, epics, novels, and *histoires* accrued a double pedagogic function in the medieval imaginary, even a doubly civilizing one. Writing for the young Archduke Charles of Austria—the future Charles V—Jean Lemaire de Belges adhered to the didactic rule of *narrandum ad probandum;* and his book, however fantastic, is inscribed within a long literary line that, beginning with the "Trojan novels" of Dares Phrygius and Dictys Cretensis, provided "European" culture (a denomination borrowed from Ernst Robert Curtius) with material it would never cease exploiting, whether for diversion or edification, until the late example provided by Fénelon's *Télémaque,* also written to educate a prince. But this tradition presents us with manifold difficulties and contradictions, beginning with those linked to the story of Paris and the judgment associated with his name.

To Christine de Pisan, things appeared quite simple: anyone with pretensions to knightly status must reject the choice made by Paris and select Minerva, the goddess of wisdom and fortitude, over Venus, the goddess of love. Such is the situation depicted by Raphael in *The Dream of Scipio:* if two figures stand in for three here, that is because Minerva, facing Venus (Juno, the austere guardian of conjugal order, seems to interest no one), presents herself as the incarnation of the *gemina perfectio* corresponding to the ancient heroic ideal. And "ideal" is the appropriate word here, if it is true that the two elements in the binary topos *sapientia/fortitudo* were understood by the Greeks to be opposites whose conflicting claims conferred upon the Homeric epic its tragic character. Achilles is not an ideal figure for Homer: he has physical strength, but the true hero also possesses wisdom, personified by Nestor. The two qualities rarely occur together, for impetuosity is the privilege of youth and experience that of maturity, if not old age; in this respect, only Odysseus seems to have attained an equilibrium between heroism, martial valor, and wisdom.[36]

Curtius understood how this opposition paralleled that in Indo-European ideology between the two aspects of kingly identity, namely those of magic and ferocity on the one hand and of wisdom and justice on the other.[37] The Middle Ages inherited this polarity through the "Trojan" novels (which, as Curtius observes, are now known to have been reworkings of Greek novels and should be understood as such) attributed to Dictys Cretensis (the *Ephemeris belli Troiani*, which dates from the fourth century) and Dares Phrygius (the *De excidio Troiae historia*, written in the sixth century). But this—following the example of Fulgentius, who drew from the first two words of the *Aenead*, *arma* and *virum*, the lesson that "all perfection consists in bodily strength and wisdom"—is to introduce a new topos, that of *sapientia et fortitudo*, in which these two qualities are not opposed to but rather conjoined with one another. Again according to Curtius, the evolutionary development leading from Homer to Dares Phrygius and Fulgentius reaches its conclusion in what Isidore of Seville (d. 633) has to say about the epic: "It is called heroic song because it tells the deeds of brave men. For hero is the name given to men who by their wisdom and courage are worthy of heaven."[38]

Thus everything necessary for Minerva to assume the double character assigned to her by Christine de Pisan was in place. "Fortitude" raises no problems, as it clearly designates strength of arms. But what is meant by "wisdom"? In the person of Aeneas, Virgil introduced a new idea based on moral virtue, namely *pietas* or *justicia*. Subsequently, in the Rome of the Caesars, culture, poetry, and eloquence would play an important role in imperial panegyric.[39] And in later developments extending from the late Middle Ages to our own day, commonplaces and prejudices of every conceivable variety would compete with serious criticism and satire in a struggle to attribute various qualities and talents to different generations and social classes, as well as to the two sexes. But as for eloquence, on which Molière's *femmes savantes* would still pride themselves, Homer had long since made it a part of the hero's arsenal: Achilles' preceptor Phoinix had set out to make his charge, as yet ignorant of "the joining of battle" and of "debate where men are made pre-eminent," "a speaker of words and one who accomplished in action."[40] To his already overburdened portrait of Paris, Lemaire de Belges added a supplementary trait, writing that, after having shown just what sort of a judge he was, he became a subtle orator. Is the fact that he won Helen's heart through verbal artifice sufficient to make this unfortunate warrior a hero of sorts—of a new sort?

* * *

"Remember Paris": the fortune of the legend of Paris in European literature demonstrates the dependence of Western culture on that of the ancient Mediterranean, and of the role played by the Middle Ages, Latin and then French, in transmitting a heritage constantly laid claim to even as it was being transformed. Everything in the *histoire* or "novel" of Troy comes to us secondhand, from its basic narrative material to the interpretative glosses on it dating from the Hellenistic period. But as to reasons underlying this fortune, they remain a completely open question, at least as regards the period after completion of the transition from epic poetry to novelistic prose. As Georges Dumézil noted, that this legend is the only one in the Greek tradition attesting the perenniality of the trifunctional ideology, far from suggesting an explanation, is itself enigmatic. We have seen that the continuity between Greek culture and its Indo-European background left marks, even if only implicit ones, on the Homeric poems, founding texts *par excellence*. But why did it do so precisely at that moment in which Western history is generally held to have commenced, if we agree with Curtius that Europe is a mere name or geographical term, if not a historical construct?[41]

A history of Greece as well as, through Virgil, of Rome, and (if we credit the "Trojan" genealogies) that of the entire Occident. A history within which Paris—to deliberately stretch a point—occupies a position comparable to that assigned in the Bible to Adam in the context of the history of humanity. For here, too, a kind of original sin—replete with the apple motif, and perhaps with a tree—serves as the narrative point of departure and determines the outcome: save that while the Bible speaks rather coyly of a "tree of knowledge," the Venus of Lemaire de Belges is more frankly suggestive when exhorting Paris not to neglect the principal in favor of the accessory: "Look upon my specious exterior. Rig the gracious ship of your free will in accordance with the indications provided by my propitious map," and, eschewing "vainglory and difficult intellection," "turn then to the left, follow the broad way taken by most human beings," and even by the gods themselves.[42]

A kind of original sin, then, or at least—seeing as such a notion would have been totally meaningless to Greeks of the pre-Christian era—an original mistake or error, a primitive sentence, a "first judgment" like a historical exordium (*rerum exordio*, to cite Apuleius once more), opening like a fault line or dark hole in which the narrative of origin becomes engulfed—along with all of the questions we might be prompted to ask concerning the role played in this instance by what Venus calls Paris's free will, to say nothing of Helen's beauty, which according to the Trojan elders was so extraordinary as to exonerate him. Two themes blend or intertwine here that might seem incompatible, even contradictory: that of the offer of "lust" or "luxury" made by Venus to her judge in hopes of swaying his decision, and that of the gift of the very liberty making him a judge in the full sense of the word, as opposed to a slave to his senses or a mere customary interpreter. A liberty that, if complete; a "free will" that, if truly free, must not simply be conceded him but must be a gift that is itself freely bestowed.

And it is in this sense that Lemaire de Belges invites his primary reader, the young archduke and future emperor, to take the adolescent Paris as an example: "When the said young prince begins to lose his childishness but is still in a pastoral state: which is to say, still possesses a sweet simplicity without boorishness or malice, then I [it is Mercury who speaks] will present him with the golden apple, which is to say with his own free will: and I will make him judge of the beauty of the three goddesses: namely Prudence, Pleasure, and Power."[43] Mercury, who in an allegorical interpretation made by Lemaire de Belges—said by him to derive from a discussion (perhaps known to him from the *Homilies of Clement*) that purportedly took place, in the presence of Saint Peter, between the future Pope Clement and a pagan philosopher named Nicetas—is assimilated to "the speech by means of which all doctrine is addressed to our understanding," which implies that his intervention consisted not in his appealing to the hero's free will, as does Venus, but rather in his conferring it upon him, a gesture that also gives him the power to change history. (And we might well wonder, along with Euripides' Helen, what Europe's future would have been if, Paris having preferred Hera or Athena to Aphrodite, the Trojans had proved victorious over the Greeks. The "history" or "story"—and no longer the myth—supposes that he might well have chosen differently: which would not preclude the possibility—this would perhaps be the height of freedom—that after having broken with the premises that might be those of his choice, the judge might well have reappropriated a part of the program of which he was the messenger.) Or, in the words of Lemaire de Belges: "Jupiter did not want to judge the matter himself, preferring to let destiny take its course, for God did not wish to deny man his free will. And also if God had condemned two of the said ways of life, he would have left only one in the world."[44]

Addressing his young imperial reader, Lemaire de Belges would have had good reason to see himself as a new Mercury: If free will there be, is it not that of subjects still too young to be implicated in their own choices? "And so the said judgment was delegated to a young shepherd of royal blood, as to one who as yet had no set way of life and so was capable of taking up any one of the three in question." History does not tell us what choice was made by the archduke and future emperor, assuming the quandary had any meaning for him.[45] But Paris? The stress placed by Lemaire de Belges on the astral signs presiding over Paris's birth leads us back to our problem: Is it legitimate to maintain that the judge was allowed to make his choice freely, given that—so we are told—the planet Venus figured prominently in his horoscope: the same Venus exercising influence "over the lower back and sexual parts" and favoring "things amorous and venereal" ("All his thoughts dwelt on love": in other words, he thought only of sex)? The signs of the zodiac reappear in Marcantonio's *Judgment of Paris* engraving after Raphael, a fact that did not escape Aby Warburg's attention. But the question surrounding Paris's choice takes on an entirely new dimension if we accept that the migration—or "displacement"—at the origin of European civilization was one of its most important long-term consequences.[46] If discontent lies at the root of civilization, at the root of history itself, then the legend of Paris figures it in an exemplary way: Why must culture, in the terms of fable, impugn as a fault—if not, I repeat, as a kind of pagan original sin—that very free choice, designated "aesthetic," from which it ostensibly arose?

Or, to frame the question differently (though still in Freudian terms): By means of what repression (under cover of what negation) has it been possible for civilization to assign itself as legendary or mythical origin—and at the very moment this fused with a certain conception of history—a "judgment" that has all the appearance of a fault, insofar as it seems explicitly to contradict the basic premise of *Kultur*, namely repression of the sexual drives? It's as though in this civilization, and in what is termed in its Western, European manifestation its "history," there has been something amiss, something odd, from the very start or origin, which in retrospect seems like a kind of slippage. As though, for there to have been any "history" at all in this sense, some such swerve or discontinuity or rupture had been necessary—namely, the excess which the Greeks called *hubris*, and which confers upon judgment its critical power, its "crisis" virulence.[47]

. . 10 . .

The Supplement: Painting, Body and Soul

Ernst Robert Curtius saw the repeated assertions in the "Trojan novels" that all of the reported actions were authentic and, in many cases, that they had been recounted by *eyewitnesses*, as one of the most characteristic features of these texts, even of novels in general. These apocryphal accounts owed much of their success to the ostensible status of their "authors" as direct witnesses of the Trojan war: Dictys Cretensis claims that he fought in the Achaean forces beside his compatriot Idomeneus, and Dares Phrygius with the Trojan army. Macrobius, in his *Satires* (IV, 6, 13), mentions the "eyewitness" or "thing seen" strategy—which he characterizes as *adtestatio rei visae*—as a means of arousing emotion. But this *topos*, which would assume considerable importance in the modern era, already appears in Virgil's *Aeneid*, in Aeneas's account of the destruction of Troy (*quaeque . . . ipse vidi*).

Doubtless there are phrases more appropriate than "*emotionally* arousing" to characterize the episode in which the shepherd Paris, dungy through and through (or blue-blooded through and through), managed, by Mercury's intervention, to have the three rival goddesses undress so that he might proceed, as Lucian would have him say, to "the most precise examination" (*to akribes tēs exetaseōs*), not having been satisfied with seeing them as they first presented themselves to him, with all of their accessories, attributes, and ornaments. The themes of "seeing" and of the "thing seen" were at work in the fable from the beginning, if only in the guise of the problem raised for the archaic Greek consciousness by a mortal's having been permitted to contemplate, with or without veils, the divine body. Lucian's Paris cuts right to the chase: *Gumnas idein boulomai*, "I want to see them naked." And Athena raises the stakes immediately, demanding that Aphrodite take off her belt, thereby prompting Aphrodite to require that Athena remove her helmet.[1] The comic tone of this passage contrasts sharply with Ovid's treatment, which introduced a trait that, as already noted, was not characteristic of Greek culture, which conceived of clothing as an integral part of beauty: Paris, in his letter to Helen, breathes not a word to her about this episode; and it is jealousy that incites Oenone, his abandoned lover, to remind him of the fatal day on which not only Venus and Juno but even Minerva (who, it is said, is more comely in armor, *sumptisquae decentior armis*) presented themselves to their judge unclothed (*venit in arbitrium nuda Minerva tuum*).[2]

Don Quixote, requested by the merchants of Toledo to be allowed to see the lady in question, or at least her portrait, before agreeing to publicly declare her beauty unequalled in the world, quips that in such circumstances the gesture would be worthless: the important thing being, on the contrary, that they believe it, affirm it, and swear to it on their arms *without seeing her*.[3] In his view, the beauty of the mistress of his thoughts would not admit of comparison. And this was because she corresponded, if not to an idea, in a quasi-Platonic sense of that word, then at least to a definition, or better yet to a postulate taken from the chivalric code that seemed to endorse strictly *a priori* judgments of taste, ones that might be qualified as apodictic, if the convictions in question weren't rooted in the singular madness of this hero of anachronism, born in an age of iron to give new life to the age of gold: an assertion of beauty accruing greater value in his eyes insofar as it was based not on material evidence but on considerations pertaining to right or code and, as such, obligatory. Those taken by Don Quixote to be knights-errant might be ready enough to judge on the basis of such tangible evidence, but what he expected of them was less a judgment of taste than a profession of faith. The consequence being that, if knights-errant there were, discussions of the relative merits of their mistresses ran as many risks of taking a bad turn as did debates around the nature of a god whose elected, whose sole legitimate interpreter, each speaker pretended to be.

It would have been out of place for Mercury to adopt the same tone in his response to Paris when the latter insisted on seeing the goddesses in the nude, for the judgment he sought from the shepherd-prince was, in principle, a matter not of deduction but of comparison (for Kant, it would be in the nature of the judgment of taste to draw distinctions, to "mark differences," *zu unterscheiden*). The key factor here being, I insist, that the arbiter should proceed *de visu*. Thus the story of Paris (like *Don Quixote* later, though in roughly inverted terms) explicitly raises the question of the privileged, and perhaps founding, relation sustained by beauty (and with it the judgment of taste) with visibility, if not with *sight* as such. By that same beauty, and even that same Platonic idea of the Beautiful as inflected by the Renaissance, which according to Panofsky entailed its descending from the supracelestial residence assigned it by Plato to settle in the human mind, specifically that of the artist, where it proceeds to function as the model for works in the process of realization. Which amounts to substituting for a metaphysical interrogation, one bearing on the paths along which Love rises, by degrees, above the desire inspired in it for beautiful bodies (to the point of contemplating what Diotima in the *Symposium* calls "the open sea of beauty" [*to polu pelagos tetrammenos tou kalou*[4]]), a questioning of the strictly anthropological character of the functioning of the *model* henceforth assigned to the Idea in the artistic and representational order described by Plato as "mimetic"[5]: If beauty is joined to the field of the visible by a link we might qualify as originary, a slippage of history as much as of thought will have effectively extended this relation to the domain of the so-called visual arts, which imitate not so much the world of appearances as the "idea," the "model," in the artist's mind during the making of a work.

Melanchthon (whom Panofsky cites) explicitly compares the Platonic Idea to the most beautiful image of the human body that Appelles could carry in his mind.[6] Now the fable of the judgment of Paris is like the metaphor of the Idea's descent into the field of the visual, in the guise of divine bodies come down from Olympus to submit themselves to the arbitration of a mortal pretending to judge them *de visu.* Save that Paris's choice of Venus is not only an indication of his libidinal or "venereal" constitution: it is also consistent with what must have been Plato's own idea of beauty and of its ties to the reign of desire: a desire, as Socrates was to say, and as Freud was to repeat, that is initiated through vision and whose displacement—of the "Idea," of bodies, but also of the object, of the drive's aim—was its motor from the start. But what of a painter setting out to paint a *Judgment of Paris*? How, other than through symbolism or allegory, can he represent the difference between the three types of beauty among which he must choose? How can he translate the moment described by Lemaire de Belges in which Paris, having been able to take in at leisure not only the splendor of her golden tresses, the *ardu* or abruptness of her black eyebrows, and the penetration of her green eyes (desire being an affair of the *gaze*), but also what might be termed her "attractions," which is to say "the soft fall of her breasts and the wide interval between them" ("la gente tressure de ses mamelles et le grand intervalle entre elles"), the sheen of her marbled abdomen, the shape of her thighs, the moment during which this body incarnating beauty as such would not admit of comparison? Further: how could he manage, this painter, to implicate the spectator in the affair without also stripping Paris of his status as judge, if not his status as subject? Would the procedure adopted by Cranach have sufficed, namely painting the story as if it were a dream (in itself a perfectly conventional strategy) in which the sleeper could give his desire free reign and multiply its—seemingly interchangeable—figures without feeling pressed to choose just one? At least this approach provides me with an occasion to open a parenthesis whose programmatic character might itself seem evidence of a *displacement:* and where are we headed, after all, if the method ostensibly presiding over our investigation, and the very purpose behind it, can be formulated only as we advance along our way—developing, becoming more precise and more richly inflected, modifying itself, and perhaps transforming itself as it changes direction (which in itself would constitute a rule of method)?

* * *

That the Renaissance, if not the Middle Ages, was able to conceive of (and represent) the choice incumbent upon Paris, like that facing Scipio and Hercules (not to mention the three doors before which Poliphilus was led by the Queen of Free Will) more or less explicitly as a *dream*—a detour allowing the introduction of the unconscious—would suffice to justify the project of an "iconology" that might be called, in the interest of brevity, "analytic": in other words, a theory, a science, a "discourse of images" that not only does not restrict itself to the conscious, perfectly masterable content conveyable by these same images or that might be deliberately associated with them, but that would be concerned primarily with the question of beauty. An iconology, a theory, a science, a "discourse of images" that, taking as its point of departure the originary connivance ostensibly maintained by beauty with the reign defined as that of the visible, if not as that of vision and representation, as well as with the reign of desire, and rejecting any notion of "applied psychoanalysis" while embracing the hypothesis of the unconscious—including its "structuralist" version, which accords pride of place to the various constraints to which the mind is subjected in the fields of myth and art—would aim (this iconology) at being focused (in its quality, precisely, as an *analytic*) on the question of representability, of *Darstellbarkeit*, to use Freud's concept: which is to say on the conditions governing, by definition, all thought pretending to manifest itself in art or dreams but that cannot succeed in doing so save by resorting to some sort of visibility. Or, to put it differently, in terms more appropriate and more adequate to the present argument: the conditions governing interpretation itself, if something like "art-work"—in a sense analogous to Freud's "dream-work"—should prove susceptible to analysis: "work" not having precisely the same meaning in the two cases, designating in dreams the process of selecting thoughts for translation into images, by and large visual ones, as well as the actual transformations effected to this end, without the involvement of aesthetic considerations per se; while in the case of art no thought can be put to work that has not been interrogated, if only momentarily, in accordance with considerations of beauty and representation. And that, in terms or forms—witness the *Déjeuner sur l'herbe*—capable of eliciting the strongest resistance, those precisely to which analysis should attend most closely, the better to master them.

Ernst Robert Curtius wrote that, "all else aside, literature is the medium of ideas, art not,"[7] an assertion for which he was much criticized by art historians, beginning with those committed to iconology as defined by Panofsky, which does not acknowledge the unconscious, at least not explicitly. Such a statement is indeed astonishing in a book dedicated to the memory of Aby Warburg, and one implementing a project dear to the creator of the library and institute that now bear his name, namely the elucidation of systems whereby traditions are transmitted, in this instance one authorizing us to consider European literature, from Homer to Goethe, as a whole, as a "spiritual unity," as Warburg's method called for the placement of the major productions of modern Western culture—as in James Joyce's *Ulysses*—against the background of ancient culture ("One is a European when one has become a *civis Romanus*"[8]).

It is understandable that a philologue of Curtius's stamp should have been irritated by the invasion of literary history by stylistic categories and periodizations ("Gothic," "Baroque," etc.) borrowed from the history of art, for it was his view that literary creation obeyed laws different from those governing creation in the visual arts. And it must be conceded that books have a status, a mode of existence, that sets them very much apart from works of painting and sculpture. The fact that one can have direct access to them at any time and place, without need of reproductions, confers on literature an unequalled liberty: for it, "all the past is present, or can become so," which means that, given its "timeless present," past literature can interfere with that of the present at any moment.[9] But despite assuming other forms, guises, and modalities, *interference* (as opposed to anachronism) is a factor in the history of the visual arts as well—in their history and not their evolution, whether that of forms or of styles. Picasso reworking the *Déjeuner sur l'herbe* is, so to speak, Manet's contemporary, just as the latter in his turn was a contemporary of Raphael and Marcantonio, and even of the ancient sculptors whose productions are invoked in their famous *Judgment of Paris* engraving.

But there is more, this time concerning the relation that art can sustain with thought. The problem is not so much one of determining whether painting and sculpture are capable of "expressing" thoughts (this question itself being biased, insofar as it presupposes that these media essentially belong to the order or domain of the *logos*, thereby precluding all possibility of passage or exchange between distinct signifying practices save in terms of *translation*[10]) as one of discerning whether a thought is or can be at work in them, and, if so, then in what forms, by what means, in accordance with what modalities and with what consequences or effects. And one of determining what is, or could be, the relation of this art-work to the thoughts that are or could be its own, just as much as its goals, which are not only a matter of transmission but also of anamnesis ("Remember Paris!"). For the project of an analytic iconology derives some of its meaning and impetus from Benveniste's hypothesis regarding linguistic reference in the Freudian discovery, which holds that, despite considerable differences in terms of substantive expression, comparisons between language and the unconscious should be made not so much on the level of language as on that of the stylistic procedures or "figures" of discourse: art, like the unconscious, disposing of a veritable rhetoric with its own tropes and syntax in which, in the cases of both painting and sculpture, the substance of expression, including its most material aspects, plays a major role, though one whose character has yet to be specified.[11]

* * *

Here again, Saint Augustine opened the way, knowing, like a new Saint Paul, how to place the weapons at his disposal—in this case, those of rhetoric—at the service of the Christian religion. And it was indeed a rhetoric, with its own tropes, if not its own syntax, that served to organize the project of "moralizing" pagan fables as well as Old Testament stories, which, as Pascal was to say, are "figures" of questions important for Christians. Tropes, like those in dreams, like those in the unconscious (the same unconscious of which art, when not its effective emissary or messenger, is happy to mimic the operations, if not to foil them), that as such require interpretation, but that, like those in dreams, like those in the unconscious, are initially produced by a labor itself constrained, through and through, by the rule of representability (as was also the case, and more explicitly, for Renaissance mythographers: the *Imagini dei Dei degli antichi* by Vicenzo Cartari offering a case in point, being an encyclopedic treatise in which, as its title indicates, figurative readings of the gods are simultaneously the end and the means—the very instrument—of the investigation: it contains not a single trait, attribute, symbol, or allegory relating to the gods that is not derived from or linked to a representation[12]). With the following caveat: whereas in psychoanalysis the first effect of interpretation is to make the image disappear from consciousness, art makes every effort, as does mythography in this case, to inscribe or impress it on the individual memory, and sometimes on the collective or institutional memory, in the material guise of a monument or a work preserved in a museum.

Paris's marked preference for a certain type of beauty corresponds—to use Freud's language in *Civilization and Its Discontents*—to a kind of "technique for living," to the choice of a way to attain happiness whose ethical dimension is avowed from the start. As early as the medieval "moralities" and the "mythologies" of Fulgentius, there is evidence of a significant slippage from the aesthetic to the ethical register, and one from the judgment of taste to moral judgment: the choice imposed upon Paris coming to seem like a decision, even a *verdict*, a pronouncement, with a privileged relation to truth insofar as the latter—as Kant would say—is a matter of obligation rather than of beauty.[13] And that being so even though Freud's theoretical elaborations go much farther, instructing us that not everything in ethics is related to a sense of obligation, and that—to cite Lacan—the genesis of the moral dimension is located nowhere else than in desire itself:[14] such is one of the lessons we might be tempted to draw from the story of Paris, should we be inclined to read it as an edifying fable.

To the extent it can be taken as a figure or, to use language still current in the Middle Ages, as an example of moral choice, and not only of aesthetic preference, the judgment of Paris takes on the character of a decision or verdict that cannot fail to effect the balance of human aspirations, insofar as it engages the question of pleasure and its place in the ethical economy. But it also retains—to a greater or lesser extent than allegory?—its force as an image, and an image (to again cite Pascal) that carries, as such, "presence and absence, pleasure and unpleasure"[15]—and carries them with a heightened valence, insofar as what is in question, in its very subject matter or "material" as much as in the artistic forms it is capable of assuming, is the economic function of pleasure, this time in the aesthetic order. Even if we restricted ourselves to the "figure" as such, the choice confronting Paris would involve beauty to an equal extent, even if each of the three goddesses had incarnated a different modality, one present in each of the others only accidentally—the same argument by which Giordano Bruno would arrive at the kind of ontological proof previously mentioned, which went much farther than Marsilio Ficino's commentary on Plato's *Symposium*.

The question of the different modalities, even the different regimes, not only of the judgment of taste but of beauty itself insofar as the latter can make itself visible—according to Plato, "sight is the keenest mode of perception vouchsafed us through the body"—leads us to the astonishing passage in the *Phaedrus* in which Socrates states: "Wisdom, indeed, we cannot see thereby—how passionate had been our desire for her, if she had granted us so clear an image of herself to gaze upon—nor yet any other of those beloved objects, save only beauty; for beauty alone this has been ordained, to be most manifest to sense and most lovely of them all."[16] How passionate indeed—if only she were representable—would be our desire for her, a desire whose phantasm is nourished by the images of art, as soon as something like thought seems to be at work in them, under the cover of beauty, something related—presence and absence, pleasure and unpleasure—to what has been designated *figure*.

* * *

It is a commonplace of the so-called emblematic literature—the "emblem" being another kind of "figure"—that seeing the body of an image awakens in the contemplating mind a desire to plumb its "soul," otherwise known as its hidden meaning.[17] Nonetheless, the hypothesis of the unconscious prohibits any marked division between images whose only function is to present what is manifestly visible and those that conventional iconology claims—to use the formulation of Cesare Ripa that has so strongly influenced its contemporary practitioners, beginning with Panofsky himself—were made "to signify something different from that seen by the eye."[18] The image of a knight in armor reclining at the foot of a tree and "envisioning" a bearded figure in theatrical garb and three nude women might well harbor a lesson or moral; but it is already an interpretive intervention, a reading into the image, of something more, or at least different, from what is readily visible there, to maintain that what we are seeing is a dream vision: if we were to hold to the letter of the image, the moment might well be that in which Paris is being awakened by Mercury.

The moral of the tale as represented by Cranach is hardly a mystery, and certainly it has not been encrypted. The ease with which the painter has conveyed in paint, and first in an engraving (to the extent that this medium is not exclusively illustrative), a reputedly "humanist" motif, casting it in a formal vocabulary devised for a northern courtly milieu, is characteristic of Cranach's art and sets him apart from Dürer, who was equally sophisticated but was directly nourished by the springs of Italian culture. It would be pointless to seek out here, beneath the chivalric trappings, a hidden meaning of Neoplatonic derivation. And it would be going too far to see these images of the judgment of Paris as alluding to the three types of life, active, contemplative, and voluptuous, evoked by Fulgentius in his *Mythologiae*. It bears repeating here that nothing—either in terms of aesthetics, ethics, or even symbolism—allows us to differentiate visually between the three goddesses, who come across less as rivals than as a renewed image of the three Graces. In the end, the moral of Cranach's pictorial fables, beginning with his images of the *Judgment of Paris*, has more to do with relations between men and women in Lutheran Reformation circles than with lessons and exercises originating in Italian humanist ones, which by contrast left their mark on a painter like Niklaus Manuel Deutsch (whose Paris, seated at the foot of a tree, facing a nude Venus holding an apple, a Minerva who wears a feathered headpiece and carries a sword and shield but is otherwise undressed, and a matronly, richly attired Juno, is himself rather sumptuously decked out, despite his shepherd's sandals, and appears in a scene that has nothing manifestly dreamlike about it, one in which mythological connotations compete with contemporary references; Figure 54) and—as we shall see shortly—on Dürer himself.[19]

There remains the matter of the seduction of the images themselves, whether produced by Cranach, Raphael, or Marcantonio, not to mention other productions generated in the wake of these "masterpieces," including Picasso's variations on Manet's *Déjeuner sur l'herbe*—a question that can hardly be dodged by an iconology dubbing itself "analytic," insofar as it must attend to what is specific to "art-work" as defined above. A work or labor that is not limited to representing or translating into images a thought content subsequently revealable by the analyst through whatever byways he or she should be pleased to invoke, but whose properly aesthetic dimension becomes the focus of a peculiarly urgent and imperious concern because what is in question in these images is the judgment of taste and—through it—of beauty, as well as the relationship sustainable by the latter with the realm of desire.

Iconology as classically defined accords pride of place to what the emblem books term "hieroglyphic" imagery, which was understood to reveal to vulgar eyes nothing more than the envelope or husk of the thought inhabiting it and transmitted by it, its being incumbent upon the initiated to discover the hidden meaning through an exercise of the intellect. But this envelope, this husk, this veil was nonetheless an integral part of

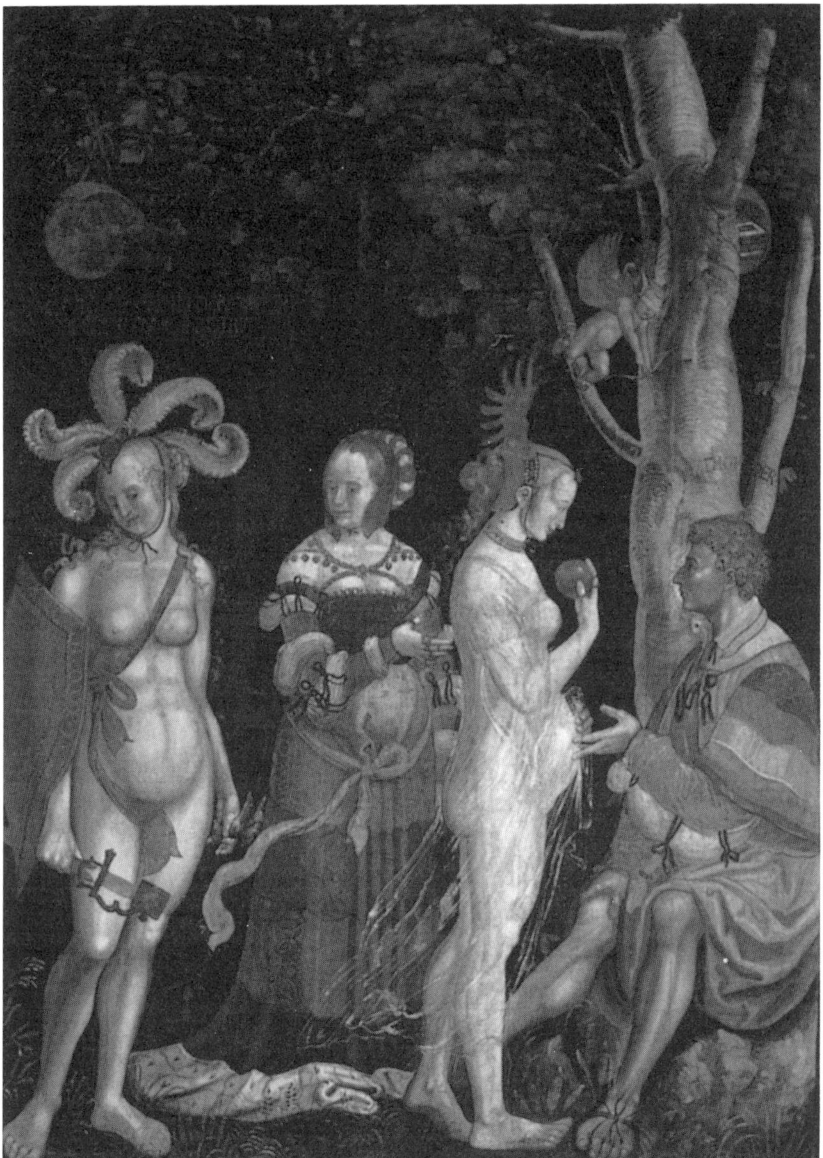

Figure 54. Niklaus Manuel Deutsch (c. 1484–1530), *The Judgment of Paris* (Basel, Öffentliche Kunstsammlung).

the mystery, if not its prime attraction, as was already explicitly maintained by Saint Augustine.[20] To this effect, Edgar Wind cites André Gide in a typically "formalist" mode: "In the great shipwreck of time, it is by their skins that masterpieces remain afloat . . . If it were not for the incomparable beauty of his prose, who would now be interested in Bossuet?"[21] However suspect the distinction implied here between form and content, the emphasis on the "skin" of masterpieces is particularly telling in the case of painting, whose thin "peel" Pontormo, in a letter to Benedetto Varchi, compared to that of an onion (*quello riciolino*), stating that the membranous quality of canvas was its principal advantage. Wind, who devoted so much attention to them, freely avowed that "mysteries" were of little interest in themselves, admitting that they merited consideration only because of their splendid expression in Renaissance art: another way of saying, before Lacan (though after Saint Augustine), that illuminating a "mystery" does not destroy its character as such (in this instance, the mystery of the masterpiece?). It is all very well for Wind, the strict-construction iconologist, to maintain that the presence, aesthetically speaking, of what he terms "unresolved residues of meaning" amounts, aesthetically speaking, to a shackling of aesthetic pleasure, raising as it does the nagging suspicion that there is more in a painting than meets the eye[22]: the important thing remains that the question of its properly aesthetic end be posed from the start of the analysis. Summoned, motivated, and justified as they are from the beginning by the seductions of specific works, those interpretations, insights, and reassessments which penetrate beyond surface structure to obtain access to their deepest substance themselves serve the pleasure principle and the beauty principle linked to it. The problem being one of determining whether art itself can have anything to say about this particular beauty, and about the mystery surrounding it: to say, or rather to render visible, in those forms and in accordance with those means that are its own. An observation that brings us back to the judgment of interest to us here, and its stakes, which, as we shall see, are also the stakes of art, and, first of all, the stakes of *painting*.

* * *

Whether an honest judge or not, Paris was faced with a difficult task, even one that required a certain cunning. For he was expected not so much to choose the most beautiful woman (*pulchriori detur*) as to express his preference among three types of beauty not only corresponding to three different paths to happiness but also linked respectively to three very different gifts: Hera, as the representative of sovereignty, offered him power; Athena, as the representative of strength, offered him victory; and Aphrodite, as the representative of love and fertility, offered him Woman. Whatever net increase in pleasure may have resulted, by opting for Aphrodite the judge pronounced in favor of a type of beauty that was quite specifically defined, at least in its difference from that of her rivals, a type of beauty that made disinterested judgment impossible. Thus it is all the more remarkable that art, from the start, has ignored the motif of the judge's corruption and concentrated instead on the three beauties identifiable by their attributes (though, as already discussed, in Greek vase painting the link between Aphrodite and Helen was often obliquely indicated by juxtaposing an image of the judgment of Paris with, on the vessel's other side, an abduction of Helen or a reunion of Helen and Menelaus). Raphael himself adhered to the simplest version of the legend (which is not to say the most economical, in the Freudian sense), but not without introducing into his composition—*per capriccio*, according to Vasari—unprecedented iconographic elements. In his description of Marcantonio's engraving, Fréart de Chambray, too, did not dream of casting doubt on Paris's competence, nor on his capacity to judge impartially. From earliest youth, had not the shepherd-prince surpassed his companions in beauty, strength, and cleverness? Was he not so beautiful that the three goddesses all agreed to submit to his decision (as though beauty, once again, amounted to a qualification in the matter of taste)? And didn't his choice fall, if not as it ought to have then at least as was only natural (desire winning out over obligation), not on the irascible Juno (how could beauty be irascible?) or on the malicious Minerva (how could beauty be malicious?) but on the agreeable Venus, who received the symbol of her victory "with modesty, accompanied by a marvelous grace"?

If Paris was able to consider Venus *agreeable*, or even *attractive*, does it follow that, in Kantian terms, this "representation" not only gave him pleasure but was devised, all too well, to *interest* him—that part of him which, according to Kant, was animal in nature, "beauty [holding] only for human beings, i.e., beings who are animal and yet rational"?[23] If Paris was incapable of judging impartially, and if it might be argued that he doesn't deserve to be called a judge at all, this is because he was not truly free, because his animal nature won out over his reason. Sartre poses the same question in different terms when he observes that one can't find a woman beautiful and desire her at the same time:[24] the question being one of determining whether this formulation, whose meaning is clear when it is used to distinguish between different forms or modes of conscious intention, can, if detached from its phenomenological context, throw some light on what I've called the paradox of Paris: Paris, who could not have risked openly desiring the goddess, but who was nonetheless sensible, "libidinous" creature that he was, to what must be called her "charms" (while in Cranach's image Cupid seems to point his arrow at Venus, it is usually aimed at Paris). But the right tone was set by Lemaire de Belges: the sparkle in the judge's eyes at the moment he announced his decision is a clear indicator of his sensual appetite, of his "unchaste desire fired by lust" ("désir non chaste, enflammé de luxure").

We could hardly expect a pre-Homeric figure to conduct himself in accordance with the principles and imperatives articulated in the *Critique of Judgement.* With respect to the norms proposed by Kant, the judgment of Paris, based as it is on a confusion between attractions or charms and beauty, has less to do with the history of taste than with its prehistory: "And yet (though beauty should actually concern only form), charms (*Reizen*) are frequently not only included with beauty, as a contribution (*als Beitrag*) toward a universal aesthetic liking, but are even themselves passed off as beauties, so that the matter of the liking is passed off as the form . . . Any taste remains barbaric if its liking requires an admixture of *charm* and *emotion*, let alone if it makes these the standard of its approval."[25] We have seen how Kant hastened to admit that such a misunderstanding had some basis in truth (*etwas Wahres zum Grunde:* something true on the most fundamental level—and by the same token necessary?). But the fact remains that, in the developed version of the myth, Venus herself does not rely solely on her beauty to guarantee her victory: not content with using her attractions to seduce her judge, she sets out to sway his decision by promising to deliver to him, should he decide in her favor, the woman she herself judges to be the most beautiful (and the most beautiful, it bears repeating here, in the same sense in which she herself pretends to surpass her rivals), her "own carnal sister," as Lemaire de Belges has her say, "the most extraordinarily beautiful woman ever born of a mother, or who ever will be." Which is to say a prize herself of the order of the admixture—or, we might say, of the *supplement*—and one resistant to any and all "sublimation": to such an extent that Paris has only to pronounce in Venus's favor to escape the position of voyeur that is his lot as judge, for Venus appeals to his desire not only through her own visible allure but by promising eventual satisfaction of his desire—a desire for beauty, a desire for love, not one for power or knowledge—through possession of an intermediary, namely, Helen.

For, although a goddess, Venus was also a woman; and it is precisely to the extent that her beauty answered to the ends of the feminine constitution that she was sure to be favored by the shepherd-prince: nature (to cite Kant's phrase once more) here being judged from a creative perspective, "insofar as it really is art, even if a superhuman one." I repeat: what is at stake in the judgment of Paris is not so much a greater or lesser degree of beauty as it is the nature of beauty itself; thus it is not difficult to understand how philosophers, moralists, and theologians have repeatedly discerned ethical content in the story. But when art takes up the motif, the image it presents of the choice among three different modes of beauty does not necessarily carry any hidden meaning. What the artist implicitly holds up to vision, in these figures depicted as divine, is the fact that he is confronted by a choice analogous to the one facing Paris, that he must himself decide in favor of one kind of beauty or another, the one chosen by Paris being particularly seductive because of its being rooted in the deepest recesses of that animal—a rational one, to be sure, but an animal all the same—to which art is addressed. But how to represent, how to signify, how to figure the supplement to which art must have recourse, namely the premium of pleasure that it promises, according to whether it favors one or another kind of beauty, one or another kind of visibility and/or legibility, or combines them in varying proportions to attain what might be called an *ars triplex*, an art unfolding on three registers, like the Neoplatonic conception of life?

I propose the following hypothesis: It was in accordance with such a program—one perfectly consistent with the modalities of Renaissance art, which was often informed by multiple and contradictory aspirations and functional considerations—that Marcantonio's print of *The Judgment of Paris* after Raphael was devised. A hypothesis justified (verified?) by its being the only one allowing us to account for the distinctive feature of this image determining its "masterpiece" status in the history of art: the presence, around the figures involved in the title episode, of several other figures that might seem to be purely decorative but that nonetheless have attracted the attention of critics as well as of other artists—beginning with Manet, who drew inspiration from four of these figures for his

Déjeuner sur l'herbe. Far from challenging the traditional interpretation of the story of Paris, the art of the Renaissance, and to an even greater extent that of the seventeenth century (see my remarks about Rubens below), systematically emphasized a choice among three types of beauty corresponding to the tripartite functional divisions of Indo-European cultures—though allowance must be made for the above-mentioned fact that in the late Middle Ages and the Renaissance Minerva was understood more as a goddess of wisdom and knowledge than of arms. Judging from Marcantonio's engraving, Raphael himself did not do otherwise. As regards "form," it might seem that art here makes no appeal to any elements other than strictly graphic ones and that it promises very little in the way of a pleasure premium. But if we consider the "invention" as presented to us, in black and white, without any other colors save those generated by the play of light and shadow (which is to say by perspective, as Fréart understood it), its most striking feature is the addition of two groups of figures that appear to be irrelevant to the focal episode, and even turn their backs on it.

If the hypothesis is accepted, the question then becomes the following: How did Raphael—assuming the *inventio* was his doing—manage to represent, to signify, to figure, by means specific to the medium of engraving, the promise implied by art—if not presupposed by it—of a premium of pleasure, a surplus-enjoyment factor (*un plus-de-jouir*) that would associate with the sensual gratification obtained through vision the intellectual gratification provided by the commentaries to which the work lent itself, and even the satisfaction associated with the prestige it had the power to bestow on its commissioner or its owner, and vice versa? And another question arises, too, one perhaps even more difficult to understand. How did the master, the director of the workshop, manage to make available to representation, signification, figuration, and by means specific to the medium of engraving, the bonus inhering in painting, the promise of a surplus-enjoyment factor seemingly implied—if not presupposed—by it? How other than by playing, precisely, on the difference separating these two visual media (which would suffice, let it be said in passing, to preclude the possibility of Marcantonio's print serving as a model for larger painted versions)?

Fréart de Chambray understood perfectly the solution adopted by Raphael. In conformity with the iconographic tradition prevailing since antiquity, the engraving makes no reference to the premiums the three goddesses offered their judge; but the image does boast certain features that are themselves "supplements" of a kind. After having described the elements with some apparent relation to "a true story," Fréart turns to the "capricious fantasies" similar to those introduced by poets, "in some sense the comrades of painters." The inscription carved on a tablet in the lower left corner of the composition, SORDENT PRAE FORMA/INGENIUM/VIRTUS/REGNA AURUM, clearly states that form, in the person of Venus, has carried the day over strength (*virtus*), which might be strength of mind (represented by Minerva), and over divine royalty (personified by Juno). But Raphael did not stop there; to the scene of judgment he added, *per capriccio*, the features and accessories that attracted Vasari's attention: the chariot of the sun, the wood nymphs, the nymphs of flowers and of springs, and the river gods, as well as vases, oars, "and other fine fantasies."[26] Or, as Fréart was to say following the description cited previously, which was primarily concerned with the four main figures and that of Mercury, "in which the entire history was adequately expressed":

> After that, the rest of this composition is but a poetic accompaniment from the painter's genius that enriches the effect of his picture: for all these nymphs with their amphoras, and the two male figures holding reeds, seated and nude, paying no attention to what is happening, indicate nothing but that Mount Ida is abundantly provided with rivers and fountains: and apparently the one leaning

> on an oar is the Xanthus River, which ran under the walls of Troy; and his neighbor is the Simois River, both of them having their sources on this same mountain, and both, after irrigating along their respective beds the Trojan countryside, joining at the mouth of the sea at the Hellespont, close to the Sigean promontory.[27]

If we take this text literally, the figures under discussion are in the nature of ornaments or *parerga*, in the Kantian sense—which is to say "what does not belong to the whole presentation of the object as an intrinsic constituent, but [is] only an extrinsic addition," though one that "increases our taste's liking."[28] In what follows, I will build upon Jacques Derrida's now classic analysis of the *parergon* and the commentaries prompted by it,[29] extending it (as is implicitly sanctioned by Derrida's own text, which invokes, for example, a *Lucretia* by Cranach[30]) to encompass the supplement authorized by direct reference to the order of representation: the question of the "supplement" as regards so-called abstract or nonrepresentational art remaining completely open.

Derrida has analyzed Kant's use in the third *Critique* of a Greek term to give an appearance of conceptual legitimacy to the notion he was discussing.[31] In fact, if we restrict ourselves to the semantic field of art, in other words to artistic literature, the word seems to have been used rather loosely in antiquity.[32] It is all the more remarkable, then, that Pliny introduced it into a confusing passage in book XXXV of his *Natural History* dealing with the role of the painter Protogenes in decorating the propylaeum of the temple of Minerva in Athens. After having depicted, in a painting that was to become famous, two figures that—according to the most plausible reading—were meant to invoke ships bearing their names, Protogenes is said to have added, to use Pliny's language, "what painters call side-pieces" (*quae pictores perergia appelant*): in this instance, small battleships intended as a reminder of his difficult beginnings in the art of painting, when he was obliged to "paint boats," and thus as an indication of how far he'd come before painting this "masterpiece." Already in Pliny, the introduction of a Greek word into the Latin text effectively shifts the focus from the anecdote being told by the author of the *Natural History* toward theoretical questions bearing on the function of such "details": these ships, doubtless depicted in the distance as a squadron accompanying the sacred galleys, must have been meant to signal a relation between the represented figures and navigation.[33]

Thus the *parergon* was associated with the ground against which the figures emerged, if not with the *scene* in which they were placed. Pliny mentions a bit farther on the case of one Serapio, an excellent decorative painter (doubtless specializing in architectural perspectives and/or landscapes) who was incapable of rendering a human being (*Hic scaenas optime pinxit, sed hominem pingere non potuit*), contrasting him with an artist named Dionysius, who painted only human figures and so came to be called *anthropographos*, or "painter of human beings."[34] (How could one not be tempted to invoke here the "wolf man's" testimony to the effect that Freud was drawn almost exclusively to painting's narrative and allegorical aspects, evincing little interest in landscape and in modern art: Freud the "anthropograph," even in his relation to painting?[35]) Now the accessories inventoried by Vasari—the female figures with their amphoras, the seated and nude men holding reeds and oars, all this "poetic accompaniment from the painter's genius" included, according to Fréart, to "enrich the effect of his picture"—effectively function as *parerga*, and even figure the latter's function. On the one hand, and Fréart states this explicitly, these figures must be read as metaphorical embodiments of the background, or at least of the landscape in which the scene of judgment ostensibly took place (the greater part of which is here invaded by a swarm of deities), as so many personifications of the many springs and rivers on Mount Ida, just as the figures painted by Protogenes personified the ships bearing their names, though perhaps indirectly, by means of what

Freud would have called a first step toward representability, these figures being themselves incarnations of cities or provinces. On the other hand—and this is doubtless the most remarkable aspect of Raphael's invention, the one that has repeatedly piqued artists' interest—these figures without any interest in what is happening and who even seem to turn their backs on the scene, like the nymph seated on the left, behind Paris, and the curiously androgynous figure whose pose is also that of Victorine Meurent in the *Déjeuner sur l'herbe* (Figures 55 and 56), these figures function, within what Fréart calls the *tableau*, as a kind of *frame:* the scene of judgment is effectively enclosed between these limiting elements, between these "borders" (one of the meanings assigned by Derrida to the *parergon*), which are like two bookends containing it. Now picture frames (*die Einfassungen der Gemälde*) are among the examples cited by Kant to clarify what he means by the "ornaments," or *parerga*, serving "to increase our taste's liking." But there are frames and frames: if the ornament (the frame) does not increase the said liking or satisfaction through its beautiful form alone but is intended, like a gold frame (*wie der goldene Rahmen*), to commend the painting to our approval, then it is called finery (*Schmuck*), and it impairs genuine beauty (*und tut der echten Schönheit Abbruch*).[36]

Which prompts the following question concerning the status of ornament, or of the *parergon.* Do the figures that, again, turn their backs on the print's eponymous scene, to which they apparently pay no attention, these nymphs and river gods pertaining to the background—if, by a singular turn, they do not themselves figure it: does this "poetic accompaniment" function like a mounting in which the scene is inserted, a setting intended to fix it, precisely, as a *scene*, and by the same token to facilitate its comprehension (*Fassung*)—in other words, do these figures make it easier for us to understand the image? Or, conversely, do they disperse our attention, directing it not toward what is revealed through this "window" the *tableau* is supposed to be (to use the Albertian metaphor, henceforth sin-

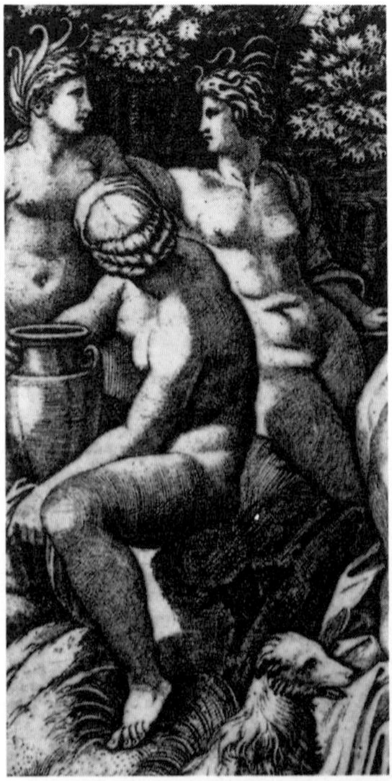

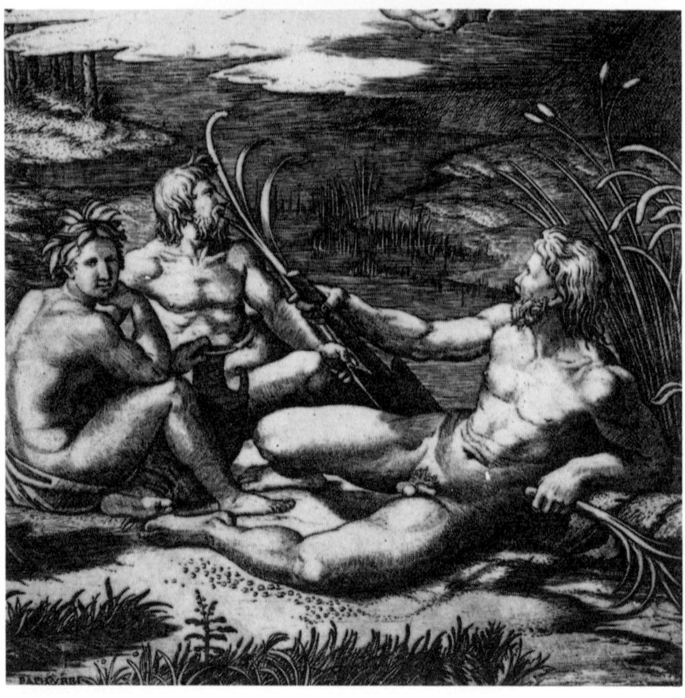

Figures 55–56. Marcantonio Raimondi, *The Judgment of Paris*, engraving after Raphael, details.

gularly stale and suspect), but rather toward the materiality of the rather overly assertive support (*châssis*) by which the "view" is framed?

* * *

In the matter of "windows," anyone looking for the only painted *Judgment of Paris* to emerge from the Raphael studio, in all likelihood at a date prior to the publication of Marcantonio's engraving,[37] will be obliged—it has not been reproduced—to visit the apartments of Julius II in the Vatican. There he will discover, in the right window embrasure of the Stanza della Segnatura, behind a heavy wooden blind obscuring it from view and inserted, beneath the inscription SUAVE, flanked by two snakes wrapped around batons, into a complex decorative scheme featuring superimposed caryatids and putti, a small scene executed in cameo and featuring, aside from the five figures essential to the fable, only the shepherd's dog. There is nothing surprising in the subject's presence here, or in its having been coupled with the *Apollo and Daphne* on the opposite side of the embrasure, for the window in question is directly beneath the *Parnassus*. In a cycle devised to exalt the ideas of the True, the Good, and the Beautiful and placed under the quadruple signs of Theology, Philosophy, Justice, and Poetry, whose personifications preside over the ceiling,[38] the *Judgment of Paris* functions here as a kind of gloss (a predictable if somewhat forced one in this context) on the idea of the Beautiful—like the Apollo (again, rather predictable here) come down from the *Parnassus* to pursue Daphne, and who reappears on the ceiling, this time above the *Parnassus*, facing Marysas, seated and holding his lyre, positioned as both victor and judge, and given a pose very like that of the shepherd-prince below, his twisting profile echoing that of Paris turning toward the trio of goddesses.

Aby Warburg was to pursue the matter further when, emulating his friend Gustav Pauli, he chose Manet as his guide in one of the archeological quests that had become his *raison de vivre*,[39] as is documented by his notes on the *Déjeuner sur l'herbe*, dictated by him to Gertrude Bing in 1929 and now in the archives of the institute in London that bears his name.[40] This great art historian and thinker reveals his attitude toward the painting in his opening words: far from denouncing the artist's irreverence toward masterpieces from the past or viewing the work as a joke in more or less questionable taste, a position quite common today, Warburg understood that the *Déjeuner sur l'herbe* is, of all "modern" paintings, the one raising the most difficult problems for anyone attempting to sort out the links between modern art and tradition. Confronted by a canvas that was to be brandished like a standard in the battle against academic virtuosity, it might seem pointless to attempt to reconstruct, along Warburgian methodological lines, the chain leading over many centuries "from Arcadia to the Batignolles quarter by way of Rousseau." Warburg invokes Manet's own explicit reference to the example (*Vorbild*) of Giorgione to support his argument that, judged objectively, with *Sachlichkeit* (a word with unmistakable "avant-garde" overtones in 1920s Germany), the grouping of dressed men and naked women in the open air had nothing revolutionary about it (whatever its possible "sexist" connotations). But why did the painter never explain his debt to Raphael? Or, to put the question in Warburg's own terms: "In this fight for the human rights of the eye" (*im Kampfe um die Menschenrechte des Auges*), why did he feel obliged to turn back and present himself as a faithful guardian of tradition? Would it not have been better to allow the work to produce its own effect unmediated (*durch seine unmittelbare Gestaltung*), such that it registered unconsciously with the public that great works are those which do not borrow their force of penetration (*ihre Durchschlagskraft*, a quasi-Freudian formulation) from a setting-aside (*Beseitigung*) of old forms but from their transformation (*Umgestaltung*)? Warburg's position here implicitly prefigures the project I have outlined for an "analytic iconology," just as it anticipates what was to become the fundamental rule of all "structuralist" aesthetic theory: namely, that what a work of art "represents" is less important than what it *transforms*.

In the matter of transformations, Warburg says nothing about Manet's citation in the *Déjeuner sur l'herbe* of a portion of Marcantonio's engraving, the group of nymphs and river gods that Raphael ostensibly devised as a poetic accompaniment to enrich his composition. But that is because the historian was preoccupied by a play of transformations subtler and otherwise consequential than the one involved in the painter's having his friends strike the poses of the river gods and recasting the nymph (in fact a singularly androgynous figure) looking toward the viewer as a young woman on the banks of the Seine—as a "French nymph," to use Warburg's phrase. If we keep in mind that Raphael himself, and/or his engraver, was working from raw material inherited from antiquity in the form of Hellenistic funerary reliefs (a fact probably unknown to Manet), the links reconstructed by Warburg take on all the appearances of a signifying chain that, over fifteen centuries, was subjected to a set of operations analogous to—when not directly involved with—those of the unconscious, and symptomatic of an evolving train of thought at work throughout (see Figure 57), a portion of which inevitably slipped through Warburg's methodological net, given its still strictly evolutionist and psychologizing character.

In this chain, the "invention" credited to Raphael (which Warburg characterized perfectly, as we shall see) occupies a singular position: in addition to persistently appealing to painters, from the start it exercised a curious retroactive influence over the models on which it was ostensibly based—beginning with the so-called *Judgment of Paris* relief (Figure 58), now incorporated into the garden facade of the Villa Medici in Rome, which Raphael might have seen in the garden of antiquities assembled by Cardinal Andrea della Valle, and which was subsequently purchased by Ferdinando de' Medici. The focus of the della Valle collection, described in inscriptions as a "pre-

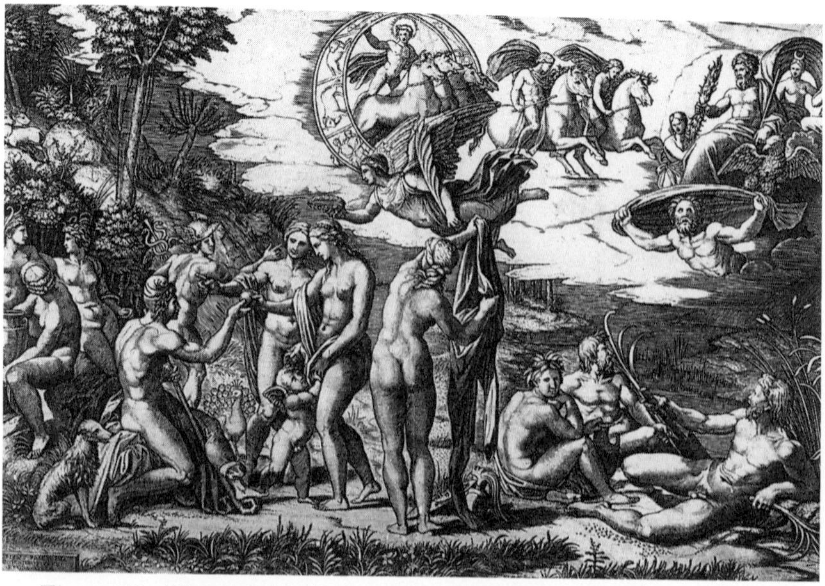

Figure 57. Marcantonio Raimondi, *The Judgment of Paris*, engraving after Raphael.

serve of antiquity" and even as the "refuge of the Graces," was perfectly consistent with Warburg's analytical approach, for the terraced garden in which it was situated had been conceived of as a visible sign of the continuity between ancient and Renaissance culture—"in memory of our ancestors, that posterity might imitate them."[41] In this context, the *Judgment of Paris* relief, actually the front panel of a sarcophagus dating from the 3d century A.D., could only take on special importance in Warburg's eyes: first, because of its subject matter; and, second, a point Warburg was to stress from the beginning of his career, because Roman sarcophagi were among the most important vehicles for the transmission of the pagan pantheon to modern culture, on occasion even being retained in Christian places of worship.[42]

When the della Valle collection was moved to the Pincian hill in 1584, the *Judgment of Paris* sarcophagus underwent a singular transformation. Ammanati's conception of the facade

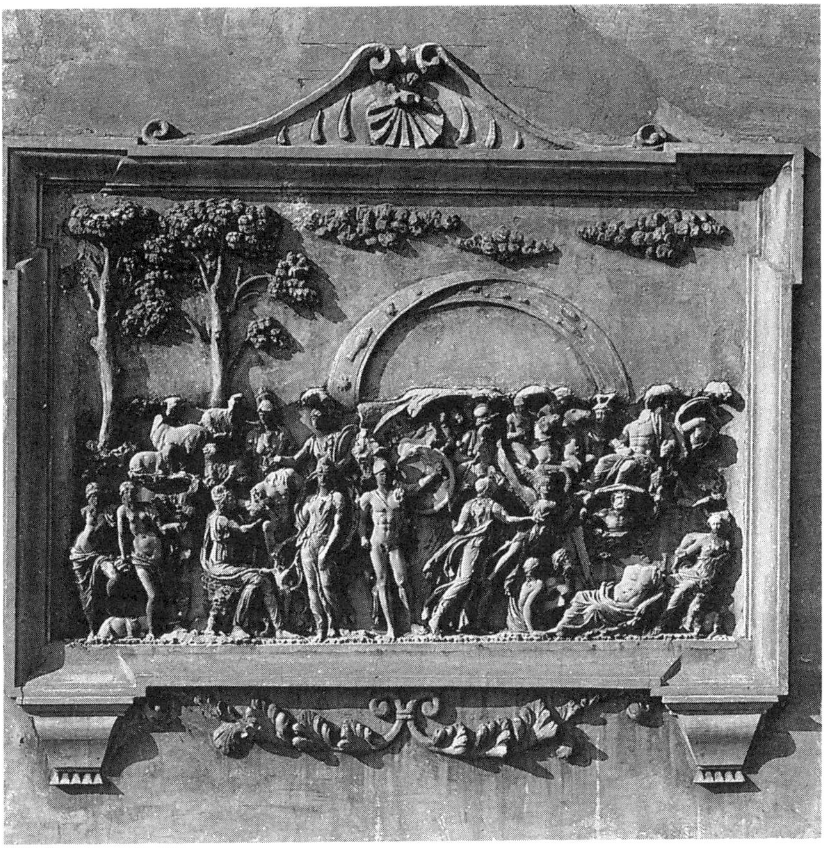

Figure 58. *The Judgment of Paris*, Hellenistic relief, second–third century (Rome, Villa Medici).

as a "wall of images," which lent itself to "montage" effects (Warburg went so far as to compare it to a "moving picture"), called for the enlargement of the relief, which was to be placed on the middle level to the right. To adapt it to this site, the sculptors produced a *pasticcio* consistent with contemporary notions of the "renewal" and even "resurrection" of ruined sculpture, going so far as to add a stucco "sky," punctuated by trees and clouds and traversed by an arc of the Zodiac modeled after Marcantonio's engraving. We might well pose questions about the significance accruing to this *Judgment of Paris* in the context of a decor devised primarily to exalt the virtues and *magnificenza* of the villa's owner, Ferdinando de' Medici. That the additions make reference to a print that was quite celebrated in this period strongly suggests that something of the program underlying Raphael's invention, according to the hypothesis advanced above, was intended to come across in this "wall of images" conceived, by and large, under the signs of religion, piety, and sacrifice: with regard to this aspect of the facade's decorative scheme, questions arise concerning both ornament, or the *parergon,* and the place here allotted beauty. (See Figure 59.)

The stucco additions visible today on the villa facade are the result of a complete restoration carried out in 1648 under the direction of Cosimo Fancelli, a Bernini student.[43] But this work did not obliterate all traces of the earlier intervention. We are here in the presence, not only of a signal example of the detours opened up by reproduction, but also of a figure that Warburg chose to inscribe, not without audacity, under the rubric "narcissism": that, doubtless, of the viewer, who takes pleasure in seeing that the tableau (in this case a *tabula sculpta*) makes a direct appeal to him; but also that of an ancient work transformed after the model of another work, a contem-

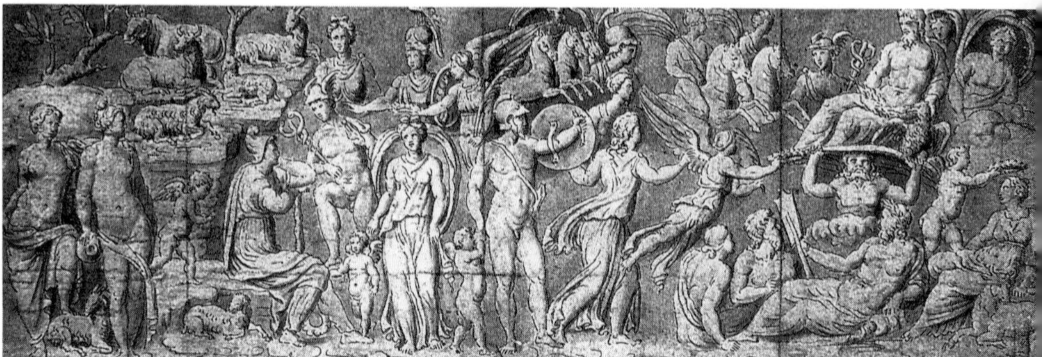

Figure 59. Étienne Delaune (?), *The Judgement of Paris,* drawing, 1575 (?), probably after the *Codex Corbugensis* (private collection).

porary one, for which it had originally served as a model, only to be subsequently caught in its mirror as if in a trap. Warburg cited as an example of "our tendency to make the narcissism of men in images the criterion of stylistic evolution" another sarcophagus, now in the Thermae Museum and formerly in the Villa Ludovisi, in which the face of the nymph looking out at the spectator is revealed to be a subsequent addition that has now disappeared.[44] However crude, this operation points to that feature of the Raphaelesque "invention" which decisively distinguishes it from its model.

The Villa Medici relief presents us with a judgment of Paris that differs from the traditional iconographic treatment of the theme (see details, Figures 60 and 61). On the left, behind Paris, seated to indicate his status as judge and handing the apple to Venus, are two naiads more than half nude—whereas Venus, by contrast, wears a long robe, her upper body framed by a billowing veil that makes her resemble Fortune, which she effectively represents for Paris. In the center of the composition is a completely nude warrior, depicted frontally, who wears a helmet and lifts his shield to the right, where the victorious goddess is about to ascend, led by a *nike*—the same winged victory figure that will crown her in the Raphael composition—and by none other than Mercury, followed by the chariot of the sun and by Minerva, identifiable by her helmet, toward Olympus, where Jupiter sits enthroned with the sky beneath his feet, his thunderbolt securely in hand. On the right of the relief, beneath this scene, is the group—consisting of a nymph and two river gods, above whom appears Tellus supporting the sky—that Raphael and Marcantonio used in their own *Judgment of Paris*, initiating a long series of paraphrases which, as we will see (and as Warburg could not), extends beyond Manet's "masterpiece" to encompass Picasso's variations on the *Déjeuner sur l'herbe*.

I will pass briefly here over Warburg's eminently psychologizing analysis of the posture of these figures, qualified by him as demi-gods associated with the earth, and shown in the

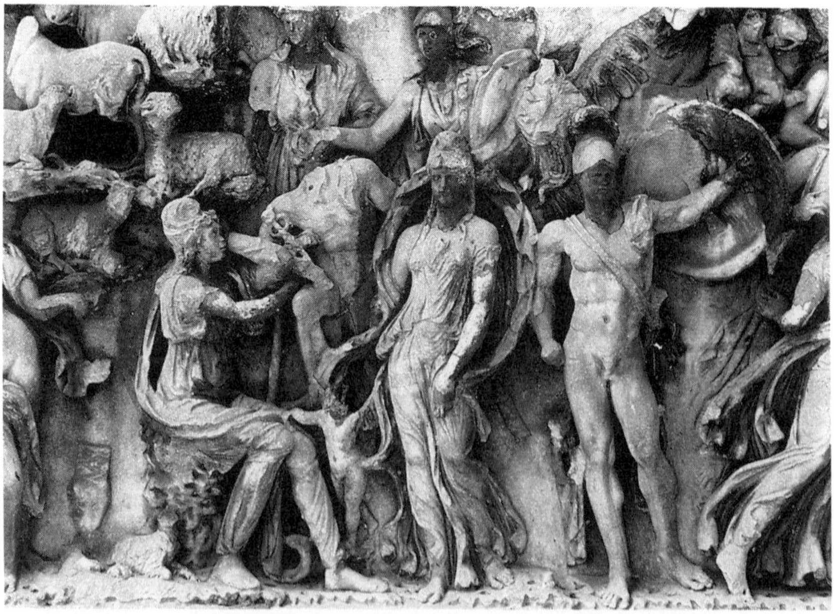

Figure 60. *The Judgment of Paris*, Hellenistic relief, second–third century, detail, central group (Rome, Villa Medicis).

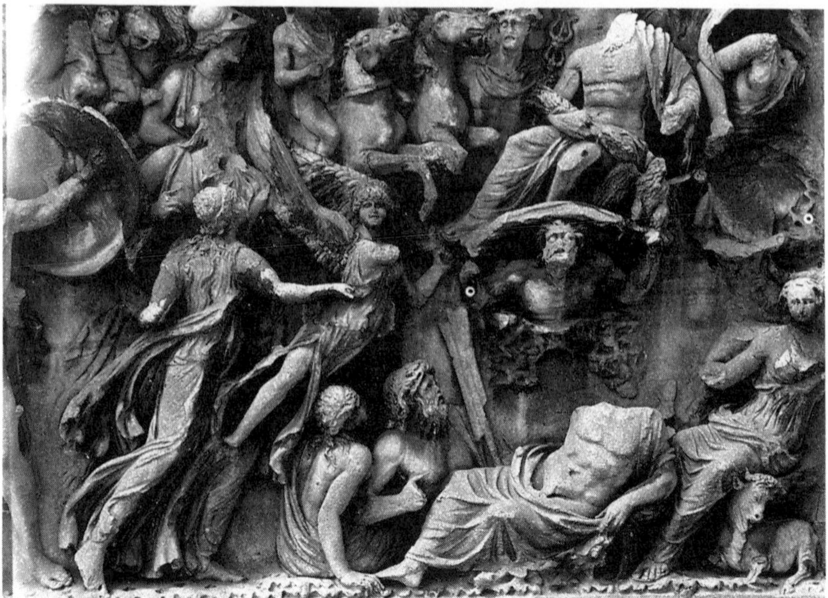

Figure 61. *The Judgment of Paris*, Hellenistic relief, second–third century, detail, right group (Rome, Villa Medicis).

Medici relief passively witnessing Venus's ascension toward Olympus: aside from the figure of Tellus, the poses of these earth-borne "demons" and "genies" scarcely evidence the desire ascribed to them by Warburg to escape the corporeal weight that was the lot of non-Olympians; but, in the context of funerary art, the ascension motif amounts to a first "moralization"—a singularly early and unexpected one—of the fable of Paris. Nonetheless, Warburg perfectly analyzed the transformations effected in the Raphaelesque "invention." First, the male figure of the helmeted hero, seen frontally and holding up his shield on the relief's central axis, has been replaced in the engraving by that of Minerva, seen from the back and removing her clothing (in the relief her helmeted figure is seen above Venus's head on the left, already half-way to Olympus). Warburg sees this substitution, which he describes as "archeologizing," but whose structural importance is unmistakable, as the sign of a first *displacement* toward the realm of plastic beauty and the pastoral idyll. Second, there is the surprising direction of the gaze of the vaguely nymphlike figure sitting just below the *nike* in the relief, who is given an oddly equivocal appearance in the print: whereas the sculpted figure looks heavenwards toward the theophany, the corresponding androgynous one in the engraving—to be replaced by an aggressively feminine one in the *Déjeuner sur l'herbe*—ignores not only the scene unfolding behind her back but even her companions, turning her leaf-crowned head toward the viewer and thus looking out of the *tabula*, from which she effectively absents herself with that same tranquil indifference which was to be characteristic of Manet's model.

Raphael and his engraver introduced still other transformations into their *Judgment of Paris* "after the antique," and they have their importance: the chariot of the sun and the Olympian Jupiter have been moved farther back in the sky, giving the composition a sense of depth precluded in the compact relief; and above all, the standing naiad behind Paris, facing the viewer, is now seated and turns her back to him, with the result that in the print the scene of judgment is effectively *framed* by the figures to either side of it. Nonetheless, Warburg was right to see in the face turned toward the viewer the essential link in the chain connecting the Hellenistic sarcophagus, Marcantonio's *Judgment of Paris* engraving, and the *Déjeuner sur l'herbe*—the new consciousness ("narcissistic," if you like) of the viewer evidenced by the "Raphaelesque" invention being increased in Manet's painting by the direct gazes of both the "French nymph" and one of her male companions. How right he was to say that the painting now fixes this viewer not in the sky but on the ground, at eye level. In light of other evidence, namely the roughly contemporary *Ecstasy of Saint Cecilia*, it is tempting to suggest that this is a typically Raphaelesque trait: whereas Marcantonio's print after this work features a Magdalen who looks heavenwards, like the nymph in the Medici relief, in Raphael's painting she looks directly at the viewer with the same distracted quality that was to characterize Manet's figure. Far from being indifferent, the "nymph" in the *Judgment*, the Magdalen in the *Ecstasy*, and Victorine in the *Déjeuner* all have the air (and the art) of vacating themselves from compositions (*tableaux*) that paradoxically derive much of their *Durchschlagskraft*, their "force of penetration," from these figures' very absence from their place.

* * *

If such is indeed the meaning of the Raphaelesque invention, then what is the nature of Manet's? Manet, whose teacher, Thomas Couture, reproached him, according to Antonin Proust, for "disturbing" the pose, going so far as to ask the model to put on some of her clothing and adopt a simpler attitude? Georges Bataille's suggestion that the author of the *Old Musician* could have instructed his models to hold poses struck "more or less haphazardly" does not hold up: scholarship has demonstrated that a year prior to the scandal of the *Déjeuner* Manet had already derived key elements of his first large-scale composition from another consecrated masterpiece, *The Drinkers* by Velázquez.[45] But the *Déjeuner*? Did Manet have only to deck out his male models in contemporary dress and ask one of them to look in his direction to justify our speaking of a "transformation"—one which, unbeknownst to the public and even to criticism, played on a literally immemorial figural configuration (*dispositif figuratif*)—explaining much of the impact, ambiguous to say the least, of his masterpiece?

With regard to the resistance, in the technical psychoanalytic sense, consistently prompted by looking at Manet's painting, even today, I have said that it seems somehow linked to the incongruous nudity of the woman who, like her Raphaelesque model, gazes out of the picture toward the viewer. But if there be any incongruity here, it will appear more clearly with the aid of a comparison. Concerning the figure replaced by Victorine Meurent, and whose androgynous character Warburg took care to point out also constituted an important transformation, we can say that she is doubly cut off from the eponymous episode of Marcantonio's engraving: first, because she pays no attention to it, even turning away from her companions to direct her gaze toward the exterior of what Fréart calls the *tableau;* and, second, because given her androgynous character she has no role to play in a debate over the nature of beauty's relation to sexual difference. And yet, if this figure thus absents herself surreptitiously from the *tableau* in which she ostensibly has her place, then the spectator or *regardant*, to use the appropriate French term from Fréart's period, would not necessarily find what he expected: for if there is to be narcissistic pleasure, desire must be among the company.

Such is not the case in the *Déjeuner sur l'herbe*. From the start, the framing of the scene precludes any idea of an intrigue unfolding in the wings, "outside of the field," or behind the figures' backs. And here it is unquestionably a woman who looks at "us," the question becoming one of determining the nature, *here*, of this "us," or of the subject (you, me, her, him) to which it is doubtless unwarranted for us to pretend that this gaze is directed, as well as the nature of its grammatical character. For this female figure, while effectively possessing all the "charms," also effectively absents herself from her ostensible place by a movement that is in a sense the opposite of the in-turning posture adopted by her companion in the background. Insofar as a bit of "psychologizing" is permissible in the wake of my earlier remarks about Warburg, it will be allowed that what seems acceptable in a pastoral idyll such as the *Concert champêtre* becomes unacceptable in what Manet called his "foursome" or *partie carrée*. Meyer Schapiro identified the real cause of scandal here, namely that two men are sitting in a glade in the company of two naked women without any current of emotion passing between the sexes.[46] But if desire is not among the company in this *partie carrée*, the same could be said of the viewer. Unlike so many paintings in which excitement generated by the sight of a (female) nude is, so to speak, represented in the painting itself in the person of (male) voyeurs taking part in the scene,[47] the woman in the *Déjeuner sur l'herbe*—like that in the *Olympia* but in accordance with a strict inversion of its terms (the nude in the *Olympia* does not absent herself from the painting but fuses with it, sinks into it as if into her own element)—keeps the viewer at a distance, if not altogether outside of the circuit, by returning his (or her) gaze, a gesture precluding all possibility of identification with the depicted figures: the perversity of this masterpiece (a perversity incommensurable with that of Ingres' *Grande Odalisque*, who also looks out at "us" but in a completely different way) attaining its apogee from the moment that the woman's absence from her place is intended to prevent the viewer or *regardant* (Poussin's term), of either gender, from taking pleasure in the play that can be operative in painting, as well as to denounce it as typically masculine (see Figures 62 and 63).

The transformation operated by Manet is thus less a matter of pose than of excision or montage, if not of collage. It remains for us, however, to characterize the operation consisting of the painter's extraction from Marcantonio's engraving of the

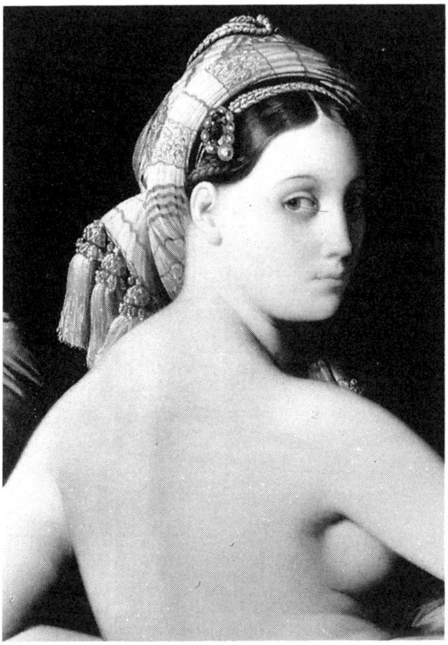

Figure 62. J. A. D. Ingres, *La Grande Odalisque*, 1814, detail (Paris, Louvre).

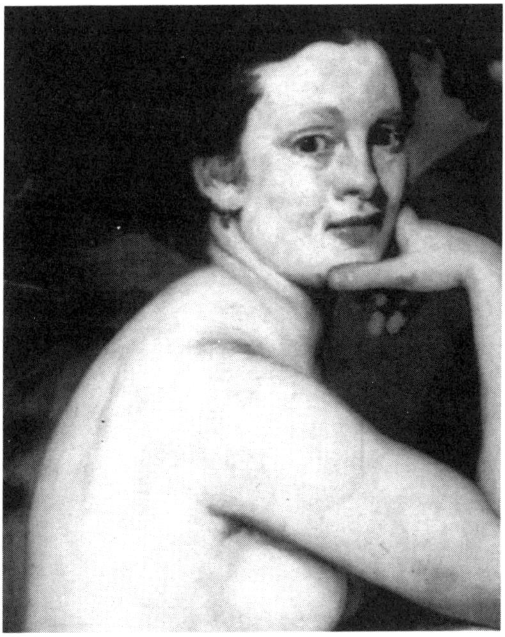

Figure 63. Edouard Manet, *Le Déjeuner sur l'herbe*, detail (Paris, Musée d'Orsay).

group serving as his model, thereby abstracting it from its original context: that of a story or fable in which the play of the male gaze over the female body performs a key role. Now it is an incontestable fact that the figures of nymphs and river gods included by the painter as a "poetic accompaniment" intended "to enrich the composition of his painting" also attracted the attention of all those who, among Raphael's successors, produced variants of his model: beginning with the anonymous sixteenth-century engraver who reproduced, juxtaposing her with the dog sitting at Paris's feet in the engraving, the nymph sitting on a rock to the left in the print, an amphora between her legs, situated behind the hero and turning her back to him "without paying any attention to what is happening," as Fréart aptly notes (Figure 64).[48] Even in the nineteenth century, Manet was not the only artist, nor the first, to be drawn to this motif. We know that Delacroix worked closely with Marcantonio's engravings until he tired of them and came to prefer unstudied photographs.[49] Of the three known study sheets from his hand after the *Judgment of Paris*, one features a rough sketch of the crouching figure of indeter-

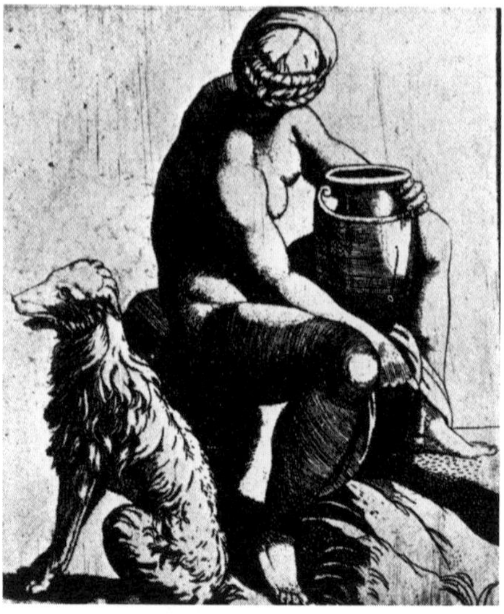

Figure 64. *Nymph with a Jug*, anonymous sixteenth-century engraving after Marcantonio Raimondi.

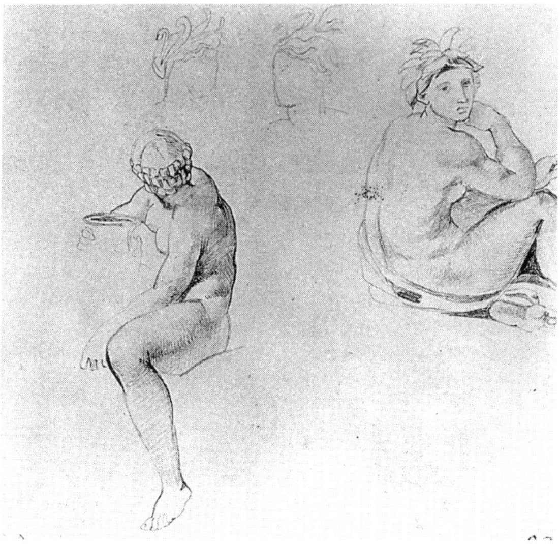

Figure 65. Eugène Delacroix, *Two Figures from "The Judgement of Paris,"* after Marcantonio Raimondi (New York, Jill Newhouse and Eric Carlson collection).

minate gender already discussed (the one whose pose is imitated by Victorine Meurent in the *Déjeuner sur l'herbe*) and another sketch of Victory in her chariot; the two other sheets concentrate on the two figures turning their backs on and framing the scene, in the manner of a *parergon* (Figure 65).[50] A drawing by Degas, dating from his brief stint at the École des Beaux-Arts, its contours seemingly traced directly from the engraving, also reproduces, in addition to some figures from the *Parnassus*, the androgynous figure—here given a clearly discernible breast—and the river god seated beside her (Figure 66).[51] And I will not fail to mention a famous drawing by Corot, the so-called *Petite Fille dans un paysage*, whose posture, including the curve of her back and her gaze directed at the viewer, seems to have been inspired by the androgyne almost line for line (Figure 67).

By working in the masterpiece's margins, Manet was only following in the footsteps of his predecessors—save that while the latter had used only the graphic resources available in printmaking and drawing, Manet removed the cited figures from their graphic context, transposing them into another: that of

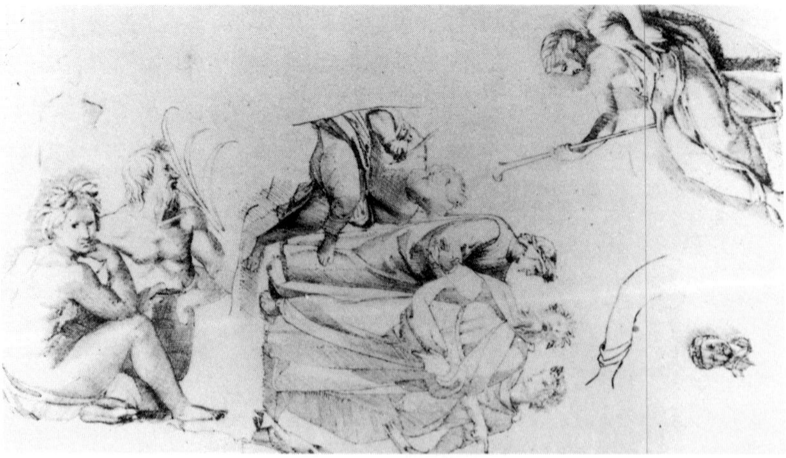

Figure 66. Edgar Degas, *Figures from "The Judgment of Paris,"* after Marcantonio Raimondi (Cambridge, Mass., Fogg Art Museum, Inv. no. 1956.10).

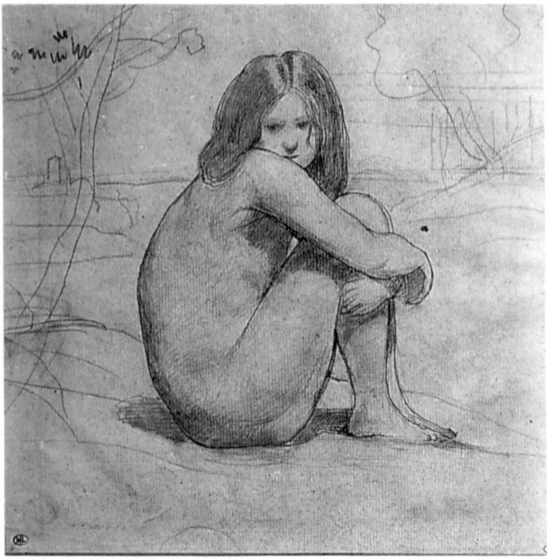

Figure 67. Camille Corot, *Petite fille dans un paysage*, charcoal with ink overtrace (Paris, Louvre, Graphic Arts Department).

painting as he understood it. Ernest Chesneau, the first critic to notice the Raphael citation, which he saw as amounting only to a "pecadillo," understood this perfectly: "What is more serious," he wrote in his account of the Salon des Refusés,

> is that M. Manet, while his tonal sensitivity is sometimes quite acute, has absolutely no idea how to draw. His taste is corrupted by a love for the bizarre, and yet he has awkward qualities that I dare—barely, in such a case—to call naive. This naiveté is not disagreeable, provided that it does not last, and that the young artist learns one day how to show us something other than fabrics that seem empty of the bodies supporting them. The figures of M. Manet unavoidably make one think of the marionettes on the Champs-Elysées: solid heads combined with limp clothing. If M. Manet's ignorance does not become systematic, we will eventually be grateful to him for having treated the live model frankly and for having taken up the brush before knowing how to wield the charcoal. He will owe—I hope—to this method a virginity of execution that is attractive and durable. If he makes a system of his clumsiness, his is a talent lost to art.[52]

The idea that in Manet painting is given precedence over drawing doubtless explains how Chesneau could see in the "live models" of the *Déjeuner* nothing but "fabrics that seem empty of the bodies supporting them." And how could the critic have borne, *in painting*, the gaze of this undressed woman, which so exemplifies the indifference that Georges Bataille maintained was central to Manet's art? "A supreme indifference, effortless and stinging; it scandalized but never deigned to take any notice of the shock it produced."[53] An indifference to everything, we might say, except painting, for that is indeed what's in question, and it is this quality, perhaps, that is responsible for the many resistances to this most intractable of masterpieces. How could Chesneau have borne this gaze: he who, maintaining that the exhibition was chock full of "horrible painting," found almost nothing to admire there except *The Adulterous Woman* by Armand Gautier, whom he praised for having treated a subject taken from his own time instead of rehashing yet again one of the themes favored by his predecessors,[54] or of—worse still—borrowing from Raphael a compositional idea in which a woman performed a role very different from that assigned her by an ethical system designed to favor specifically masculine interests?

The accordance to painting of a precedence over all other considerations partially explains the uneasiness prompted by looking at the *Déjeuner sur l'herbe*, and this aspect of the work is not unrelated (assuming my hypothesis is correct) to Raphael's agenda in choosing the judgment of Paris as the subject of what might properly be called a preliminary essay in the art of the *reproducible*—an essay that, as such, was governed by specific rules. Manet's operation in "lifting" a figural grouping from Marcantonio's engraving for use in the *Déjeuner* was a kind of experiment to test the limits of representability: the role of the woman in this configuration, her calculated "absence," constituting the best illustration of the system's inherent deficiencies, prompting the addition, by way of compensation, of the *parergon*, the "supplement."[55]

What might have been the intention behind Raphael's providing his engraver with a drawing conceived of specifically for reproduction? The additions, remarked by Vasari though without his realizing that they were more in the nature of a transformation, amount to a clear articulation of a theoretical point of view: it is as though Raphael meant to signal by this gesture that prints should not restrict themselves to the kinds of signifying operations most commonly associated with graphic representations, and to whose reproduction prints readily lent themselves. By showing Venus prevailing over her rivals, and above all over Minerva, who is placed on the composition's central axis, Raphael reiterated in his own way the celebrated formula used by Alberti to mark the distinction between painting and mathematics: whereas geometry has need only of points without extension, of lines without thickness, of surfaces without texture, art requires "a fatter Minerva."[56] And Raphael cast his demonstration in black and white, without recourse to color, using exclusively the means proper to drawing and to the print reproducing it, and through the subtle rearrangement of a consecrated iconographic model—a rearrangement that, in truth, might very well have been inscribed under an invocation of the "grey-eyed goddess," of Minerva, if the latter, although having laid aside her helmet and shield, weren't still in the process of disrobing.

According to Marcantonio's engraving, it might seem that as regards "form"—the same form that Kant held should proceed above all from drawing—art promises no "charms" and eschews all appeal to supplemental elements, beginning with color, which is a privilege of painting. And what are the stakes when art, or to stick with the question that has been our primary focus up to this point, what are the stakes when painting sets out to represent, in other words to stage, to repeat, to rehearse the judgment of Paris, using only those means available to engraving? It's as though the painter intended this gesture as a reminder, a silent one, that painting has roots outside of the realm of taste, of "pure" form, and that it has an inalienable "barbaric" component. When figured by the means available to painting, the scene can function as a theoretical proposition, or at least as an aesthetic one: namely, that art is inextricably linked to desire, and that it is governed by the pleasure principle. Other forms of beauty might be linked to various kinds of pleasure. But painting, as a *cosa mentale*, can address the mind as well as the senses, prompting a kind of pleasure consistent with understanding, perspicacity, and erudition. It can also combine diverse approaches to beauty, promising the viewer a premium of sensual pleasure (a "surplus-enjoyment factor") even as it manipulates highly sophisticated iconographic materials, and providing intellectual satisfaction even as it concentrates on visible forms. But Fréart is nonetheless on target when, breaking explicitly for the first time with a well-established moralizing tradition, he congratulates Paris for having chosen, in the person of Venus, a type of beauty that associated modesty with the grace of pure form, to say nothing of other decidedly lesser *charms* (ones less modest and pure). Note that the properly artistic dimension of the choice facing Paris is underlined by the presence of Mercury, who had long been regarded, at least in the Northern countries, as a patron of artists.

Whatever one might think of the position traditionally assigned the *Déjeuner sur l'herbe* at the beginning of modern painting or modern art, it remains significant (perhaps we should say "symptomatic") that Manet worked, like many others before him, in what should be termed the margins of classical art. It is common knowledge that modern art accords privileged status to what is supposed to have been "supplemental" to classical art (I use the conditional construction advisedly, theory and practice having diverged more or less consistently on this point): namely, color, materials, texture, and everything pertinent to non-form, if not to the formless (*l'informe*), to unprecedented types of formal organization, to *Gestaltung*. In other words, Manet did not simply repeat a masterpiece, simultaneously citing and parodying it in a knowing studio joke, with the intention of producing a masterpiece in his turn, even one that might justly be characterized as "modern." If in the history of modern painting the *Déjeuner sur l'herbe* corresponds to a—singularly perverse—kind of origin or point of departure, this is so to the extent that the painter was here deliberately working at the margins, operating on the supplement of the masterpiece (the "symbol" or figure of which is, in the Raphael, a landscape, a conventional example of which genre here, too, provides the backdrop): a masterpiece that, like Raphael's work, is intimately related, through the fable providing its subject, to the question of the judgment of taste, which leads us back to the problem raised at the beginning of our inquiry, that of beauty—of a beauty that, in this instance, must be termed "modern."

. . 11 . .

Turns, Returns, and Dodges

"The three goddesses are too nude."

On the ceiling of the Farnese Gallery in Rome, in one of the three large *quadri riportati* along its longitudinal axis, the Apple of Discord makes an entrance that has not been sufficiently remarked—and a conspicuous entrance it is, too, with Mercury plunging headlong, trumpet in hand, to give the apple to Paris, who is seated on a rock, grasping a long shepherd's staff in one hand and extending his other to receive this gift from heaven, while his dog, sitting beside him, looks up at the incongruous apparition with fury in his eyes (Figure 68). The scene includes no reference to the judgment to come, nor any indication of the events leading up to and following it, at a greater or lesser chronological remove. Paris receives the apple, the sign of his election, the way others receive the martyr's palm, devoid of emotion. It is true that, unlike the beholder, he is ignorant of the consequences; but this same beholder, however cultivated or well informed, might find himself wondering about the significance in this context of evoking a moment in the story of Paris never previously represented, at least autonomously—a moment as opposed to an episode, for the image results from what might be called, once again, a process of abstraction, entailing as it does the elimina-

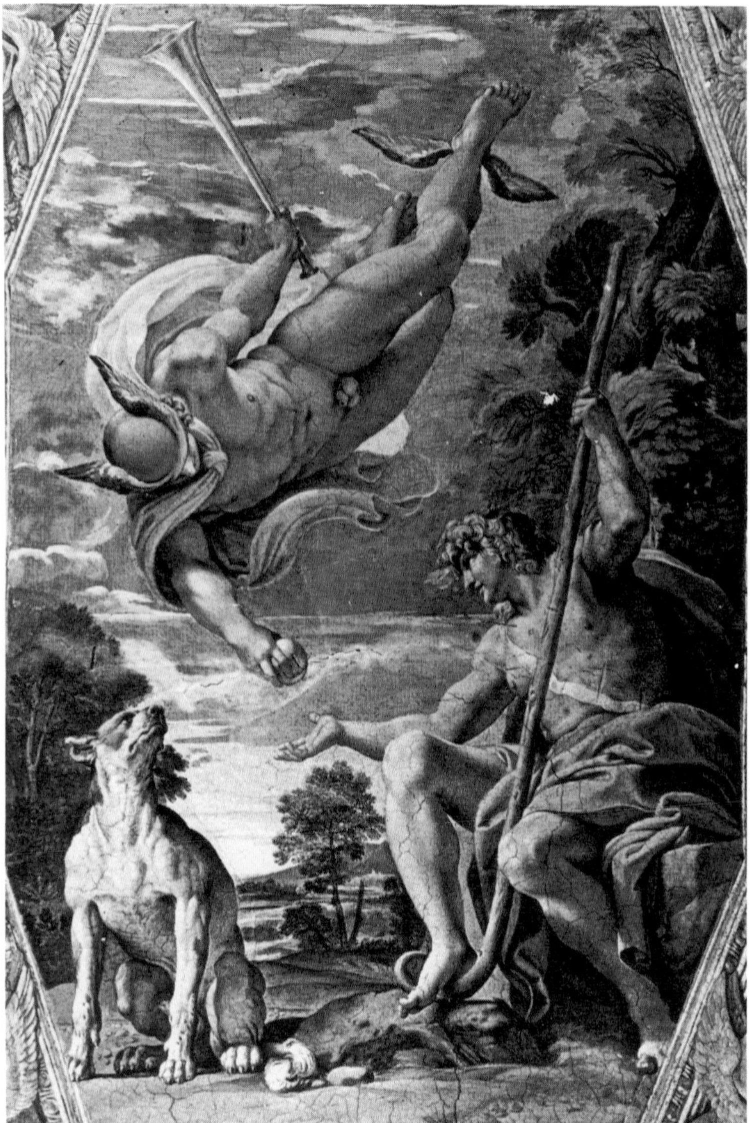

Figure 68. Annibale Carracci, *Mercury and Paris*, fresco, 1597–1600 (Rome, Palazzo Farnese).

tion of the object of the competition (the three women) and a spectacular highlighting of the judge's selection.[1]

What is the meaning of this image, and of its prominence, in the context of the iconographic subtleties of the Farnese Gallery? Charles Dempsey has demonstrated that Bellori's interpretation of its program holds up only in very general terms, since the original meaning of the loves-of-the-gods cycle on the ceiling, which was executed over a relatively short period of time by Annibale Carracci himself, was subsequently inflected, even substantially altered, when his students, working under his direction, reworked the stucco relief elements on the walls to allow for the addition of the two large compositions—*Perseus and Andromeda* and *Perseus and Phineus*—on which Bellori based his reading of the program as celebrating the victory of virtue over vice,[2] with Domenichino then supplementing the pairs of putti already in the corners of the vault with four Virtue figures (Justice, Temperance, Strength, and Charity, in the final bays of the long walls), adding as well the *Virgin with a Unicorn*, an allegory of chastity. The loves-of-the-gods images accrue a singular valence in this context, as Bellori himself realized, a consequence of there having been two successive painting campaigns (ceiling 1597–99, walls ca. 1604–8) governed by programs whose intentions were quite different, if not completely at odds with one another.[3] Paradoxically, the prominence here accorded the Paris story might seem consistent with Bellori's moralizing interpretation: Had not the theme of Paris's *choice* been traditionally associated with the thematic focus of another frescoed ceiling, the one in the young Cardinal Farnese's Camerino, painted by the same Annibale shortly after his arrival in Rome, which is organized around a depiction of Hercules seated at the crossroads between Vice and Virtue?

Conceived of by Fulvio Orsini, court librarian and mentor to the young cardinal, the decor of the Camerino is an allegorical panegyric cast in the mode of the *speculum principis*, the mirror of virtues of the ideal prince. It includes figures of the

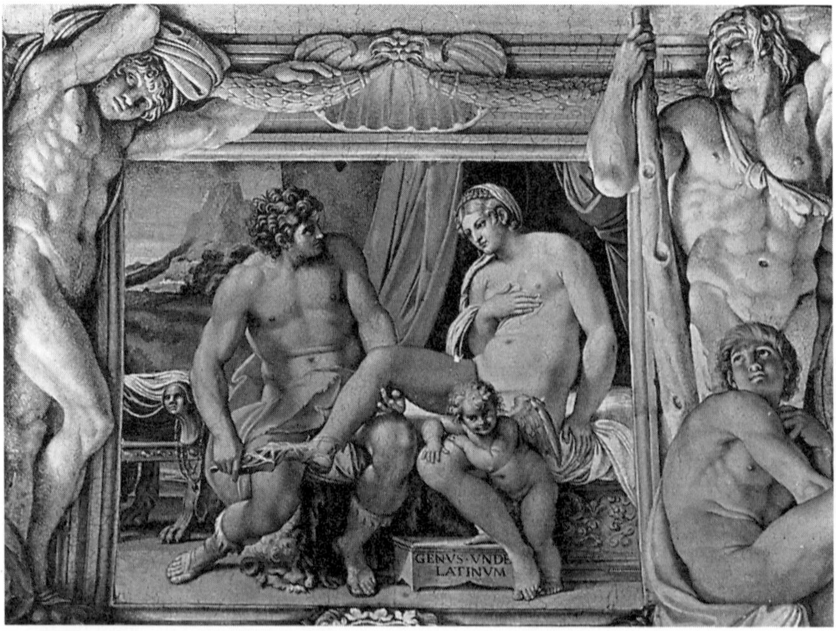

Figure 69. Annibale Carracci, *Venus and Anchises*, fresco (Rome, Palazzo Farnese).

four cardinal Virtues (Justice, Prudence, Strength, and Temperance), accompanied by corresponding narrative scenes in the lunettes: *Ulysses and the Sirens*, *Ulysses and Circe*, and, finally, providing a hint of the large compositions subsequently to be executed on the walls of the gallery, a *Perseus Decapitating the Medusa*, in the presence of Mercury, who personifies Reason, and Minerva, who lifts up the shield of Prudence.[4] Things are very different on the ceiling of the Farnese Gallery, painted by Annibale immediately after the Camerino: far from evoking virtues at odds with Paris's unfortunate decision but consistent with princely responsibilities, the three large *quadri riportati* disposed along the ceiling's length illustrate, as Dempsey has shown, the all-conquering power of love, which masters gods and mortals alike, including Venus herself—the whole cycle being dominated by a triumph of Bacchus and drunkenness, and treated in a pointedly playful and satirical style similar to

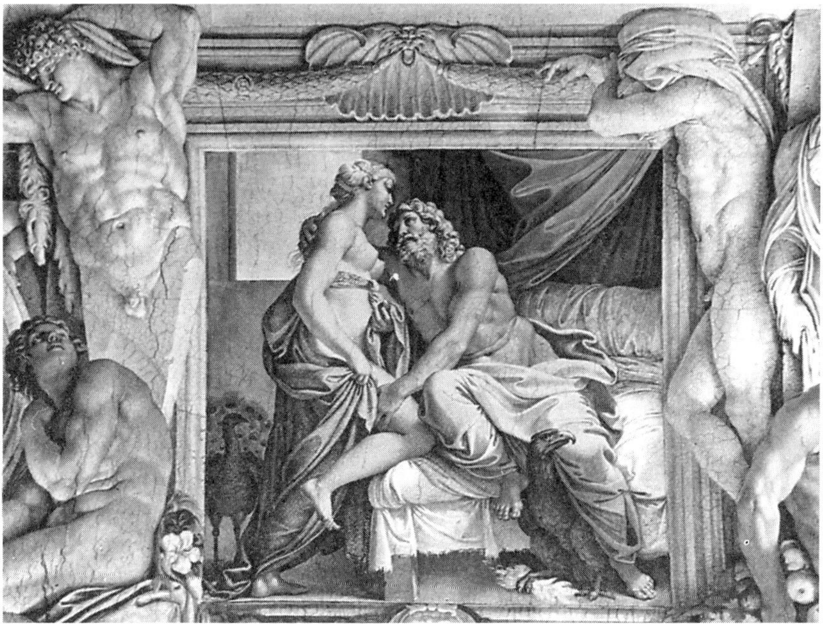

Figure 70. Annibale Carracci, *Jupiter and Juno*, fresco (Rome, Palazzo Farnese).

that adopted by Raphael in his decor for the entrance loggia of the Farnesina, across the Tiber, where the subject is not so much Cupid and Psyche as it is the jealousy of Venus and her own capitulation in the face of love.[5]

Among the four small *quadri integrati* set into the illusionistic architectural elements along the "frieze"—punctuated by terms and atlantes in grisaille and contrasting *ignudi*—ringing the vault, joining the *Paris and Mercury* and a depiction of Diana receiving wool from Pan, are two other images deserving of our attention: the first (Figure 69) represents Anchises all but kneeling at the feet of Venus, whose sandal he is removing (but, perhaps more than male subjection and the fruit of their union, which is recalled by the inscription below, *Genus unde Latinum* ("The origin of the Latin race"), a phrase that here acquires a satirical edge and is the only reference to the Trojan epic in the cycle, this image evokes the situation to which

Venus had been reduced when, according to the Homeric Hymn to Aphrodite, Jupiter decided to make her as vulnerable as the gods to the power of love[6]); and the second (Figure 70) shows Juno easing onto the bed of Jupiter, who leans back indolently, having allowed his thunderbolt to fall to the floor, while his eagle, nestling between his legs, looks out at the viewer with an indignant air very much like that of Paris's dog (a motif inspired, like the overall conception of the scene, by the depiction of Venus and Jupiter in Raphael's loggia at the Farnesina).

The image takes its subject from a famous passage in the *Iliad*, already discussed, in which Hera, having decided to distract Zeus so that the Achaians can gain the upper hand on the battlefield, sets out "to array herself in loveliness" such that her divine husband would be "taken with desire to lie in love with her next her skin, that she might be able to drift an innocent warm sleep across his eyelids, and seal his crafty perceptions."[7] Apparently suspecting that her own *charis* would prove insufficient to achieve this end, Hera goes to Aphrodite, her enemy in the Trojan conflict, and asks her, under false pretenses, to give her "loveliness and desirability, graces with which you overwhelm mortal men, and all the immortals"—a request that the "laughter-loving" goddess (*philomeidēs*) could hardly refuse: Did not Hera sleep in the arms of Zeus, the supreme master? "She spoke, and from her breasts unbound the elaborate, pattern-pieced zone (*keston imanta poikilon*), and on it are figured all beguilements (*oi thelktēria panta*), and loveliness (*philotetes*) is figured upon it, and passion of sex is there (*imeros*), and the whispered endearment (*parphasis*) that steals the heart away even from the thoughtful." Aphrodite places this object in Hera's hands, then calls her by name and says: "Take this zone, and hide it away in the fold of your bosom. It is elaborate, all things are figured therein. And I think that whatever is your heart's desire shall not go unaccomplished."[8]

This "ribbon" (*imas*), belt, zone, or "girdle" (*kestos*) of Aphrodite is visible in Annibale's fresco, knotted just beneath

Hera's voluptuous breasts.[9] It also appears in Lucian's playlet, in which Minerva requires that Aphrodite remove it when they undress before their judge. Thus this ribbon, belt, zone, or "girdle" functions as an element of the *parergon*, and so is ornamental. But there is more: it also figures as a binding, and in two different senses. First, it is designed to seduce by means of guile, *mētis*, as indicated by the epithet *poikilos* that is applied to it: Detienne and Vernant have demonstrated that its elusive character follows from the most intimate nature of the *mētis*, which is multiple and ever-changing, fertile in invention, surprise, and enigma, all of which it uses to secure its hold over its object. "Her sinuous *mētis*, her skill in setting traps, her insatiable desire to deceive and seduce make Aphrodite a goddess to be feared in equal measure by both gods and men,"[10] one who, presiding over amorous unions and accompanied by Love, Desire, and the Graces, and having been born from the foam of the sperm (*aphros*) escaping from the severed genitals of her father, is possessed of a power that is ambiguous—like that of eloquence, of which she is the mistress.[11] But Aphrodite is caught in her own trap when Hephaistos, the deceived husband, throws his net over her and Ares in an adulterous coupling; and she is also subject to constraints imposed by her very function, as is shown by Hera's deceitful borrowing of her belt to outwit Zeus's vigilance, thereby assuring the victory of the Greeks over the Trojans. The interpretation of Venus's belt current in the Middle Ages was rather similar: according to Lemaire de Belges (who did not know Greek and read Homer in Latin translation), what he called the *Ceston* (from the Latin *cestus*, girdle) was forged by Dame Nature to constrain lascivious Venus "through shame and conjugal laws": it was not so much a belt of chastity as one of control, of repression, and the goddess was supposed to wear it only for legitimate nuptials (as Juno was authorized to use it in seducing her husband). "And this is why every other kind of congress between woman and man is called incest, when Venus is not wearing the *Ceston* belt,"[12] as she was not in her encounter with Paris—an encounter that might be called "incestuous" in this sense, since it violated, at least symbolically, the prohibition reputed to be at the root of culture.

The two other small *quadri riportati*, *Hercules and Omphale* and *Diana and Endymion*, are quite appropriate in a loves-of-the-gods cycle, as are the pseudo-*Galatea* and the *Cephalus and Aurora*, as well as the two episodes featuring Polyphemus and Galatea at either end of the vault and the *Triumph of Bacchus and Ariadne* in its center. But what of the *Mercury and Paris*? Dempsey thinks the rationale for its presence here becomes apparent when it is considered in tandem with the symmetrically placed *Diana and Pan*, as both represent gifts from heaven to earth. But this argument does not hold up, as the latter image features a gift in the other direction, from earth to heaven (Pan's offering to Diana of immaculate wool), and its companion a gift from heaven to earth, making for a kind of circular, up-and-down movement that frames the horizontal composition of the *Triumph*.[13] From an iconographic perspective, the important thing about these two images is that in both of them the gift in question functions as a token in an interaction with erotic implications. This is straightforward in the case of Pan's seduction of Diana; as for Paris, the gift of the apple establishes, for better or worse, his position as judge in a trial whose outcome is predetermined, as the context of the decor as a whole makes clear. Mercury's function here is to place the apple in circulation, thereby symbolically initiating a play of exchanges presided over by Love and in whose network various partners become trapped, as instanced by Anchises's removal of Venus's sandal and the knotted "girdle" under Juno's breasts. And there is more: Mercury places it in circulation, this apple, as an indicator that erotic relations between gods and mortals are at an end and that another kind of history is about to begin.

But what of the *Cestus*? What of this supplement to attractions that, whether those of Juno or Venus, were already quite eloquent in themselves? The Greek word *kestos* designates something that is quilted or embroidered and, thus, by extension a belt with ornament of a variegated character appropriate to Aphrodite, as it figures the elusive nature of her attractions, her charms. If Aphrodite could maintain that this ribbon contained all charms (in every sense of the word) as well as tenderness and the most passionate desire, that is because the Greek term *imeros* designates not only desire but also the attractions that inspire it. The problem being to determine the nature of these eventually deceptive charms, represented as "artificial," added to those declared to be "natural." To determine the relation between those artful attractions inherent in the *poikilos* and others that are less colored, more plastic, despite their participating in form only in its plural aspect. To determine the nature of this "more" (when they are supplementary) or this "less" (when Venus is obliged to do without them, falling back on the allure and charm of her forms, again in the plural). The same question is posed by the decor of the Farnese Gallery, and in particular by its ceiling, which plays, in a literally exemplary way, on the notion of the *parergon:* beginning with its accentuation of the status and function of the frame and of framing in the constitution of these images, which, though painted in fresco (as are the frames themselves and the ensemble of the decor, including its feigned architectural armature), present themselves as canvases either "added" (to the decor), "integrated" (into the decor), or "superimposed" (*sovraposti*)—when, that is, they don't get in the way of the framing elements, or even with one another (see Figure 71). For the very fact that paintings, even fictive ones, can be *added* to a decor made up of stuccos, garlands, shells, masks, and bronze medallions as well as reliefs, statues, and architectonic elements (including the herms and atlantes punctuating the false frieze) which are themselves illusionistic attests to the singularity of the mimetic economy: these paintings that are not paintings, these fictive canvases that resemble real ones, "hung" from walls that are not walls (their flat surfaces are made to appear as though they extend to the top of the false

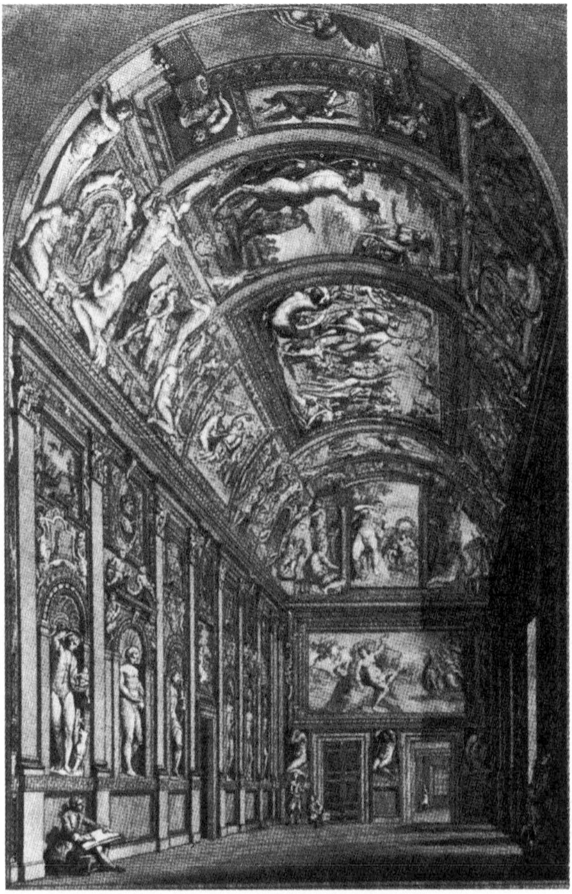

Figure 71. View of the Farnese Gallery, nineteenth-century print by Pietro Bettelini after an etching by Giovanni Volpato.

frieze, which is actually painted on the vault), do not so much constitute as *represent* the supplement from which the ensemble of the decor supposedly derives its meaning—as though (note well: *as though*) the iconographic dimension corresponds in the end to a kind of surplus value.

Philippe Morel has proposed a magisterial analysis of what he calls the syntactical structure of this decor, even of its semiology, showing how its novelty derives from a pointed split or fracture between two distinct orders of representation: a narrative one, contained within the traditional limits of painting, and an ornamental one, operative throughout the ceiling's different levels. One cannot simply maintain, like Donald Posner, that the ornamental component here prevails over the iconographic program.[14] If "decor" there be, in this instance, it operates as a *system*, as a play of exchanges, governed by strict rules of opposition, inversion, and substitution, between the different representational registers, which means that the iconographic program accrues its true meaning—like a suite or "gallery" of paintings—by way of a decor treated illusionistically, while the "paintings" themselves are given a fictive quality that is somewhat paradoxical, as it derives in equal measure from an evocation of the thinness of their support and the massiveness of their gilt frames. But these frames, which define the limits of the "paintings," are produced by the decor, by the ornament. And it follows from this that the beholder finds himself implicated not so much in the detour of the said "paintings" as in that of the ornamental framework, which, as I have said, is treated illusionistically, *da sotto in su*, and "lit" in a way consistent with the gallery's natural light. But the best illustration of the system's economy is that furnished—*à la limite*, to use Morel's phrase—by the pairs of putti (Eros and Antéros) placed at the four corners of the vault "behind" the false frieze, standing on a balustrade beyond which we glimpse patches of blue sky. As a result of operations central to the scheme's conception, which encompasses both fictive decor and fictive canvases, these putti are situated at a frontier between two spaces, one that is aerial and exterior and another that is architectonic and interior, while in symbolic terms they occupy points of juncture between the ornamental and narrative orders: "they escape the limits of the *tableau* but interpellate or designate the content."[15]

In this context, the obligatory reference to Raphael, and above all to the Raphael of the Farnesina, which was doubtless very much in Annibale's mind during the execution of the gallery,[16] prompts us to reformulate the problem of the presence, in this place and in this scheme, of the *Mercury and Paris.* The depiction of the delivery to Paris of the apple, the sign of his election, from which all explicit reference to the object of the debate has been abstracted, signifies that in principle his choice is open: the moment of freedom is, as it were, suspended, seized, fixed by the operations of painting, like Mercury in his headlong plunge. And while the overall context might well predispose us to think that Paris is by this action *bound,* caught in a trap, as he would soon be obliged to place the apple in circulation once more, if not to give it to Venus, the judgment expected of him remains first and foremost an aesthetic judgment: *pulchriori detur,* "to be given to the most beautiful." This *Mercury and Paris,* a fresco made to seem like a painting on canvas, brings to mind Marcantonio's engraving, which Fréart describes with reference to a painting it was to, if not reproduce, then at least represent (to the point of taking its place): when considered in the context of the overall scheme, Annibale's image, like the figures introduced in the print *per capriccio,* raises the question of what is, or might be, the function of the supplement, of the *parergon,* with regard to beauty. As if to amplify this problematic, on a lower level, on the real walls of the Farnese Gallery, there are two images—like a recall to order, or to reality—of a powerful force, namely, the Medusa: the white of the bodies petrified by the sight of her head contrasting markedly with the heros' pink complexion, just as do the white "stone" terms and atlantes in the "frieze" with the fleshy *ignudi* (Figure 72).

According to the classic version of the legend, Hermes, messenger of the gods, did nothing more than again place in circulation, on Jupiter's orders, the apple tossed by Eris, the goddess of Discord, onto the gods' banquet table at the wedding of Peleus and Thetis, instructing Paris to give it in turn to the goddess judged by him to be "the most beautiful" of the three. This last point is important if we accept that the constraints governing the fable manifest, in the final analysis, a properly

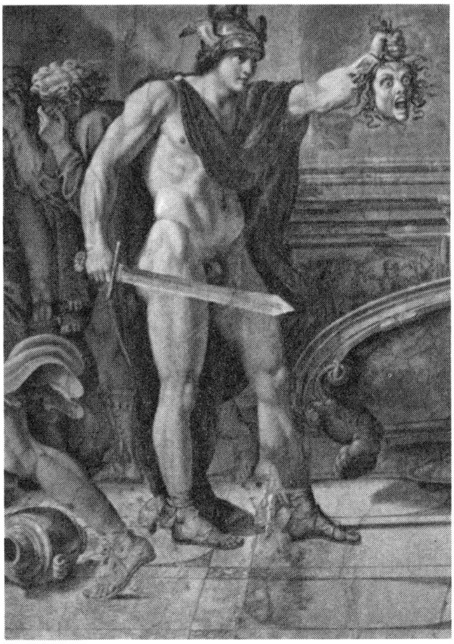

Figure 72. Annibale Carracci, *Perseus and Phineus*, fresco (Rome, Palazzo Farnese).

mythic dimension: if so, the choice in question would be not only an instance—rare in the Greek world—of the trifunctional schema so central to Indo-European ideology; it would also be consistent with the rule of rights and interests current in Archaic societies, which are premised on an exchange of gifts that, while in theory voluntary, is in fact compulsory.[17] My reference here to Marcel Mauss's "Essay on Gifts" being justified by an allegory transmitted by Seneca in which the group of the three Graces, so akin to that of the three goddesses, as I have been emphasizing, is seen to figure the three successive moments in the gift cycle: giving, receiving, and bestowing, in turn.

In this context, it is tempting to interpret the three rivals' promises to their judge less as an attempt to sway him than as a way of investigating the process initiated by the bestowal of the apple, as an effort to place it within a general framework of exchange. But a problem arises, one that has less to do with the promises than with the apple itself, for it seems to have first appeared in literature, if not in art, relatively late. Many authors of the pre-Christian era, mostly of the second rank, exploited the theme of the three promises, and Albert Severyns even sees the account of the Paris story offered by the grammarian Apollodorus as proof that the episode had taken its definitive form in the *Cyprian Lays*, the previously discussed lost poem postdating the writing down of the Homeric poems, from which it took several themes, configuring them into a kind of prelude to the *Iliad.* The passage in question mentions the three promises as well as Eris's tossing of the apple (the latter apparently an interpolation).[18] By contrast, the summary of events prior to the *Iliad* given by another grammarian, Proclus, in his *Chrestomathy*—of all Byzantine Homeric manuscripts, the one closest to the poem—makes no mention of the apple, referring only to Aphrodite's promise.[19] And even this is only obliquely invoked, which Severyns sees as an indication there was no need to enter into the details because all readers could be expected to the know the story. But then the same argument could be used regarding the apple. The fact remains, however, that the latter first appeared in texts of the Roman era: in Lucian, who characterized it as an "invention of the poets," and in Apuleius's *Golden Ass*, where the judgment of Paris provided the story for the musical pantomime already mentioned, which Gombrich believes inspired the program of Botticelli's *Primavera.*[20] Ovid, however, doesn't mention the apple in his account of the judgment of Paris in the *Heroides.*[21] And it was only in the *Clementine Homilies* (second century), whose unknown author was a contemporary of Lucian, that an allegorical interpretation of the episode was first proposed, the one that was retained by Lemaire de Belges.[22]

Continuing to explore the relevance of the gift and countergift model, we must ask: does the above information suggest that the motif of the Apple of Discord may have been introduced after the fact to counter the theme of the three promises? There is hard evidence to refute this interpretation: archeologists have discovered Etruscan mirrors of the fourth and third centuries B.C. and, above all, an ivory comb found at Sparta, from level Laconian I (700–635 B.C.), which show, along with the earliest known depiction of Athena as helmeted, Paris holding out to Aphrodite a spherical object that must be an apple (Figure 73).[23] While the motif could have appeared in art—if only the "industrial" or commonplace variety—before it made its way into literature, Severyns is inclined to dismiss this possibility, arguing that the apple shown here in Paris's hand is not that of Discord but that of Victory, an apple analogous to those awarded the winners in the Pythian games. *Mēlon sēma nikēs*, the apple as sign of victory: the generic quality of this motif facilitated its subsequent integration into all sorts of contexts, including erotic ones: it came to be used, for example, as a token by which a lover acknowledged a woman's triumph over him.[24]

Raphael depicts Aphrodite, and Fréart de Chambray describes her, as receiving this prize "with a modesty accompanied by all the grace one can imagine." And how could it be otherwise, if we concur with Lessing that, for both sculptors

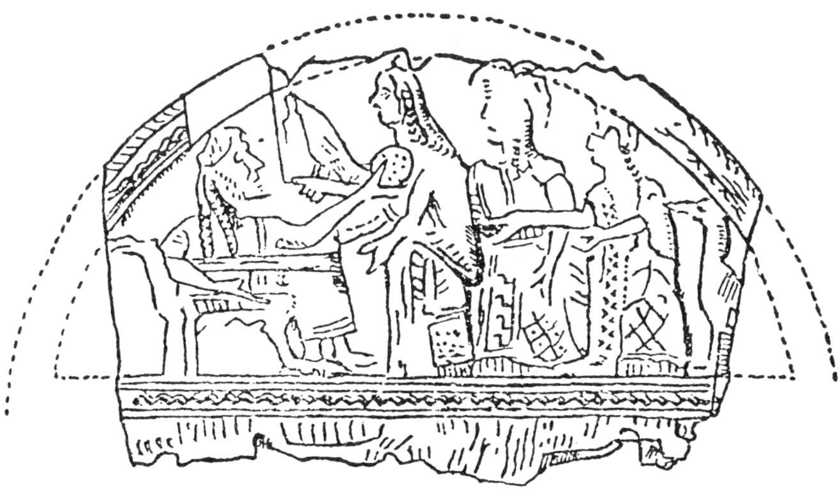

Figure 73. *The Judgment of Paris*, ivory comb found at Sparta (eighth–seventh century B.C.). Drawing by R. M. Dawkins (1929).

and painters, Venus is the goddess of Love? "Hence he must give her all the modest beauty and all the graceful charm which delight us in an object we love and which we therefore associate with our abstract conception of love. The slightest deviation from this ideal makes its form unrecognizable to us. Give it beauty, but with more majesty than modesty, and we have not a Venus, but a Juno. Give it charms, but those which are more commanding and masculine than graceful, and we have not a Venus, but a Minerva. Worst of all, a wrathful Venus, a Venus driven by fury and the desire for revenge, is, to the sculptor [and to the painter] a complete contradiction in terms, for love as such is never wrathful or vengeful."[25]

The painted image must be identifiable otherwise than by its name, for the "unrecognizability" (*das Verkennen*) mentioned by Lessing corresponds to an error with regard to person (or personification). Such is not the case in poetry, for it can always resort to *naming*. "To the artist [the gods] are personified abstractions which must always retain the same characteristics if they are to be recognized. To the poet, on the other hand, they are real, acting beings who, in addition to their general character, possess other qualities and feelings which, as circumstances demand, may stand out more prominently than the former." The poet can speak of Venus and can even pronounce her name, ascribing actions to her explicitly, but the artist must present her such that vision and understanding can ascertain that she is indeed the goddess of Love: in other words, such that neither her actions nor her attributes impede this identification. "To the poet . . . , Venus is, to be sure, Love, but she is also the goddess of Love who has, besides this characteristic, her own individual personality and hence must be just as capable of the impulses of aversion as those of affection. It is no wonder, then, that in his depiction she is inflamed with indignation and rage, especially when offended love itself has excited these feelings in her."[26]

Ernst Gombrich, following Aby Warburg, has rightly insisted on the ambivalence of the figure of Venus in the Renaissance, and even of the title "the Goddess of Love," pointing out the multiple and even contradictory meanings of this "symbol" during the period.[27] Limiting ourselves to present concerns, the same Venus whom Christine de Pisan exhorted her aspiring knight to set aside in favor of Minerva would be used in quattrocento chivalric poetry both as an allegory of courtly love and as the name of a planet that supposedly held sway over pleasure, love, the return of spring, and the sanguinic temperament. But in the matter of love, it was not the image so carefully fabricated by humanists that was the most popular: beginning with Marsilio Ficino, who in his commentary on the *Symposium* expounded the Platonic theory of the "two Venuses" and the two forms of "furor" they were reputed to embody.[28] According to Gombrich, it is Filarete who was the first to mention a painting of Venus depicting her in a way consistent with nascent Renaissance traditions, in this instance in a Temple of Vice, where she appears in the company of Bacchus and Priapus, emerging from the foam on a shell, crowned with myrtle, carrying a dove, and exclaiming: "All you, old and young, rich and poor, who have an instrument like that of Priapus, come visit our convent where you will be well received by us" (this inscription being translated into several languages—Latin, Italian, Greek, Hungarian, German, French, etc.—to assure its general accessibility[29]). Cartari says much the same thing in his *Imagini dei Dei:* Venus is less the goddess of Beauty—which was placed under her charge, and was bestowable by her on anyone she saw fit—than the Goddess of Desire and Lust, planting in men's hearts libidinous impulses and lascivious appetites: this being so because she is the overseer of reproduction, in which capacity she presides, with Hymen and Juno, at human nuptials, whose ultimate goal is generation by means of carnal intercourse.[30]

Formulating this question in terms of representability, as does Cartari,[31] it would seem that Venus must be depicted in the nude: not to make her visible in all her beauty, but because "intercourse is better and more agreeably accomplished without clothes than when wearing them"—unless, as Cartari suggests, we discern a moral intention here and see Venus's nudity as signifying that everything, both body and soul, is placed at risk by surrendering to the voracity of lascivious women, which leads to one's becoming prey to *furti amorosi*, to furtive libidinal impulses: as evidenced by the suspicious stain left on Praxiteles' Cnidian Aphrodite by an overly ardent visitor, an indelible mark of his concupiscence (in Pliny's words, *eiusque cupiditatis indicem maculam*).[32] But Cartari's Venus is victorious as well as lascivious: he cites the epigram from Ausonius in which Minerva addresses a statue of Venus representing her as armed, in Sparta, in terms consistent with my argument:

> The moment has come to end this
> Quarrel, which has made you so proud,
> And to accept Paris as judge: to which [Venus]
> Responded, ah! shameless one, so you hope
> To carry the day by arms over me, who
> Has already conquered you nude, and without arms?[33]

A lascivious Venus, yes. A victorious Venus, yes. But a furious Venus? Could it be that there aren't any images of an "enflamed" Venus (which is not the same as saying there are not images of Venus that excite desire: Gombrich cites the famous letter from Aretino to Federico Gonzaga about Sanovino's Venus, which is said to fill with desire the mind—and not the heart—of all who contemplate it.[34])? Could it be that such images are not possible because they are at odds with the dictates of *representability* and would necessarily lead to misunderstandings? The question at issue here is, precisely, how to set the parameters of an iconology that would not limit itself to the forms of "ideal" beauty, one that could accommodate a relation to beauty other than a "sublimated" one. But does such an iconology make sense in the absence of anger and rage? Botticelli has given us a Venus who is wide awake, mistress of herself as well as of the putti playing with the arms of Mars, who slumbers beside her. This Venus is akin to Cranach's. But

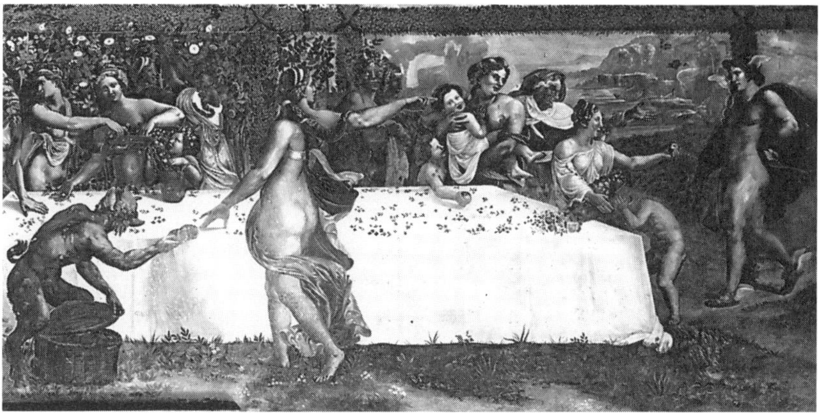

Figure 74. Giulio Romano, *The Wedding Banquet of Psyche*, fresco, detail (Mantua, Palazzo del Te, Psyche Room).

the authority appropriate to the victorious goddess (even in the absence of arms) is still more clearly evident in the decor of the Psyche Room in the Palazzo del Te, in Mantua. There, in its fresco of the banquet at the wedding of Cupid and Psyche (largely executed by Giulio Romano himself, in the service of the same Federico Gonzaga to whom Aretino addressed his letter; Figure 74), Venus strides across the foreground—her girdle riding high above her waist—and twists backwards, gesturing imperiously toward a table at the right onto which a youth has just emptied the contents of a basket, from which a woman has taken an apple, offering it to Mercury, who is close by; it is as though Aphrodite were saying in an aside, as a kind of historical gloss: "Make no mistake, this is a gift that is destined for me, and that eventually will come to me, in another fable, another '*histoire*'; these apples are mine, and I take Mercury as witness to what I say, for he, too, will be of the party!"

If we concede that the events following those narrated in the *Cyprian Lays* and leading to Troy's destruction resulted from a deliberate plan on Zeus's part, then it follows that Discord herself was only an instrument in his hands—and that her presence alone at the banquet would have sufficed to initiate a quarrel between the three goddesses, even if she had tossed the

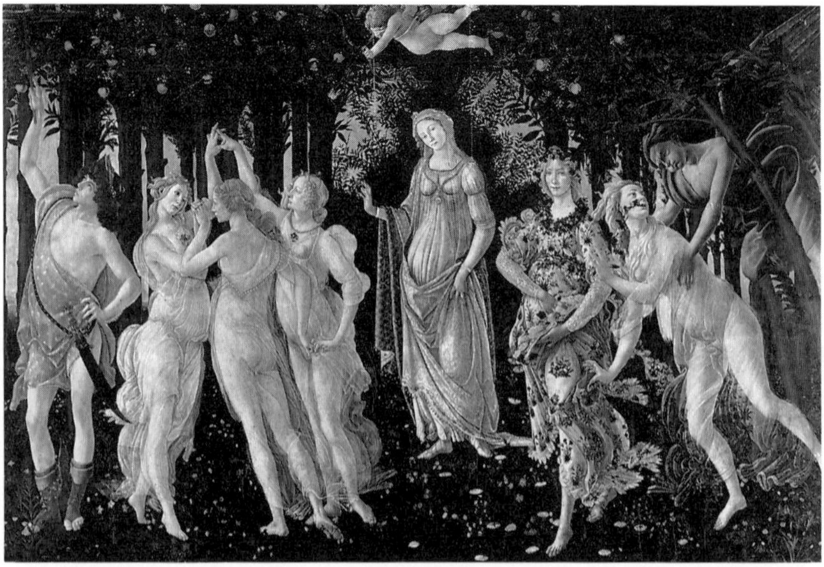

Figure 75. Sandro Botticelli, *La Primavera*, 1478 (Florence, Uffizi).

apple without saying a word, or had exclaimed "To be claimed by the most beautiful!," or if the apple had borne a similar inscription. Paradoxically, the Neoplatonists saw this same Love—which, according to Christine de Pisan, was fraught with traps to be avoided by those wishing to escape Discord's clutches ("Erys la deese de discorde / Maulv sont ses liens et sa corde / Les noces peleus troubla / Dont puis maintes gents assembla")—as an instrument of that Concord symbolized by the three Graces, who, so tenderly intertwined, adorn Venus's cortege in Botticelli's *Primavera* (Figure 75). The same judgment of Paris in which Christine de Pisan saw an illustration of Discord's misdeeds would be cited by Marsilio Ficino as a cautionary tale demonstrating the nature of good choice: in his view, Paris, instead of selecting one of the options presented him, should have embraced all three, in an image of the *triplex vita* advocated by him.[35]

The Apple of Discord is also visible in one of Dürer's most beautiful and enigmatic engravings, which is dated 1497 and

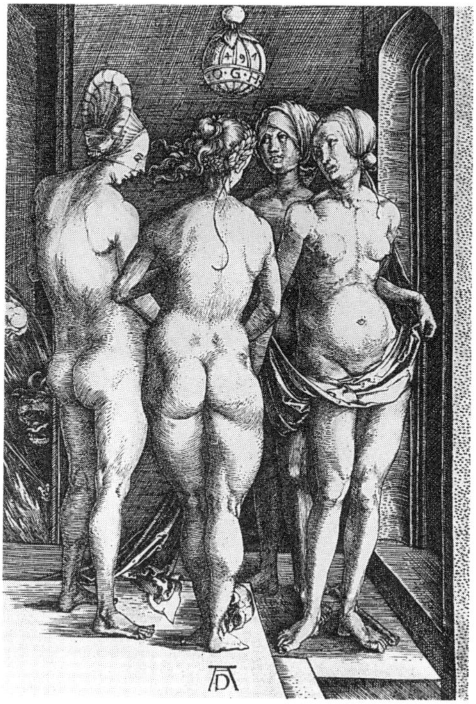

Figure 76. Albrecht Dürer, *Discordia* (formerly known as *The Four Witches*), engraving, 1497.

was exhibited at the Nuremberg quincentenary exhibition under the title *Discordia* (Figure 76). Assessment of this image is complicated by the fact that a print, after Dürer's engraving, made by Nicoletto da Modena around 1500 is explicitly presented as a *Judgment of Paris:* the three goddesses are identifiable by their respective attributes and the apple bears the inscription *pulchriori detur.* Such is not the case in Dürer's image, and the three letters OGH on the ornamented globe suspended above its group of four women have been variously interpreted since Eugène Duthuit proposed that they referred to the motto of Discord (*Odium Generis Humanis*).[36] Jessie Poesch saw this engraving as an image, not of the choice offered to Paris, nor of the judgment itself, but rather of the result of his choice, a reading she based on the presence of a skull at the feet of the central figure, identified by her as Venus, and by the glimpse of Hell visible at the left.[37] Panofsky did not find this interpretation congenial, rejecting Poesch's suggestion that the image shows the three rival goddesses along with Discord herself in the background and retaining the description he had proposed in his great book on Dürer, namely that it is an enigmatic group akin to that of the three Graces, or perhaps directly modeled after a classical source.[38]

Poesch's hypothesis is oddly similar to one proposed by Gombrich in connection with Botticelli's *Primavera.* To be sure, Gombrich rejects the argument put forward in a nineteenth-century guidebook, whose readers were bluntly informed that the title of this first great mythological painting of the Renaissance was *The Judgment of Paris.*[39] But movement from this last theme to the group of the three Graces is easily accomplished by metonymy, especially if texts such as Apuleius's are taken into consideration. Gombrich's subtle and attractive hypothesis is that the *Primavera* was devised as a kind of visual lesson—one consistent with ideas about pedagogy proposed by humanists like Ficino, who argued that making virtue's beauty visible was preferable to describing it in words—for the young Lorenzo di Pierfrancesco de' Medici, the cousin of Lorenzo the Magnificent (and the model for Alfred de Musset's "Lorenzaccio"): led in front of the painting he would have, in Gombrich's words, "completed the context" by positioning himself as the recipient of Venus's address while retaining his freedom of choice, like Paris. That Ficino's letter to this same *Laurentius minor* (cited by Gombrich in support of his argument) instructs him not to have contempt for Venus, who is assimilated to *Humanitas*—that is, to the ideal of refinement and culture that was to replace the chivalric one for the Florentine merchant class—in his own astrological "heaven,"[40] does not preclude our being tempted to see the two other female figures on the right as Juno, sumptuously attired, and Minerva, whom an aerial being is trying to disrobe, as in numerous *Judgment of Paris* images, beginning with those by Rubens. At least their appearance invites such speculation, assuming we don't push it too far, a temptation that has not always been

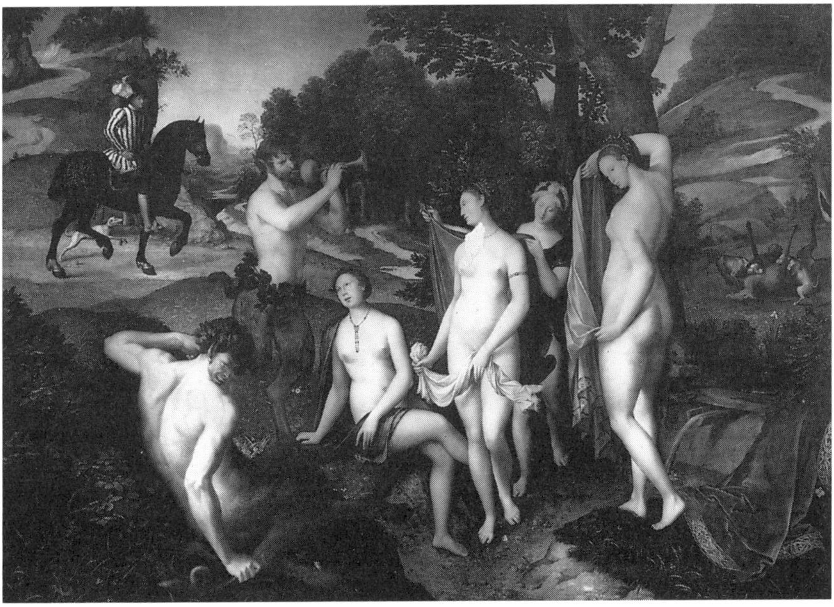

Figure 77. François Clouet (c. 1505–72), *The Bath of Diana* (Rouen, Musée des Beaux-Arts).

resisted in attempts to read the three Graces or three rival goddesses into Dürer's engraving. Sometimes confusion of this kind has been deliberate, as in *The Bath of Diana* by François Clouet (Figure 77), in which the goddess is surrounded by two other female figures who might be her rivals, forming with her a group that tends to evoke the three Graces or even the group of the three goddesses in Marcantonio's print, while in the background Acteon is depicted as a fancy-dress knight not unlike Cranach's Paris, even in his being vouchsafed a remarkable vision.

But the three Graces—whom Apuleius made dance to the sound of a flute in Venus's train and whom Cartari, developing this idea, placed on Venus's chariot, showing the goddess of love holding the apple awarded her by Paris in her right hand, and in her left hand the three apples (smaller ones) sometimes exhibited by the three Graces and symbolizing them (Figure

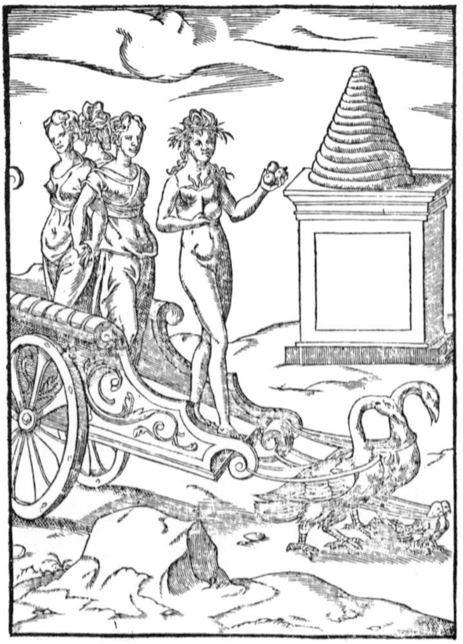

Figure 78. *The Chariot of Venus*, woodcut from Vincenzo Cartari, *Imagini dei dei degli antichi* . . . (Lyon, 1581), p. 446.

78)—resist univocal interpretation. We have seen how the Charites were originally an undifferentiated triad, a sign of multiplicity (as the heads of a three-headed monster could sometimes be) as opposed to a single figure's unity and a couple's binarity. It was only in an allegory long regarded as of Stoic origin, though it was in fact derived from a lost treatise on liberality by Chrysippus, that the three women were individuated in such a way that they could no longer appear to be interchangeable.[41] While the generic term used to designate them is richly suggestive in a Christian context, the Graces have not always prompted interpretations as positive as those proposed by the humanists. In the *Ovide moralisé*, we read that the warm and humid atmosphere associated with Venus makes her an image of the voluptuous life and that the three Graces in her train are symbols of the three sins linked to her: luxury, pride (or infidelity), and avarice (a trait subsequently taken up by Cartari[42]). But the text then goes on to assign them a positive meaning, as do most medieval writings on allegory.[43] A reading of Dürer's print as a depiction of Satanic "Graces" is perhaps just as closely linked to the "moralizing" tradition as one construing it as a representation of four witches (*Die vier Hexen*).

But the important point for my present argument lies elsewhere, namely in the precise configuration of the three Graces, which has influenced that of the three rival goddesses in depictions of the *Judgment of Paris.* The image of Venus's chariot in Cartari's publication is remarkable in that the three Graces turn their backs to one another and hold hands, much like the three women who make up the central pillar of Giovanni Pisano's pulpit in Pisa Cathedral, all the more "trinitarian" in that their arms and shoulders abut one another in an arrangement diametrically opposed to that adopted in Botticelli's *Primavera*, in which the three figures face one another. Neither of these formulas is of classical derivation. This is not the place for a detailed account of the discovery of the first ancient depictions of the three Graces and their influence in the quattrocento;[44] for present purposes we need only bear in mind that in *Della pittura* Alberti recommends Seneca's description of such a group to his artist-readers and that this text appeared a half-century before the discovery, in Rome, followed by much hoopla, of the Hellenistic marble group sent to Siena in 1502 and then prominently installed in the Piccolomini Library. Raphael himself adhered to this schema, hereafter understood to be of antique origin, in his small pendant to *The Dream of Scipio:* two of the Graces face the viewer, while the third (in the center) is seen from the back, as in the fresco from Pompeii now in the National Museum in Naples, as well as on the medal of Pico della Mirandola—the very Pico who would subsequently recommend that only one of the Graces be represented frontally and two from the back, the first being assimilated to permanence and perfection, which are not reflexive, and the other two embodying, respectively, will and understanding, which are reflexive and to which correspond the

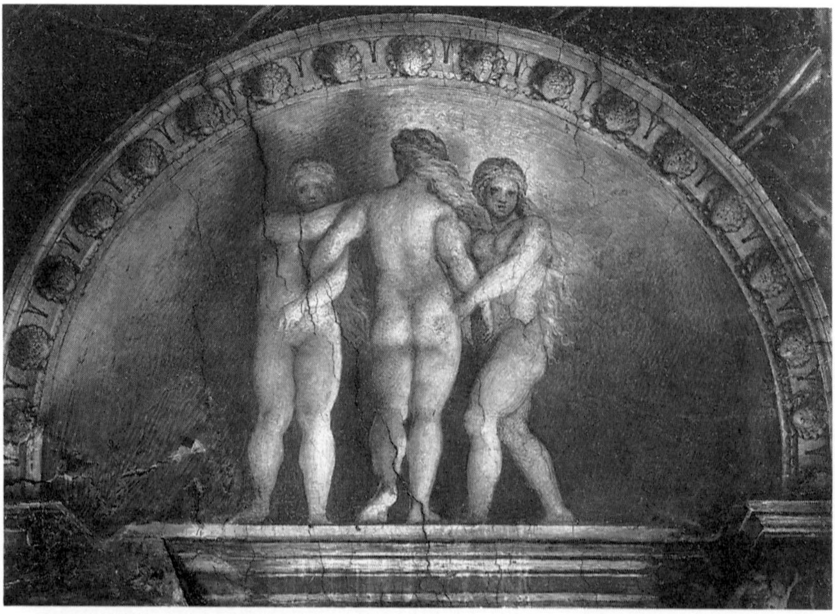

Figure 79. Correggio, *The Three Graces*, fresco, 1519 (Parma, Camera San Paolo).

splendor illuminating the latter and the desire animating the former ("reflexivity" here implying a reversed position).[45] The illustration in Valeriano's *Hieroglyphica* represents them nude but refashioned along lines set by late-medieval precedent, with the first of the Graces seen from the back, the second frontally, and the third in profile—the intention being, according to Edgar Wind, to *amplify* Seneca's argument such that the three figures signify, respectively, giving "without ostentation," receiving "publicly" and openly, and returning in a way that "hides" the restitution but "exhibits the benefit obtained."[46] It was in accordance with this model or program, in all its dissymmetry, that Corregio devised his group for a lunette in the Camera di San Paolo in Parma (Figure 79), and the same compositional idea also appears in a stucco medallion in the Vatican Loggie. While Cartari's trio of Graces turns on itself, for the greater pleasure of the beholder,[47] in these latter works all three principal views of the female body (front, back, profile) are seen within a single composition, and in a continuous chain.

* * *

Questions pertaining to Venus's authority and, through her, to that of beauty necessarily prompt others concerning the authority of the masterpiece, as well as that of the name attached to it, of the *auctoritas* of its author, and these queries in turn bring us to an interrogation of imitation and reproduction. In the matter of author's rights, Marcantonio's engraving is not an isolated case, far from it: many prints carry both the name of the engraver and that of the painter furnishing its design or model. It is nonetheless a remarkable example, for two reasons. First, as regards what we would call "copyright" today, its "invention" is explicitly assigned to Raphael. Second, long before attracting Manet's attention, the Raphael/Marcantonio *Judgment of Paris* served as a model for numerous drawings and prints more or less faithful to the original, when not themselves derived from paraphrases: as was an engraving by Jean Mignon (Figure 80), the first in a series of six representing episodes from the Trojan war, which was directly copied from a drawing by Luca Penni (discussed in chapter 6) in which the nymphs and their companions look directly toward the scene of judgment in the foreground: the engraver having accentuated the composition's "pastoral" aspect by eliminating the *nike* figure crowning Venus and emphasizing the rustic quality of the landscape, fitting it out with a shepherd's cottage reminiscent of Serlio's "satyric scene."[48] By contrast, other mannerist printmakers would increase the erudite complexity of Marcantonio's engraving: a large print dated 1555 by Giorgio Ghisi, though it bears the "copyright" mark of Giovanni Battista Bertani, shows Juno and Minerva having stepped down from their chariot, accompanied by putti trying to disrobe them, while Venus remains in hers (Figure 81). The nymphs

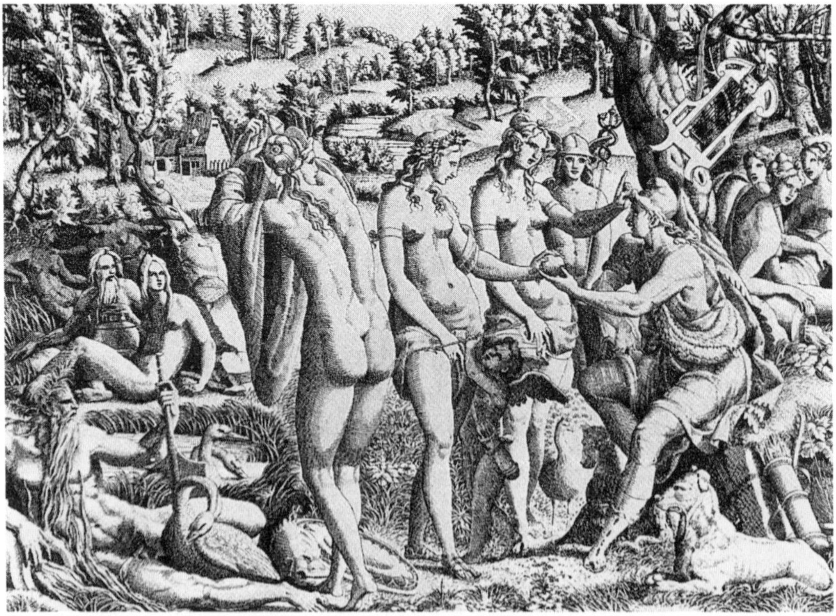

Figure 80. Jean Mignon, *The Judgment of Paris*, engraving after Lucca Penni, c. 1545.

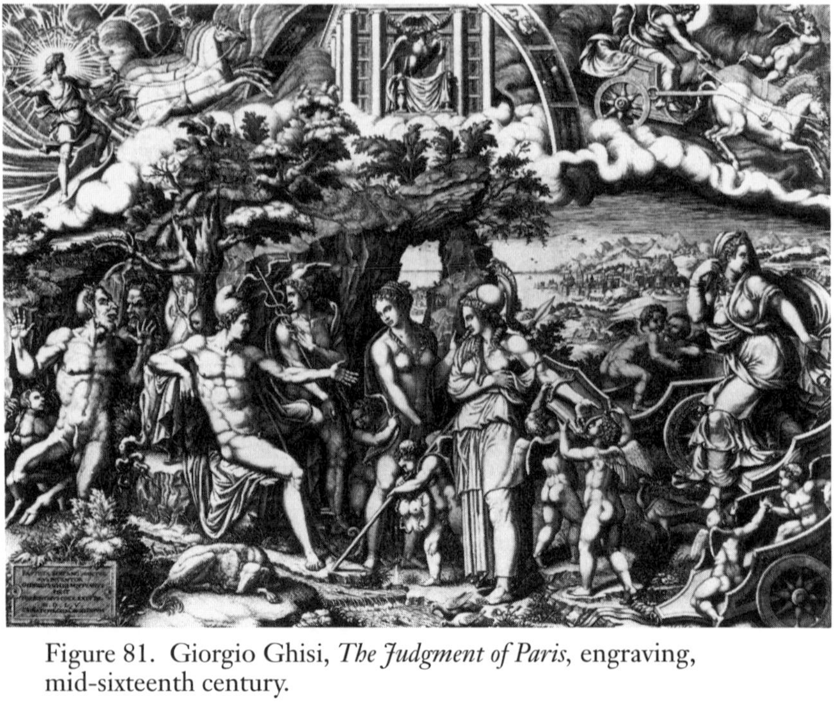

Figure 81. Giorgio Ghisi, *The Judgment of Paris*, engraving, mid-sixteenth century.

and river gods have been replaced by grimacing fauns, but the "sky" here is occupied by a zodiac rainbow analogous to that in Marcantonio's print, though it is flanked by the chariots of both the sun and the moon.[49]

It is in the field of the so-called minor or decorative arts that the Raphael/Marcantonio composition—in the form, let it be remembered, of a "reproductive" engraving—was most faithfully imitated, in whole or in part. The judgment of Paris frequently appears on furniture or objects, often small, somehow linked with personal adornment: enamels, majolicas, *cassone* panels, medals, bronzes, tapestries, and even Chinese porcelains (see Figures 82 and 83). Surely it is significant that the oldest known image of the theme is on a comb, the one from Sparta previously discussed. The widespread use on such objects of the Marcantonio composition "after" Raphael only increased the motif's popularity, thereby complicating the task of artists and, to an even greater degree, of craftsmen.[50] Consider, for example, the tapestry woven at the Gobelins factory in the last years of the seventeenth century (Figure 84): a particularly interesting case, as it belongs to a series begun in 1683, when Louvois succeeded Colbert as superintendent of the king's buildings, that depicts *mythological subjects* in compositions derived from Raphael and Giulio Romano. A painting by Michel Corneille the Younger (1642–1708) recently acquired by the Lyon Museum provides us with a link between the probable working methods in Raphael's studio and those used at the Gobelins factory (Figure 85): Jean-Claude Boyer has demonstrated how this painting *en petit*, to use the contemporary expression, functioned as an intermediary between preliminary sketches after Marcantonio's engraving (as well as a drawing in the Jabach collection) and the final full-scale cartoon. Subsequently, Madame de Maintenon required that the figures be clothed, and between 1700 and 1703 the necessary changes were made, apparently—judging from a drawing in Montpellier—with Corneille's collaboration.[51]

To return to painting, we should not neglect to mention the

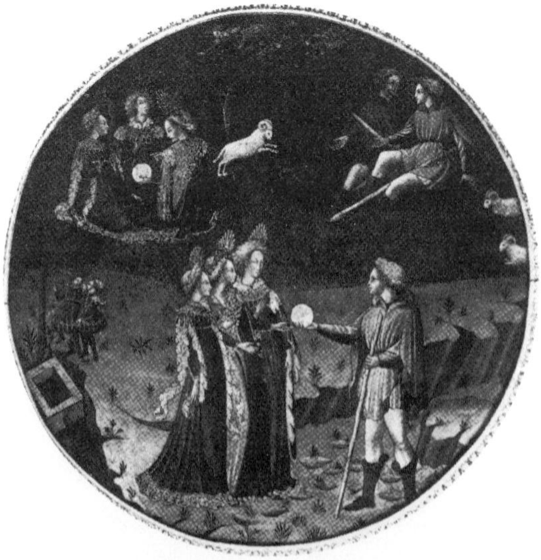

Figure 82. *The Judgment of Paris*, tondo, fifteenth century (Florence, Bargello Museum).

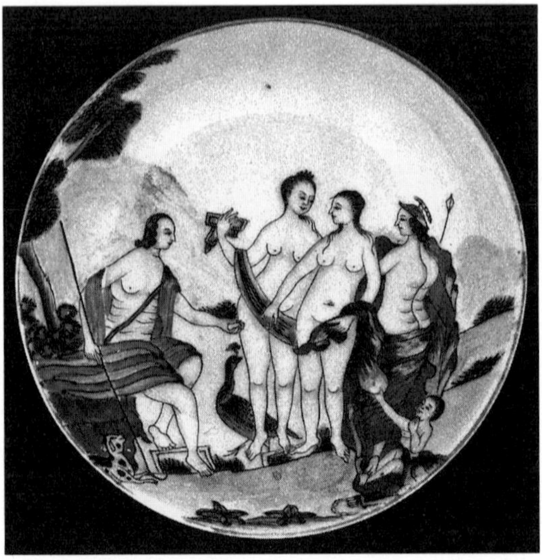

Figure 83. *The Judgment of Paris*, India Company porcelain, c. 1750 (private collection).

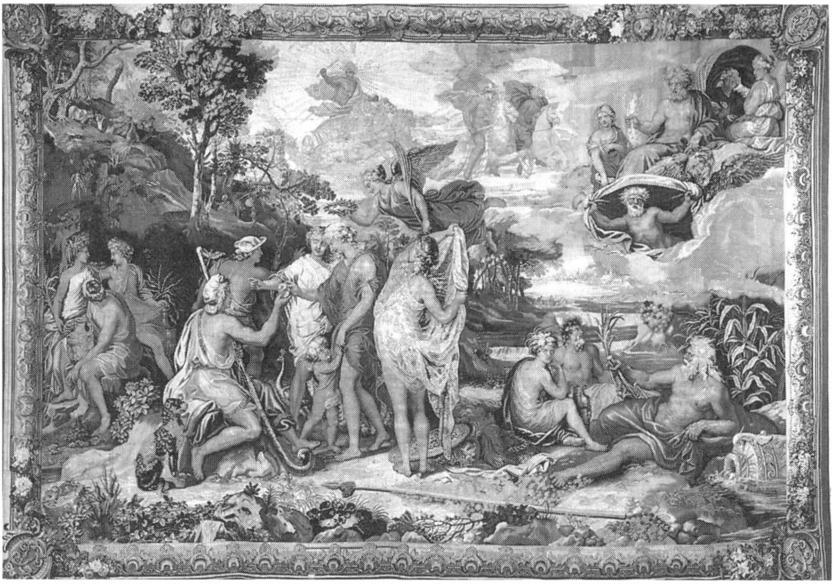

Figure 84. *The Judgment of Paris*, Gobelins tapestry, 1691–1703 (Paris, Mobilier National).

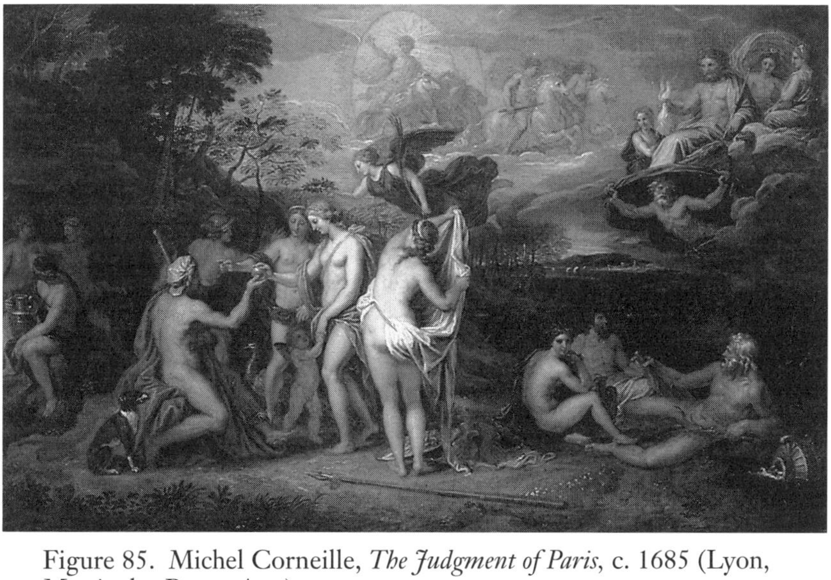

Figure 85. Michel Corneille, *The Judgment of Paris*, c. 1685 (Lyon, Musée des Beaux-Arts).

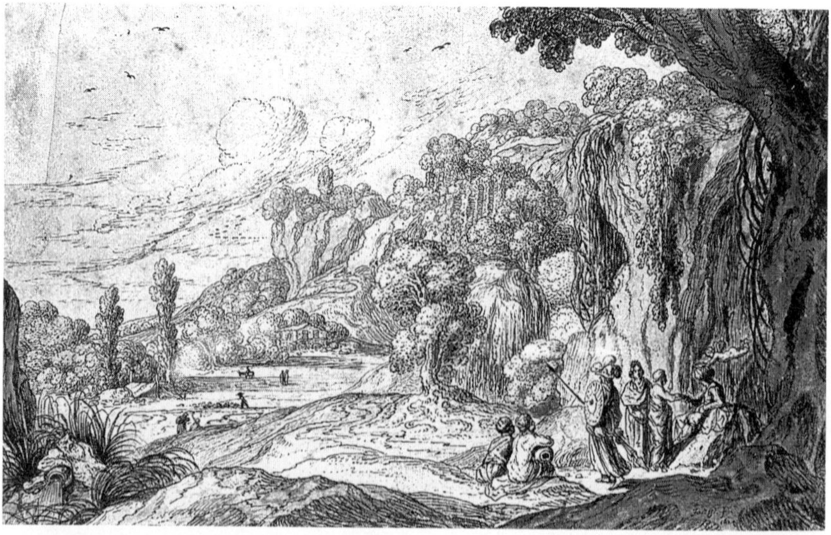

Figure 86. Jacob Pynas (c. 1585–after 1656), *Landscape with the Judgment of Paris*, pen and wash drawing (Paris, Louvre, Graphic Arts Department).

Judgment of Paris in the Villa d'Este, in Tivoli, which Aby Warburg thought provided a missing link between Marcantonio's engraving and Manet's *Déjeuner sur l'herbe*. In this seventeenth-century Dutch version, the "nymph" and the river gods are contemplating nothing more stirring than a herd of cattle.[52] The move toward a pastoral mode is further evidenced by *Landscape with the Judgment of Paris* by Jacob Pynas (Louvre, cabinet des dessins; Figure 86): here the landscape—the *parergon*—is emphasized to such a point that it becomes relatively autonomous, but, even so, Marcantonio's composition has left its traces in the form of the two seated observers, one of whom is undressed and holds a jug in her lap.[53] In Gombrich's words, "the transformation into the pastoral was complete and the way was open for Manet to recharge [the composition] with a novel revolutionary *pathos*."[54]

Not all Renaissance artists followed Raphael's example, however. In his youth, Marcantonio himself had engraved another *Judgment of Paris* with only four figures and patently inspired by German models, though its group of goddesses is not unrelated to the classical three Graces configuration: Venus, with wings sprouting from her hair, exhibits her prize, while Minerva holds up what seems to be a mirror, and Paris, leaning on a curious axe-like implement, stares vacantly in front of him, apparently ignoring the three rivals (Figure 87).[55] A drawing by Francesco Francia in the Albertina in Vienna, probably also dating from 1505–6, also features only these same four figures (Figure 88). But in this case, Paris, completely nude and crowned with foliage, sits on a cornice fragment and holds the apple, while the three goddesses surrounding him are given unusual attributes identifying them as allegories of, respectively, the contemplative, active, and erotic life: Minerva, on the left, dressed in a long tunic, carries a large horn from which flames emerge; Juno, on the right, nude and seen from the back, carries an arms-bearing trophy; and Venus, facing us in the center, also nude, carries a lyre.[56]

We should not allow the singular fate subsequently awaiting Raphael's invention to mislead us: it was not the elements and figures added *per capriccio* but rather the central group of the myth's protagonists in that composition (sometimes reduced to four) that first attracted the attention of artists depicting the judgment of Paris. And although the Raphaelesque prototype played a role in the affair, this was only to the extent that it entered, directly or otherwise, into competition with that of the three Graces: the three goddesses forming a closely intertwined trio in which their rivalry is obscured, or in which the winner stands apart, having already been singled out. Raphael's most direct successor, Giulio Romano, introduced this latter idea in the decor, executed by his studio against a dark ground, for the small Sala dei Metamorfosi in the Palazzo del Te in Mantua (Figure 89): Paris, seated in the center and wearing a Phrygian cap, Mercury at his side, turns toward the left to present the apple to Venus, who is accompanied by Cupid, while on the right her two unlucky rivals withdraw, one of them turning back to make a menacing gesture:[57] the torsion

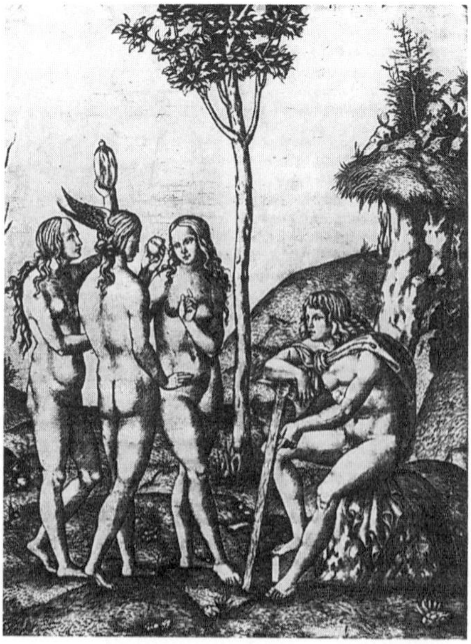

Figure 87. Marcantonio Raimondi, *The Judgment of Paris*, engraving, c. 1504–5.

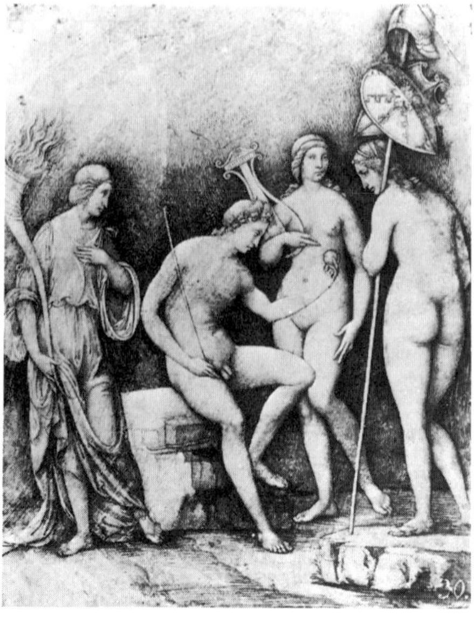

Figure 88. Francesco Francia, *The Judgment of Paris*, pen drawing, c. 1505 (Vienna, Albertina).

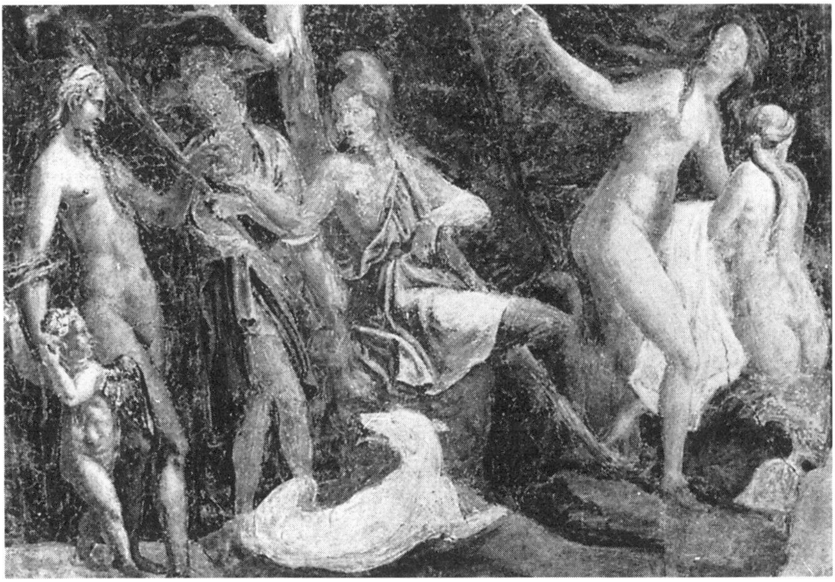

Figure 89. Giulio Romano, *The Judgment of Paris*, fresco (Mantua, Palazzo del Te, Sala dei Metamorfosi).

in Paris's body brings to mind that given his figure in the small *Judgment of Paris* in the Stanza della Segnatura.[58]

But it is Rubens who, after Cranach, offers us the most developed example of real work with the *Judgment of Paris* theme, which occupied him throughout his life, from his Italian voyage to his final years: painter's work if ever there was, as this subject offered him opportunities to demonstrate his gifts for treating the nude; artist's work, in the degree to which the celebration of beauty here prevails over ethical considerations; but commissioned work, too, for Burgundian court traditions, and even memories of the "Trojan novel" by Jean Lemaire de Belges, remained very much alive in Rubens's milieu. It is all the more remarkable, then, that his first *Judgment of Paris* (Figure 90), painted in 1600 (probably the year of his departure for Italy) and executed in a palette redolent of the Antwerp school, retains something of Raphael's composition: while the eccentric treatment of Paris, seen from the back and twisting

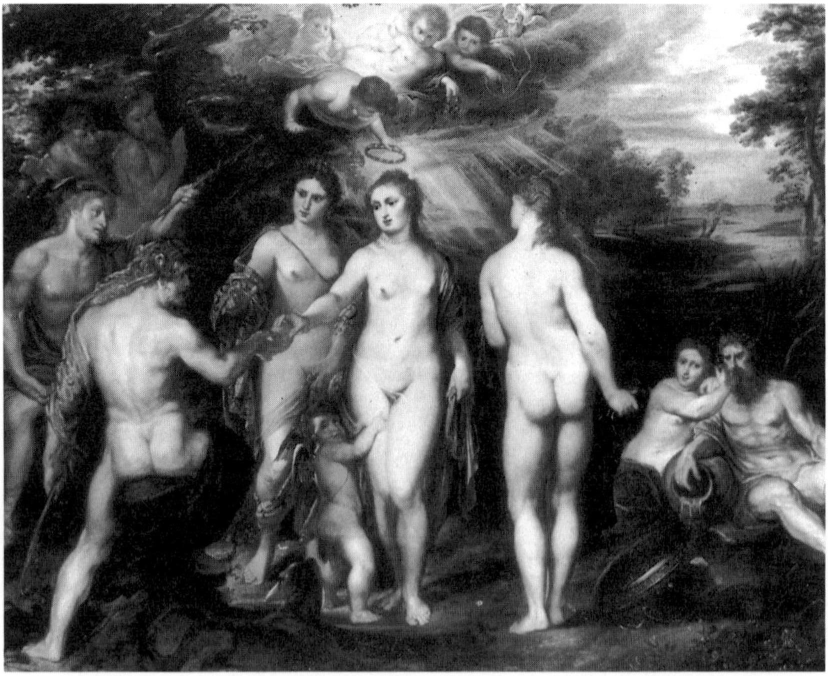

Figure 90. Peter Paul Rubens, *The Judgment of Paris*, 1600 (London, National Gallery).

to the right, owes something to Giulio Romano, if not to his master, the group of the three goddesses and, especially, the nymph and river god observing the scene, seated on the bank to the right, are clearly derived from Marcantonio's engraving, the three rivals being configured—with two positioned frontally and one seen from the back, in an *aab* rhythm—in a variation on the scheme of the antique three Graces, a recurrent motif in Rubens's work.[59] The small oil sketch in Vienna includes only the five principals: here, too, Paris is seen from the back and twists toward the right, but Minerva arrives from the same side in profile—making for an *aac* rhythm—and surrenders her robe to a putto.[60]

I will only discuss those paintings of the judgment theme by Rubens that are now in London, Dresden, and Madrid—and not, among others, the composition reproduced in *Sight and*

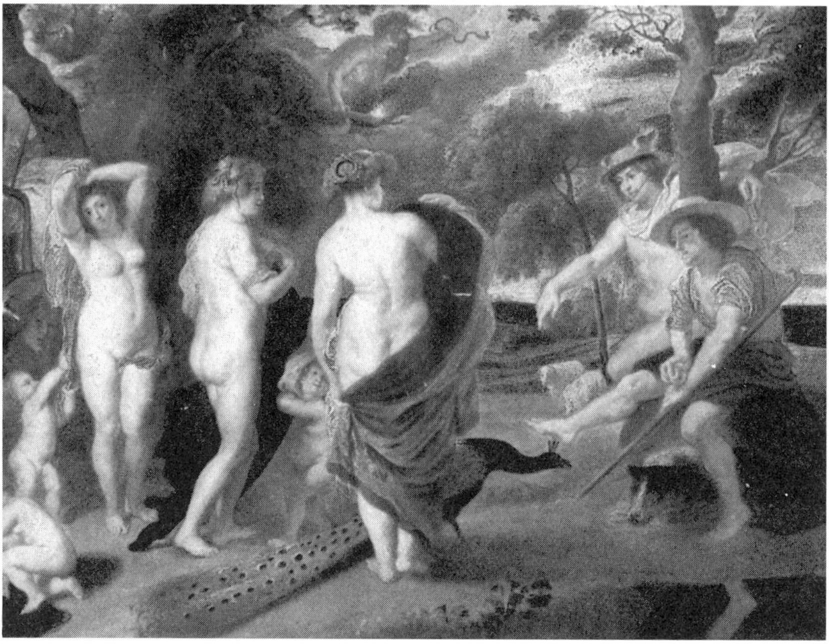

Figure 91. Peter Paul Rubens, *The Judgment of Paris*, 1625 (Dresden, Gemäldegalerie).

Smell by Jan Breughel I.[61] The Dresden canvas, dated about 1625 (Figure 91), reverses the composition such that Paris is seated on the right, under a tree behind which Mercury is visible. Juno, accompanied by her peacock, which is already picking a fight with the shepherd's dog, is seen from the back, much of her body hidden by a great purple mantle. Venus is seen in profile, and Minerva from the front (a surprising touch, given that she is the chaste goddess), her arms lifted to remove her clothing, with—once more—the aid of a putto, another of which is active in the lower left corner. Behind her, at the very edge of the picture (like Satan in Dürer's engraving), is the shield with the Gorgon's head and an owl. The nymph and river god have disappeared, but a trio of satyrs, relegated to the upper left corner, observe the scene, while Discord appears in the sky, a lighted torch in one hand and a snake in the other.[62]

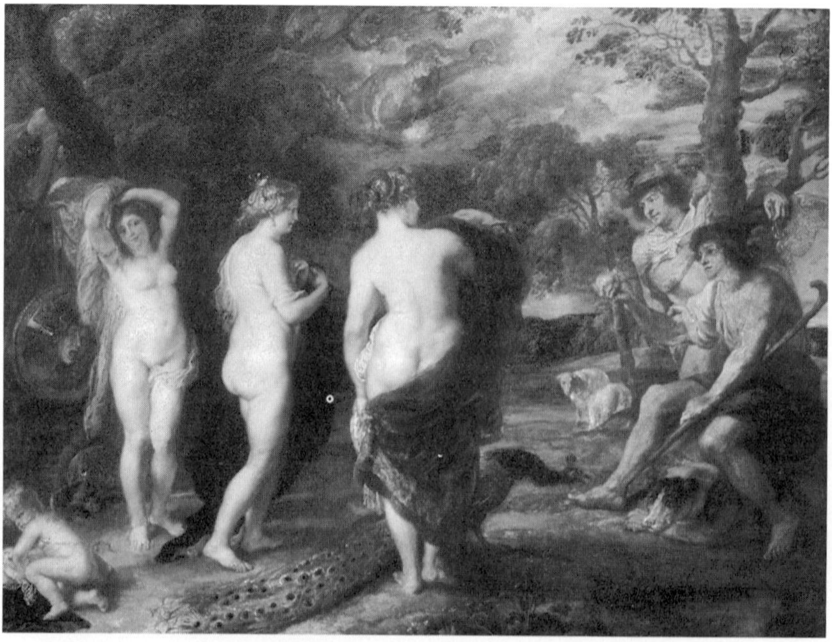

Figure 92. Peter Paul Rubens, *The Judgment of Paris*, 1632–35 (London, National Gallery).

Ten years later (around 1632 to 1635 or 1636) Rubens painted another painting, now also in London, largely based on that in Dresden. It is tempting to identify this work with the Rubens *Judgment of Paris* from the Orléans gallery described by Roger de Piles when it was in the collection of the duc de Richelieu, although his text differs in several respects from the work as we see it today; but these discrepancies might well be explained by a number of repaintings that have been revealed by X-rays. In the Dresden painting, Paris, wearing a straw hat, holds the apple in his lap, and the overall composition is consistent with de Piles's description: "The painter has chosen the moment immediately after the goddesses have disrobed, and in which Mercury signals them to approach their judge, who is beside him. All three are standing but present different views, and each is accompanied by distinguishing tokens."[63] In the second National Gallery canvas (Figure 92), Paris is bareheaded and

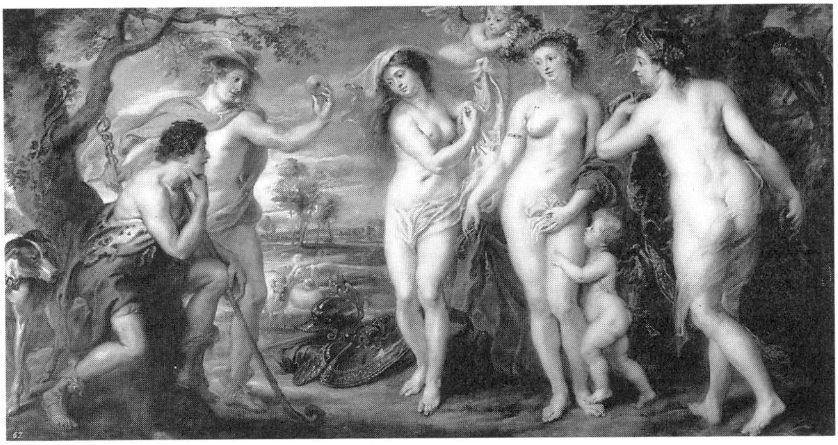

Figure 93. Peter Paul Rubens, *The Judgment of Paris*, 1638 (Madrid, Prado).

holds the apple in his right hand, which he extends toward the goddesses, but in such a way that it is impossible to determine its intended recipient; as in the Dresden composition, Mercury has positioned himself behind a tree. This is one of the passages that was repainted; the changes are significant, including the introduction of the outstretched hand, although the trio of goddesses was not affected by them. But another set of repaintings excised both the satyrs and the putto helping Minerva to disrobe, and also gave wings to the putto crouching in the lower left corner, transforming him into Cupid.[64]

The last work in the series, the *Judgment of Paris* in the Prado (Figure 93), was painted in 1638–39, a year or two before the artist's death, perhaps for the Torre de la Parada hunting pavilion (where *The Wedding of Peleus and Thetis* [Figure 94] by Jordaens also hung). Paris reverts to the left of the composition, a decision accentuating the act of judgment itself as opposed to the entry of the goddesses, as in the Dresden and London canvases. But it is Mercury who here holds up the apple, while Paris, leaning forward on his cane, his hand under his chin, is thoroughly absorbed in his "most precise" examination, to use Lucian's phrase. Given the objects of his scrutiny, his intent

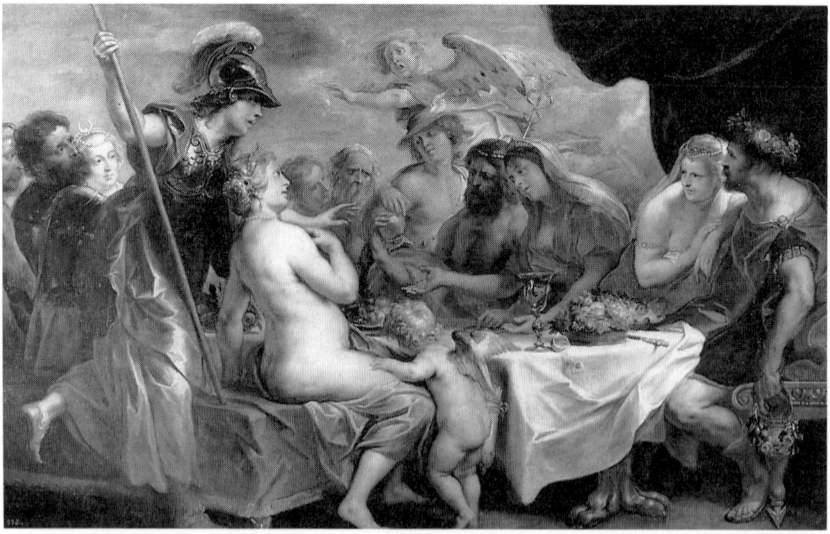

Figure 94. Jacob Jordaens, *The Wedding of Peleus and Thetis* (Madrid, Prado).

concentration is not surprising: the three goddesses present themselves to their judge in the brightest light, their pale flesh, while not petrified, seeming somehow unreal in its marked difference from the swarthy complexion of the two male figures. The Infante Ferdinand, Governor of the Low Countries, was most astute when, in the same letter in which he informed his brother Philipp IV that Rubens had finally completed the canvas and that all painters agreed it was his finest work, he offered his own opinion—comparable to Madame de Maintenon's vis-à-vis the Marcantonio engraving—that it had a single flaw: "The three goddesses are too nude."[65]

In showing beauty as desirable, painters have two options: they can represent an object that vividly conveys this idea, one that perhaps even functions for the beholder himself as an object of desire (as Sansovino's Venus supposedly did); or they can depict an object such that it functions for one or several figures *within* the image as an object of desire. The two options are not mutually exclusive, of course: a single object can appeal

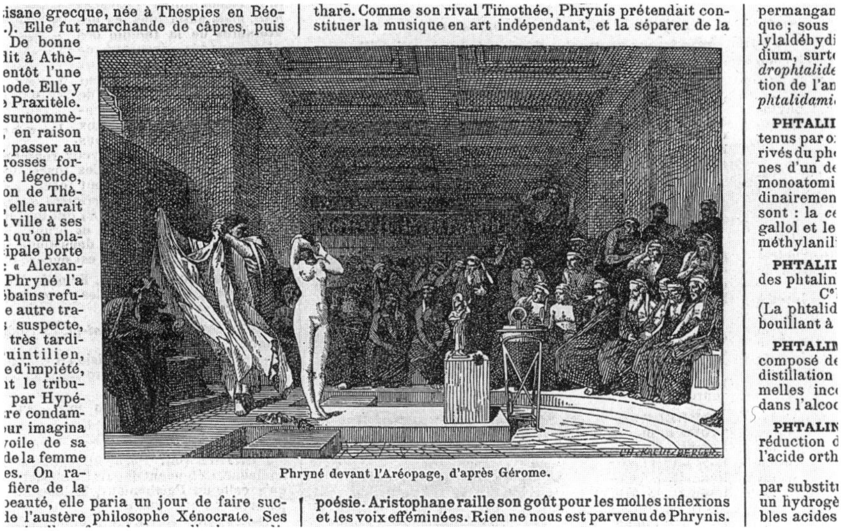

Figure 95. Jean-Léon Gérôme, *Phryne before the Areopagus*, 1861, as reproduced in *Grand Larousse illustré*.

simultaneously, in ways that should raise suspicion, to the represented desire of the other, in the guise either of voyeurism (*Susanna and the Elders*) or of violence (*The Rape of the Sabine Women*, *Tarquin and Lucretia*), and to the desire of the beholder, which can only be reinforced by the erotic circuitry within the painting. One particularly cunning instance of this double play is the "masterpiece" by Gérôme, *Phryne before the Areopagus*, in which the lawyer unveiling his client's charms before the stupefied assembly functions as a kind of supplementary operative (see Figure 95). Much the same could be said about depictions of the judgment of Paris, before which everyone, to a greater or lesser extent, finds himself cast as judge and/or voyeur.

Rubens is masterful at manipulating this double relation of desire. The Madrid painting, the last in the series, is something of a *tour de force* in the degree to which it insists on the judge's rapt attention to the objects before him even as it presents to the spectator all of the complementary charms—the "different views" mentioned by Roger de Piles—of the three rivals, who are configured in a rhythmic variation on the classical three Graces motif (*aab*, with two of the goddesses facing us and one seen from the back, as opposed to the *aba* arrangement). Almost all, that is: veils obscure the genitals of the two frontal figures, although Minerva is unusually exposed here. In the Dresden and London paintings, the female divinities are seen in three distinct "views" (*acb*, another variation on the three Graces motif), whereas the earliest *Judgment* in the series proposes the sequence *aac:* but here it is Minerva who is seen in profile. By the beholder, that is: as Jacob Burckhardt observes in his *Memories of Rubens* (though this applies only to the second and third paintings in the series), Venus, being the only one of the three goddesses to face Paris directly, was thereby assured victory.[66] To be sure, Venus is partly obscured from Paris's gaze by a thick mantle; nonetheless, the shepherd-prince is situated such that he sees her from the front, whereas both Minerva and Juno present themselves to him in profile, which means that there is no chance of his seeing their genitals (the clear implication of Burckhardt's observation). As Fréart de Chambray wrote with regard to the "perspective" in Marcantonio's engraving:

> The subject of this story treating of vision, and Paris, among all the other figures, being the principal exerciser of this function, the painter could not have positioned his point of view more judiciously than as identical with that from the eye of Paris, who has been depicted in profile in order to show that he should only have, precisely, one [eye], as we learn from the optics of the geometers, who represent vision in the form of a radiating pyramid with the eye at its point.[67]

With regard to the level of depth "where the three rivals are," that which "carries degradation toward Paris's eye," as Fréart puts it, the key consideration is the play of the "different views" of the three rivals' respective self-presentations. As we have seen, the latter group lends itself to such a distribution, and to variations on the three Graces model. The classical *paragone* trope comes to mind: doubtless painting can rotate an object so as to present its various aspects in simultaneous if discreet representations, without there being any need for the beholder to move in order to see them, as is the case with sculpture. The ancient Greeks already took delight in turning in their hands, like kinetoscopes (a word deriving from *kinema*, movement, and *skopein*, to examine), cups bearing friezelike depictions of the three goddesses and their guide in procession.[68] The movement with which Rubens instills them, the kind of dance so beautifully performed by them in the Madrid painting, is but a way of signifying that the drive can attain its aim only *en faisant le tour* of its object: *tour* being used here, as in Lacan's *Four Fundamental Concepts*, "with the ambiguity it possesses in French, meaning both *turn*, the limit around which one circles, and *trick*."[69] So true is it—a point well worth repeating—that this object is but the presence of a void, a lack, and that nothing will ever satisfy the drive, unless it be to circle around the eternally absent object.[70] Or, to cite Plotinus, a more ethereal source, and one doubtless closer to what has functioned, under the banner of Neoplatonism, as the dominant discourse of art history: "He who wishes to speak with precision cannot name the ultimate, but only circle around it."[71]

* * *

It follows from the preceding that the historical fortune of Marcantonio's *Judgment of Paris* print after Raphael is paradoxical. The figures added to the scene *per capriccio*, beginning with those turning their backs, have had a singular attraction for artists studying the image (even Rubens, as is shown by his *Nymphs and Satyrs* in the Prado; Figure 96). But the judgment scene has retained considerable seductive power, too, if only because of the opportunities it affords for depicting three beautiful female nudes. Should a painter be inclined to set it

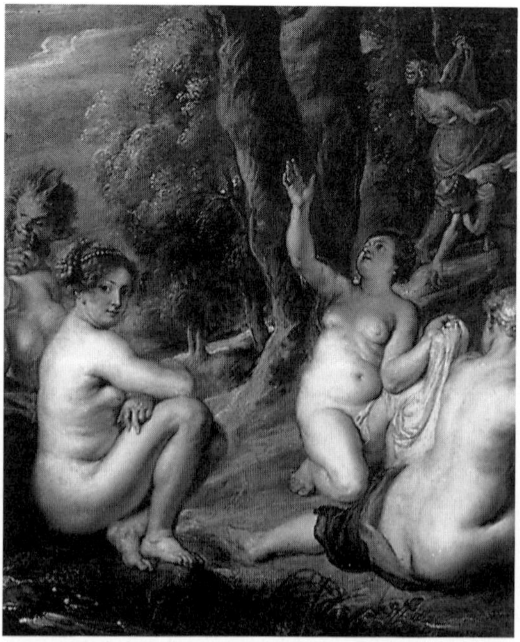

Figure 96. Peter Paul Rubens, *Nymphs and Satyrs*, 1637–40, detail (Madrid, Prado).

within a larger framework, it is the banquet of the gods, at the wedding of Peleus and Thetis, which is best suited to his purpose, providing an agreeable background—such depictions often including figures, and in the foreground, that are reminiscent of the nymphs and river gods in Raphael's composition (see Figure 97).

Rubens himself, after having paid early tribute to Raphael's treatment, reverted to the traditional iconography, with its five principal figures: Paris, Mercury, Juno, Minerva, and Venus. And Renoir, too, adhered to this model in his two versions of the *Judgment of Paris* dating from 1908 and 1914—specifically, to the version of it in Rubens's last treatment of the theme, which he would have seen during his visit to the Prado in 1892. He was doubtless drawn not only to its composition but also to its forthright depiction of a "fatter Minerva," to cite once

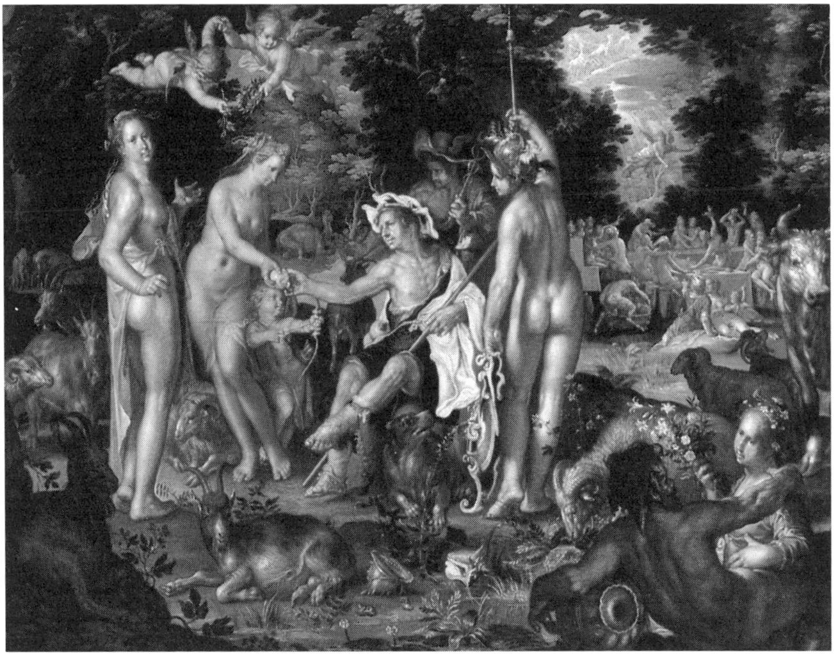

Figure 97. Joachim Wtewael, *The Judgment of Paris* (London, National Gallery). Note that the wedding of Peleus and Thetis is visible in the background.

more Alberti's remark about the dictates of painting. Curiously, in Renoir's versions it is Paris who seems androgynous—partly, it would seem, because the artist asked Gabrielle to pose for this figure (Figure 98).[72] And, no less curiously, if we think of the antique reliefs which so palpably influenced these works, the second one (now in the Hiroshima museum, a fact that carries its own resonance) seems to have been the model for the *Victorious Venus* sculpted by Richard Guino on Renoir's instructions, as well as for a relief, also executed by Guino, that was exhibited at the Paris Triennale in 1916: Renoir having finally tried his hand at sculpture, like Raphael tried his at engraving, through an intermediary.

But the motif that was to be most fully exploited in nineteenth and twentieth-century art—in various postures and

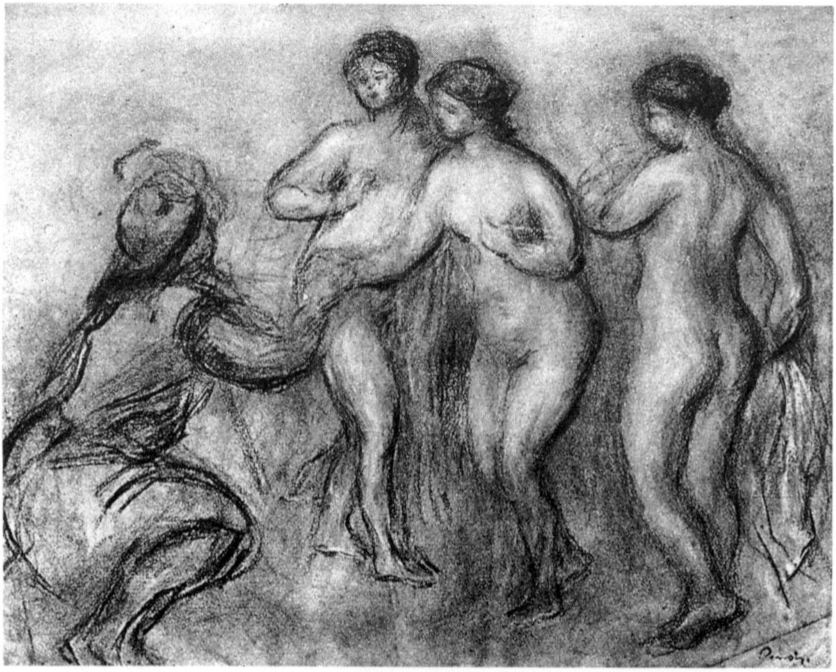

Figure 98. Auguste Renoir, *The Judgment of Paris*, pastel, 1908 (Washington, DC, Phillips Collection).

guises, some of them unexpected—(Delaunay's *Three Graces* are directly cited from Pompeii) is that of the female trio: as in Seurat's *Les Poseuses* (Figure 99), which has been compared so often with the Hellenistic *Three Graces* relief which entered the Louvre in 1878, as well as with *Women by the Sea* by Puvis de Chavannes (1879 Salon), Meyer Schapiro having gone so far as to draw a parallel between the painter's work on this "three-body" motif and that of contemporary mathematicians then attempting to devise equations for the mutual attraction of three heavenly bodies.[73] In the matter of gravitation, it is difficult to conceive of a law to which the *Poseuses* constellation would be subject: to the left is a seated woman, seen from the back; in the center, a standing woman seen frontally, her linked hands blocking our view of her genitals, her legs separated (Schapiro playfully suggests that there is an affinity between

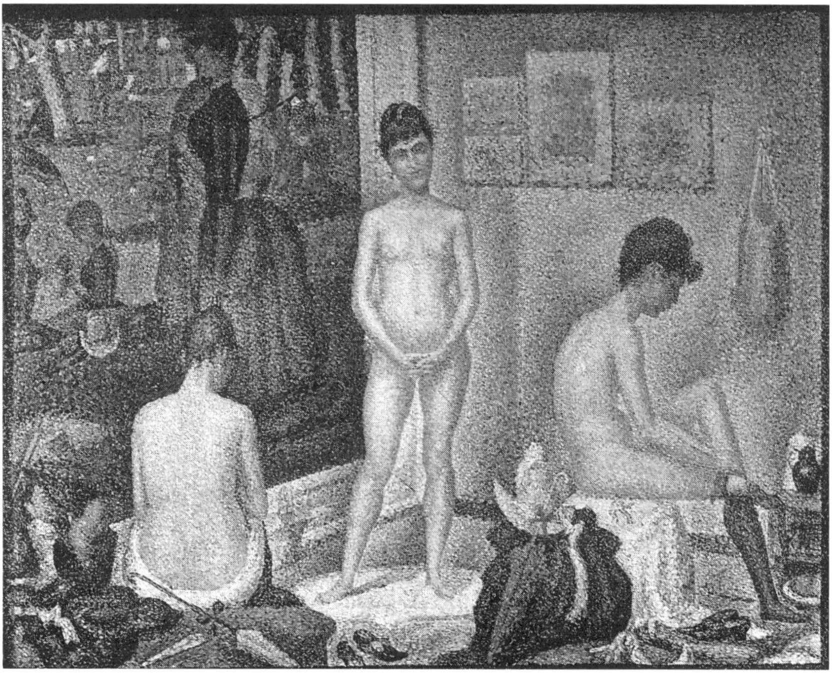

Figure 99. Georges Seurat, *Les Poseuses*, 1886–88 (Merion, Penn., Barnes Foundation).

their contours and those of the Eiffel Tower, another favorite Seurat motif[74]); and to the right, another seated woman, this one in profile, removing her stockings, turning her back on the two others as well as on the *Grande Jatte*, which is leaning against the studio wall.

Seurat's *Poseuses* contains no allusion to the theme of choice. It would have been otherwise if the three women had been situated in a brothel instead of a studio, but their poses would have been inappropriate for a moment of choice in such a context, and likewise in a depiction of prostitutes waiting for customers, or relaxing between them, a subject that fascinated Toulouse-Lautrec, although Paris's adventure would be obliquely invoked in drawings and caricatures by Picasso and Georges Grosz on the theme of prostitution (see Figures 100 and 101). But here we are dealing with no more than the myth's

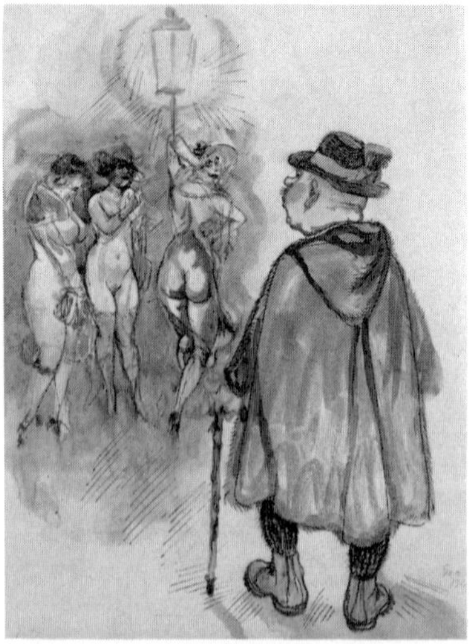

Figure 100. George Grosz, *Sirens*, watercolor (present location unknown).

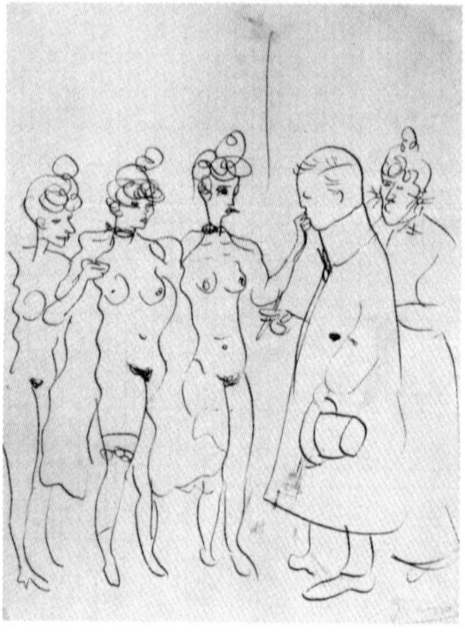

Figure 101. Pablo Picasso, *At the Brothel: The Choice*, drawing (present location unknown).

externals, as was already the case with Cézanne: and not in the painting often called *The Judgment of Paris*[75]—whose correct title, *The Amorous Shepherd*, has been restored by Schapiro—nor in the early canvas showing three clothed men in the company of three naked women on a riverbank, but rather in an-

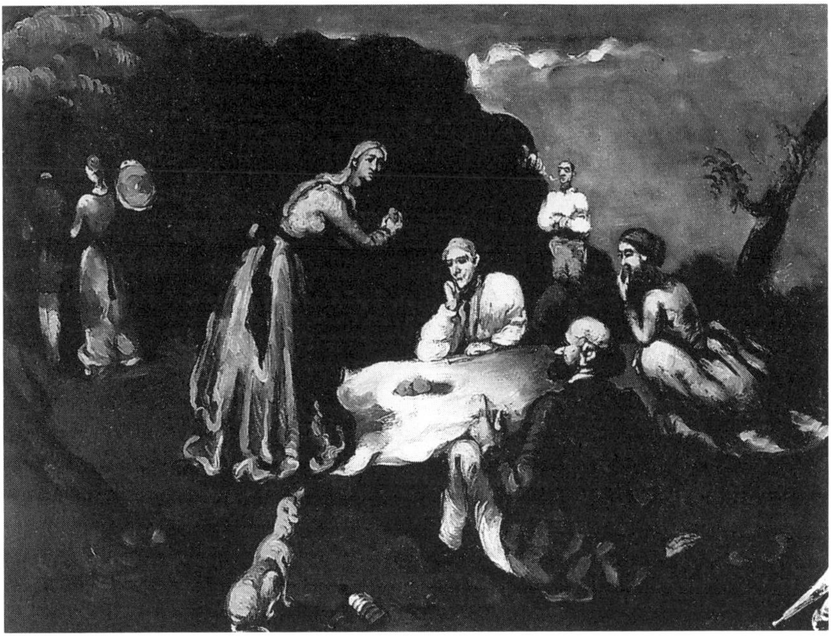

Figure 102. Paul Cézanne, *Le Déjeuner sur l'herbe*, 1869–70 (private collection).

other *Déjeuner sur l'herbe* (Figure 102), painted by Cézanne around 1870–71, in which he seems to have depicted himself, as he had already done in a small painting, *A Modern Olympia*, explicitly inspired by the Manet even as it evokes a client's reverie in a brothel: there are three women and four men here, one of whom is somewhat withdrawn and another implied to be "talking," as in Manet's *Déjeuner*.[76] Three women, one of them exiting on the arm of one of the men, another raising a hand to her mouth, and the third, in the center, her long blond hair untied, gesturing authoritatively with an apple—one of three—taken from the tablecloth. A *Déjeuner sur l'herbe*, or a *Judgment of the Goddesses*—a *Theōn Krisis*, to use Lucian's phrase? Perhaps as much the latter as the former, for Cézanne seems to suggest in this work something that only Kafka would say without equivocation: it is not the man who judges but rather the woman (though Kafka goes on to note: "Who can claim to know the judge's secret thoughts?").[77]

All of the above would not suffice to justify the place assigned the *Déjeuner sur l'herbe* at the beginning of modern painting: as its threshold, its originary "masterpiece." It fell to Picasso, repeating the operation he had already applied to Velázquez's *Las Meninas*, to interrogate the work and, by methods that must be termed analytic (even though they employ only the means available to painting), reconfigure the threads of the story, his set of variations on Manet's painting effectively representing what we might call, borrowing a term from chemistry, its precipitate. After the *Young Women on the Banks of the Seine*, *The Women of Algiers*, and *Las Meninas*, he turned to the *Déjeuner:* what might be called the logic behind his choice of these works—as conjugated in the increasing amount of time devoted to each series (a few weeks for the Courbet, three months for the Delacroix, four months for the Velázquez, and no less than two years for the Manet)—testifying to a deepening engagement and increasingly high stakes. What started as little more than an exercise, a way of measuring himself against canonical masterpieces—a reciprocal testing, if you will—evolved in the *Las Meninas* series into an investigation of the configuration of paintings generally, and the *Déjeuner sur l'herbe* subsequently served as a pretext for manipulations and associative explorations that would not cease until they had led Picasso back to the operation that had prompted Manet's masterpiece in the first place. The numbers speak for themselves: whereas Picasso produced forty-five variations on *Las Meninas*, there are two hundred drawings and twenty-five paintings in his *Déjeuner* series, as well as a handful of linoleum prints and cardboard maquettes for monumental sculptures (see Figure 103).

There was something frankly experimental about Picasso's work with *Las Meninas:* in his set of variations on Velázquez's great composition, he set out more or less systematically to

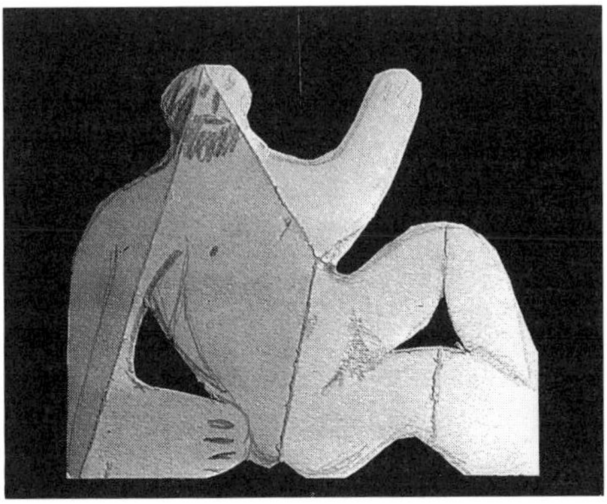

Figure 103. Pablo Picasso, *Reclining Man*, maquette for sculpture, charcoal on cut paper, 26 August 1962 (Paris, Musée Picasso).

determine the functions, respectively, of the mirror reflecting the heads of the royal couple and the open door at the back of the painting.[78] He would proceed similarly, in many respects, with the *Déjeuner.* In the month of August 1959, in Vauvenargues, Picasso began by executing four drawings after the Manet, more or less faithful ones, though in the last of these sheets, the seated man to the left, closest to Victorine Meurent, has disappeared (see Figures 104 and 105). This "second man" would subsequently reappear, though usually relegated to a marginal position, shown reading, for example, leaving the spotlight to the seated man on the right, most often depicted at the foot of a tree and cast—to cite Douglas Cooper—as the "talker,"[79] which makes him the dominant figure. Unless the country outing becomes, as it did in April–July 1961, a swimming party (Figure 106; Cooper notes in this connection that Manet had originally entitled his painting *Le Bain*); or the scene of Manet's "foursome" or *partie carrée*—as he himself called it—did not take an overtly pornographic turn, as it did in a series of drawings which critics have long conspicuously ignored.

From that point forward, the general configuration was set,

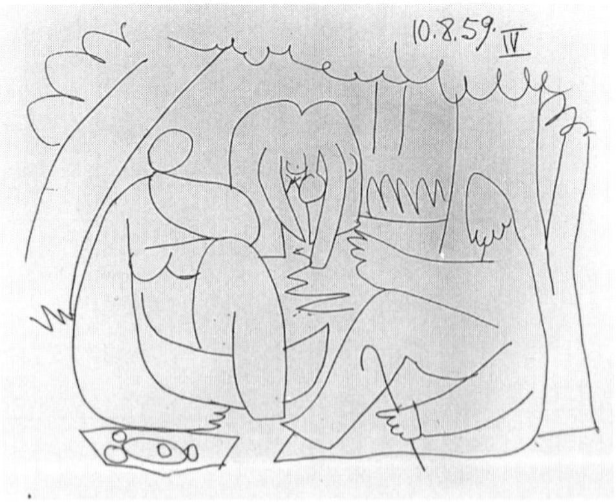

Figure 104. Pablo Picasso, *Le Déjeuner sur l'herbe*, drawing, 10 August 1959 (present location unknown).

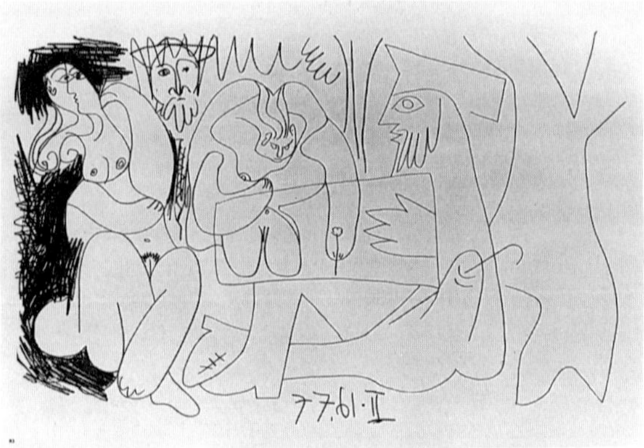

Figure 105. Pablo Picasso, *Le Déjeuner sur l'herbe*, drawing, 7 July 1961 (present location unknown).

though Picasso inflected it in ever-new ways, his variations being constantly reinforced by repetition—as in psychoanalysis, which Freud maintained should proceed *wie absichtlos*, as if without a premeditated plan.[80] A man, the "talker," is always present in his assigned place, though his appearance varies: sometimes he is bearded and wears a hat, at other times he is clean-shaven and bald, and at others still he is reduced to a simple silhouette, though he usually has a cane, most often with a curved handle. A woman always faces him, sometimes seated, sometimes reclining, on occasion spreading her legs to reveal her carefully delineated genitals to the spectator, at

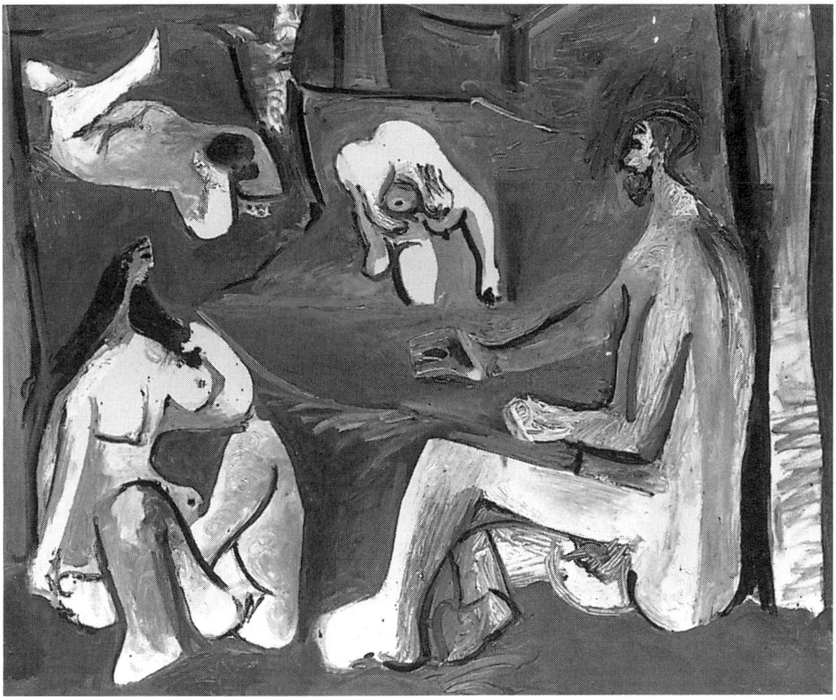

Figure 106. Pablo Picasso, *Le Déjeuner sur l'herbe*, oil on canvas, 13 July 1961 (Paris, Musée Picasso).

whom she thus gazes with all of her "eyes." This pair always suggests another theme dear to Picasso, that of "the painter and his model" (at least once, in a drawing dated 29 December 1961, a strange easel-like object is introduced into the picture). There is a second woman, too, at least some of the time, who occasionally takes the place of the first: she is the analogue to Manet's "bather" (similar to other such figures by Picasso himself), eventually assuming monstrous proportions, and leaning forward not to splash herself but to pick a flower. Finally, we arrive at the series of six large canvases painted between 30 July and 10 August 1961, in which the couple formed by the "talker" and the seated nude delineate with the "bather" a tri-

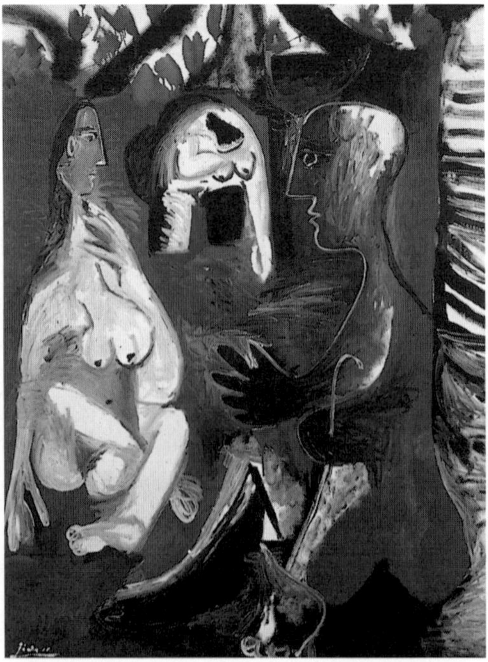

Figure 107. Pablo Picasso, *Le Déjeuner sur l'herbe*, oil on canvas, 30 July 1961 (Humlebaeck, Louisiana, Museum of Modern Art).

angle contained within the edges of a now vertical-format canvas (see Figures 107 and 108). Here again, the "talker" varies in appearance, his image assuming an unmistakable resemblance to self-representations of the painter on two occasions, while his placement—seated at the foot of a tree and holding a cane or staff—irresistibly brings to mind the shepherd Paris. Admittedly the "talker" does not hold an apple. But the gesture with which, in the culminating canvas, the "bather" at the triangle's summit seems to place a flower in his outstretched hand constitutes a direct link with the theme of Venus's promise to her judge, and evokes the pleasure premium she offered him. It is as though (but this "as though" seems to emanate from the painting itself, associatively, like the "lesson" Gombrich at-

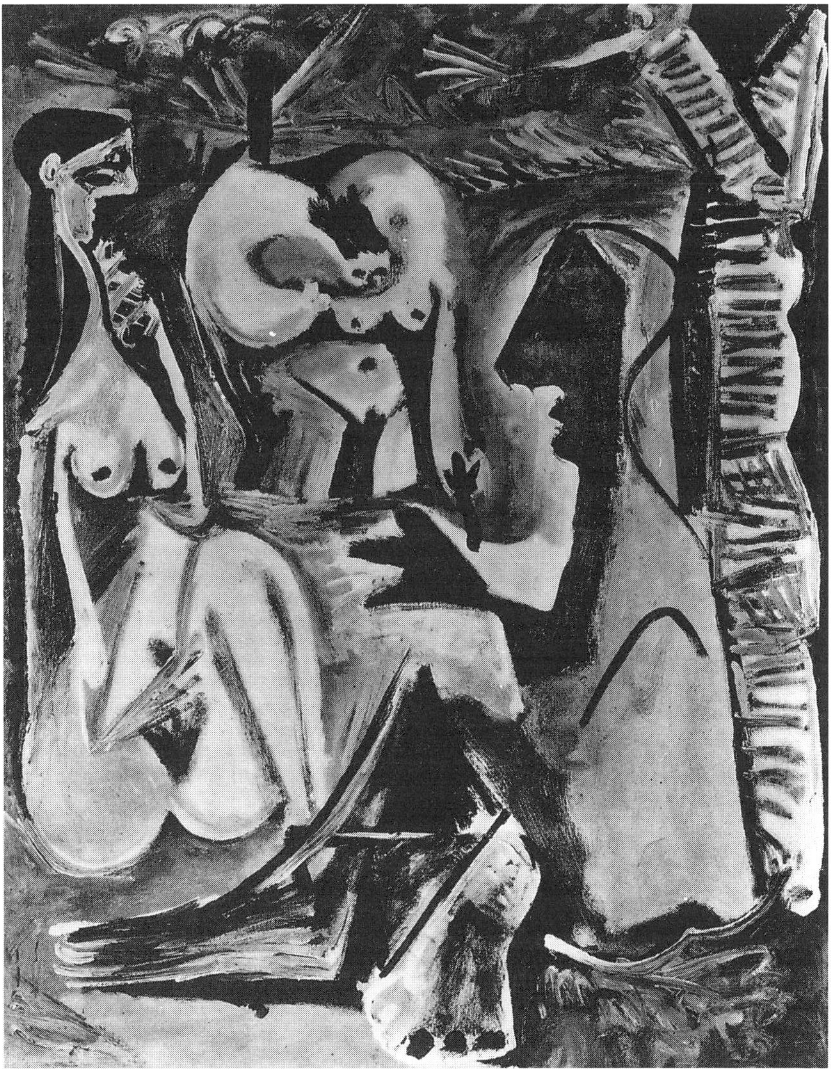

Figure 108. Pablo Picasso, *Le Déjeuner sur l'herbe*, oil on canvas (?), 10 August 1961 (present location unknown).

tributes to the *Primavera*); it is as though the fable or myth in whose margins Manet, following Raphael's example, chose to work, here returned, under disguise, in the supplement itself, in the very *parergon* from which the image, like Marcantonio's engraving, derives its force as a picture or *tableau*.

. . 12 . .

Paris Judged: The Reverse Side of the Picture

In his work with the *Déjeuner sur l'herbe*, Picasso managed to bring together all of the strands in this complex braid—to reconfigure these strands, which were already quite twisted, by folding the braid back on itself in order to arrive, in a crucial experiment, at the "precipitate" already discussed. And it is indeed a braid of intermingled strands that has progressively taken form in the preceding pages—as opposed to a Warburgian series, in which each link must be riveted securely into place for the chain of transformations to acquire its full demonstrative force. A braid, or better yet a *décor*, one as intricate as that devised by the Carracci for the Farnese Gallery, and one whose power should be measured in the terms of fiction as well as of *mise en scène* or staging: the staging of painting, the fiction of the picture or *tableau;* but also the staging of fiction and the fiction of staging. For the configuration assumes an inherently analytic dimension from the moment the function allotted to the "supplement" is made to encompass, beyond its visible surface, what might be taken to constitute its back: as on the vault of the Farnese Gallery, where the series of *quadri riportati* cast shadows onto an elusive background,[1] the images deriving their identity as paintings or tableaux from their frames, which themselves stand out against this background. A braid, a decor, then, in which simultaneity and imbrication prevail over sequentiality and succession, and in which a rejection of all evolutionary models and all linear methods of explication is implied. But a configuration, as well, in which both Freudian and Kantian references can perform contextual or framing functions, to the point of acting as a "supplement" analogous to that determining the fiction of the *tableau*, or the staging of painting—its having been primarily in such pictorial guise that the judgment of Paris has concerned us here.

(We might invoke another "decor" in this context, that of the painter's studio, with its canvases resting on easels or on the floor or turned against the wall; its pots of paint; its brushes; its odds and ends, perhaps a mask; books and catalogs; postcards; photographs on the wall, in the way reproductions of the *Déjeuner sur l'herbe* might well have been pinned up at Vauvenargues, or elsewhere—so many fragments or sketches of a history cobbled together by the artist for his personal use: a history conceived *ad hoc*, mobilizing diverse bits and pieces that accrue meaning and acquire a destination only through the work of painting.)

If the enterprise of this book has occasionally seemed frankly experimental, this is largely due to the object it set out to investigate. While Picasso's work in his *Déjeuner* series is in many ways analogous to that of the myth which resurfaces in its themes and images, we cannot in this instance draw a clear line between the results of conscious deliberation and those of operations determined by the unconscious, for the nature of the play of art is such as to preclude unequivocal distinctions of this kind. Such work is not unprecedented. As we have seen, a reduction—from three to two—of the options offered Paris had long since been effected, having been facilitated by the fusion, in Minerva's person, of the two virtues Strength and Wisdom. Raphael provided us with an example in his small panel *The Dream of Scipio*, in which the trio formed by Minerva, the sleeping hero, and Venus clearly echoes that in its

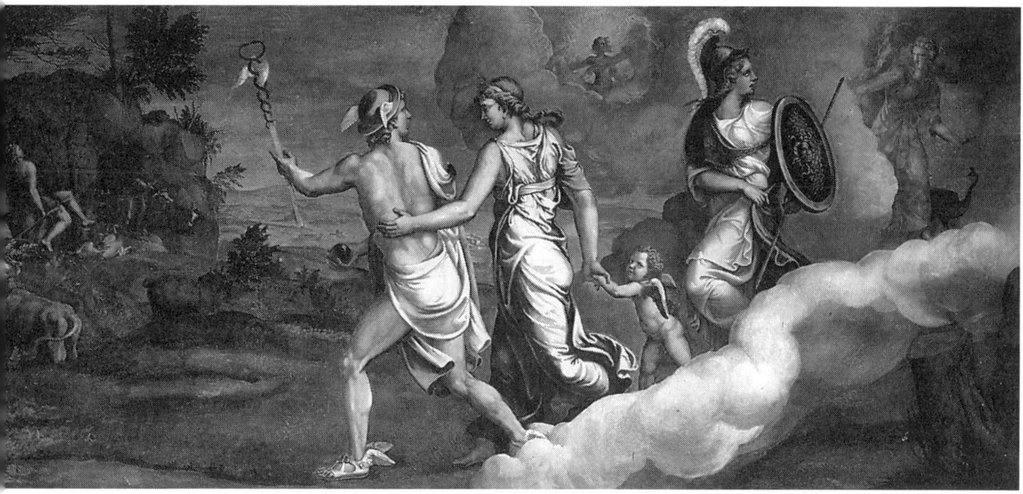

Figure 109. Giulio Romano and assistants, *The Judgment of Paris*, fresco, 1536–39 (Mantua, Ducal Palace, Trojan Room).

pendant, *The Three Graces.* But it was in the Trojan Room of the Ducal Palace in Mantua that Juno's subsequent pictorial fate was set (Figure 109). Reviving the ancient motif of the goddesses in procession, Giulio Romano here depicted them descending on a cloud and, led by Mercury, caduceus in one hand and apple in the other, heading toward Paris, who is asleep under a tree in the background in the midst of his herd. Venus is in the foreground, her left arm prominently placed around Mercury's waist, while Minerva, fully armored, turns toward Juno, who seems to hesitate some distance behind, and urges her to join them. Watteau was to use a similar schema in his *Judgment of Paris* (Figure 110), even though his painting represents a later moment in the story: here Venus and Minerva are in the foreground while Juno, identifiable by her peacock, is visible in the upper right corner moving away, looking back at the scene with a finger raised to her lips (a gesture that brings to mind the Cézanne discussed above).

Given the essentially erotic content of the myth, chivalric ideology could encourage its adepts to hope that Minerva

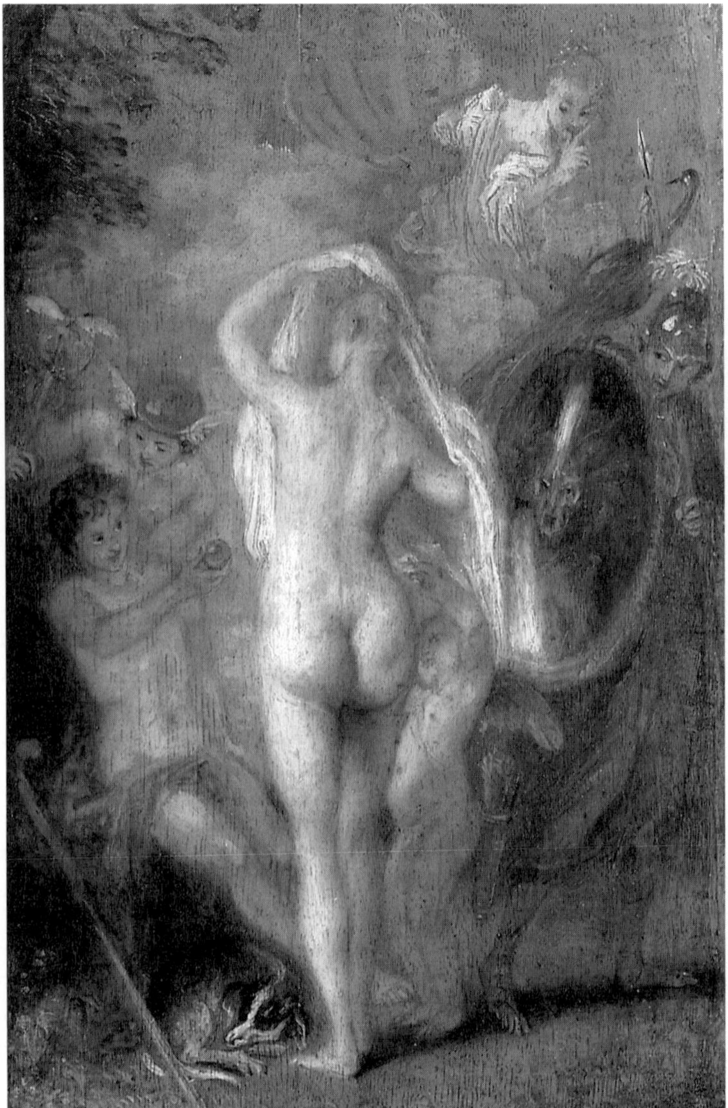

Figure 110. Antoine Watteau, *The Judgment of Paris*, oil on wood, 1720 (Paris, Louvre).

might seize the apple from Venus, but it had little positive to say about Juno, the guardian of conjugal law. In Lucian's playlet *The Judgment of the Goddesses*, Aphrodite asks whether Paris is married, fearing that if so he might be more difficult to seduce. In his *Heroides*, Ovid provides the shepherd-prince with a companion, the nymph Oenone; both faithful and good, she is apparently intended to function as a counterweight to the negative image of the bad woman, the temptress. But despite the ubiquity of this oppositional schema in the Middle Ages, Juno's lot was not to improve. Another playful retelling of the judgment of Paris story, in *L'Astrée* (1607–27) by Honoré d'Urfé, still has Venus—the woman most beautiful to the senses, and to taste—carrying the day, though the author describes his heroine's irritation at being obliged to display herself in the nude before her judge (here disguised as a shepherd), and shows her as animated by a kind of hatred for the love preventing her from seeking revenge for this offense against her modesty: as though the two lovers had been unable to submit to the constraints imposed by the fable and so were reduced to playing out the "judgment of the goddesses" scenario for themselves.[2]

We have seen that, according to Kafka, it is the woman who judges in the end, and Watteau manages to indicate this without resorting to the crude tactic of reversing the roles, of establishing a woman in the judge's position and providing her with three svelte men to assess. Instead, Watteau's Paris is relegated to the lower left, diagonally opposite the withdrawing Hera, and strikes a note very different from that of the attentive judge to whom Mercury concedes in most earlier depictions: seated, inclined slightly backwards, eyes uplifted to look at the looming Venus, who exhibits herself in a way that clearly conveys her domination of him, he surrenders the apple to her like one conquered, while Mercury looks over his shoulder. But the most surprising thing here is the precise placement of Venus, who, as Pierre Rosenberg has rightly noted, is seen from the back, "while from Rubens to Renoir artists treating this subject have shown her from the front"[3] (or, as we have seen, in profile, as was already the case in Marcantonio's engraving). Venus, aligned with the composition's vertical axis, exposes her genitals directly to Paris, but her face is obscured from him by a veil or robe which she lifts above her blond head, its hair knotted at the back, while Cupid draws aside its lower portion to reveal an unimpeded view of her private parts, that he might reach his decision *en toute connaissance de cause*. Paris's looking toward a face that is largely hidden from him alters nothing: here, as in Rubens's *Judgment of Paris* in the Prado, Paris sees her frontally while we see her from the back. The result being, as Burckhardt notes, a depiction of the moment in which she secures her victory (*und damit ist auch ihr Sieg entschieden*)—evidence, if you will, that Paris was not permitted to deliberate at leisure and that Venus was assured the prize simply by exposing her genitals to him.[4]

This reading of the Watteau is further supported by the fact that the two rival goddesses are clothed, either having previously shown themselves to Paris or never having done so. As we have seen, Juno flies away, a finger to her lips: as though there were something about this transaction that neither could nor should be spoken. Then again, it may be that she is already plotting revenge, but she seems far less fierce than the figure of Minerva. Helmeted, dressed in a long dark robe and leaning on her spear, she too moves away to leave center stage to Venus, partly hidden behind a large shield on which appears a menacing image of the Gorgon's head, much as in the Medici relief, Watteau here reviving—unconsciously?—an antique motif unknown to Raphael. (Despite the seeming anachronism, it might be worth pointing out that this Minerva seems very much like a Walkyrie, for in German *-küre* [from *Walküre*] would seem to be etymologically related to the old verb *kiesen* [other forms being *kur* and *gekoren*], which means precisely "to choose."[5])

Pierre Rosenberg observes that this little panel has often been compared with the Rubens *Judgment of Paris* then in Paris (the later of the versions now in London; see Figure 92), two motifs from which were drawn by Watteau on a sheet in an English private collection. The Goncourts call this work an *esquisse*, and it is indeed similar in technique to Rubens's oil sketches: like the latter, it is painted on wood with little in the way of preliminary surface preparation and includes passages of the artist's working the paint with the tip of his brush handle while it was still wet.[6] But the links with Rubens's composition only make the transformation operated by Watteau, the singular *tour* or turn he gave its figures, all the more remarkable. There is no longer any question of "different views" of the female body. And if we can speak of a *tour* here, this is only in relation to Venus's body, which constitutes a unique intervention in the *Judgment of Paris* iconographic tradition. This nude, seen from the back, irresistibly evokes the woman entering the shop—also seen from the back, her head inclined to the left—in *The Sign of Gersaint*, which was painted by Watteau at about the same time, in his final years (Figure 111).[7] But the nude figure, although rotated, is reminiscent of the image of Beauty in Cesare Ripa's *Iconology* (Figure 112), which presents us with a nude woman whose head is largely obscured by a cloud but who emanates light—as does Watteau's Venus, whose luminous aura sets her apart from the half-lit figures around her. All of which is consistent with Ripa's accompanying text, as translated for the French edition by Jean Baudoin: "It is no less difficult to paint her than to look at her without being dazzled by the rays of light surrounding her. And although she does not willingly listen to the praise bestowed upon her by Renown, who cannot laud her overmuch, nonetheless both of their heads are enveloped by clouds."[8]

What then did he see, this Paris to whom all possibility of free choice would seem foreclosed? And what is the significance of Watteau's having turned Ripa's image of Beauty 180 degrees? What did Paris see, as opposed to the beholder, who is denied a view of it, just as the opportunity to *faire le tour* of the object is denied him? Then again, is it? While Juno moves

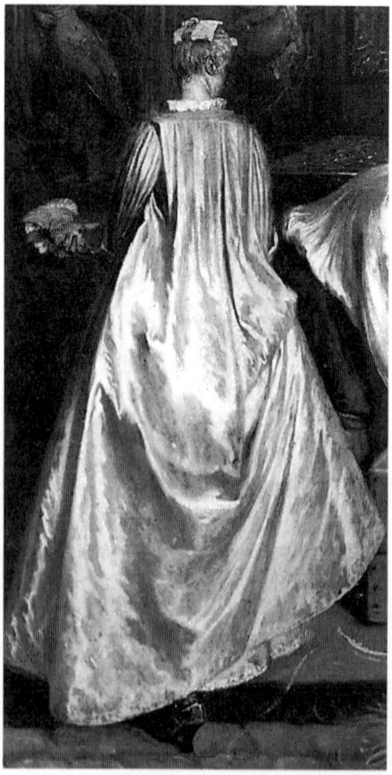

Figure 111. Antoine Watteau, *L'Enseigne de Gersaint*, oil on canvas, 1720, detail (Berlin, Schloss Charlottenburg).

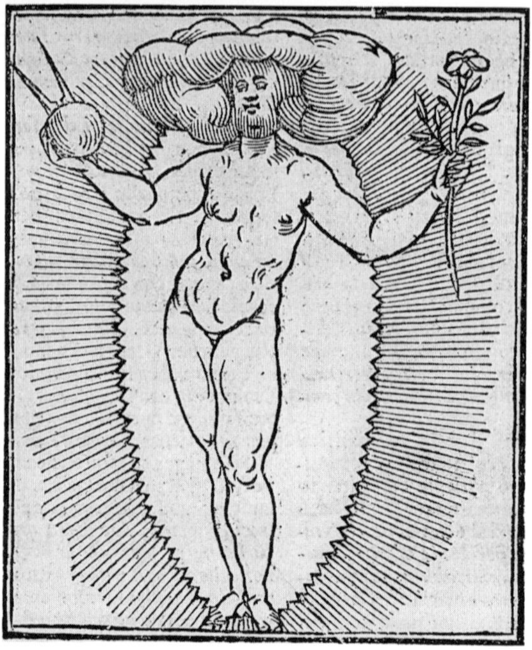

Figure 112. *Bellezza*, emblematic figure from Cesare Ripa, *Iconologia* (Rome, 1593).

away, holding a finger to her lips as if to signal that what must not be shown also must not be spoken (though her stare *indicates* it, there being no question, despite the summary handling, of the direction in which she and the other faces look), we see this airborne goddess in profile, more or less. And it is frontally (more or less) that we are shown Minerva's face, as well as that of the Gorgon on her shield, which gives off brilliant white reflections suggestive of lightning. Minerva's eyes, like those of the Gorgon, are fixed on the same object as that from which Juno seemingly cannot look away: as though both rivals, and the Gorgon as well, had been reduced to confirming the judgment in favor of Venus, Paris himself having no choice but to declare which of the three goddesses delivered the strongest "final judgment" or "last sentence" (*das Schlussurteil*). In the end, it is the woman who judges; but as Kafka wrote, who can claim to know this judge's secret thoughts?

What Paris saw is also what is being contemplated by the servant kneeling in front of her mistress in *La Toilette intime*, which was painted by Watteau a few years earlier (Figure 113). According to René Démoris, the doubled or relayed looks at the sexual object built into the structure of this painting—and into a few other female nudes by this artist, as well as into depictions of *Susanna at the Bath* and Gérôme's *Phryne before the Areopagus*—makes it quite audacious,[9] for here the beholder is invited to project himself onto the figure of the voyeur within the painting, thereby vicariously gaining access to a full view of the said object. Thus, it might be maintained that this *Toilette* is "obscene," like several other "works [Watteau] thought insufficiently distant from this genre" and which, according to the comte de Caylus, he wanted brought to him a few days before his death "in order to burn them: which he did."[10] The engraving by Philippe Mercier, which Jean de Jullienne omitted from his published collection of prints after the master's work, presumably because he found the image indecorous, differs markedly from the original, the engraver having placed a piece of cloth over what the tricentenary exhibition catalog calls "her

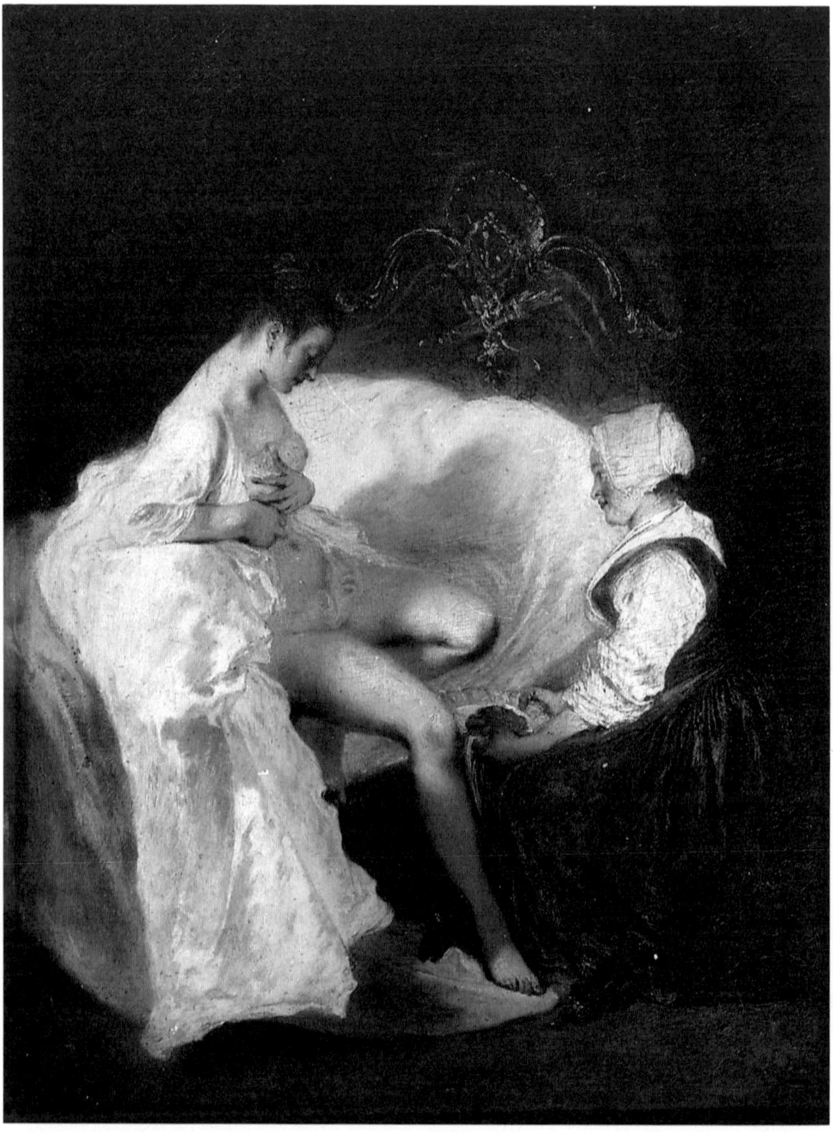

Figure 113. Antoine Watteau, *La Toilette intime*, oil on canvas, 1717 (private collection).

most intimate parts" (which are scarcely visible even in the painting). If this *Toilette* is indeed obscene, it is so to the extent that it renounces—to use the language in the catalog entry—equivocation and innuendo. But it is no more "pornographic" than are more recent variations on the same theme. For pornography begins precisely where painting (or photography) stops: with the *tour*, in the sense of "trick," that consists of suggesting through visual means that the judge (or the camera) is permitted to contemplate something that the beholder cannot actually see.

Thanks to Minerva's determined stride toward the right, what is visible to the beholder, as a kind of stand-in for what Paris alone can see (even Mercury lowers his eyes), is the Gorgon's face, emblazoned on her shield like a mask—which is only appropriate, given the sacred power operating through masks, which can assume no form other than this one, full-frontal exposure of their physiognomy being one of their fundamental characteristics.[11] One might even argue that it is because the Gorgon can only be represented frontally that Venus is here shown from the back and that the contrast between the latter's tied-up tresses and the former's wildly disordered snake-hair is not accidental.[12] But it is above all the play of cross-references between the face of Gorgo and the image of the female genitals, operative through displacement and substitution, that is important here. Vernant discusses this dynamic in connection with the strange figure of Baubo, a benign old woman whose jokes and obscene gestures managed to distract Demeter from her pain at having lost her daughter: "Comparison of the texts recounting this episode with the statuettes from Priene representing a female figure reduced to a face that is also the female genitals suggests the following reading of Baubo's gesture of lifting her robe to expose her private parts: what Baubo shows Demeter is her genitals made-up to look like a face, a face in the form of the female sexual organs—sex made mask, we might say. When made to grimace, this genital-face seems to laugh, and the goddess laughs in

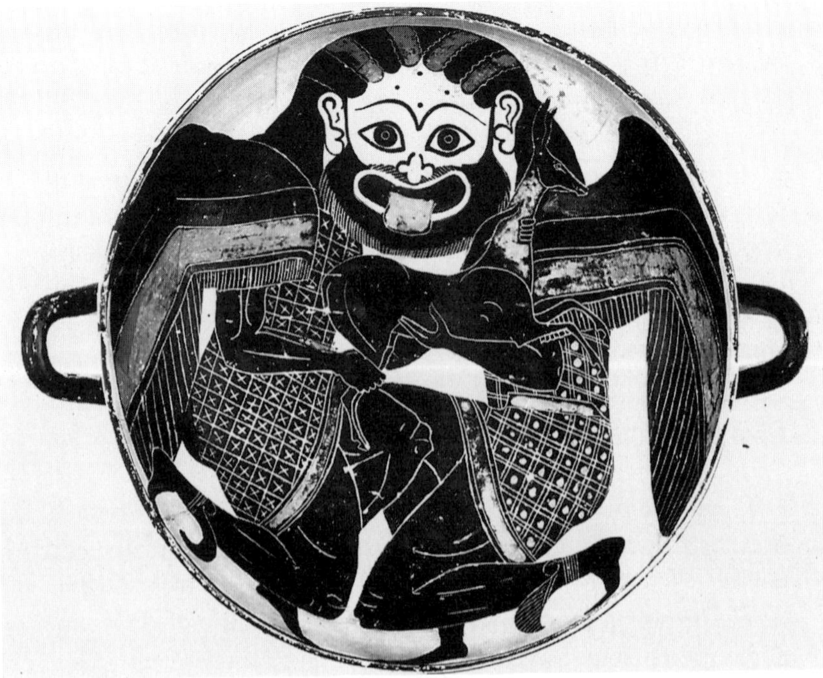

Figure 114. *Gorgo*, attic black-figure kylix (Copenhagen, Ny Carlsberg Gliptotek).

turn, just as the horrific scowl of the Gorgo answers to the terror of those who look at her" (see Figure 114).[13]

Marcel Detienne has shown how in the nineteenth century mythology began to be constituted as a science from the moment fable ceased to function as a pretext for playful jokes and came to seem, rather, like a morass of mad propositions, wild utterances, and absurd statements. "In asserting its authority as a science of the scandalous . . . in taking as its object the infamous, the monstrous, and whatever makes it shudder with horror, the new Mythology presents us with the spectacle of a double movement whereby that which repels also attracts," much like "the 'machine' hidden in the Greek *skandalon:* a snare in which a lure was placed."[14] Detienne's analysis of the idea of "scandal" and the vocabulary used to describe it is applicable, word for word, to that other scandal provoked by the exhibition of Manet's *Déjeuner sur l'herbe* at the Salon des Refusés; and it was not only the laughter which greeted it that took part in the operations of the "machinery" in question.[15]

We should not find it surprising that stories known for so long, ones that had repeatedly occasioned renewed pleasure, suddenly began to seem scandalous. The science of mythology was itself complicit in this development, for it set out to determine reasons for the scandal as well as for the pleasure. Jean-Pierre Vernant's research on the figure of Gorgo[16] does more than push back the boundaries of "indecency" (to those of pornography, we might say, if this word had any meaning in the present context); it goes beyond the "scandalous" component of "scientific" mythology to access, on the other side of the fable literature's apparent disorder, the very root of the scandal: namely, the network of constraints and the play of oppositions on which rest, at the deepest level, *zum Grund*, the logic of myth and the economy of the polytheistic system. The semantic opposition between fable and mythology is characteristic of a culture deriving many of its themes and motifs, many of its figures, images, and emblems, from fable[17]: so much is clear even if we do not raise questions about the secret pleasures obtainable in this way. This opposition collapses, however, when fable ceases to function as a code granting access to the world of the culture but continues to be perpetuated in its classic form: then the knowledge bearing on myths tends to become more rigorous and scientific. But this process does not drain its object of all of its seductive powers. Quite the contrary: it is perhaps in such moments that myth's inherent "aesthetic" dimension becomes most evident, most pregnant.

It remains the case, however, that even in the classical period there was a clear divergence between the level of narration and that of myth per se: a distinction based on constraints operative at this level and which also function in the field of representation, although in the latter instance they remain largely unconscious. I will cite but one example: the fate of the Gorgon's mask in depictions of the judgment of Paris. Whereas Raphael and Giulio Romano represent Minerva's shield in profile or in three-quarter view, Rubens presents it to us frontally, implying it to be a metonymic extension of Minerva's body—which might seem surprising, given that she is usually described as the most chaste of the three rivals. Watteau does likewise, at least as regards the two faces of Minerva and Gorgo. But the constraint—not a narrative but a specifically visual constraint—determining a frontal presentation of the Gorgon is not without its effects on the rest of the configuration. Watteau simply accepts the consequences imposed by the system: as the Gorgo requires frontal presentation, he finds himself more or less obliged to rotate his figure of Venus 180 degrees. As a result, the horrific mask functions for the beholder, through a process of displacement, as a substitute for the most immediate object of the scopic drive—that same object a mere view of which would seem to have assured Venus's victory.

The return or reemergence, from beneath the surface of the story as it has assumed visual form, of constraints bestowing on this story some of its force and seductive power also manifests itself in another way: in the final inefficacy of all attempts to propose another ending for the story or to ascribe some meaning to it other than its original one. Fréart de Chambray understood this perfectly well, having been the first to endorse Paris's choice unreservedly. And we have seen that Picasso himself was not immune to pressures enforcing the reemergence of the judgment theme in the margins, in the supplement. It should by now be clear that I believe the work of myth or myth-work—in the sense of Freud's dream-work—to be an insistent presence in the visual field and that this ongoing dynamic justifies the project of an iconology encompassing the unconscious as well as engaging the questions of representability and of beauty (unless I have formulated the problem backwards, a more fruitful approach being to investigate the role of visual art in the work of myth, in its double articulation on the aesthetic and representational registers).

This dimension is present and active in the psychoanalytic text itself, whether in the form of the great murder-of-the-father myth inscribed by Freud at the beginning of civilization—characterized by Lacan as a *reconstructed* secular mythology more credible than the "revealed" one,[18] although Freud curiously fails to invoke it in *Civilization and Its Discontents*—or in the perhaps overly celebrated passage on the quasi-mythological status of drive theory.[19] If Lacan—to invoke him again—criticizes the use in this context of the word "myth," preferring the term "fiction,"[20] this is because he wishes to stress that Freud regarded the drive as a *Grundbegriff*, a concept (or fiction) that was *fundamental*. But myth itself is linked to this *Grund* or ground from the moment it presents itself, not as a kind of preamble to a future science, nor as a confused sketch or metaphorical substitute for a concept, but as a reminder, addressed as much to the conceptual and scientific registers as to any other, of *another* dimension—a reminder issuing from the *Grund*, the ground, the root. When Freud characterizes the theory of the drives as "our mythology," he is not maintaining that the energies investigated by psychoanalysis under this rubric can only be conceptualized in mythological terms; rather, he is suggesting that these energies are tied to what is most atavistic in man, and that they cannot be transcended, either existentially or philosophically. What is most atavistic, not what is most "primitive." Myth should not be exclusively, and reductively, associated with an earlier stage in the intellectual development of humanity: it also participates in an ongoing archeological project of re-discovery, of re-*invention*. To become persuaded that, even today, the human spirit should pass through a "mythology" of one kind or another, we need not turn to so-called primitive populations, as did Edward Burnett Tylor and advocates of the "new mythology"[21]: we need only consider what might be the profound motivations underlying the current work of anthropologists and historians of religion, to say nothing of the scenes and figures animating this "fiction," which is the theory of the drives, or of the conceptual displacements that are their corollaries. But the fact that mythologists can implicate themselves as subjects in their research certainly does not preclude their yielding to the logic of the system, the better to illuminate it: didn't Plato already censure those who defame the gods and heroes (*tois amartanousi peri muthologian*) by treating myths like fables with which one can do as one pleases, those who fail to reflect properly on themselves?[22]

And what of Paris? What then did he see, which we are permitted to see, through another kind of displacement, only the reverse: not Venus's back or "foundation" but the equivalent of Gorgo's mask? In Ovid's *Heroides*, Paris, addressing Helen, recalls a dream of his mother Hecuba when she still carried him in her womb: "It seemed to her, in an image of sleep (*visa est sub imagine somni*), as though a gigantic flaming torch emerged from this womb. Terrified, she rose; she recounted the frightening things she had seen in the night to old Priam, and he told them to the soothsayers. The soothsayers proclaimed that Ilion would be consumed by the fire of Paris." And Paris concludes: "This torch designated she who today inflames my heart."[23] This dream is extraordinary, as is Paris's retelling of it here, for he condenses into a figure of extraordinary violence what Freud described as the three necessary stages in the relation of man to woman, or the three stages through which, in the course of his life, the image of the mother should pass: childbearer, companion, and destroyer. Or to put it another way: the mother herself, the beloved (according to the *Épître à Othéa*) chosen after her pattern, and lastly the Mother Earth mother who receives him once more.[24]

What Paris saw on Mount Ida (but *to see* is here another name for blinding) was that same womb from which he emerged, the bearer of a flame that was to consume him, and all of Troy with him. An image as horrifying as it was fascinating, an *eloquent* image,[25] like that of the Medusa, its substitute for the beholder, including the latter's relation to castration. The alternatives—signaled by Courbet's *L'Origine du Monde* as well as by Duchamp's *Étant donnés*,[26] though it was already familiar to Greek vase painters—are clear: either a body without a head, reduced to a torso but with its genitals fully visible; or this face, the sight of which turns one to stone. While Watteau's Paris can see Venus's sex but not her face, the beholder sees the Gorgon's head, but cut off, separated from its body and fixed to Minerva's shield, the painter having taken care, like Caravaggio, to present it at a slight tilt, its gaze directed toward Venus.[27] But the beholder, the *regardant*, had best not think he has escaped the trap set for him by the painting and this horrific visage: doubtless he runs no risk of being turned to stone, but his look is relayed, through that of the Medusa, to the object of which the painting reveals only the back (and for which the Gorgon is, I repeat, a substitute). Namely the object seen by Paris, who, judging from Watteau's painting, hasn't been petrified: if there is an erection here (that erection which Freud, in his celebrated text "The Head of the Medusa," maintains has a reassuring effect—fear of the Gorgon being fear of castration, the beholder stiffens to persuade himself that he still has a penis[28])—it is Venus herself, who towers upright before her judge. Is he petrified, this judge? That would be going too far: he settles back submissively, surrendering to the power of Eros as here embodied in a woman.

Thus Watteau produced in this oil sketch a remarkably precise image of the displacement on which the judgment of beauty is premised: a displacement of the genitals (which have not participated in the development of human forms toward beauty) onto secondary sexual characteristics; a displacement of the sexual organs onto the face; a displacement of the unformed onto the formed; but also a displacement of form onto the *parergon*, the "supplement" making it possible to conceptualize form in its very difference (*en sa différence même*). Does Paris's having ceded to a fascination with lack and the unformed, to the point of chaos, justify our denouncing him as a savage, a barbarian, a slave? And, conversely, does the mastery of form attained by the Greeks mark them as free men? The place allotted Gorgo in their pantheon prompts us, following Vernant's example, to ask questions about the way the ancients attempted—precisely—to *give form* in their religious universe to the experience of the absolutely *other*, of which the Gorgon is the emblem: "no longer human beings different from the Greeks, but something radically different from human beings per se: in place of the other man, the other of man."[29] An "other" whose presence is manifest, and active, even in the "same."

In his study "The Theme of the Three Caskets," Freud noted that the Greek Aphrodite was not without ties to hell (nor, it should be added, without links to castration, born as she was of sperm emitted by the severed genitals of her father, Saturn). Although early on she ceded her cthonic role to other divinities (Persephone, Artemis, the three-bodied Hecate, etc.), her "antique ambivalence," her connection to the atavistic, did not altogether disappear: "The goddess of Love herself, who now took the place of the Goddess of Death, had once been identical with her."[30] The choice offered to Paris was fixed from the start, from the moment the judge took it to be his destiny: Venus is to Paris as Cordelia is to Lear. And while psychoanalysis pretended, through Freud, that it had nothing to say about beauty, "less in any case than about any other subject," the muteness—only relative, as we have seen—in which it chose to cloak itself regarding this point was never (as is sometimes the case in dreams) anything but another way of signifying what always has the last word. Which suffices to confer an eminently tragic significance (or should we say: eminently mythic?) on the function of beauty, and on its enigma. For it bears repeating: although the beautiful (*le beau*, masculine) is all gender, beauty (*la beauté*, feminine) is all sex.

. . . . .

Notes

Abbreviations of Frequently Cited Sources

GW	Sigmund Freud, *Gesammelte Werke chronologish geordnet*, 17 volumes (London: Imago Press, 1940–1952).
LOEB	*The Loeb Classical Library*, edited by T. E. Page, W. H. D. Rouse et al. (London: William Heineman Ltd.; Cambridge: Harvard University Press, 1912–).
SE	*The Standard Edition of the Complete Psychological Works of Sigmund Freud, translated from the German under the General Editorship of James Strachey in collaboration with Anna Freud.* 24 volumes (London: The Hogarth Press and The Institute of Psycho-Analysis, 1953–73).
Judgment/Pluhar	Immanuel Kant, *Critique of Judgment*, translated by Werner S. Pluhar (Indianapolis: Hackett Publishing Company, 1987).
LEMAIRE/STECHER	Jean Lemaire de Belges, *Oeuvres*, edited by August Jean Stecher, 4 volumes (Geneva: Slatkine, 1969 [reprint of 1882 edition]).
Le Séminaire	*Le Séminaire de Jacques Lacan*, edited by Jacques-Alain Miller, in progress (Paris: Seuil).

Seminar Jacques Lacan, *The Seminar of Jacques Lacan*, standard English-language edition of the texts as edited in the original French by Jacques-Alain Miller, various translators, in progress (New York: W. W. Norton).

Chapter One

1. "Leider weiss auch die Psychoanalyse uber die Schönheit am wenigsten zu sagen." See Sigmund Freud, *Das Unbehagen in der Kultur* (1929), vol. 14 of *Gesammelte Werke chronologish geordnet*, 17 volumes (London: Imago Press, 1940–1952), hereafter cited as *GW*, p. 441 [*Civilization and Its Discontents*, vol. 21 of *The Standard Edition of the Complete Psychological Works of Sigmund Freud, translated from the German under the General Editorship of James Strachey in collaboration with Anna Freud*, 24 volumes (London: The Hogarth Press and The Institute of Psycho-Analysis, 1953–73), p. 30, hereafter cited as *SE*.]

2. Freud, "Das Interesse an der Psychoanalyse" (1913), *GW*, vol. 8, p. 416 ["The Claims of Psycho-Analysis to Scientific Interest," *SE*, vol. 13, pp. 187–88].

3. "The hypothesis of there being unconscious mental processes paves the way to a decisive new orientation in the world and in science." See Freud, *Vorselungen zur Einführung in die Psychoanalyse* (1916–17), *GW*, vol. 11, p. 15 [*Introductory Lectures on Psychoanalysis*, *SE*, vol. 15, p. 22]. "As a 'depth psychology,' a theory of the mental unconscious, [psychoanalysis] can become indispensable to all the sciences which are concerned with the evolution of human civilization and its great institutions such as art, religion, and the social order." See Freud, *Die Frage der Leienanalyse* (1926), *GW*, vol. 11, p. 283 [*The Question of Lay Analysis*, *SE*, vol. 20, p. 248]. Freud even asserted that "neurotic illness holds the hidden key [*den Schlüssel*] to mythology as well." See Freud, "Die psychogene Sehstörung in Psychoanalytischer Auffassung" (1910), *GW*, vol. 8, p. 100 ["The Psycho-Analytic View of Psychogenic Disturbance of Vision," *SE*, vol. 11, p. 217].

4. Jacques Lacan, *Le Séminaire de Jacques Lacan*, edited by Jacques-Alain Miller, in progress (Paris: Seuil), vol. 7, *L'Éthique de la psychanalyse* (Paris: Seuil, 1986), p. 279, hereafter cited as *Le Séminaire* [Jacques Lacan, *The Seminar of Jacques Lacan*, standard English-language edition of the texts as edited in the original French by Jacques-Alain Miller, various translators, in progress (New York: W. W. Norton), vol. 7, *The Ethics of Psychoanalysis*, translated by Dennis Porter (New York and London: W. W. Norton, 1992), p. 238, hereafter cited as *Seminar*].

5. Cf. Sarah Kofman, *The Childhood of Art: An Interpretation of Freud's Aesthetics*, translated by Winifred Woodhull (New York: Columbia University Press, 1988).

6. To her father, who has asked her what she might have to say to convince him to give her a larger portion of his realm than her sisters, Cordelia responds only "Nothing, my lord."—"Nothing?"—"Nothing." And Lear presses her further: "Nothing will come of nothing; speak again." Cf. Freud, "Das Motiv der Kästchenwahl" (1913), *GW*, vol. 10, p. 29 ["The Theme of the Three Caskets," *SE*, vol. 12, p. 295].

7. Lacan, *Séminaire*, p. 14 [*Seminar*, vol. 7, p. 7].

8. Freud, *Das Unbehagen*, in *GW*, vol. 14, p. 433 [*Civilization*, in *SE*, vol. 21, pp. 75–76].

9. Cf. Konrad Lorenz, "Naturschönheit und Daseinkampf," in *Kosmos*, vol. 58 (1962), pp. 340–48, and *On Aggression*, translated by Marjorie Kerr Wilson (New York: Harcourt, Brace, and World, 1966), chapters 1 and 2. It was the "beauty" of coral fish that initially prompted Lorenz to attempt to discover the *reason* for their brilliant coloring. While the positivism which currently prevails dismisses as anachronistic any attempt to assess works of art of the past by our own contemporary criteria, in view of forcing us to consider them with eyes and in terms which might be those of their own era, what then are we to make of the enthusiasm which prompts ethnologists to speak of the "beauty" of certain animals and even ask questions about this beauty, whereas the animals in question have no word by which to designate it?

10. Freud, *Das Unbehagen*, in *GW*, vol. 14, p. 433 [*Civilization*, in *SE*, vol. 21, p. 75].

11. "Hier kann man den interessanten Fall anschliessen, dass das Lebensglück vorwiegend im Genusse der Schönheit gesucht wird, wo immer sie sich unseren Sinnen und unserem Urteil zeigt, der Schönheit menschlicher formen und Gesten, von Naturobjecten und Landschaften, künstlerischen Formen und selbst wissenschaftlichen Schöpfungen." Ibid., p. 441 [*SE*, vol. 21, p. 82].

12. Ibid., p. 439 [*SE*, vol. 21, p. 80].

13. "Die Ersatzbefriedigungen, wie die Kunst sie bietet, sind gegen die Realität Illusionen." Ibid., p. 433 [*SE*, vol. 21, p. 75].

14. "Weiss ihn als Lustquelle und Lebensströstung." Ibid., p. 439 [*SE*, vol. 21, p. 81].

15. Ibid., p. 433 [*SE*, vol. 21, p. 75].

16. "El primo [libro], tutto matematico, dalle radici entro la natura fa sorgere questa leggiadra et nobilissima arte." See Leone Battista Alberti, *Della pittura*, edited by Luigi Malle (Florence: G. C. Sansoni [1950]), Prologue, p. 54 [*On Painting*, translated by John R. Spencer (New Haven: Yale University Press, 1966), p. 40]. On the vision that, in Cézanne, gains access to the roots, "this side of constituted humanity," cf. Maurice Merleau-Ponty, "Cézanne's Doubt," in *Sense and Non-Sense*, translated by Hubert L. Dreyfus and Patricia A. Dreyfus (Evanston: Northwestern University Press, 1964), pp. 9–25, and *L'Oeil et l'esprit* (Paris: Gallimard, 1964).

17. Lou Andreas Salomé, *Correspondance avec Sigmund Freud*, French trans. (Paris, 1970), pp. 32–33 [*Sigmund Freud and Lou Andreas-Salomé: Letters*, edited by Ernst Pfeiffer, translated by William and Elaine Robson-Scott (London: Hogarth Press and the Institute of Psycho-Analysis, 1972)].

18. Freud, "Formulierungen über die zwei Prinzipien des psychischen Geschehens" (1911), in *GW*, vol. 8, pp. 236–37 ["Formulations Regarding the Two Principles of Mental Functioning," *SE*, vol. 12, pp. 224]. For additional comments along these lines, cf. *Vorlesungen zur Einführung in die Psychoanalyse*, in *GW*, vol. 11, pp. 390–91 [*Introductory Lectures on Psychoanalysis*, in *SE*, vol. 16, pp. 375–76]. Freud himself noted that Otto Rank had developed similar ideas in his book *Der Kunstler. Ansätze zu einer Sexualpsychologie* (Vienna: International Psychoanalytic Association, 1907).

19. Ibid., p. 238 [*SE*, vol. 12, p. 225].

20. Freud, *Das Unbehagen*, in *GW*, vol. 14, p. 436 [*Civilization*, in *SE*, vol. 21, p. 78].

21. Ibid., p. 439 [*SE*, vol. 21, p. 81].

22. Ibid.

23. Ibid.

24. "Ein Nutzen der Schönheit liegt nicht klar zu Tage, ihre kulturelle Notwendigkeit ist nicht einzusehen, und doch könnte man sie in der Kultur nicht vermissen." Ibid., p. 441 [*SE*, vol. 21, p. 82].

25. "Einzig die Ableitung aus dem Gebiet des Sexualempfindens scheint gesichert; es wäre ein vorbildisches Beispeil einer zielgehemmten Regung." Ibid., pp. 441–42 [*SE*, vol. 21, p. 83 (Strachey does not render the conditional in this last passage, which I have restored—Trans.)].

26. "Die 'Schönheit' und der 'Reiz' sind ursprünglich Eigenschaften des Sexualobjekts. Es ist bemerkenswert, dass die Genitalien selbst, deren Anblick immer erregend wirkt, doch fast nie als schön beurteilt werden, dagegen scheint der Charakter der Schönheit an gewissen sekundären Geschlechtsmerkmalen zu haften." Ibid. [*SE*, vol. 21, p. 83].

27. Freud, *Drei Abhandlungen zur Sexualtheorie*, preface to the 4th edition (1920), in *GW*, vol. 5, p. 32 [*Three Essays on the Theory of Sexuality*, in *SE*, vol. 7, p. 134].

Chapter Two

1. "Es scheint mir unzweifelhaft, dass der Begriff des 'Schönen' auf dem Boden des Sexualerregung wurzelt und ursprünglich das sexuell Reizende ['die Reize'] bedeutet. Es steht im Zusammenhange damit, dass wir die Genitalien selbst, deren Anblick die stärkste sexuelle Regung hervorruft, eigentlich niemals 'schön' finden können." See Freud, *Drei Abhandlungen*, in *GW*, vol. 5, p. 55 [*Three Essays*, in *SE*, vol. 7, p. 156].

2. Ibid., p. 48 [*SE*, vol. 7, p. 149].

3. "Der optische Eindruck bleibt der Weg, auf dem die libidinöse Erregung am häufigsten geweckt wird, und auf dessen Gangbarkeit—wenn diese teleologische Betrachtungsweise zulässig ist—die Zuchtwahl rechnet, indem sie das Sexualobjekt sich zur Schönheit entwickeln lässt." Ibid., p. 55 [*SE*, vol. 7, p. 156].

4. Ibid., p. 60 [*SE*, vol. 7, p. 160].

5. Ibid., p. 57 [*SE*, vol. 7, p. 158].

6. Lacan seems to have acquired *L'Origine du monde* during the Second World War. He then asked his brother-in-law André Masson to paint a little curtain to hide it. Cf. the catalog of the exhibition *Courbet Reconsidered* held in Brooklyn and Minneapolis in 1988 (New Haven: Yale University Press, 1988), pp. 176–78. According to Charles Léger (*Courbet* [Paris: G. Crès, 1929] pp. 115–16), Baron François de Hatvany, of Budapest, purchased the painting from the dealer Bernheim-Jeune toward 1910. At that time, it was in a double frame which could be closed and locked and was covered by a small panel representing a snow-covered castle, which was purchased by another Hungarian aristocrat, one Baron Herzog.

7. "Die mit der Kultur fortschreidetende Verhüllung des Körpers hält die sexuelle Neugierde wach, welche danach strebt, sich das Sexualobjekt durch Enthüllung der verborgenen Teile zu ergänzen, die aber ins Künstlerische abgelenkt ('sublimiert') werden kann, wenn man ihr Interesse von de Genitalien weg auf die Körperbildung im ganzen zu lenken vermag." See Freud, *Drei Abhundlungen*, in *GW*, vol. 5, p. 55 [*Three Essays*, in *SE*, vol. 7, p. 156].

8. Ibid., p. 49 [*SE*, vol. 7, p. 150].

9. "Wir werden so angewiesen, die Verknüpfung zwischen Trieb und Objekt in unseren Gedanken zu lockern. Der Geschlechtstrieb ist wahrscheinlich zunächst unhabhängich von seinem Objekt und verdankt wohl auch nicht den Reizen desselben seine Entstehung." Ibid., p. 46 [*SE*, vol. 7, p. 148].

10. Ibid., p. 48, note 1 (added in 1910) [*SE*, vol. 7, p. 149].

11. Plato *Symposium* 210c.

12. Ibid., 212a.

13. Freud, *Drei Abhandlungen*, in *GW*, vol. 5, p. 46 [*Three Essays*, in *SE*, vol. 7, p. 149].

14. Ibid., p. 47 [*SE*, vol. 7, p. 148].

15. Freud, "Triebe und Triebschicksale" (1910), in *GW*, vol. 10, p. 215 ["Instincts and their Vicissitudes," in *SE*, vol. 14, pp. 122–23]. On the object with which we can have dealings only in its form as the "objet petit a," see Lacan's comments on "La pulsion partielle et son circuit," in *Le Séminaire*, vol. 11, *Les Quatre Concepts fondamentaux de la psychanalyse* (Paris: Seuil, 1973), pp. 162–65 ["The Partial Drive and Its Circuit," in *Seminar*, vol. 11 (*The Four Fundamental Concepts of Psycho-Analysis*), translated by Alan Sheridan (New York: W. W. Norton, 1978), pp. 174–84].

16. "Il ne faut jamais lire Freud sans avoir les oreilles dressées.

Quand on lit des choses pareilles, ça doit tout de même les faire bouger un peu." See Lacan, *Séminaire*, vol. 11, p. 153 [*Seminar*, vol. 11, *Four Fundamental Concepts*, p. 168].

17. Freud, *Drei Abhandlungen*, in *GW*, vol. 5, p. 111 [*Three Essays*, in *SE*, vol. 7, p. 209].

18. Freud, *Das Unbehagen*, in *GW*, vol. 14, pp. 458–59 [*SE*, vol. 21, pp. 99–100].

19. Ibid., p. 458 [*SE*, vol. 21, p. 99].

20. Cf. André Leroi-Gourhan, *Gesture and Speech*, translated by Anna Bostock Berger (Cambridge: MIT Press, 1993), chapter 1, "The Image of Ourselves," pp. 3–24.

21. Freud, *Drei Abhandlungen*, in *GW*, vol. 5, pp. 68–69 [*Three Essays*, in *SE*, vol. 7, p. 169].

22. Freud, "Die psychogene Sehstörung in psychoanalystischer Auffassung" (1910), in *GW*, vol. 8, p. 97 ["The Psycho-Analytic View of Psychogenic Disturbance of Vision," in *SE*, vol. 11, p. 213].

23. Freud, *Das Unbehagen*, in *GW*, vol. 14, pp. 458–59 [*Civilization*, in *SE*, vol. 21, pp. 99–100].

24. ". . . infantile amnesia, which turns everyone's childhood into something like a prehistoric epoch and conceals from him the beginnings of his own sexual life . . ." See Freud, *Drei Abhandlungen*, in *GW*, vol. 5, p. 76 [*Three Essays*, in *SE*, vol. 7, p. 176].

25. Lacan, *Le Séminaire*, vol. 11, pp. 70 ff. [*Seminar*, vol. 11 (*The Four Fundamental Concepts*), pp. 67 ff.].

26. In a note added to the second of the *Three Essays* in 1920, Freud stresses that "In biological discussions it is scarcely possible to avoid a teleological way of thinking, even though one is aware that in any particular instance one is not secure against error." See Freud, *Drei Abhandlungen*, in *GW*, vol. 5, p. 85 [*Three Essays*, in *SE*, vol. 7, p. 184].

27. Ibid., p. 57 [*SE*, vol. 7, p. 158].

28. "Wir fordern, das der Kulturmensch die Schönheit verehre, wo sie ihm in der Natur begegnet, und sie erstelle an Gegenständen, soweit seiner Hände Arbeit es vermag." See Freud, *Das Unbehagen*, in *GW*, vol. 14, p. 452 [*Civilization*, in *SE*, vol. 21, p. 92].

29. "Eine psychoanalytische, di. genetische Ableitung." Ibid., p. 425 [*SE*, vol. 21, p. 65].

30. "Aber der Nützen erklärt uns das Streben nicht ganz. Es muss noch etwas anderes im Spiele sein." Ibid., p. 453 [*SE*, vol. 21, p. 94].

31. Ibid., pp. 451–52 [*SE*, vol. 21, p. 92].

32. Ibid., p. 459 [*SE*, vol. 21, pp. 99–100].

33. Freud, *Drei Abhandlungen*, in *GW*, vol. 5, p. 51 [*Three Essays*, in *SE*, vol. 7, p. 152].

34. "Ein Verweilen bei diesem intermediären Sexualziel des sexuell betonten Schauens kommt in gewissen Grade den meisten Normalen zu, ja es gibt ihnen die Möglichkeit, einen gewissen

Betrag ihrer Libido auf höhere künstlerische Ziele zu richten." Ibid., pp. 55–56 [*SE*, vol. 7, pp. 156–57].

35. Ibid., p. 61 [*SE*, vol. 7, pp. 161–62]. Freud, in a letter to Fliess dated 3 January 1897, had already indicated his interest in the perversions, envisaging placement of this citation from the prelude of Goethe's *Faust* ("From Heaven, through the world, to Hell") at the head of a chapter on sexuality in a work he was then planning (*The Complete Letters of Sigmund Freud to Wilhelm Fliess, 1877–1904*, edited by Jeffrey Masson [Cambridge, MA: Belknap Press of Harvard University Press, 1985], p. 220). Walter Benjamin also emphasized, from a perspective quite distinct from that of psychoanalysis, the mixture of high and low inherent in art, going so far as to affirm that "every work of art is simultaneously a document of barbarism" ("Edward Fuchs, Collector and Historian," French trans., *Macula*, no. 3–4 [1978]: 45). But it is William Blake who went the farthest in this direction, boldly proclaiming, in *The Marriage of Heaven and Hell* (note the Goethean title), that "the genitals [are] beauty" (*The Complete Poetry and Prose of William Blake*, edited by David V. Erdman [New York: Anchor Books, 1988], p. 37).

36. Freud, "Die psychogene Sehstörung," in *GW*, vol. 8, pp. 98–99 ["The Psychoanalytic View," in *SE*, vol. 11, p. 216]. On all of these questions, and that of "representability" in general, cf. Patrick Lacoste, *L'Étrange Cas du professeur M.: Psychanalyse à l'écran* (Paris: Gallimard, 1990).

37. Lacan, *Le Séminaire*, vol. 11, p. 151 [*Seminar*, vol. 11 (*Four Fundamental Concepts*), p. 166].

38. "If we bring together the paradoxes that we just defined at the level of *Drang*, at that of the object, at that of the aim of the drive, I think that the resulting image would show the working of a dynamo connected up to a gas-tap, a peacock's feather emerges, and tickles the belly of a pretty woman, who is just lying there *for beauty's sake* [*pour la beauté de la chose;* my emphasis]. Indeed the thing begins to become interesting from this very fact, that the drive defines, according to Freud, all the forms of which one may reverse such a mechanism. This does not mean that one turns the dynamo upside-down—one unrolls its wires, it is they that become the peacock's feather, the gas-tap goes into the lady's mouth, and the bird's rump emerges in the middle." Ibid., p. 154 [*Seminar*, vol. 11 (*Four Fundamental Concepts*), p. 169].

Chapter Three

1. References to Kant are rare in Freud's work; they evidence his concern to clarify how the hypothesis of the unconscious might be substituted for that of the Kantian *a priori* by "going beyond" it and articulating it in genetic terms. Thus spatiality is conceived of not as

pure intuition but as deriving by projection from the extension of the psychic apparatus as such: "The psyche has extension but knows nothing about it" (cf. Freud, *Résultats, idées, problèmes*, vol. 2, 1921–38 [Paris, 1985], p. 288).

2. "Man muss nicht im mindesten für die Existenz der Sache eingenommen, sondern in diesem betracht ganz gleichgultig sein, um in Sachen des Geschmacks, den Richter zu spielen." See Immanuel Kant, *Kritik der Urteilskraft*, part 1, section 2 ["In order to play the judge in matters of taste, we must not be in the least biased in favor of the thing's existence but must be wholly indifferent about it." Immanuel Kant, *Critique of Judgment*, translated by Werner S. Pluhar (Indianapolis: Hackett Publishing Company, 1987), p. 46, hereafter cited as *Judgment*/Pluhar].

3. Ibid.

4. "Diejenigen, welche immer nur auf das Geniessen ausgehen . . . sich gerne alles Urteilens überheben." Ibid., section 3 [*Judgment*/Pluhar, pp. 47–48].

5. Roland Barthes, *The Pleasure of the Text*, translated by Richard Miller (New York: Hill and Wang, 1975), p. 21 [trans. altered].

6. Jacques Derrida, "Parergon," in *The Truth in Painting*, translated by Geoff Bennington and Ian McLeod (Chicago: University of Chicago Press, 1987), p. 48.

7. "Da doch Schönheit ohne Beziehung auf das Gefühl des Subjekts für sich nichts ist." Kant, *Kritik*, part 1, section 9 [*Judgment*/Pluhar, pp. 61–64].

8. Cf. Freud, "Formulierungen," in *GW*, vol. 8, p. 233 ["Formulations," in *SE*, vol. 12, pp. 221]; and "Die Verneinung," in *GW*, vol. 14, p. 12 ["Negation," in *SE*, vol. 19, pp. 235–36].

9. "In Wirklichkeit bedeutet die Ersetzung des Lustprinzips durch das Realitätsprinzip keine Absetzung des Lustprinzips, sondern nur eine Sicherung desselben." See Freud, "Formulierungen," in *GW*, vol. 8, pp. 235–36 ["Actually the substitution of the reality principle for the pleasure principle implies no deposing of the pleasure principle, but only a safeguarding of it." See "Formulations," in *SE*, vol. 12, p. 223].

10. Kant, *Kritik der Urteilskraft*, part 1, section 13 [*Judgment*/Pluhar, pp. 68–69].

11. Ibid.

12. Freud, "Beiträge zur Psychologie des Liebeslebens. II. Uber die allgemeinste Erniedrigung des Liebeslebens" (1912), in *GW*, vol. 8, p. 90 ["On the Universal Tendency to Debasement in the Sphere of Love (Contributions to the Psychology of Love II)," in *SE*, vol. 11, p. 189].

13. Jacques Lacan, *Le Séminaire*, vol. 7, p. 11 [*Seminar*, vol. 7 (*The Ethics*), p. 3].

Chapter Four

1. Kant, *Kritik der Urteilsckrft*, book 1, sec. 2 [*Judgment*/Pluhar, pp. 45–46].

2. Jean-François Lyotard, *Lessons on the Analytic of the Sublime (Kant's "Critique of Judgement," [sections] 23–29)*, translated by Elizabeth Rottenberg (Stanford, CA: Stanford University Press, 1994), p. 3.

3. Friedrich Nietzsche, *Unfashionable Observations*, translated by Richard T. Gray (Stanford: Stanford University Press, 1995).

4. Immanuel Kant, *Beobachtungen über das Gefühl des Schönen und Erhabenen* (1764), section 3 [*Observations on the Feeling of the Beautiful and Sublime*, translated by John T. Goldthwait (Berkeley: University of California Press, 1960), pp. 76–96].

5. Ibid. [*Observations*, p. 80].

6. ". . . what I have to observe and explain in the sensing of the beautiful is only the appearances." Ibid. [*Observations*, p. 85].

7. Ibid. [*Observations*, p. 84].

8. Ibid. [*Observations*, p. 91].

9. "Die Natur wird nicht mehr beurteilt, wie sie als Kunst erscheint, sodern sofern sie wirklich (obzwar übermenschliche) Kunst ist." See Kant, *Kritik der Urteilskraft*, book 1, sec. 48 [*Judgment*/Pluhar, pp. 179–80].

Chapter Five

1. *Manet*, catalog of an exhibition held in Paris and New York in 1983 (New York: The Metropolitan Museum of Art, 1983), entry on *Le Déjeuner sur l'herbe*, no. 62, by Françoise Cachin.

2. P. G. Hamerton, "The Salon of 1863," *Fine Arts Quarterly Review* (October 1863); as cited by John Rewald, *The History of Impressionism*, 4th ed. (New York: Museum of Modern Art, 1973), p. 85.

3. Sigmund Freud, "Der Moses des Michelangelo" (1914), in *GW*, vol. 10, p. 185 ["The Moses of Michelangelo," in *SE*, vol. 13, p. 222].

4. Freud, "Das Unheimliche" (1919), in *GW*, vol. 12 ["The Uncanny," in *SE*, vol. 17, p. 225].

5. In his review of what he called the *Salon des Vaincus* or "Salon of the Vanquished," Ernest Chesneau feigned to express regret for the public's behavior in this exhibition containing so many "horrible paintings": "The real spectacle was offered by the spectators . . . We would have preferred a bit more moderation in their laughter . . . One doesn't laugh at one's sick friends, one cares for them" (*L'Art et les artistes modernes en France et en Angleterre* [Paris: Didier, 1864], pp. 182, 197). The painter Cazin, himself one of the *refusés*, was more explicit still: "It was as though those in the exhibition had been court-martialed. One entered a chamber of horrors, as at Madame Tussaud's in London. Visitors expected to laugh, and laugh they did,

from the moment they set foot in the door . . . Manet, in the innermost room, made them split their sides with his *Déjeuner sur l'herbe*" (as cited by Adolphe Tabarant, *Manet et ses oeuvres* [Paris: Gallimard, 1947], p. 67).

6. Cf. Marcel Detienne, *The Creation of Mythology*, translated by Margaret Cook (Chicago: University of Chicago Press, 1986), pp. 13 ff.

7. Meyer Schapiro, "The Apples of Cézanne: An Essay on the Meaning of Still-Life," in *Selected Papers II. Modern Art, Nineteenth and Twentieth Centuries* (New York: Braziller, 1978), pp. 8–9.

8. "The Bath, the Majo, and the Espada are fine sketches, I'll concede that. There's a certain liveliness in the tone, a certain frankness in the touch that have nothing vulgar about them. But then? Is this drawing? Is this painting? M. Manet thinks he's being firm and powerful, but he's only being hard; oddly, he's as soft as he is hard" (Jules Castagnary, "Le salon des Refusés," *L'Artiste* [15 August 1863]: 16).

9. "A 'Bréda prostitute,' as nude as can be, impudently makes a spectacle of herself between guardians as fully clothed and cravated as she is naked . . . These two figures seem like vacationing students determined to assert their manhood; and all my attempts to decipher this unseemly conundrum have proved vain." See Louis Étienne, *Le Jury et les exposants—salon des Refusés* (Paris, 1863), p. 30.

10. "It is hard to believe that M. Manet borrowed from one of Raphael's compositions. But alas, this is all too true! One need only compare his *Déjeuner sur l'herbe* to a certain group in the *Judgment of Paris*" (Chesneau, *L'Art et les artistes modernes*, p. 190, note 1).

11. Wayne Andersen makes the amusing suggestion that the figure extends his index finger to serve as a perch for the sparrow nestling in the upper reaches of the painting, a hypothesis that at least draws attention to the presence of this bird ("Manet and the Judgment of Paris," *Art News* 72 [February 1973]: 63–69).

12. Gustav Pauli, "Raphael und Manet," *Monatshefte für Kunstwissenschaft*, I (January–February 1908): 53–55. Cf. Ernst Gombrich, *Aby Warburg: An Intellectual Biography*, 2d ed. (Chicago: University of Chicago Press, 1986), pp. 273–77.

13. "Monsieur Manet will have talent on the day he learns drawing and perspective; he will have taste on the day he ceases to choose subjects in view of their scandalous content. It is not our purpose here to deliver a lecture on moral questions as they relate to the fine arts, but we cannot regard as perfectly chaste a work in which a woman seated in the woods, surrounded by students in berets and coats, is clothed only in the shadows of the leaves. This is a question of subordinate interest, but I must express regret, more than for the composition itself, for the intention that inspired it. Monsieur Manet wants to attain celebrity by *shocking the middle class.* Assaulting the modesty of M. Prudhomme is a source of delight for this young brain

given to foolery . . . But today M. Prudhomme can no longer be scandalized, he laughs at these youthful excesses and enlists the others who are laughing in his cause" (Chesneau, *L'Art et les artistes modernes*, p. 190).

14. "A curious lack of imagination repeatedly led Manet to 'borrow' from other artists. Many of his works, if not based directly on old masters, were at least inspired by remembrance (Manet had travelled extensively), by reproductions, prints, etc. Although Manet himself rarely made any allusions to his sources, he often used them with so little disguise that it would have been easy to identify them had anybody cared to do so. But in Manet's case the whole question seemed of little importance, since what mattered was not the subject but the way in which he treated it. He found in the works of the past only compositional elements; he never copied, because only his inspiration, not his talent, needed an occasional guide" (Rewald, *The History of Impressionism*, p. 86).

15. Alan Bowness, "A Note on Manet's Compositional Difficulties," *Burlington Magazine* 103 (June 1961): 276–77.

16. Jules et Edmond de Goncourt, *Manette Salomon* (1864–66), chapter 7; as cited by Françoise Cachin in *Manet*, exhibition catalog, no. 62, p. 170.

Chapter Six

1. Michael Fried, "Manet's Sources: Aspects of His Art, 1859–1865," *Artforum* 7 (March 1969): 40.

2. "La première feuille qui porta le nom de Raphaël hors d'Italie, et qui fit connaître a tous les peintres de son siècle, qu'il était leur Coriphée, fut la noble et fameuse Estampe du Jugement de Pâris, ou Raphaël fit une heureuse tentative pour lui, et pour son élève Marc-Antoine, que depuis il continua de l'entretenir en ce même emploi: et à cet effet il lui dessina tout-exprès plusieurs autres belles choses, que nous n'aurions, peut-être, point vues sans cette occasion, parce qu'il ne les a jamais peintes." See Roland Fréart, Sieur de Chambray, *Idée de la perfection de la peinture* (Geneva: Minskoff, 1973 [reprint of 1662 edition]), pp. 23–24.

3. Mantegna was without doubt the first to realize that engravings could secure a much wider audience for an artist's work than paintings, though in his case we cannot speak of reproduction, except insofar as his students took up some of his motifs in their own productions. It was by means of his engravings, and those of his school, that Dürer first had contact with the Italian Renaissance. Cf. Jay A. Levenson, Konrad Oberhuber, and Jacquelyn L. Sheehan, *Early Italian Engravings from the National Gallery of Art* (Washington, DC: National Gallery of Art, 1977), pp. 165 ff.

4. Karl Marx and Frederick Engels, *The German Ideology*. vol. I, "The Leipzig Council," III, "Saint Max," in Karl Marx and Frederick

Engels, *Collected Works*, various translators (London: International Publishers, 1975—), vol. 5 (1976), p. 393.

5. "There is no history of politics, law, science, etc., of art, religion, etc." (ibid., I, "Feuerbach," p. 92). "Religion, the family, the state, law, morality, science, art, etc. are only *particular* modes of production and therefore come under its general law . . . The history of *industry* and the *objective* existence of industry as it has developed is the *open* book of the essential powers of man, man's psychology present in tangible form; up to now this history has not been grasped in its connection with the *nature* of man, but only in an exterior utilitarian aspect, for man, moving in the realm of estrangement, was only capable of conceiving the general existence of man—religion, or history in its abstract and universal form of politics, art, literature, etc.—as the reality of man's essential powers and as *man's species-activity*." See Marx, "Economic and Philosophical Manuscripts" (1844), in *Karl Marx: Early Writings* (New York: Vintage Books, 1975), pp. 349, 354.

6. "Ma tornando a Marcantonio, arrivato in Roma intaglio in rame una bellisima carta di Raffaello da Urbino, nella quale era una Lucrezia Romana che si uccideva, con tanta diligenza e bella maniera, che, essendo subito portata da alcuni amici suoi a Raffaello, egli si disposa a mettere fuori in istampa alcuni disegni di cose sue; e appresso un disegno che gia avea fatto del giudizio di Paris, nel quale Raffaello per capriccio aveva dignato il carro del sole, le ninfe de'-boschi, quelle delle fonti, e quelle de'fiumi, con vasi, timoni ed altre belle fantasie attorno; e cosi risoluto, furono di maniera intagliate da Marcantonio, che ne stupi tutta Roma." See Giorgio Vasari, *Le Vite de piu eccellenti pittori, scultori et architecttori*, edited by Gaetano Milanesi, 9 vols. (Florence: G. C. Sansoni, 1906), "Vita di Marcantonio Bolognese e d'altri intagliatori di stampe," vol. 5, p. 411.

7. "Avendo dunque veduto Raffaello lo andare nelle stampe d'Alberto Durero, volonteroso ancor egli di mostrare quel che in tale arte poteva, fece studiare Marco Antonio Bolognese in questa practica infinitamente." Ibid., vol. 1, p. 354 ("Vita di Raffaello da Urbino").

8. ". . . pero non ottenne altro, se non che Marcantonio non facesse più il nome nè il segno sopradetto d'Alberto nelle sue opere." Ibid., vol. 5, p. 406 ("Vita di Marcantonio").

9. Cf.: Stefania Massari, "Il Cinquecento," in *Raphael invenit: Stampe da Raffaello nelle collezioni dell'Istituto Nazionale per la Grafica*, exhibition catalog by Grazia Bernini Pezzini, Stefania Massari, and Simonetta Prosperi Valenti Rodino (Rome: Quasar, 1985), p. 10; and Konrad Oberhuber, "Raffaello e l'incisione," in *Raffaello in Vaticano*, catalog of an exhibition held in Vatican City in 1984–85 (Rome: Electa, 1984), pp. 333–42. The indication RAPH URBI / INVEN / MAF appears at the lower left in the second state of the *Judgment of Paris* engraving.

10. Sigmund Freud, "Der Moses des Michelangelo" (1914), in *GW*, vol. 10, p. 185 ["The Moses of Michelangelo," in *SE*, vol. 13, p. 222]. On this point, cf. my article on this celebrated text by Freud, "Le gardien de l'interpretation," originally published in *Tel Quel*, no. 44 (Winter 1971): 70–84, and no. 45 (Spring 1971): 82–96; it will be included in a forthcoming collection.

11. Henri Zerner, "Introduction," in *Tout l'oeuvre peint de Raphaël* (Paris: Flammarion, 1969), p. 7.

12. Massari, *Raphael invenit*, pp. 9–10, 242.

13. Ibid., "Stampa di traduzione," p. 10.

14. The idea of the *translatio*, in the sense of a transferral implying passage from one expressive medium to another, does not seem to have figured in humanist discourse, which was preoccupied, in the matter of literary translation, with a strictly rhetorical parallel with painting. Cf. Michael Baxandall, *Giotto and the Orators: Humanist Observers of Painting in Italy and the Discovery of Pictorial Composition, 1350–1450* (Oxford: Clarendon Press, 1971), pp. 24–27.

15. "L'invenzione, la quale fa mettere insieme in istoria le figure a quattro a sei a dieci a venti, talmente che si viene a formare le battaglie e l'altre cose grandi dell'arte." See Vasari, *Vite*, vol. 1, p. 173 [*Vasari on Technique*, translated by S. Maclehose, edited by G. Galdwin Brown (New York: Dover Books, 1960), p. 210].

16. Cf. Massari, *Raphael invenit*, p. 660, fig. 23.

17. Re a small monochrome panel—doubtless a studio work—in the window embrasure underneath the *Parnassus* in the Vatican Stanze della Signatura, whose decor was completed in 1511, see below, chapter 10.

18. Cf. Hubert Damisch, *The Origin of Perspective*, translated by John Goodman (Cambridge, MA: MIT Press, 1993), pp. 25–26.

19. ". . . la pauvre peinture [en fût] réduite à l'estampe, je pourrais dire mieux à la sépulture (si, hors de la main des Grecs, quelqu'un l'a jamais vue vivante). . . ." (Nicolas Poussin, letter to Chantelou dated 7 April 1647; in *Correspondance*, edited by Charles Jouanny, *Archives de l'Art Français*, new series, vol. 5, 1911 [reprint Paris, 1968], p. 354).

20. Vasari, *Vite*, vol. 1, p. 173 [*Vasari on Technique*, p. 210].

Chapter Seven

1. ". . . absolument nécessaire, pour en pouvoir faire une discussion raisonnable, de savoir les circonstances de cette histoire poétique" (Roland Fréart, Sieur de Chambray, *Idée de la perfection de la peinture* [Geneva: Minskoff, 1973 (reprint of 1662 edition)], p. 24).

2. "Lisez l'histoire et le tableau, afin de connaître si chaque chose [était] appropriée au sujet" (Nicolas Poussin, letter to Chantelou dated 28 April 1639; in *Correspondance*, edited by Charles Jouanny, *Archives de l'Art Français*, new series, vol. 5, 1911 [reprint Paris, 1968], p. 21). On the meaning of this statement, cf. Louis Marin, *To*

Destroy Painting, translated by Mette Hjort (Chicago: University of Chicago Press, 1995), pp. 30 ff.

3. "Pâris, fils du roi Priam, ayant été exposé sur le Mont Ida, incontinent après sa naissance, et abandonné aux bêtes sauvages (à cause d'un songe funeste, et fatal à sa patrie, que sa mère Hécube fit de lui durant sa grossesse) fut recueilli par un des bergers de la contrée, qui l'éleva comme son enfant. Ce jeune prince inconnu à son nourricier, et à soi-même, par une secrète vertu de son sang royal, se rendit dès ses premières années si parfait, qu'il surpassait tous les autres de son âge, en force, en beauté, en adresse, et en tout ce qu'il y avait de recommandable parmi eux. Cela, jusqu'ici, a quelque apparence d'une véritable histoire: mais les poètes, qui sont en quelque façon les camarades des peintres, y ont ensuite mêlé plusieurs fantaisies capricieuses; et disent qu'en ce temps-là tous les dieux ayant été convies aux noces de Pélée avec Thétis, hormis la seule déese Discorde; cette malicieuse, pour se venger du mépris qu'on avait d'elle, jeta secrètement dans la foule de l'assemblée, une pomme d'or, sur laquelle était écrit, *Soit donnée à la plus belle.* Mercure, le plus intrigue de tous les dieux, l'ayant aperçue la ramassa, et lisant tout haut l'adresse de ce pernicieux présent, alluma tant de jalousie entre les déeses, qui se piquaient d'être belles, que Jupiter même ne voulut pas en être le juge, de peur d'offenser sa femme Junon, s'il se prononçait en faveur d'une autre; ou de paraître suspect et intéressé, s'il l'eût préférée. Les seules rivales de Junon, furent la fière Minerve, et l'agréable Vénus. Si bien que cette question étant remise, du commun consentement des trois prétendantes, au jugement du royal berger Pâris (qui était lui-même pour lors un parfait modèle de beauté), Mercure lui fut incontinent dépêché de la part de Jupiter, avec cette pomme, qu'il devait donner à celle des trois qu'il jugerait être la plus belle. / Voilà ce que Raphaël s'est proposé de représenter dans ce dessin; ou, par une considération générale, et presque toujours nécessaire, il a placé les principales figures du sujet au milieu de son ordonnance; et les a fait voir dans une grande variété d'aspects, et d'expressions; car Minerve toute remplie de dédain de n'avoir pas eu le prix qu'elle prétendait, tourne le dos à son juge, avec une contenance de mépris extrême. Vénus, en faveur de qui la sentence fut prononcée, est au milieu de ses deux rivales, recevant le gage de sa victoire, avec une modestie accompagnée de toute la grâce que se peut imaginer. Le peintre a voulu nous la faire voir par le profil, qui est le côté le plus avantageux, pour montrer la forme et la régularité des parties d'un beau visage. Junon, la plus orgueilleuse des prétendantes, outrée de dépit de n'avoir pas été préférée, parait s'emporter contre Pâris, qui néanmoins ne témoigne pas d'en être ému, et demeurant sur son siège, assis comme il appartient à la qualité de juge qu'il tient là, donne son arrêt, avec la pomme fatale, qui causa ensuite tant de désordres parmi la Grèce, et enfin la ruine entière de

la déplorable ville de Troie, lieu de naissance de Pâris. Cette dernière déese paraît de front, comme plus audacieuse que les deux autres: et Raphaël les a dessinées expressément toutes trois en des aspects différents, pour donner autant qu'il était possible de contraste à ses figures. Je remarque même encore en celle du berger Pâris quelque variété dans son profil d'avec celui de Vénus: car si cette belle nous découvre dans son profil une partie de son sein, Pâris au contraire se montre par le côté des épaules, tant notre peintre est exact à faire que chaque partie de son tableau soit diversifiée. / Outre ces quatre figures principales, ou toute l'histoire était suffisamment exprimée, il a encore introduit Mercure en une démarche qui donne visiblement à entendre, qu'ayant achevé sa commission, il est prêt de retourner dire à Jupiter quel en a été l'événement, et qui est la bienheureuse que la victoire aurait couronnée." Fréart de Chambray, *Idée de la perfection de la peinture*, pp. 24–28.

4. Cf. above, chapter 6.

5. "La storia è summa opera del pittore." See Leone Battista Alberti, *Della pittura*, edited by Luigi Malle (Florence: G. C. Sansoni [1950]), book III, p. 111 [*On Painting*, translated by John R. Spencer (New Haven: Yale University Press, 1966), p. 95].

6. Marcel Detienne, *The Creation of Mythology*, translated by Margaret Cook (Chicago: University of Chicago Press, 1986), chapter 7, pp. 124–34.

7. Ibid., pp. xi–xii.

8. It was under this rubric that Dumézil elected to discuss the judgment of Paris in a work exploring the relations between myth and epic. See Georges Dumézil, *Mythe et épopée*, I, *L'Idéologie des trois fonctions dans les épopées indo-européens* (Paris: Gallimard, 1968), p. 10.

9. Homer *Iliad* 24.25–30 (Richard Lattimore, trans. [Chicago: University of Chicago Press, 1951]).

10. Cf. Albert Severyns, *Homèrè*, 3 vols. (Brussels: Office de la Publicité, 1944–48), vol. 3, *L'Artiste*, p. 84, note 4; and the more developed discussion by the same author in his *Le Cycle épique dans l'école d'Aristarque* (Liège: Imp. H. Vaillant-Charmanne; Paris, E. Champion, 1928), pp. 261–64.

11. Dumézil, *Myth et épopée*, I, p. 633.

12. Ibid., p. 583.

13. Cf. Albert Severyns, "Pomme de discorde et Jugement des déesses," in *Phoibos*, vol. 5 ("Mélanges Joseph Hombert"; 1950–51), pp. 145–72.

14. Aristotle *Poetics* 7.1450b–1451a.

15. Nicole Loraux has demonstrated convincingly how the discourse of politics, of the city or *polis*, being predicated on the exclusion of women, implied that the body and sexuality were exclusively female provinces. As though there were but one sex, the female sex. As though women were "*all sex, and men all gender*" [my emphasis, as

this distinction is crucial on both theoretical and practical levels], this embodiment of the human genus, this male example or paradigm whose virility could not be tainted by anything feminine, gaining a decisive advantage by having neither body nor sexuality, the *soma* with civic obligations existing only in the context of the satisfaction of said obligations (Nicole Loraux, *The Experiences of Tiresias: The Feminine and the Greek Man*, translated by Paula Wissing [Princeton: Princeton University Press, 1995], p. 10).

16. Homer *Iliad* 3.442–46, 399–415 [Lattimore trans.].

17. Severyns, "Pomme de discorde et Jugement des déesses," p. 155.

18. Apollodorus, *The Library*, translated by James George Frazer, in *The Loeb Classical Library*, edited by T. E. Page, W. H. D. Rouse et al. (London: William Heineman Ltd.; Cambridge: Harvard University Press, 1912–), hereafter cited as LOEB, 2 vols. (1921), vol. II, pp. 172–73 (*Epitome*, III, 2–3). This summary of the *Cyprian Lays* is known as the *Cypria.*

19. "One will not look for the original text, *because it doesn't exist*" (Marcel Mauss, *Manuel d'ethnographie* [Paris: Payot, 1947], p. 98; cited by Detienne, *The Creation of Mythology*, p. 37).

20. Cf. François Jouan, *Euripède et les légendes des Chants cypriens: Des origines de la guerre de Troie à l'"Iliade"* (Paris: Société d'édition "Les Belles Lettres," 1966).

21. Sophocles, fragment 361 P, cited by Jouan, *Euripède et les légendes des Chants cypriens*, pp. 106–7. Cf. Karl Reinhardt, "Das Parisurteil" (1938), in *Von Werken und Formen* (Godesberg: H. Küpper, 1948), pp. 11–36.

22. Cf. Jean-Pierre Vernant and Pierre Vidal-Naquet, *Myth and Tragedy in Ancient Greece*, translated by Janet Lloyd (New York: Zone Books, 1988).

23. Euripides *Iphigenia in Aulis*, lines 71–75. Cf. *The Complete Greek Tragedies*, edited by David Grene and Richard Lattimore, 4 vols. (Chicago: University of Chicago Press, 1959), vol. 4, p. 300.

24. Ibid., lines 1400–1403: ibid., p. 371.

25. "Donc Pâris, à vingt ans, monte sur l'Ida; / Il rencontre trois déesses qui le prennent pour arbitre. / 'Qui de nous trois est la plus belle?' / Sais-tu ce que lui offrait Pallas / pour acheter son jugement? / La Grèce, tout simplement. Avec l'appui d'Athéna / il aurait conquise en un tournemain. / Et Héra: 'Si je gagne tu auras l'Asie entière / et les confins de l'Europe.' / Cypris, en cas de victoire, n'a rien promis / sauf moi. Elle m'a décrite, elle a gagné." From *Les Troyennes*, an adaptation of Euripides' play by Jean-Paul Sartre (Paris: Gallimard, 1965), pp. 98–99. [There is an English-language version of the Sartre/Euripides *The Trojan Women* by Ronald Duncan (London: H. Hamilton [1967]), but it takes considerable liberties with Sartre's text. I have used my own rendering—Trans.].

26. Euripides *The Trojan Women* 918–31. Cf. *The Complete Greek Tragedies*, vol. 3, p. 646 (trans. Lattimore).

27. Homer *Iliad* 1.318–48. "The fall of Troy will be the conclusion of a concatenation of events which, like the prehistory of the Trojan War, begins with the stealing of a woman" (Ernst Robert Curtius, *European Literature and the Latin Middle Ages*, translated by Willard R. Trask [Princeton: Princeton University Press, 1953], p. 170).

28. Dumézil, *Myth et épopée*, I, p. 44.

29. Moses I. Finley, "Lost: The Trojan War," in *Aspects of Antiquity: Discoveries and Controversies* (New York: Viking Penguin, 1968), p. 36.

30. Eric Auerbach, "Ulysses' Scar," in *Mimesis: The Representation of Reality in Western Literature*, translated by Willard R. Trask (Princeton: Princeton Univ rsity Press, 1953), pp. 13–14.

31. Ibid., pp. 14 ff.

32. Moses I. Finley, *The World of Odysseus* (London: Pelican Books, 1967), p. 26.

33. Ibid., pp. 32–33.

34. Ibid., pp. 25–26.

35. Finley, "Lost: The Trojan War," p. 36. Pierre Vidal-Nacquet cites the following example to illustrate how archeology, even when it embraces a nationalist agenda, remains in thrall to myth: before the former Yugoslavia had reduced its own monuments to rubble, it would have been feasible to explore the possibility that Homer's Troy might have been situated not in Turkey but rather on the more civilized banks of the Neretva, between Split and Dubrovnik; but this thesis has found no more support among the Albanians than it has among the Greeks and the Turks (Pierre Vidal-Nacquet, *Les Juifs, la mémoire et le présent* [Paris: F. Maspéro, 1981], p. 47).

36. Finley, *The World of Odysseus*, p. 10.

37. Ibid., p. 56.

38. Herodotus, *The History*, book II, sections 112–15; *Euterpes*, part II, 120 ff.

39. Cf. Christoph Clairmont, *Das Parisurteil in der antiken Kunst* (Zurich: Im Selbstverlag des Verfassers, 1951); Irmgard Raab, *Zu den Darstellungen des Parisurteils in der griechischen Kunst* (Frankfurt and Berne: Lang, 1972); Karl Schefold, *Götter und Heldensagen der Griechen in der spätarchäischen Kunst* (Munich: Hirmer, 1978), pp. 186 ff.

40. As on a very beautiful stamnos in Detroit (Clairmont, K 135).

41. See also the amphora in the museum in Hanover (Clairmont, K 90).

42. Attic black-figure amphoras in the Lyons museum (Clairmont K 14) and the Thorwaldsen Museum in Copenhagen (K 57), etc.

43. Tripod pyxis in the Athens Museum (Clairmont K 47); Attic

red-figure vase in the British Museum (K 153), etc.; depictions of the judgment of Paris could sometimes assume a caricatural form, as in an amphora now in Berlin (K 21), similar in tone to literary evocations of the event in authors such as Lucian.

44. Tripod pyxis in the Louvre (Clairmont, K 45), an amphora in Florence (K 63), etc. Cf. Karl Schefold, *Götter und Heldensagen der Griechen*, pp. 186–87.

45. Clairmont, K 40. Cf. John Davidson Beazley, *Attic Black-Figure Vase Painters* (Oxford: Clarendon Press, 1956), p. 58, no. 122; *The Development of Attic Black-Figure*, rev. ed. (Berkeley: University of California Press, 1986), pp. 20–22; and Aliki Kauffmann-Samaras, "Le 'peintre C,' peintre novateur de la céramique attique, dans la collection du Louvre," *La Revue du Louvre* 37, nos. 5–6 (December 1987): 340–55. On "swift wind-footed Iris," cf. *Iliad* 15.200.

46. Clairmont, *Das Parisurteil*, pp. 97–100.

47. Cf. the amphora recently reassembled in the Athens Museum (NM 1004, c. 570–560); Schefold, *Götter und Heldensagen der Griechen*, pp. 186–87, fig. 250.

48. Homer *Iliad* 24.257.

49. In the Hellenistic period, the judgment of Paris was frequently represented in mural painting, notably in Pompeii, and rather less frequently in mosaics. A fine example of the latter is the floor from Antioch now in the Louvre: it shows Paris seated in a rocky landscape, at the foot of a column superimposed on a tree and surmounted by a statue of Eros; the three goddesses are before him, Athena standing and the two others seated. Cf. *Catalogue des mosaïques romaines et paléochrétiennes du musée du Louvre* (Paris: Éditions de la Réunion des musées nationaux, 1978), catalog no. 43, pp. 87–92.

50. Clairmont, *Das Parisurteil*, p. 99.

51. Cf. Laura Slatkin, "Genre and Generation in the *Odyssey*," *Mētis* 1 (1986): 259–68.

52. Cf. The "secret things" formulated by Zeus "apart from the rest of the gods" (*Iliad* 1.549) only gradually become manifest. And it is only in book 20 that the prohibition against the gods' intervention in the war between the Greeks and the Trojans is formally lifted.

53. Dumézil, *Mythe et épopée*, I, p. 581.

54. Ibid., p. 582.

55. François Jouan points out that in epics the function of the cowherd was frequently allotted to members of royal families: beginning with Anchises, the beloved of Venus, whose story is not without analogy to that of Paris. Cf. Jouan, *Euripède et les légendes des Chants cypriens*, p. 100.

56. Ibid., pp. 104–7.

57. Ibid., p. 57.

58. Ibid., p. 57.

59. Cf. Nicole Loraux, *The Experiences of Tiresias*, pp. 220–26.

60. Homer *Iliad* 5.428–29.
61. Ibid., 14.187–224; cf. also below, chapter 11.
62. "A decisive advance was made on the day, around 1950, when I realized that the 'tripartite ideology' was not necessarily accompanied, in the life of a society, by the *real* tripartite division of this society, in accordance with the Indian model; that on the contrary, it could be only (no longer be, never have been anything but) an ideal and, at the same time, a way of analyzing, of interpreting the forces assuring the flow of the world and the life of men" (Dumézil, *Mythe et épopée*, I, p. 15).
63. Ibid., pp. 58–59.

Chapter Eight

1. *The Judgement of the Goddesses* (*Theōn krisis*), LOEB, Lucian, 8 vols., translated by A. M. Harmon (1927–67), vol. 3, pp. 383–409.
2. At the beginning of the sixteenth century, Jean Lemaire de Belges posed this same question implicitly in his *Illustrations des Gaules et singularitez de Troie:* Jupiter being disinclined to assume the task, his young minion, Ganymede of Troy, whispered that he should assign it to his cousin Alexander, "descended in any case from the gods" (cf. Jean Lemaire de Belges, *Oeuvres*, edited by August Jean Stecher, 4 volumes (Geneva: Slatkine, 1969 [reprint of 1882 edition]), hereafter cited as LEMAIRE/STECHER, book I, chap. 30; vol. 1, p. 224). On Lemaire de Belges and his "Trojan novel," cf. below, chapter 9.
3. "Venus huic erat utraque nota" ["He knew both sides of love"]. Ovid *Metamorphoses* 3.323 [LOEB, 2 vols., translated by Frank Justus Miller (1916), vol. 1, pp. 146–47].
4. Xenophanes, fragment 14, as cited by Jean-Pierre Vernant, "Mortels et immortels: le corps divin," in *L'Individu, la mort, l'amour: Soi-même et l'autre en Grèce ancienne* (Paris: Gallimard, 1989), p. 7.
5. Ibid., pp. 7–39.
6. A code, it must be said, that is of singular complexity. On the basis of his study of the vocabulary of "corporeality" in the Archaic period, Vernant has been able to establish that the pre-Socratic Greeks had no conception of the opposition between soul and body so prevalent from Plato on, just as they had no conception of that between the material and the spiritual from which proceeds the stigma of illusion attaching to the concept of the body so central to the subsequent Western tradition: they had no single word designating the body as an organic unity serving all of the individual's various physical and mental functions, but they did have at their disposal quite a few words referring to specific aspects of this body (its qualities as living or dead, as anatomical or signifying), and naming them—instinctive as well as reflexive qualities, emotive as well as cognitive ones. But it remains to be determined how such a symbolic

system was able to function, and how it was used by the Greeks to, in Vernant's words, "conceptualize man's relation to the gods under the double sign of both self and other."

7. Ibid., pp. 36–37.

8. Homer *Iliad* 5.339–42 [Lattimore trans.]. On Ares, also wounded during the same engagement, in the belly, by Diomedes, whose spear had been guided by Athena (ibid., 856–57); Ares, the killer of men who, if a god could die, would have succumbed to the mortal treatment inflicted on him by the sons of Aloeus (ibid., 385–91); cf. Nicole Loraux, "Le corps vulnérable d'Arès," *Le temps de la réflexion*, vol. 7 (1986), "Corps des dieux," pp. 335–54.

9. Vernant, *L'individu*, p. 18.

10. Homer *Iliad* 14.314–17 and 3.441–42 [Lattimore does not render the beginning of these two passages identically, but they are indeed identical in the Greek, as Damisch asserts—Trans.].

11. Vernant, *L'individu*, pp. 16, 28.

12. Ibid., p. 17.

13. Ibid., p. 38.

14. Homer *Odyssey* 5.217–18 [Lattimore trans.]; cited by Vernant, *L'individu*, p. 28.

15. Ibid., p. 38.

16. Ibid., p. 32.

17. Ibid.

18. "Gumnas idein boulomai" ["I want to see them naked"]: "The Judgement of the Goddesses," LOEB, Lucian, vol. 3, sec. 9, pp. 396–97. One can only concur with Jules de Goncourt: "The most stunning modernity amazes and charms in Lucian. This Greek of the end of Greece and the twilight of Olympus is our contemporary in both soul and spirit. His Athenian irony initiated 'Parisian humor' [*la 'blague de Pâris'*]." See Edmond de Goncourt and Jules de Goncourt, *Journal: Mémoires de la vie littéraire*, 3 vols. (Paris: R. Laffont, 1989), vol. 3, p. 92 (entry dated 31 December 1858).

19. LOEB, Ovid, *Heroides*, translated by Grant Showerman, 2d ed. revised by G. P. Gould (1977), "Paris to Helen," 16.64–74, pp. 202–3 ["And at the self-same time, three goddesses—Venus, and Pallas, and with her Juno—set tender feet upon the sward. I was mute, and chill tremors had raised my hair on end, when 'Lay aside thy fear!' the winged herald said to me; 'thou art the arbiter of beauty [*arbiter es formae*] to vanquish the other two!' And, lest I should refuse, he laid command on me in the name of Jove, and forthwith through the paths of ether betook him toward the stars"].

20. "Qua Venus et Juno sumptisque decentior armis / Venit in arbitrium nuda Minerva tuum" ["When Venus and Juno, and unadorned Minerva, more comely had she borne her arms, appeared before you to be judged"]: ibid., "Oenone to Paris," 5.35–36, pp. 60–61.

21. Cf. Homeric Hymn to Aphrodite, 1.170–90, cited by Vernant, *L'individu*, p. 32 [LOEB, *Hesiod: The Homeric Hymns and Homerica*, translated by Hugh G. Evelyn-White (1959), pp. 418–19].

22. Nicole Loraux, "What Tiresias Saw," in *The Experiences of Tiresias: The Feminine and the Greek Man* (Princeton: Princeton University Press, 1995), pp. 211–26. There is at least one surviving vase (an Italian krater now in the Louvre) on which the figure of Tirésias is associated with an image of the judgment of Paris (cf. Christoph Clairmont, *Das Parisurteil in der antiken Kunst* [Zurich: Im Selbstverlag des Verfassers, 1951], p. 98, note 57; catalog K 184).

23. Cf. C. Calvi, "Il piatto d'argento di Castelvino," *Aquilea nostra* 50, (1979): 355–56, and Nicole Loraux, *The Experiences of Tiresias*, pp. 220–23.

24. Jérôme Carcopino, *De Pythagore aux apôtres: Études sur la conversion du monde romain* (Paris: Flammarion, 1956), pp. 24 ff.

25. Homer *Iliad* 3.166 [Lattimore trans.]. Earlier in the narrative, Hector praises the hero, though reproaching him for a certain slackness and lack of resolve (6.521–23).

26. Ibid., book 17.

27. Sallust the Platonist (Sallustius), *Péri théôn kai kosmon (De diis et Mundo)*, English bilingual ed., *Sallustius Concerning the Gods and the Universe*, translated by Arthur D. Nock (Cambridge: Cambridge University Press, 1926), sec. 4, pp. 6–7.

28. Cf. François Jouan, *Euripède et les légendes des Chants cypriens: Des origines de la guerre de Troie à l'"Iliade"* (Paris: Société d'édition "Les Belles Lettres," 1966).

29. Euripides, *The Women of Troy*, v. 931–37; [*The Complete Greek Tragedies*, edited by David Grene and Richmond Lattimore, 4 vols. (Chicago: University of Chicago Press, 1959), vol. 3, p. 646 (Lattimore)].

30. Emile Benveniste, *Indo-European Language and Society*, translated by Elizabeth Palmer (Coral Gables, FL: University of Miami Press, [1973]), p. 387 [translation modified].

31. Cf. Louis Gernet, *Recherches sur le développement de la pensée juridique et morale en Grèce (étude sémantique)* (Paris: Leroux, 1917), pp. 86 ff., 448–51.

32. As Gernet stresses, Greek justice long retained the imprint of interfamilial strife: *agon* designated simultaneously a combat, a competition, and a judicial struggle, while *krinein* always implied only the idea of struggle (*Recherches*, p. 90, note 106).

33. Apuleius, *The Golden Ass*, book 10.33, LOEB, translated by W. Adlington, revised by S. Gaselee (1935), pp. 532–33.

34. Cf. Albert Severyns, *Recherches sur la Chrestomathie de Proclos*, 4 vols. (Paris: Droz, 1938–63), vol. 4, pp. 77–85.

35. The advice offered by the council made no mystery of the strong impression made by Helen on the so-called Ancients: "'Surely

there is no blame on Trojans and strong-greaved Achaians if for long time they suffer hardship for a woman like this one. Terrible is the likeness of her face to immortal goddesses. Still, though she be such, let her go away in the ships, lest she be left behind, a grief to us and our children'" (*Iliad* 3.156–60 [Lattimore]).

36. Gernet, *Recherches*, p. xiii.

37. "The definition of taste on which I am basing this [analysis] is that it is the ability to judge the beautiful." See Kant, *Kritik der Urteilskraft*, Book I, note to the title of the "First Moment of a Judgment of Taste, as to its Quality" [*Judgment*/Pluhar, p. 43].

38. "Paris, as you are beautiful yourself (*epeidē kalos te ãutos ei*), and are ignorant of nothing concerning love (*kai sophos ta erōtika*), Zeus asks that you decide which of the three goddesses is the most beautiful (*dikasai tais Theais, ētis autōn ē kallistē estin*)" (LOEB, Lucian, vol. 1, pp. 384–85).

39. On the "savage" as "body of pleasure" (*corps de jouissance*), cf. Michel de Certeau, "Archéologie du discours ethnographique," *Semiotica* 7, no. 4 (1973): 373.

40. Kant, *Kritik der Urteilskraft*, section 3 [*Judgment*/Pluhar, p. 48].

41. "Te vigilans oculis, animo te nocte videbam, / Lumina cum placido victa sopore iacent. / Quid facies praesens quae nondum visa placebas? / Ardebam, quamvis hinc procul ignis erat" (LOEB, Ovid, *Heroides*, 16.101–4, pp. 204–5).

42. Cf. Stephen W. Hawking, *A Brief History of Time from the Big Bang to Black Holes* (New York and Toronto: Bantam Books, 1988).

43. Sigmund Freud, "Das Motiv der Kästchenwahl," in *GW*, vol. 10, pp. 23–37 ["The Theme of the Three Caskets," in *SE*, vol. 12, pp. 291–301].

44. Georges Dumézil, *Mythe et épopée*, I, *L'Idéologie des trois fonctions dans les épopées indo-européens* (Paris: Gallimard, 1968), pp. 580–601.

45. Ibid., p. 591.

46. Ibid.

47. Cf. below, chapter 10.

48. Edgar Wind, *Pagan Mysteries in the Renaissance*, 2d ed. (London: Faber, 1968).

49. Saint Augustine, *Retractiones*, I, xiii; as cited by Wind, *Pagan Mysteries*, p. 21.

50. "Oportet . . . ut Creatorem . . . Trinitatem intelligamus, cuius in creatura, quomodo est, apparet vestigium" (Saint Augustine, *De Trinitate*, VI, x, 12; as cited by Wind, *Pagan Mysteries*, pp. 41–42.

51. Saint Augustine, *De Trinitate*, IX–XV.

52. Wind, *Pagan Mysteries*, pp. 26–52.

53. Fulgentius, *Mythologiarum ad Catum presbyterum libri III*, II, 1, "De iudicio Paradis." Cf. Jean Seznec, *The Survival of the Pagan Gods*

(Princeton: Princeton University Press, 1953), p. 89, and Wind, *Pagan Mysteries*, pp. 81–82.

54. "Tres esse vitam, nemo ratione vivens dubitat, contemplativam, activam, voluptuosam. Quoniam videlicet tres ad felicitatem vias homines eligerunt, sapientiam, potentiam, voluptatem. Nos autem sapientiae nomine quodlibet artium studium, religiosumque ocium intelligimus. Sub appellatione potententiae authoritatem in gubernatione civili pariter atque militari, divitiarumque affluentiam et splendorem gloriae, negotiosamque virtutem comprehendi putamus. Sub voluptatis denique cognomento quinque sensuum / oblectamenta et laborum curarumque declinationem, contineri non dubitamus. Primum igitur poetae Minervam, Secundam vero Junonem, Tertiam denique Venerem nominaverunt. Tres olim apud Paridem de pomo aurea, id est, de palma et victoria certaverunt. Consultante videlicet Paride secum, quam / de tribus potissimam ad felicitatem eligerit, elegit denique voluptatem, cum vero sapientiam / spreverit, et potentiam, merito inprudenter felicitatem sperans, incidit in miserias" (Marsilio Ficino, *Opera omnia* [Basel, 1576], p. 919). Wind, who cites this passage (which was also known to Ernst Gombrich, cf. "Botticelli's Mythologies: A Study in the Neo-Platonic Symbolism of his Circle," in *Symbolic Images: Studies in the Art of the Renaissance* [London: Phaedon, 1972], p. 54), points out that the comparison of rulers' judgment with that of Paris subsequently became a standard formula of Renaissance courtly panegyric, citing a notable example in which the object of flattery is Queen Elizabeth of England (cf. J. D. Reeves, "The Judgement of Paris as a Device of Tudor Flattery," *Notes and Queries*, vol. 199, [1954]: an allegorical portrait of Elizabeth, now at Hampton Court, in which the queen puts the three goddesses to shame because, as an inscription makes clear, she combines in herself the gifts which they possess only separately; cf. Charles Henry Collins Baker, *Catalogue of the Pictures at Hampton Court* [Glasgow: R. Maclehose and Company, Ltd., 1929], p. 47, no. 635, as cited by Wind, *Pagan Mysteries*, p. 83, note 7).

55. Seznec, *Survival of the Pagan Gods*, pp. 85, 104.

56. Athanasius Kircher, *Oedipus Aegyptiacus*, 4 vols. (Rome: ex. Typ. Vitalis Mascardi, 1652–54), vol. 2, p. 76; as cited by Mario Meunier in the "Prolegomena" to his French translation of Sallustius.

57. Sallust the Platonist (Sallustius), *Peri theon kai kosmon (De diis et Mundo)*, English bilingual ed., *Sallustius Concerning the Gods and the Universe*, sec. 4, pp. 6–7. Cf. Franz Cumont, "Salluste le Philosophe," *Revue de Philologie* 14 (1892): 49–56.

58. Sallust the Platonist (Sallustius), *Peri theon kai kosmon (De diis et Mundo)*, English bilingual ed., *Sallustius Concerning the Gods and the Universe*, sec. 3, pp. 4–5. On this author, cf. the Emperor Julian, "To

the Cynic Heraclaeios," 9 in LOEB, *The Works of the Emperor Julian*, translated by Wilmer Cave Wright, 3 vols. (1913–23), vol. 2, pp. 102–3: "For nature loves to hide her secrets, and she does not suffer the hidden truth about the essential nature of the gods to be flung in naked words to the ears of the profane. Now there are certain characteristics of ours that derive benefit from that occult and unknown nature, which nourishes not our souls alone but our bodies also, and brings us into the presence of the gods, and this I think often comes about by means of myths; when through riddles and the dramatic setting of myths that knowledge is insinuated into the ears of the multitude who cannot receive divine truths in their purest form" (cited by Mario Meunier in the introduction to his edition of *De diis et mundo* by Sallustius).

59. Paris, Bibliothèque nationale, Ms fr. 143. Cf. *Manuscrits à peintures en France du XIII*[e] au XVIe siècle, catalog of an exhibition held in Paris in 1955 (Paris: Bibliothèque nationale, 1955), catalog no. 344, pp. 162–63.

60. "Pero a quella si deve esser consecrato il pomo spherico, come chi è tutto in tutto." See Giordano Bruno, *Des fureurs héroïques* (*Degli heroici furori*), bilingual French-Italian ed. with translation by Paul Henri Michel (Paris: Belles Lettres, 1954), pp. 278–81.

Chapter Nine

1. Francesco Colonna, *Hypnerotomachia Poliphili*, critical edition by G. Pozzi and L. Ciapponi, 2 vols. (Padua: Editrice Antenore, 1965), vol. 1, p. 127. Cf. André Chastel, "Le *Polyphile* d'Alde Manuce dans une réédition savante," *Le Monde*, 20 August 1965.

2. LOEB, Seneca, *Moral Essays*, translated by John Basore, 3 vols. (1928–35), vol. 3, *De Beneficiis*, pp. 12–13 (cited by Edgar Wind, *Pagan Mysteries in the Renaissance*, 2d ed. [London: Faber, 1968], p. 28 ff.); Leone Battista Alberti, *Della pittura*, edited by Luigi Malle (Florence: G. C. Sansoni [1950]), book III, p. 105 [*On Painting*, translated by John R. Spencer (New Haven: Yale University Press, 1966), p. 91].

3. Love starts from beauty and ends in voluptuousness: "Amor igitur in voluptatem a pulchritudine desinit," Ficino, *De amore*, II; cited by Wind, *Pagan Mysteries*, p. 43.

4. "In nel posteriore el magno Iupiter uno solerte pastore in suo loco iudice collocava, excitato da esso proximo ad uno lepidissimo fonte dormiente, ove a tre nude et formosissime dee feceva iudicio; el quale, dal'operoso Cupidine seducto, alla sua facetissima genitrice el pomo consentiva" (Colonna, *Hypnerotomachia Poliphili*, pp. 156–57). "En celle de derriere Jupiter commettoit en sa place un Berger de subtil esprit qui dormoit sur une fontaine, & vouloit ce dieu qu'il jugeast du different survenu entre trois déesses s'estant despouillees nues devant sa face: & comment ce Berger seduict par Cupido, donna

sentence en faveur de Vénus sa mere, luy adjugeant la pomme d'or, comme à la plus belle & la plus excellente a son gré" (French edition, fol. K iij). ["In the one behind Jupiter was a shepherd of subtle mind who slept at a fountain, its being this god's will that he settle in his stead a dispute among three goddesses who displayed themselves naked before him: and how this shepherd, seduced by Cupid, declared in favor of Venus his mother, awarding her the golden apple, thus indicating that according to his inclination she was the most beautiful and the most excellent."]

5. Erwin Panofsky, "Hercules am Scheidewege und andere antike bildstoffe in der neueren Kunst," *Studien der Bibliothek Warburg*, vol. 18, Leipzig/Berlin, 1930. Cf. Christoph Clairmont, *Das Parisurteil in der antiken Kunst* (Zurich: Im Selbstverlag des Verfassers, 1951), p. 98. On the emblematic value of this motif in the context of Panofsky's work, see Hubert Damisch, *The Origin of Perspective*, translated by John Goodman (Cambridge, MA: MIT Press, 1993), chapter 1, "At the Crossroads," pp. 3–20.

6. Panofsky, "Hercules am Scheidewege," pp. 142 ff. I plan to address the problems raised by the identification of this group with the classical allegory of the Graces in another context.

7. Wind, *Pagan Mysteries*, pp. 81 ff.

8. Ibid., pp. 80 ff.

9. Admittedly, the choice here is among not three but four possible routes ("At this point he came to a road that forked off in four directions, and at once he thought of those crossroads where knights-errant would pause to consider which path they should take. By way of imitating them, he halted there for a while . . ." [Miguel de Cervantes Saavedra, *The Ingenious Gentleman Don Quixote of la Mancha*, translated by Samuel Putnam (New York: Viking, 1963), p. 45]). But it will be clear to readers of the preceding chapter in Cervantes' novel that, as Lacan recommended, Don Quixote knew how to count higher than two, to three and even four ("the knight, without saying a word or asking favor of anyone, once more adjusted his buckler and raised his lance, and if he did not break the second mule driver's head to bits, he made more than three pieces of it by dividing it into quarters" [ibid., p. 39]).

10. Wind, *Pagan Mysteries*, pp. 89 ff.

11. Hollstein H 104. Cf. Panofsky, "Hercules am Scheidewege," pp. 59 ff. and 99 ff., as well as Dieter Koepplin et al., *Lucas Cranach*, catalog of an exhibition held in Basel in 1974, 2 vols. (Basel, 1974), vol. 2, pp. 621–22, no. 528.

12. Cf. Jean-Claude Schmitt, "Bildhaftes Denken: Die Darstellung biblischer Traüme im mittelalterlichen Handschriften," in Agostino Paravicini and Giorgio Stabile, eds., *Traüme im Mittelalter: Ikonologische Studien* (Stuttgart and Zurich, 1989), pp. 9–24.

13. According to Lemaire de Belges, these were slippers or socks

like those worn by comedic actors, or like the clogs worn by the three rival goddesses after discarding all other articles of clothing, "pour que l'herbette poignante n'offensa leurs plantes tendres et doucettes" ("so that the greensward would not offend the soft and tender soles of their feet").

14. Martha Lethner, "Das 'Iudicium Paradis de pomo aureo' des Iakobus Locher Philosomus," Ph.D. diss. (Vienna, 1951); as cited by Koepplin et al., *Lucas Cranach*, vol. 2, p. 622.

15. Koepplin et al., *Lucas Cranach*, vol. 2, p. 614.

16. Ibid., pp. 618–20.

17. Ibid., vol. 2, pp. 616–17. On the judgment of Paris in the *Ovide moralisé*, cf. Carla Lord, "Three Manuscripts of the *Ovide moralisé*," *Art Bulletin* 57 (1975): 161–75, esp. p. 166 and figs. 17–18.

18. Cf. Richard Forster, "Neue Cranachs in Schliessen," *Schliessens Vorzeit* 7 (1898): 269; as cited by Max Friedlander and Jakob Rosenberg, *The Paintings of Lucas Cranach* (Ithaca: Cornell University Press, 1978), no. 41, p. 79.

19. Cf. Seznec, *Survival of the Pagan Gods*, pp. 214, 306–7. On Jean Lemaire, cf. Alphonse Bayot, *La Légende de Troie à la Cour de Bourgogne* (Bruges: Impr. de L. de Plancke, 1908); Georges Doutrepont, *Jean Lemaire de Belges et la Renaissance* (Brussels: M. Lamertin, 1934).

20. A Latin inscription exhorts the viewer to take in with his own eyes the disastrous consequences of Paris's illicit loves, here painted as they might have been by Zeuxis. Cf. Sylvie Béguin, "Deux tableaux allemands des collections du Louvre," *La Revue de l'Art* 9 (1959): 25–28.

21. Cf. *La Bouche de vérité*, Heinz Kisters collection, Kreuzlingen.

22. Johannes Kymaeus, *Von des Priester Ehestand* (Wittenberg, 1533). Cf. Koepplin et al, *Lucas Cranach*, no. 242, vol. 1, pp. 359–60.

23. Ibid., vol. 2, pp. 562–65.

24. About 1512–14: Cologne, Wallraf-Richartz Museum; cf. Friedlander and Rosenberg, *The Paintings of Lucas Cranach*, no. 41, p. 77.

25. Cf. *Venus with Cupid Stealing Honey* (see Figure 49 in the text) in the Borghese Gallery, signed and dated 1531 (ibid., no. 245, p. 118), or *Venus Outdoors* in the Louvre, signed and dated 1529 (ibid., no. 242, p. 118), etc.

26. Signed and dated 1531, Paris, Seligmann collection; ibid., no. 250, p. 119.

27. Around 1537, Saint Louis Art Museum; ibid., no. 258, p. 120.

28. Signed and dated 1538, Basel, Öffentliche Kunstsammlung; ibid., no. 253, p. 120.

29. *Reclining Water Nymph* (see Figure 51 in the text) signed and dated 1534, Liverpool, Walker Art Gallery; ibid., no. 259, p. 121.

30. (See Figure 52 in the text.) Signed and dated 1526; ibid., no. 191, p. 107.

31. Cf. Doutrepont, *Jean Lemaire de Belges et la Renaissance.*

32. Jean Lemaire de Belges, *Illustrations des Gaules et Singularitez de Troye* (Paris, 1512), book I, chap. 31; cf. LEMAIRE/STECHER, vol. 1, pp. 236–39.

33. See Christine de Pisan, *Livre de la Cité des dames* and *Lettres sur le Roman de la Rose* (1401–1402), where she defends her sex against the calumnies of Jean de Meung. The first of these titles has been translated: *The Book of the City of Ladies,* translated by Earl Jeffrey Richards (New York: Persea Books [1982]).

34. See above, chapter 8.

35. Christine de Pisan, *Les cent hystoires de Troye: L'Epistre de Othéa, déese de Prudence, envoyee à l'esprit chevalereux Hectore de Troye* (Paris, 1522) ("Les choses nécessaires a haute vaillance chevalereuse, et qui peuvent s'acquérir par bonne école"; "par science et non par essai").

36. Cf. Ernst Robert Curtius, *European Literature and the Latin Middle Ages,* translated by Willard R. Trask (Princeton: Princeton University Press, 1953), chap. 9, "Heroes and Rulers," esp. pp. 170–73.

37. Cf. Georges Dumézil, *Mitra-Varuna: An Essay on Two Indo-European Representations of Sovereignty,* translated by Derek Coltman (New York: Zone Books, 1988), p. 177.

38. As cited by Curtius, *European Literature and the Latin Middle Ages,* p. 175.

39. Ibid., p. 176.

40. Homer *Iliad* 9.440–43 [Lattimore].

41. Curtius, *European Literature and the Latin Middle Ages,* p. 6.

42. LEMAIRE/STECHER, vol. 1, pp. 246–47: "Areste ton plaisant aspect sur la speciosite dont je suis decoree." "Esquippe le gracieux navire de ton franc arbitre selon la demonstration de ma carte propice," and, ignoring "vaine gloire" and "difficile intellecture," "tourne donc a gauche, ensuys le grand chemin usite de la plus part des humains."

43. Ibid. ("Quand le dit enfant jeune Prince commencera a vuider de puerilite, et sera encore en estat de pastoureau: cestadire, de douce simplesse sans rusticite ne malice, alors ie lui présenteray le pomme d'or, cestadire, son propre franc arbitre: et le feray juge de la beauté des trois déeses: cestasavoir Prudence, Plaisance et Puissance"). The precis at the head of chapter 35 on page 269 begins as follows: "Explication tant morale, comme philosophalle et historialle des Noces dessus escrites: ensemble du Jugement de Pâris en plusieurs sortes, avec la figure du ciel, qui fut la naissance de Pâris" ("An explanation, as much moral as philosophical and historical, of the above-described wedding: together with the judgment of Paris in several respects with the figure of the sky, which was the birth of Paris").

44. Ibid., p. 272 ("Jupiter n'en voulut point juger, pour ce que dieu laisse faire le cours aux destinees, et ne veut tollir à l'homme son

franc arbitre. Et aussi si Dieu eut contemne deux des dites manieres de vivre, il n'en eust laisse qu'une au monde.") It will be remembered that in *The Dream of Poliphilus* it is the Queen of Free Will who leads the hero to the three doors among which he must choose.

45. At least one important indicator suggests that Charles V did not embrace the chivalric ideal to which Francis I remained faithful. Charles owed his victory over the latter at Pavia to his singularly modern conception of warfare: the French king continued to view battle as a kind of tournament. Cf. Jean Giono, *Le Désastre de Pavie* (Paris: Gallimard, 1963), which also contains astute observations on the Emperor's libidinal investments, especially as regards food.

46. Like another model, also mythological or legendary (one I intend to discuss elsewhere), namely the rape of Europa or Europe, which is reiterated in that of Helen: Europe, which figures in the iconography of the "parts of the world," of which for some time—before the Americas entered the picture—there were only three, like the three Graces and the three rival goddesses (cf. Bartolomé Bennassar and Lucie Bennassar, *1492: un monde nouveau?* [Paris: Perrin, 1991]).

47. In a seminar we taught together, during which I presented some of the material in this chapter, Jacques Derrida observed that this legendary genealogy of Europe had been subjected to a kind of philosophical *relève* or sublation in Husserl's aptly named *Krisis:* Under the sign of the "crisis" then being experienced by European humanity, phenomenology undertook a return to the forgotten Greek origin of philosophy, with the intention of reactivating it through an act of freedom—the history of European humanity being intimately coupled, through Plato, Descartes, and Kant, with a history of judgment, its being incumbent upon us, as previously suggested in Kant's third *Critique*, to conceptualize its ante-predicative foundations as well as the freedom that is its condition and horizon [The work in question is: Edmund Husserl, *The Crisis of European Sciences and Transcendental Phenomenology*, translated by David Carr (Evanston: Northwestern University Press, 1970)].

Chapter Ten

1. Lucian, *The Judgement of the Goddesses* (*Theōn Krisis*), secs. 9–10; LOEB, vol. 3, pp. 398–99.

2. Ovid *Heroides* 5.33–36; LOEB, pp. 60–61.

3. Miguel de Cervantes Saavedra, *The Ingenious Gentleman Don Quixote of la Mancha*, translated by Samuel Putnam (New York: Viking, 1963), I, 4.

4. Plato *Symposium* 210d.

5. Erwin Panofsky, *Idea: A Concept in Art Theory*, translated by Joseph J. S. Peake (New York: Harper and Row, 1968).

6. "Certum est, Platonem ubique vocare Ideas perfectam illus-

trem notitiam, ut Apelles habet in animo inclusam pulcherrimam imaginem humani corporis." Philipp Melanchthon, *Ennaratio libri I. Ethicor. Arist.*, chap. 6; as cited by Panofsky, *Idea*, p. 6.

7. Ernst Robert Curtius, *European Literature and the Latin Middle Ages*, translated by Willard R. Trask (Princeton: Princeton University Press, 1953), p. 14.

8. Ibid., p. 12.

9. Ibid., pp. 14–15.

10. Curtius's argument (ibid., p. 14) that every new translation of the Homeric poems gives them new life, while, if the Parthenon frieze had been destroyed, it would have been impossible for us to have any idea of it, also holds, *mutata mutandis*, for ancient painting: While it is possible to derive some notion of what these works *represented* from Philostratus's ostensible descriptions of them, we would have been unable to reconstitute ancient perspective on the basis of these same ekphrastic texts. And if thought is indeed at work in art, perspective provides the best example of this.

11. Cf. Emile Benveniste, "Remarks on the Function of Language in the Freudian discovery," *Problems of General Linguistics*, translated by Mary Elizabeth Meek (Coral Gables, FL: University of Miami Press, [1971]), pp. 65–75.

12. Vicenzo Cartari, *Le Imagini dei Dei degli Antichi nelle quali si contengono gl'Idoli, Riti, Ceremonie, & altre cose appartenenti alla Religione de gli Antichi* (Lyon, 1581).

13. Kant, *Bemerkungen zu den Beobachtungen über das Gefühl des Schönen und Erhabenen, Nachlass*, vol. 7 (Berlin, 1942), p. 70.

14. Lacan, *Le Séminaire*, vol. 7, p. 11 [*Seminar*, vol. 7 (*The Ethics*), p. 3].

15. "Presence et absence, plaisir et déplaisir": Blaise Pascal, *Pensées*, Brunschvicg ed., fragment 678.

16. Plato *Phaedrus* 250d (Hackforth trans.).

17. Cf. Paolo Giovio, *Dialogo dell'imprese militari e amorose* (1551), edited by Maria-Luisa Doglio (Rome: Bulzoni, 1978).

18. "Le Imagini fatte per significare una diversa cosa da quella che si vede con l'occhio," Cesare Ripa, *Iconologia* (Rome, 1593), "Proemio."

19. Edgar Wind (*Pagan Mysteries in the Renaissance*, 2d ed. [London: Faber, 1968], p. 252, note 45) cites the case of Conrad Celtes, a Viennese humanist—Cranach had first been active in Vienna—who, having learned of the Italian craze for pagan trinities, chose to display this knowledge in a singularly pedantic and obvious way by providing the woodcut engraver Hans Burgkmair with a pyramidal emblem (intended to honor the Emperor Maximilian) on the theme *discordia/concors* with Paris's "triadic" judgment as its base: Discord hands the apple to Paris, *errando dicitur philosophia*, while Mercury brandishes the caduceus, emblem of concord.

20. "Vela faciunt honorem secreti": cf. André Marrou, *Saint Augustine et la fin de la culture antique* (Paris: É. de Boccard, 1938), pp. 448 ff.; as cited by Wind, *Pagan Mysteries*, p. 10.

21. Wind, *Pagan Mysteries*, p. 14.

22. Ibid., p. 15.

23. Kant, *Kritik der Urteilskraft*, part I, sec. 5 [*Judgment*/Pluhar, p. 52].

24. Jean-Paul Sartre, *L'Imaginaire* (Paris: Gallimard, 1948), p. 246.

25. Kant, *Kritik der Urteilskraft*, part I, sec. 13 [*Judgment*/Pluhar, p. 69 (translation modified—TRANS.)].

26. See above, chapter 6.

27. Roland Fréart, Sieur de Chambray, *Idée de la perfection de la peinture* (Geneva: Minskoff, 1973 [reprint of 1662 edition]), p. 28: ("Après cela, le reste de cette composition n'est plus qu'un accompagnement poétique du génie du peintre, pour enrichir l'ordonnance de son tableau: car toutes ces nymphes avec leurs cruches, et les deux figures d'hommes nus et assis, tenant des roseaux à la main, sans témoigner aucune attention à ce qui se passe, ne veulent dire autre chose sinon que le Mont Ida est très abondant en fleuves, et en fontaines: et apparemment celui qui s'appuie sur un aviron, est le fleuve Xanthe, qui allait border les murs de Troye; et son voisin est le fleuve Simoïs, lesquels ont tous deux leurs sources dans le même mont, et arrosant par divers détours la campagne de la Troade, se vont enfin joindre à l'embouchure de la mer hellespontique, près le promontoire de Sigée").

28. Kant, *Kritik der Urteilskraft*, part I, sec. 14 [*Judgment*/Pluhar, p. 69–72].

29. On this problematic and its treatment in the *Critique of Judgement*, cf. Jacques Derrida, *La Vérité en peinture* (Paris: Flammarion, 1978), "Parergon," pp. 44–94 [*The Truth in Painting*, translated by Geoff Bennington and Ian McLeod (Chicago: University of Chicago Press, 1987), pp. 37–82].

30. Ibid., p. 67 [*The Truth*, p. 57].

31. Ibid., pp. 63 ff. [*The Truth*, pp. 54 ff.].

32. Derrida characterizes several uses of the word "parergon" by Plato and Aristotle as follows: "It is what the principal subject *must not become*, by being separated from itself" (Plato *Laws* 766a; *Theaetetus* 184a); "*one must avoid* letting the *parerga* get the upper hand over the essentials" (Aristotle *Nichomachean Ethics* 1098a 30). Ibid. [*The Truth*, p. 54].

33. Pliny the elder *Natural History* 35.101; I have used the French critical edition by Jean-Michel Croisille, (Paris: "Les Belles Lettres," 1985), p. 79 and notes on pp. 213–14 [LOEB, Pliny the elder, *Natural History*, ten vols., translated by H. Rackam et al. (1938–62), vol. 9, pp. 336–37]. Cf. also Adolphe Reinach, *Recueil Milliet* (Paris: C.

Klincksieck, 1921 [new ed. Chicago: Ares, 1981]), p. 364, note 1. On the beginnings of Protogenes and the meaning to be ascribed the phrase *naves pinxisse*, cf. Croisille, p. 213, note 4. It would seem that Protogenes began his career either by painting boats or by painting *on* boats, decorating them with emblems that might themselves be seen as "supplements" (*parasema, episema*). Pliny is here referring to the current practice of painting warships, shipping vessels, and even rough-hewn boats, "for even objects exposed to danger were decorated" (ibid., p. 49).

34. Pliny the elder *Natural History* 35.113 [LOEB, vol. 9, pp. 344–45].

35. Muriel Gardiner, ed., *The Wolf-Man by the Wolf-Man* (New York: Basic Books, 1971), p. 145.

36. Kant, *Kritik der Urteilskraft*, part I, sec. 14 [*Judgment*/Pluhar, p. 72].

37. The decoration of the apartments of Julius II started with the Stanza della Segnatura, whose cycle, begun in 1508, was completed in 1511, as is attested by inscriptions in the *Parnassus* fresco and on the architrave of the window under the Virtues lunette. Cf. Pierluigi de Vecchi, *The Complete Paintings of Raphael* (London: Weidenfeld and Nicolson, 1969), p. 100.

38. Cf. André Chastel, *Art et Humanisme à Florence au temps de Laurent le Magnifique* (Paris: Presses universitaires de France, 1959).

39. "Manet walks ahead of me with a guiding torch, and I will follow him" ("Manet tritt mit der Führerfackel vor mich hin, und ich werde folgen."). Cited by Ernst Gombrich, *Aby Warburg: An Intellectual Biography*, 2d ed. (Chicago: University of Chicago Press, 1986), p. 273.

40. "Manet's *Déjeuner sur l'herbe*. Die vorpragende Funktion heidnischer Elementargottheiten für die Entwicklung modernen Naturgefühls." An Italian translation of the complete text has now been published: "Il *Déjeuner sur l'herbe* di Manet. La funcione prefigurante delle divinita pagane elementari per l'evoluzione del sentimento moderno della natura," *aut aut*, no. 100–200, January–April 1984, pp. 40–45. Gombrich's book, *Aby Warburg*, contains extended passages in both the original German and English translation.

41. Cf. Fritz-Eugen Keller, "Les reliefs de la façade sur jardin," in *La Villa Medicis*, 3 vols. (Rome: French Academy in Rome, 1989–92), vol. 2, edited by André Chastel and Philippe Morel, pp. 412–42. I have drawn freely from the information provided by this excellent study on the Villa Medici's "wall of images" and the place of the *Judgment of Paris* in it.

42. This function was discussed in an book by Anton Springer, *Bilder aus der neueren Kunstgeschichte* (2d rev. ed., Bonn: Adolf Marcus, 1886 [first published 1867]), whose first chapter is entitled "The Continuing Influence of the Antique in the Middle Ages" (pp. 3–40).

Warburg doubtless consulted this volume while preparing his dissertation on Botticelli; cf. Gombrich, *Aby Warburg*, p. 49.

43. Keller in *La Villa Medicis.*

44. Cited Italian trans., p. 44 (as in note 40, above). Cf. C. Boert, *Die antiken Sarkophag-Reliefs* (Berlin, 1890), vol. 2, p. 17.

45. Georges Bataille, *Manet*, translated by Anstryn Wainhouse and James Emmons (rev. ed., New York: Skira, 1983), p. 36.

46. See above, chapter 5.

47. Beginning with the classic Susanna and the elders theme, images of which, as has been demonstrated by Mary D. Garrard, lend themselves to a kind of sexual exploitation all the more at odds with the purported moral of the tale because artists and patrons tended to identify with the male figures rather than with that of the heroine. Cf. Mary D. Garrard, "Artemisia and Suzanna," in Norma Broude and Mary D. Gerrard, *Feminism and Art History: Questioning the Litany* (Harper and Row: New York, 1982), pp. 146–71.

48. Cf. Stefania Massari, *Raphael invenit: Stampe da Raffaello nelle collezioni dell'Istituto Nazionale per la Grafica*, exhibition catalog by Grazia Bernini Pezzini, Stefania Massari, and Simonetta Prosperi Valenti Rodino (Rome: Quasar, 1985), p. 345, no. 6; ill. on p. 803.

49. "After dinner, they [Pierret and Riesener] looked at the photographs I owe to Durieu's kindness. I had them perform an experiment that I had done myself, without thinking, two days earlier: after having examined these photographs of nude models, some of whom were rather wretched and poorly proportioned, producing a disagreeable effect, I laid out Marcantonio's engravings for them to look at. We experienced a feeling of repulsion, almost of disgust, due to the lack of correction, the mannerism, the unnatural quality, despite the quality of the style, the only thing that is admirable, but which we could no longer admire in this moment" (Eugène Delacroix, *Journal*, 21 May 1853; new edition [Paris: Plon, 1980], p. 350).

50. The two first sheets are in the museum in Besançon. The third, of higher quality, was included in the 1988 exhibition at The Drawing Center, New York, *Creative Copies: Interpretive Drawings from Michelangelo to Picasso*, curated by Egbert Haverkamp-Begemann and Carolyn Logan (New York: Harper and Row, 1988: no. 59, pp. 194–95); at that time it was in the collection of Jill Newhouse and Eric Carlson in New York. It would seem to date from the years in which Delacroix was working on the murals for the Palais Bourbon, which is to say around 1840. Cf. Sarah Lichtenstein, "Delacroix Copies after Raphael," *Burlington Magazine* 113 (1971): 525–33 (part I) and 593–603 (part II; see figs. 35 and 36); and also, by the same author, "More about Delacroix' Copies after Raphael," ibid., vol. 119 (July 1977): 503–4.

51. Fogg Art Museum, Cambridge (Mass.), Inv. no. 1956.10 Cf. *Creative Copies*, no. 60, pp. 196–97.

52. Ernest Chesneau, *L'Art et les artistes modernes en France et en Angleterre* (Paris: Didier, 1864), pp. 189–90.
53. Georges Bataille, *Manet*, p. 73.
54. Chesneau, *L'Art et les artistes modernes.*
55. Derrida, *La Vérité*, p. 67 [*The Truth*, p. 57].
56. "Noi, perche vogliamo le cose essere poste da vedere, per questo useremo quanto dicono piu grassa Minerva." See Leone Battista Alberti, *Della pittura*, edited by Luigi Malle (Florence: G. C. Sansoni [1950]), p. 55. "A fatter Minerva" and not "a fatter Venus," if indeed it is true that geometry has more to do (*à voir*) with reason than with desire. [Spencer renders this passage rather flatly as "Since we wish the object to be seen, we will use a more sensate wisdom" (*On Painting*, translated by John R. Spencer [New Haven: Yale University Press, 1966], p. 43); but see his useful discussion of the term in his introduction (ibid., pp. 18–20)].

Chapter Eleven

1. In his *Education of Marie de Medicis* (Figure 115), Rubens repeated the "plunging Mercury" motif (Michelangelo's Christ figure in his *Conversion of Saint Paul* and Caravaggio's angel conveying the martyr's palm to Saint Matthew have similar airborne poses), but in the presence of three women—not three goddesses but the three Graces, who have stopped dancing to present their gifts to the future queen of France.

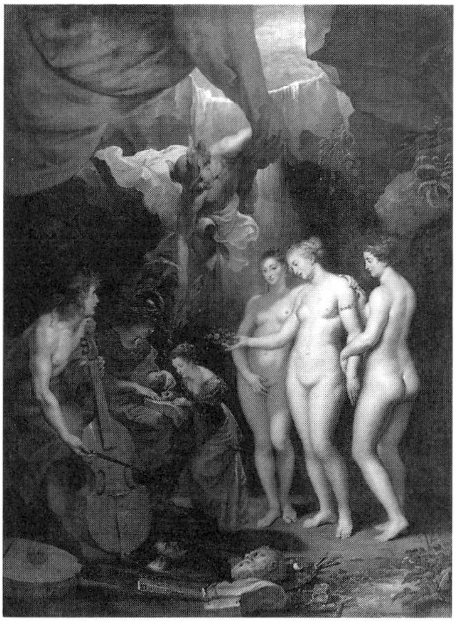

Figure 115. Peter Paul Rubens, *The Education of Marie de Medicis*, oil on canvas, 1622–25 (Paris, Louvre).

2. Giovan Pietro Bellori, "Vita di Annibale Carracci pittore bolognese," in *Le vite de'pittori, scultori e architetti moderni,* Rome, 1672; critical ed. by Evelina Borea (Turin: G. Einaudi, 1976), pp. 57–77.

3. Charles Dempsey, "Annibale Carrache au Palais Farnese," in *Le Palais Farnese,* 2 vols., (Rome: École Française de Rome, 1980), pp. 269–311.

4. Ibid., p. 272.

5. Ibid., pp. 290 ff.

6. "But upon Aphrodite herself Zeus cast sweet desire to be joined in love with a mortal man, to the end that, very soon, not even she should be innocent of a mortal's love; lest laughter-loving Aphrodite should one day softly smile and say mockingly among all the gods that she had joined the gods in love with mortal women who bare sons of death to the deathless gods, and had mated the goddesses with mortal men." See LOEB, Hesiod, *Homeric Hymns and Homerica,* pp. 408–9.

7. Homer *Iliad* 14.162–65 [Lattimore].

8. Ibid., 14.198–221 [Lattimore]. Cf. Marcel Detienne, *Les maîtres de vérité dans la Grèce archaique* (Paris: F. Maspéro, 1967), pp. 64–65. Book 1 of the *Iliad* shows an Achilles full of anger because of a woman "à la belle ceinture" who is taken from him [namely, Briseis].

9. "Sa precieuse ceinture dont elle estoit ceinte, s'appelle Ceston par les nobles poètes . . ." (LEMAIRE/STECHER, vol. 1, p. 242).

10. Marcel Detienne and Jean-Pierre Vernant, *Cunning and Intelligence in Greek Culture and Society,* translated by Janet Lloyd (Atlantic Highlands, NJ: Humanities Press, 1978), p. 285 [trans. altered]. Cf. the "Homeric Hymn to Aphrodite," 34–44 and 249–51, in LOEB, Hesiod, *Homeric Hymns and Homerica,* pp. 408–9, 422–23.

11. Detienne and Vernant, *Cunning and Intelligence,* p. 66 and note 55 on pp. 96–97; Detienne, *Les maîtres de vérité,* pp. 65–66. Cartari says the same thing, writing that the Arcadians called Aphrodite the "plotter" and "contriver," the first eloquence having been that of young lovers trying to persuade their beloveds to surrender to their desire and so discover for their pleasure a thousand things previously unknown ("E la prima eloquenza fu de gl'innamorati, quali cercarono di persuadere alle amate giovani, che fooero facili à desiderii liro, e per piacere anch'essi à quelle trovarono mille belle cose, che prima non erano conosciute," [Vicenzo Cartari, *Imagini dei dei,* p. 455]). Note that a homonymous Greek term, *parphasis,* designates both "seductive propositions" and the inner parts of the female genitals.

12. "Et a ceste cause toute autre convention qui se faict de femme a homme est appelee inceste, quand Vénus n'y a point la ceinture Ceston" [LEMAIRE/STECHER, vol. 1, p. 242].

13. Cf. Philippe Morel, "Le système décoratif de la Galerie Farnese: Observations sur les limites de la représentation," in *Les Carrache et les décors profanes,* acts of a colloquium held by the École Française in Rome in 1986 (Rome: École Française de Rome, 1988), p. 116.

14. Donald Posner, *Annibale Carracci: A Study in the Reform of Italian Painting around 1590*, 2 vols. (London: Phaidon, 1971), vol. 1, chap. 8, pp. 93–112.

15. Morel, "Le système décoratif de la Galerie Farnese," p. 122.

16. Dempsey, in *Le Palais Farnèse.*

17. Marcel Mauss, "Essai sur le don: Forme et raison de l'échange dans les sociétés archaïques," in *Sociologie et anthropologie*, preface by Claude Lévi-Strauss (Paris: Presses Universitaires de France, 1950), p. 147.

18. The corresponding passage in Apollodorus's *Library* is lost; we know only the summary account of it in the *Epitome Vaticanus*, which is quite explicit: "But afterwards Alexander carried off Helen, as some say, because such was the will of Zeus, in order that his daughter might be famous for having embroiled Europe and Asia; or, as others have said, that the race of the demigods might be exalted. For one of these reasons, [Discord] threw an apple as a prize of beauty to be contended for by Hera, Athena, and Aphrodite; and Zeus commanded Hermes to lead them to Alexander on [Mount] Ida in order to be judged by him. And they promised to give Alexander gifts. Hera said that if she were preferred to all women, she would give him the kingdom over all men; and Athena promised victory in war, and Aphrodite the hand of Helen. And he decided in favor of Aphrodite." Cf. LOEB, Apollodorus, *The Library*, pp. 171–73. The Greek word *melon* may have been introduced into a late copy (from the twelfth century?) in place of *neikos* ("quarrel"). Cf. Albert Severyns, "Pomme de discorde et jugement des déesses," in *Phoibos*, vol. 5 ("Mélanges Joseph Hombert"; 1950–51).

19. "Zeus deliberates with Themis about how to conduct the Trojan war. Eris arrives as the gods are celebrating the wedding of Peleus. She arranges a contest opposing Athena, Hera, and Aphrodite, to determine which of the three was the most beautiful. Zeus orders them brought before Alexander, who lives on Mount Ida, to be judged. Excited by the prospect of marrying Helen, Allexander gives his preference to Aphrodite." Cf. Albert Severyns, *Recherches sur la Chrestomathie de Proclos*, 4 vols. (Paris: Droz, 1938–63), vol. 4, p. 77. Proclus refers to Aphrodite as "the initial cause of the amorous inspiration that penetrates all things and that leads all lives issuing from her towards the beautiful" (*Theol. Plat.*, 6.22).

20. Ernst Gombrich, "Botticelli's Mythologies: A Study in the Neo-Platonic Symbolism of his Circle," in *Symbolic Images: Studies in the Art of the Renaissance* (London: Phaedon, 1972). Apuleius's *Golden Ass* enjoyed a considerable vogue in the Quattrocento: Apuleius was the first classical author published in Italian translation, in a magnificent Roman edition which appeared in 1469 (ibid., p. 46 and note 58).

21. *Heroides*, XVI, "Paris to Helen," 53–88; LOEB, Ovid, pp. 200–203.

22. In the Hadrianic period, Ptolomy Chemnos proposed a very different rationalist interpretation: the three goddesses are said to have quarreled not over an apple but over a handsome lad they wanted, respectively, as their priest (cf. Severyns, *Recherches*, p. 158).

23. Richard McGillivray Dawkins, *The Sanctuary of Artemis Orthia at Sparta* (London: McMillan and Co., Ltd., 1929), p. 223, pl. CXXVII.

24. Severyns, *Recherches*, pp. 161–63.

25. Gotthold Ephraim Lessing, *Laocoon: An Essay on the Limits of Painting and Poetry*, translated by Edward Allen McCormick (Baltimore: Johns Hopkins University Press, 1984), chap. 8, pp. 50–54, esp. pp. 52–53.

26. Ibid.

27. Gombrich, *Symbolic Images*, pp. 40 ff.

28. Marsilio Ficino, *De Amore*, second discourse, sec. VII, p. 1326.

29. Antonio Averlino, known as Filarete, *Trattato di architettura*, book 18, fol. 148 verso [*Treatise on Architecture*, translated by John R. Spencer, 2 vols. (New Haven: Yale University Press, 1965), vol. 2, p. 254]. Gombrich, *Symbolic Images*, pp. 39–40.

30. "Fu dunque Venere seconde le favole la Dea della libidine e della lascivia, come ch'ella mandasse nel cuore dei mortali i libidinosi desiderii, e gli appetiti lascivi, e che à questi con l'aiuto suo si desse il desiderato compimento . . . & a costei dettero parimento gli antichi, oltre Himeneo, Giunione, la cura della nozze, percioche queste si fanno, accioche ne seguiti il carnale congiungimento, onde ne habbia da seguitare poi la generatione de i figliuoli. Fu la bellezza anchora data a guardia a Venere, si ch'ella potesse darla, et torre come pareva a lei" (Cartari, *Imagini dei dei*, p. 443).

31. "Prima che disegnare la imagine di Venere, voglio fare uno schizzo della natura sua: perché sarà di non poco giovamento a conscere la ragione di diverse cose, che in quella diro poi" (Ibid.)

32. Ibid., p. 448; cf. Pliny the elder, *Natural History*, 36.21; LOEB, vol. 10, pp. 16–17.

33. "Vedendo a Sparta Pallade, la bella / Venere armata à guisa di guerriera, / Hor, dissé, è tempo da terminar quella / Lite, ch'andar ti fa cotanto altiera / E siane pur giudice Paris: & ella / Rispose, ah temereria, dunque spera / L'animo tuo vincer hor me armata, / Che nuda già ti vinsi, e disarmata?" Ausonius, as cited by Cartari, *Imagini dei dei*, p. 456. For the original Latin, cf. LOEB, Ausonius, translated by Hugh G. Evelyn White, 2 vols. (1919–21), vol. 2, pp. 192–93.

34. "Credo che messer Iacobo Sansovino rarissimo vi ornera la camera d'una Venere si vera e si viva che empie di libidine il pensiero di ciaschuno chi lamira." See Pietro Aretino, letter to Federico Gonzaga, 6 October 1527 (as cited by Ernst Gombrich in "Zum Werke Giulio Romano," *Jahrbuch der kunsthistorischen Sammlungen in Wien*, new series, vol. 7 [1934], pp. 79–104 [this citation on p. 95]).

35. Albert Severyns cites a curious passage in the *Exegese de l'Iliade* by Jean Tzetzes (1140), in which this "loquacious scholar" recounts what he himself calls an "idiotic story," declaring it to be untrustworthy: Paris was in reality an orator who had published a pamphlet drawing a parallel between the three goddesses, maintaining Aphrodite's superiority and proclaiming the inevitability of Love's triumph over Discord. Subsequent misinterpretations of this *archeogonie*, the story goes, generated a set of legends linking the marriage of Peleus and Thetis to the Trojan war, and including the judgment of Paris.

36. Eugène Duthuit, *Manuel de l'amateur d'estampes* (Paris, 1888), p. 197. Cf. catalog of the exhibition *Albrecht Dürer 1471–1971* held in Nuremberg in 1971 (Munich: Prestel Verlag, 1971), pp. 270–72, no. 514.

37. Jessie Poesch, "Sources for Two Dürer Enigmas," *Art Bulletin* 46 (1964): 78–82.

38. Cartari (*Imagini dei dei*, p. 468) maintained that the three Graces were sometimes four, but Panofsky refuted this assertion. Cf. Erwin Panofsky, *The Life and Art of Albrecht Dürer*, 2d ed. (Princeton: Princeton University Press, 1945), p. 70, and *Problems in Titian, Mostly Iconographic* (New York: New York University Press, 1969), pp. 136–37, note 66.

39. Gombrich, *Symbolic Images*, p. 55.

40. Ibid., pp. 41–42.

41. Wind, *Pagan Mysteries*, p. 28. I am grateful to Jean-Pierre Vernant for suggesting this idea to me, especially as it clarifies the absence of the three Graces from Freud's list of triads illustrating what Dumézil has called "dramas of choice."

42. "Et pour ce dist on qu'elle conceüt cupidon, le dieu d'amour, c'est-a-dire la concupiscence de la chair pour cause que pour sa chaleur et moiteur on dit ceste étoile esmouvoir la concupiscence de la chair . . . Ces trois demoiselles qui tiegnent compagnie à Vénus sont troy pechez, qui frequentent la prosperite et volupte des choses. C'est assavoir: luxure, orgueil et avarice." Cf. Jeanette Theodora marin Van T'Sant, *Le Commentaire de Copenhague de l'Ovide moralisé* (Leiden, 1929), pp. 36–37, cited by Cornelis de Boer, "*Ovide moralisé*"; *poème du commencement du quatorzième siècle publié d'après tous les manuscrits connus*, 5 vols. (Amsterdam: J. Müller, 1915–38), vol. 5.

43. "Autre moralite se puet icy assigner. Ces troy pucelles sont troy vertus theologales. C'est assavoir: foy et esperance et charite" (Ibid.).

44. Cf., among the most recent bibliography, Heinz Ladendorf, *Antikenstudium und Antikencopie* (Berlin: Akademie-Verlag, 1953).

45. Pico della Mirandola, commentary on the *Canzone d'Amore* of Beniveni (Venice, 1522), II, chap. 15; as cited by Gombrich, *Symbolic Images*, p. 56.

46. Pierio Valeriano, *Hieroglyphica*, LIX; as cited by Wind, *Pagan Mysteries*, p. 32.

47. ". . . e nel rivolgere quello orbe, o palla, o circolo che sia, pare che porgano mirabile diletto a riguardanti" (Cartari, *Imagini dei dei*, p. 468.

48. Adam von Bartsch, *Le peintre graveur*, 21 vols. (Wurzburg: Verlagsdruckerei Wurzburg, 1920), vol. 16, p. 404, no. 72.

49. Ibid., vol. 15, p. 408, no. 60.

50. Cf., for example: the majolica plates reproducing either the central group or the entire composition now in the Louvre or the Sèvres manufactory (cf. Jeanne Giacomotti, *Catalogue des majoliques des musées nationaux* [Paris: Réunion des musées nationaux, 1974], nos. 1001, 1020, and 1021, ill.); that in Urbino, the work of Guido Dorantino (1539); that in the Musée Conde in Chantilly (cf. G. Liverani, "La fortuna di Raffaello nella maiolica," in Mario Salmi, *Raffaello* [Novara: Istituto Geografico de Agostini, 1968], p. 701, fig. 23); a sixteenth-century Venetian bronze in the Capodimonte Museum in Naples (cf. Louis Dunand and Philippe Lemarchand, *Les Compositions de Jules Romain intitulées "les Amours des dieux," gravees par Marc-Antoine Raimondi*, I [Lausanne: Institut d'iconographie, 1977], p. 258, fig. 539); and an amusing series of Chinese porcelains now in the Musée de la Compagnie des Indes, in Port-Louis.

51. Jean-Claude Boyer, "Le Jugement de Paris de Michel Corneille," *Bulletin des musées et monuments lyonnais*, no. 1 (1991): 30–37.

52. Gombrich, *Aby Warburg*, p. 276 and pl. 53c.

53. Cf. *Le Paysage en Europe du XVI*^e^ au XVIIIe siècle, exhibition catalog, Paris, Musée du Louvre, 1990, p. 34, no. 23.

54. Gombrich, *Aby Warburg*, p. 276.

55. Bartsch, *Le peintre graveur*, vol. 14, p. 339.

56. Cf. *Bologna et l'umanesimo 1490–1510*, catalog of an exhibition held in Bologna and Vienna in 1988 (Bologna: Nuova Alfa Editoriale, 1988), p. 262, no. 67.

57. This composition is repeated, in reverse and in a much wider format allowing for greater distance between the two groups, in a fresco originally in the Palazzo Torelli in Mantua (now in the Castelvecchio Museum in Verona), also executed by Giulio Romano's studio. Cf. Sergio Marinelli, "Gli affreschi di palazzo Torelli a Mantova," *Quaderni di Palazzo Te*, no. 2 (January–June 1985): 28–34.

58. Cf. above, chapter 10.

59. Most scholars agree that this painting, rediscovered in 1966 and now in the National Gallery in London, is by Rubens: in addition to an oil sketch in Vienna, several related preparatory drawings survive (in the Louvre and the Metropolitan Museum). Cf. Michael Jaffe, "Rubens in Italy Part II: Some Rediscovered Works of the First Phase," *Burlington Magazine* 110 (1968): 174–87, and Gregory Martin, *The Flemish School, circa 1600–circa 1900* (London: National Gallery, 1970), pp. 213–15.

60. Heribert Hutter, *Peter Paul Rubens in der Gemäldegalerie der Akademie der bildenden Künste in Wien* (Vienna: Akademie der Bilden-

den Künste, 1977), pp. 6–7. Leo van Puyvelde rejects this sketch, which has also been attributed to the young Van Dyck. See his *The Sketches of Rubens*, translated by Eveline Winkworth (London: K. Paul, Trench, Trubner and Co. Ltd., 1947).

61. Prado, no. 1405.

62. The same figure also appears in the large *Judgment of Paris* in London. The catalog of the National Gallery (Martin, *The Flemish School, circa 1600–circa 1900*, pp. 154–55) identifies her as the fury Alecto. In his description of paintings in the Galerie d'Orléans, Roger de Piles recognized her as Discord.

63. Bernard Teyssèdre, "Une collection française de Rubens au XVIIe siècle: le Cabinet du Duc de Richelieu décrit par Roger de Piles (1676–1681)," *Gazette des Beaux-Arts*, 6e per., vol. 112, no. 1138 (November 1963): 241–99.

64. It makes little sense to invoke Lucian's playlet in connection with this painting—as does the entry in the National Gallery catalog, where it is suggested that the Dresden and London canvases as we see them today correspond to two successive moments of the myth: that in which Mercury asks the goddesses to disrobe, and that in which Paris awards the apple to Venus.

65. Letter from the Cardinal-Infante Ferdinand to Philipp IV, 27 February 1638. Cf. Hans Gerhard Evers, *Peter Paulus Rubens* (Munich: F. Bruckmann, 1942), p. 440, and, by the same author, *Rubens und sein Werk: Neue Forschungen* (Brussels: De Lage Landen, 1944), pp. 89, 91.

66. "Kann nur sie durch Paris von vorn gesehen werden, und damit ist auch ihr Sieg entschieden." See Jakob Burckhardt, *Erinnerungen aus Rubens*, new ed. (Vienna and Leipzig: Bernina Verlag, 1937), p. 138.

67. "Le Sujet dont il s'agit en cette histoire étant de la Vue, et Pâris, entre toutes les autres Figures, faisant principalement cette fonction, le Peintre ne pouvait pas colloquer plus judicieusement son point de vue qu'à l'oeil de Pâris, qu'il a même pour cet effet représenté de Profil, afin de montrer encore par là qu'il n'y en doit avoir qu'un précisément, comme les Géomètres l'enseignent dans l'Optique; où ils représentent la Vision par une forme de pyramide radieuse, à la pointe de laquelle est l'oeil." See Roland Fréart, Sieur de Chambray, *Idée de la perfection de la peinture*, (Geneva: Minskoff, 1973 [reprint of 1662 edition]), pp. 36–37.

68. Cf. Françoise Frontisi-Ducroux, *Le Dieu-masque, une figure du Dionysos d'Athènes* (Paris: Découverte and Rome: École Française de Rome, 1991), pp. 118–19 ff.

69. Lacan, *Le Séminaire*, vol. 11, p. 153 [*Seminar*, vol. 11 (*The Four Fundamental Concepts*), p. 168 (translation modified)].

70. On the relation between the drive and its object, cf. above, chapter 2.

71. Plotinus *Enneads* 9.3–4.

72. "Voyez, Vollard, comme elle ressemble à un garcon! Depuis toujours je voulais faire un Pâris. Je n'avais jamais pu trouver de modèle, quel Pâris j'aurai là!" See Ambroise Vollard, *En écoutant Cézanne, Degas, Renoir* (Paris: B. Grasset, 1938), p. 251.

73. Meyer Schapiro, "Seurat," in *Selected Papers II. Modern Art, Nineteenth and Twentieth Centuries* (New York: Braziller, 1978), p. 105.

74. Ibid., pp. 107–9.

75. Schapiro, "The Apples of Cézanne: An Essay on the Meaning of Still-Life," *Modern Art*, pp. 1–5.

76. Cf. Lawrence Gowing et al., *Cézanne: The Early Years (1859–72)*, catalog of an exhibition held in London, Paris, and Washington (New York: Abrams, 1988), pp. 25–27, 172.

77. Franz Kafka, *Letters to Milena*, translated by Philip Boehm (New York: Schocken Books, 1990), p. 16.

78. Cf. Hubert Damisch, *The Origin of Perspective*, translated by John Goodman (Cambridge, MA: MIT Press, 1993), pp. 432–39.

79. Douglas Cooper, *Pablo Picasso: Les Déjeuners* (Paris: Éd. Cercle d'Art, 1962), p. 10.

80. Cf. Hubert Damisch, "*Wie absichtlos:* le Faire, le Croire, la Ruse, la Théorie," *Nouvelle Revue de psychanalyse* 18 (Fall 1978): 55–73. But note that several of the analogies with the game of chess proposed in this article are mistaken and/or misleading.

Chapter Twelve

1. Philippe Morel, "Le système décoratif de la Galerie Farnese: Observations sur les limites de la représentation," in *Les Carrache et les décors profanes*, acts of a colloquium held by the École Française in Rome in 1986 (Rome: École Française de Rome, 1988), pp. 116–17.

2. Honoré d'Urfé, *L'Astrée*, part I, book 4: "Finally, unable to delay any longer, I was obliged to do it, but my God! When I think on it, I still die for shame: I had thick hair that covered me almost completely, my only ornament being the garland he had given me the preceding day . . . Judge, wise Diana, to what I had been reduced; for love prevented me from revenging my modesty, and in any case shame turned me against love." ("Enfin, ne pouvant plus dilayer, j'y fus contrainte, mais mon Dieu! quand je m'en souviens, je meurs encore de honte: j'avais les cheveux espars, qui me couvroient presque toute, sur lesquels pour tout ornement je n'avais que la guirlande que le jour au paravant il m'avait donnée . . . Jugez, sage Diane, quelle je devins lors; car amour me deffendoit de venger ma pudicité, et toustefois la honte m'animoit contre l'amour" [Honoré d'Urfé, *L'Astrée*, 5 vols. (Lyon: P, Masson, 1925–28)]).

3. Cf. *Watteau 1684–1721*, catalog of an exhibition held in Paris and Washington, DC, in 1984–85 (Paris: Réunion des musées na-

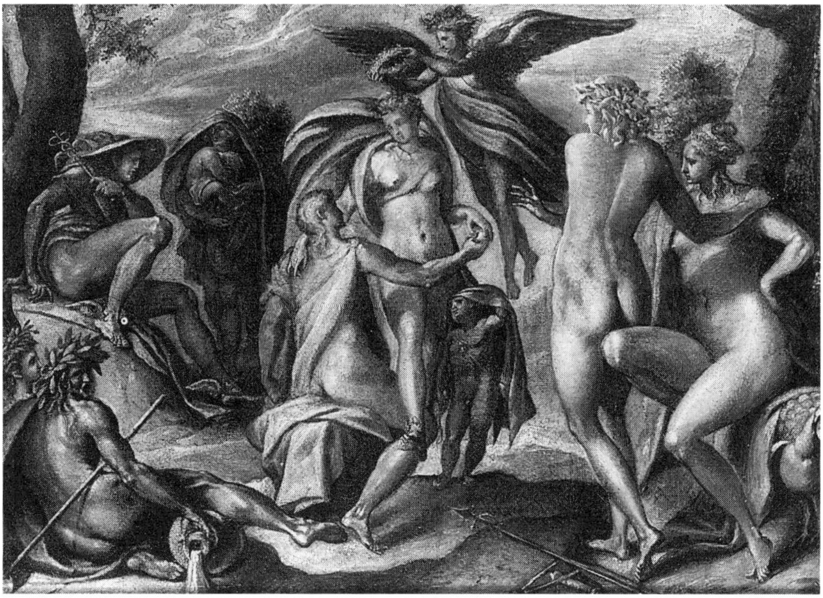

Figure 116. Anthonie Blocklandt, *The Judgment of Paris*, grisaille, c. 1570–80 (Paris, Louvre).

tionaux and Washington: National Gallery of Art, 1984), pp. 417–18, no. 64.

4. A small panel by Anthonie Blocklandt (Figure 116), executed in Utrecht in the 1570s and recently acquired by the Louvre, features the opposite arrangement: here Paris is seen from the back while Venus, who is urging herself on him, is seen from the front, her genitals obscured from our view by the judge's extended arm (*Nouvelles acquisitions du département des peintures (1987–1990)* [Paris: Réunion des musées nationaux, 1991], pp. 42–43).

5. In German mythology, the *Walküre*—"she who chooses"—"elects" from those perishing in battle the heroes worthy of Walhala. Cf. the note by Bertrand Féron in the French volume of essays by Freud (*l'Inquiétante Étrangeté et autres essais* [Paris: 1985], p. 71).

6. On this technique, which in French is designated by the phrase *à la hampe*, cf. Segolene Bergeon, "Quelques points de technique picturale," in *Antoine Watteau (1684–1721): The Painter, His Age, and His Legend* (Paris and Geneva: Ed. Champion-Slatkine, 1984), pp. 137–38.

7. Rosenberg mentions a drawing in the Louvre, attributed to Rubens, that is very close to Watteau's Venus (R.F. 2028; cf. *Dessins de Rubens*, catalog of an exhibition at the Cabinet des Dessins of the

Louvre, 1959, no. 20, fig 3). And it is again Rubens who provides us with a link between Watteau's *Judgment of Paris* and his *Enseigne de Gersaint:* the same dog, more or less directly inspired by the one in *The Coronation of Marie de Medicis,* is found in both of these works. Note that in the *Judgment* this dog is quite similar to the one in the Rubens, whereas he appears in the lower right corner of the *Sign* in a mirror reversal.

8. "Il n'est pas moins difficile de la peindre que de la regarder, sans être eboui des rayons que lui donne la Renommee, qui n'en peut parler assez dignement, l'une et l'autre neanmoins ont la tete enveloppe d'un nuage." See Jean Baudouin, *Iconologie, ou explication nouvelle de plusieurs images, emblèmes et autres figures hiéroglyphiques . . . tirées des recherches et des figures de Cesare Ripa* (Paris, 1644), p. 29. Cf. Hubert Damisch, *Théorie du nuage: Pour une histoire de la peinture* (Paris: Flammarion, 1972), p. 83 [translation forthcoming].

9. René Démoris, "Watteau, le paysage et ses figures," in *Antoine Watteau (1684–1721): The Painter, His Age, and His Legend,* p. 161.

10. A. C. de Trubières, comte de Caylus, "Vie de Watteau," in Pierre Champion, *Notes critiques sur les vies anciennes d'Antoine Watteau* (Paris: E. Champion, 1921), p. 110; as cited by Rosenberg in *Watteau,* exhibition catalog, p. 334. The same "Vie de Watteau" is included in Pierre Rosenberg, ed., *Vies anciennes de Watteau* (Paris: Hermann, 1984), pp. 53–91, where the cited passage appears on p. 85.

11. Jean-Pierre Vernant, *La Mort dans les yeux: Figures de l'autre en Grèce ancienne* (Paris: Hachette, 1985), pp. 29–32. As Vernant notes, there is an exhaustive study of materials relating to Baubo (who is discussed below): Maurice Olender, "Aspects de Baubo, textes et contextes antiques," *Revue de l'histoire des religions* 7 (1985): 3–55. [An English translation (by Robert Lamberton) of an abbreviated version of this essay has been published: M. Olender, "Aspects of Baubo: Ancient Texts and Contexts," in *Before Sexuality: The Construction of Erotic Experience in the Ancient Greek World,* edited by David M. Halperin, John J. Winkler, and Froma I. Zeitlin (Princeton: Princeton University Press, 1990), pp. 83–113.]

12. According to Vernant, in Athenian culture young women's hair, when left untied, was understood to assimilate them to wild fillies, thereby indicating their savagery, and Athenian males acted accordingly: "By cutting the hair of newly wedded brides, not only were these untamed fillies domesticated, they were purged of that element of savagery that Athena and Artemis, the two virgin goddesses precluded from marrying, retained in their different ways" (Vernant, *La Mort,* p. 46).

13. Ibid., p. 33.

14. Marcel Detienne, *The Creation of Mythology,* translated by

Margaret Cook (Chicago: University of Chicago Press, 1986), pp. 13–14 [translation modified].

15. Things are very different today: *La Toilette intime* was placed on the cover of the recent volume of articles on Watteau whose publication was sponsored by two prestigious institutions: the Centre national de la recherche scientifique, in Paris, and the Center for Advanced Study in the Visual Arts, which is affiliated with the National Gallery in Washington (*Antoine Watteau [1684–1721]: The Painter, His Age, and His Legend*).

16. Cf. Jean-Pierre Vernant, *Figures, idoles, masques* (Paris: Julliard, 1990).

17. "The semantic difference between fable and mythology can be formulated as the difference between a generalized and stabilized interpretative system and a rational investigation of that interpretive system according to other standards of validity." See Jean Starobinsky, "Fable and Mythology in the Seventeenth and Eighteenth Centuries," in *Blessings in Disguise; or, The Morality of Evil*, translated by Arthur Goldhammer (Cambridge, MA: Harvard University Press, 1993), pp. 169–93 and notes on pp. 228–29 (this citation on p. 173).

18. Lacan, *Le Séminaire*, vol. 7, p. 14 [*Seminar*, vol. 7 (*The Ethics*), p. 5].

19. "The theory of the [drives] is so to say our mythology. [Drives] are mythical entities, magnificent in their indefiniteness." See Freud, *Neue Folge der Vorlesungen zur Einführung in die Psychoanalyse* (1932), in *GW*, vol. 15, p. 101 [*New Introductory Lectures on Psychoanalysis*, in *SE*, vol. 22, p. 95].

20. Lacan, *Le Séminaire*, vol. 7, p. 19 [*Seminar*, vol. 7 (*The Ethics*), p. 12].

21. Detienne, *The Creation of Mythology*, pp. 12 ff.

22. Plato *Phaedrus* 243a. Cf. the preface by Léon Robin in the Budé edition (Paris: 1970), p. xxviii.

23. Ovid *Heroides* XVI, "Paris to Helen"; LOEB, Ovid, *Heroides*, pp. 200–203.

24. Freud, "Das Motiv der Kästchenwahl," in *GW*, p. 37 ["The Theme of the Three Caskets," in *SE*, vol. 12, p. 301].

25. Note that the homonymous Greek term *paraphasis* designates both "deceiving," "seductive words," and the interior of the female genitals. Cf. above, chapter 11.

26. Cf. Jean Clair, *Méduse: Contribution à une anthropologie des arts du visuel* (Paris: Gallimard, 1989).

27. In the words of Louis Marin: "the *Head of Medusa*, a full-face portrait, but not entirely" (*To Destroy Painting*, translated by Mette Hjort [Chicago: University of Chicago Press, 1995], p. 119). Marin's analysis of Caravaggio's *Medusa* as a painting of *decapitation*, and the aporias resulting from this, is exemplary.

28. Freud, "Das Medusenhaupt" (1922), in *GW,* vol. 17, pp. 47–48 ["The Medusa's Head," in *SE,* vol. 18, pp. 273–74]. On psychoanalytic interpretation as itself a trap for the interpreter, cf. Louis Marin, *To Destroy Painting,* pp. 145–49.

29. Vernant, *La Mort dans les yeux,* p. 29.

30. Freud, "Das Motiv der Kästchenwahl," in *GW,* vol. 10, p. 34 ["The Theme of the Three Caskets," in *SE,* vol. 12, p. 299].

Index

Page references to illustrations are indicated by **boldface** type.

Photo Credits

Figures

1: Ornans, Musée Courbet
2: Paris, Lauros Giraudon; © 1995 C. Herscovici, Brussels / Artists Rights Society (ARS), New York
4: Paris, Réunion des musées nationaux
5: Paris, Réunion des musées nationaux
6: Paris, Réunion des musées nationaux
7: Madrid, Museo del Prado
9: Paris, Réunion des musées nationaux
10: Paris, Bibliothèque nationale
11: Paris, Bibliothèque nationale
14: Paris, Réunion des musées nationaux
16: Paris, Réunion des musées nationaux
17: Paris, Réunion des musées nationaux
19–22: Paris, Réunion des musées nationaux
23–26: Paris, Bibliothèque nationale
32: Paris, Anderson Giraudon
37: Paris, Réunion des musées nationaux
39: London, National Gallery
42: Copenhagen, Statens Museum for Kunst

43: Basel, Robert von Hirsch
44: New York, Metropolitan Museum
45: Karlsruhe, Staatliche Kunstalle
47: Saint Louis, Saint Louis Art Museum
54: Basel, Hinz
55–57: Paris, Bibliothèque national
62: Paris, Réunion des musées nationaux
63: Paris, Réunion des musées nationaux
64: Paris, Flammarion
67: Paris, Réunion des musées nationaux
74: Paris, Alinari Giraudon
75: Paris, Giraudon
77: Rouen, Ellebé
79: Paris, Anderson Giraudon
82: Nantes, Yves Bruneau
83: Nantes, Yves Bruneau
84: Paris, Mobilier national
85: Lyon, Studio Basset
86: Paris, Réunion des musées nationaux
89: Paris, Réunion des musées nationaux
93–94: Madrid, Museo del Prado
96: Madrid, Museo del Prado
99: Paris, Giraudon
100: © 1996 Estate of George Grosz/Licensed by VAGA, New York, NY; Paris, Giraudon
101: © 1995 Artists Rights Society (ARS), New York / SPADEM, Paris
103: © 1995 Artists Rights Society (ARS), New York / SPADEM, Paris; Réunion des musées nationaux
104: © 1995 Artists Rights Society (ARS), New York / SPADEM, Paris; Réunion des musées nationaux
105: © 1995 Artists Rights Society (ARS), New York / SPADEM, Paris; Réunion des musées nationaux
106: © 1995 Artists Rights Society (ARS), New York / SPADEM, Paris; Réunion des musées nationaux
107: Humlebaeck, Louisiana, Museum; © 1995 Artists

Rights Society (ARS), New York / SPADEM, Paris

108: © 1995 Artists Rights Society (ARS), New York / SPADEM, Paris

109: Paris, Alinari Giraudon

110: Réunion des musées nationaux

115: Réunion des musées nationaux

116: Réunion des musées nationaux